Psychological Reactance

A Theory of Freedom and Control

Psychological Reactance

A Theory of Freedom and Control

Sharon S. Brehm
Jack W. Brehm

Department of Psychology
University of Kansas
Lawrence, Kansas

1981

ACADEMIC PRESS

A Subsidiary of Harcourt Brace Jovanovich, Publishers

New York London Toronto Sydney San Francisco

ACADEMIC PRESS, INC.
111 Fifth Avenue, New York, New York 10003

United Kingdom Edition published by
ACADEMIC PRESS, INC. (LONDON) LTD.
24/28 Oval Road, London NW1 7DX

Library of Congress Cataloging in Publication Data

Brehm, Sharon S.
    Psychological reactance.

    Bibliography: p.
    Includes index.
    1. Psychological reactance. I. Brehm,
Jack Williams. II. Title.
BF632.5.B73 1981   153.8   81-12796
ISBN 0-12-129840-X   AACR2

PRINTED IN THE UNITED STATES OF AMERICA

81 82 83 84   9 8 7 6 5 4 3 2 1

None can experience stint
Who Bounty—have not known—
The fact of Famine—could not be
Except for Fact of Corn—

Want—is a meagre Art
Acquired by Reverse—
The Poverty that was not Wealth—
Cannot be Indigence

EMILY DICKINSON

Contents

Preface

When we set out to write this book, we knew it would involve considerable time and effort. We wanted to review and integrate some 15 years of research on reactance theory, and we realized this would be a task of no small magnitude. In retrospect, however, we failed to appreciate the full scope of the undertaking that would eventually develop. Although the core of the theory—and, thus, of the present book—rests on laboratory-based social psychological research conducted by a number of American social psychologists, the theory has also been examined, discussed, and applied in a wide variety of other contexts. Exploring these areas of theoretical relevance led us to look at research and theory in clinical and developmental psychology; had us consider applied research in several different fields; introduced us to (for us) such esoterica as Gilles de la Tourette syndrome, antilittering campaigns, and the *Journal of Obstetrics and Gynecology*; forced us to call on our friends for translations; and made one of us pay more attention to individual differences than he would ever have believed possible.

It has been, then, an enlightening experience for us, and we hope that at least some of what we have learned has been conveyed to the reader. We have attempted to examine reactance theory in all its complexity and generativity. The fundamental tenets of the theory and research relevant to these tenets are discussed in considerable detail. Subsequently, we examine a number of special topic areas to which the theory seems especially relevant. Individual and gender-linked differences in reactance processes also are considered as well as developmental aspects of reactance. In the chapters on applications of the theory, we focus on clinical applications, societal problem solutions, and power relations in the real world. Finally, we have tried to place reactance theory in a broader theoretical context by examining impression management formulations of the theory and by comparing reactance to other theoretical models in which the notion of control plays a central role.

In view of the range of the material that we have covered, we expect that the present volume will appeal to readers with many different interests. For a full understanding of the theory and its possibilities as an explanatory device, we would, of course, recommend a complete reading of the book. In addition, however, readers may well wish to emphasize areas of interest to them—e.g., developmental psychology, clinical applications, applied research. We have tried to organize the book in such a way that the material relevant to special interests can be easily located while still presenting it in the appropriate context of the theory as a whole. Our hope is that the book can serve as a comprehensive presentation of the theory, a demonstration of the theory's relevance to a wide range of topic areas in a variety of fields, and a source of theoretical stimulation for social scientists and their students.

Having alluded briefly to the burden we have placed on our friends, we can be a great deal more explicit. A number of colleagues have been extremely helpful to us in the writing of this book. Richard Archer, C. Daniel Batson, Larry Beutler, Charles Carver, Shirley Feldman-Summers, John Harvey, Madeline Heilman, Darwyn Linder, Judson Mills, Timothy Smith, Marsha Weinraub, Stephen West, Robert Wicklund, Sharon Wolf, Stephen Worchel, and Camille Wortman read and commented on earlier versions of the chapters in this book. As is customary in such endeavors, we want to thank them for the improvements that resulted from their assistance, point out that they by no means agree with everything we have written, and absolve them from any blame attaching to deficiencies in our work. Special assistance was provided by the following individuals: Elizabeth Holtzman was perservering and meticulous in tracking down relevant literature; Thomas Hill and Sharon Wolf gave us superb and vitally important translations of, respectively, the German and French sources that we have included; and Jacqueline Christie kept her sanity and ours with incredible good humor in the face of the avalanche of rough drafts that needed to be transformed into typed copy.

We also want to express our appreciation to the General Research Fund of the University of Kansas, which provided support for the initial development of this book. Finally, we would like to thank each other: for hard work, a minimal number of reactance-inducing statements, and a lot of faith.

CHAPTER 1

Introduction: Freedom, Control, and Reactance Theory

When the press predicted that Mr. [President] Johnson
would get rid of all the Kennedy men in the White House,
he invited them all to stay, and when he was later praised
for doing so, he gradually let almost all of them resign.
[JAMES RESTON, The New York Times, November 28, 1965.]

Why would a president of the United States apparently modify his plans regarding top administrative posts simply in order to cross up the press? What is there about predictions by the press that would produce such effects on behavior? Would press reports always produce oppositional behavior, or would they do so only under certain circumstances? Was President Johnson simply unique in the way he responded, or did his behavior represent a common response in human behavior?

That President Johnson was not unique in acting contrary to what the press said he would do can be seen in the plethora of examples of oppositional behavior from everyday life. For example, when desegregation sit-ins and demonstrations began in North Carolina in the 1960s, the owner of a television repair shop in Chapel Hill, James Botsford, closed his shop rather than give in to the demands of the demonstrators (Durham Morning Herald, 1963). In explaining his action, Botsford noted that he had been raised in the North and was in sympathy with blacks. What he objected to, he said, was the attempt to force him to operate his business in a particular way. In fact, in response to the desegregation demonstrations, Botsford actually instituted a segregationist policy in his own business.

What about the opposite side of the coin? If forcing something on someone can lead to opposition, can withholding something lead to increased desirability? In the realm of interpersonal attraction, people certainly seem to believe that this is the case. Playing hard to get is surely one of the world's oldest strategies in romantic interactions. Variations on this theme range from the admonishment not to be "too easy" to the more elaborate advice supposedly given by Jack Bouvier to his daughter Jacqueline. According to Stephen Birmingham's (1978) biography of Mrs. Onassis, "The mating dance that Jack Bouvier described involved a woman offering a man a little something, then withdrawing it, then offering him something else, and then withdrawing that. . . . Tease a little. Be mysterious. . . . Remember La Gioconda and her strange, disturbing, eternally provocative smile [p. 33]."

And then there's the example of a friend of ours who was trying to get his children to eat leafy green vegetables. Appeals to "it's good for you," starving children in China and even Popeye having all failed dismally, our friend finally discovered a tactic that would work: He would bring to the dinner table elaborate dishes of spinach et al., which he and his wife would eat with great enjoyment and firmly forbid the children to have. At first, the children watched with amused interest. Soon, however, they asked if they could have some. Showing great reluctance, our friend eventually "gave in."

What these examples illustrate is that people frequently act counter to restrictions or pressure that is put on them. President Johnson showed that he did not have to do what the press said he was going to do, Botsford did exactly the opposite of what desegregation demonstrators were trying to accomplish, a suitor's desire is thought to be enhanced when the romantic object plays hard to get, and our friend's children did not want to be kept from eating a particular food. In a word, the individuals in these examples acted so as to protect or restore their freedom and control.

Especially during the last decade, freedom and control have become popular concepts in the behavioral sciences. Although the meanings and usages of these terms have increased correspondingly with their popularity and with the number of scientists attending to them, a dominant theme can be discerned in the growing body of theory and research addressing these concepts. This theme holds, generally speaking, that to have control or freedom is good and beneficial to the individual, while not to have control or freedom is bad or potentially harmful. Though this assertion is practically a truism and could hardly be refuted on logical grounds, it fails to be an accurate representation of the major thrust of the experimental evidence. Rather, what much of the evidence shows is that threat to control or freedom has important psychological consequences, and these consequences may be either beneficial or harmful. It is these psychological consequences of threat to or loss of control or freedom with which the present volume is concerned.

Just what sort of freedom and control are of interest and what constitutes a threat to them? We can illustrate this point by referring to people's experiences in making a major purchase—buying a car, a house, a special item of clothing, etc. The freedoms contained in the situation of making a purchase include the possibility of having or not having each relevant item. An individual who wishes to purchase a car, for example, may consider a Ford, Honda, Chevrolet, Toyota, and Volkswagen. The individual who has unlimited money could buy one or more of each, and presumably might do so if each had some especially valuable characteristic not belonging to any of the others. Such an affluent individual has the freedoms to have or not have each of the five different cars.

How might these freedoms be threatened? In general, any event that increases the perceived difficulty of having or of not having a potential outcome threatens the exercise of a freedom. In different words, the individual's control over each potential outcome is threatened or reduced by an increase in the perceived difficulty of attaining an outcome. The person who contemplates buying the five different cars could thus have one or more of his freedoms threatened in a number of ways. For example, import quotas imposed on foreign cars could make it more difficult to obtain Hondas, Toyotas, and Volkswagens. A strike at General Motors could increase the difficulty of obtaining a Chevrolet. Unusually high sales of Fords could deplete the supply of that particular item, at least temporarily. Coming from an entirely different realm, social influence attempts could increase the difficulty of attaining particular outcomes, as when a Ford salesman says that a Volkswagen is a rotten car, or one's friend says that a Honda is the only good car on the road. Finally, of course, if the individual's affluence suddenly decreases such that it is no longer possible to buy more than one car, the individual's control over and freedom to have four of the cars is lost altogether. In all of these examples, the individual's freedom or control in regard to particular outcomes is made more difficult to exercise. These examples, then, bring us to the question of interest; namely, what are the psychological consequences of having one's freedom or control threatened or reduced?

The theory of psychological reactance (Brehm, 1966, 1968; Wicklund, 1974) outlines a set of motivational consequences that can be expected to occur whenever freedoms are threatened or lost. The theory stipulates what constitutes a freedom, how freedoms can be threatened or eliminated, and how the ensuing motivational state (psychological reactance) will manifest itself. In general, the theory holds that a threat to or loss of a freedom motivates the individual to restore that freedom. Thus, the direct manifestation of reactance is behavior directed toward restoring the freedom in question. For example, a person can be expected to try to exercise the freedom. The individual who discovers that import quotas have been placed on Hondas will exhibit increased motivation to buy a Honda by trying all of the dealers she can locate, and perhaps by purchasing the car from a dealer much further from her home than she would normally like to do. In addition to direct behavioral consequences, reactance affects the subjective attractiveness of potential outcomes. Having learned that Hondas are subject to import quotas, the individual will perceive the Honda to be more attractive or desirable than before receipt of this information.

The arousal of reactance, according to the original formulation, is maximal when a freedom is eliminated altogether. That is, even when there is no way to restore the freedom, reactance is aroused and has the consequence of making the lost option more desirable. If true, this state of affairs—wanting something that one cannot have—would presumably be frustrating and unpleasant to the individual, and from an intuitive point of view, would not seem to be a particularly adaptive way for individuals to respond. This theoretical problem has been dealt with in part by a recent modification of the theory. Wortman and Brehm (1975), noting the research on "learned helplessness" that demonstrates a "giving up" when outcomes are uncontrollable, suggested that giving up can be the end product of an elimination of a freedom. Implicit in this argument is that the individual gives up the freedom (to attain a particular outcome) and thereby does not experience reactance. Presumably, however, giving up a freedom occurs only when the individual becomes absolutely convinced that there is no way to restore the freedom.

Reactance theory, as outlined to this point, has a wide variety of implications for the understanding of behavior. It suggests that individuals will sometimes be motivated to resist or act counter to attempted social influence, such as in mass persuasion or in psychotherapy; that individuals may resist having their personal space or their privacy invaded; that they may resist favors that tend to obligate them; and that they can even threaten and eliminate their own freedoms and thereby increase the difficulty of choice when they have to choose one from among two or more alternatives.

The implications of the theory are further enriched by some additional principles. When, for example, a child is told that he must clean up his room, whether or not the child will experience reactance is a function of how firmly the child believes that he has the freedom *not* to clean up his room. The child who has unfailingly had to clean up his room will not perceive the freedom not to do so and will experience no reactance. The child who is usually allowed to leave his room in a mess will hold the freedom not to clean up the room rather firmly and should experience a great deal of reactance. The principle here is that a freedom is an expectancy and can be held with more or less certainty. Reactance can be aroused in a person only to the extent that the individual believes he or she has a freedom or control over a potential outcome.

A second principle concerns the importance of the freedom that is threatened or eliminated. When an individual is told not to select one of two attractive choice alternatives, the amount of reactance aroused by this threat will depend on the importance or attractiveness of the alternatives. Where the alternatives are trivial in importance, such as the choice in a lunch line between an apple and an orange, relatively little reactance will be aroused. Where the alternatives are important, however, such as the choice between a Ford and a Toyota, a great deal of reactance can be aroused. In short, the greater is the importance of the freedom that is threatened, the greater will be the amount of reactance aroused by any given threat.

A third principle holds that the amount of reactance aroused by a given threat is a direct function of the number of freedoms threatened. A child who is told by a parent not to chew gum at the dinner table should experience less reactance than a child told by a parent never to chew gum. The latter dictum eliminates the freedom to chew gum at all times, while the former eliminates only a single freedom, to chew gum during dinner.

Dependent on the third principle is the fourth and final one. It is that freedoms can be threatened by implication, and therefore, that the magnitude of reactance is increased when implied threats occur. When a newly married woman is told by her husband that he wants to spend a night out with his male friends, she may experience reactance not so much in regard to losing the company of her husband for the one night but rather in response to the implied threat that he will be leaving her alone many nights in the future. Similarly, if a secretary is told not to eat snacks while working, the reactance aroused in him may be due more to the implied threats that neither should he chew gum, drink coffee, or smoke while working than to the loss of the freedom to snack.

Because it is easy for people to infer implications of restrictions, reactance arousal by virtue of implied threats may be a frequent and powerful source of problems in human relations.

These four principles stipulate the main determinants of the magnitude of reactance and together indicate the conditions under which reactance-induced changes in the attractiveness of potential outcomes and attempts to restore freedom should occur. In Part I, Chapters 2, 3, and 4 detail the operation of these principles and examine the relevant experimental evidence. The behavioral and subjective effects of reactance are delineated in Chapter 5.

Following these theoretically oriented chapters, the theory's implications for a variety of specific topic areas are considered in Part II. Chapter 6 examines persuasion and attitude change, Chapter 7 discusses social power and interpersonal relationships, and reactance in decision-making processes is dealt with in Chapter 8. The literature on reactance and individual differences is reviewed in Chapter 9, an impression management version of reactance theory is discussed in Chapter 10, and Chapter 11 considers the implications of reactance theory for the understanding of a variety of issues in developmental psychology. Sex differences in the reactance literature are described and discussed in Chapter 12. In Part III, three chapters review the application of reactance theory to real world problems: clinical applications (Chapter 13), social problems (Chapter 14), and power relations (Chapter 15). The range of topics examined in these chapters reflects the diversity of research findings relevant to the theory and stands, we believe, as a clear indicator of the power and cogency of the theoretical formulation.

The volume then returns in Part IV to more purely theoretical considerations with Chapter 16 on the relationship between reactance theory and the concept of control. That chapter explores some of the many meanings of control and control motivation. For the present, however, and for the text up to that chapter, the reader should be aware that there is a definition of "control" that is equivalent to that of "freedom" as used in reactance theory. It is that control is the ability to affect the probability of occurrence of a potential outcome. To the extent that one has this ability, one has a freedom. To the extent that this ability is reduced, exercise of the freedom is made more difficult. Hence, reduction in control arouses reactance, and reactance impels the individual to try to restore control. What is noteworthy about this conception of control is that, like the definition of freedom, it is specific in regard to a particular outcome.

The concluding chapter, Chapter 17, focuses on some of the more complex and unresolved theoretical issues that have been raised in the course of the book. It is hoped that this discussion will serve to highlight the interplay of various theoretical principles and to stimulate future research efforts. Indeed, the single most important goal of this entire volume is to generate future research on reactance theory and related psychological processes. In the long run, the merit of this book should be judged in terms of whether or not this goal is achieved.

PART I
The Theory

CHAPTER 2

Freedoms and
Threats to Freedoms

All theories must start somewhere and, formally speaking, where they start is with one or more basic propositions that we call assumptions. A theoretical assumption is the "given" that, once accepted, permits construction of theoretical hypotheses that will be subject to empirical test. In and of themselves, assumptions are not tested. We allow the theorist some givens in order that the game might begin. The outcome of any theoretical enterprise is judged in terms of various properties (e.g., cumulative supporting evidence, heuristic value) of the elaborations permitted by the original assumptions.

In a strict sense then, the truth or falsehood of an assumption is irrelevant. Theories can and have been constructed (e.g., pre-Copernican theories of a terrocentric universe) that were extremely useful and that, we know now, were based on assumptions that were patently false. According to at least some philosophers of science, such occurrences should not ruffle the hearts and minds of good scientists. Still, most theorists want to believe that their theoretical assumptions are true, and every theorist needs to specify his or her assumptions in the clearest form possible. If an assumption begins the game, it also defines the subsequent particulars of that game.

Considered in this context, the theory of psychological reactance seems quite straightforward. There is one major assumption and this assumption appears to have been adequately defined in the initial presentation (Brehm, 1966) of the theory. Unfortunately, however, it is precisely this assumption that seems to have generated considerable confusion in the understanding and application of the theory. In this chapter, we shall try to clarify the theory's basic assumption and attempt to distinquish between reactance and various related conceptual positions. We will not (indeed, cannot) try to prove the assumption; we will try to define it as sharply as possible.

FREE BEHAVIORS

Reactance theory is based on the notion of free behaviors. The theory's assumption initially was stated as follows.

> It is assumed that for a given person at a given time, there is a set of behaviors any one of which he could engage in either at the moment or at some time in the future. This set may be called the individual's "free behaviors." Free behaviors include only acts that are realistically possible. . . . In general, we may say that for specified behaviors to be free, the individual must have the relevant physical and psychological abilities to engage in them, and he must know, by experience, by general custom, or by formal agreement, that he may engage in them. . . . It should be noted that the concept of "behavior" is intended to include any conceivable act [Brehm, 1966, pp. 3–4].

It is critical to note that this assumptive statement is placed in terms of specific freedoms, not general freedom. Contrary to some interpretations (e.g., Dowd, 1975), the freedoms addressed by the theory are not "abstract considerations," but concrete behavioral realities. If a person knows that he or she can do X (or think X, or believe X, or feel X), then X is a specific, behavioral freedom for that person.

Characteristics of Freedoms

Knowledge That a Freedom Exists

But the person must *know* that he or she *can* do X. Knowledge and ability are the prerequisites for a behavioral freedom. The importance of knowledge in establishing a freedom was demonstrated in an experiment by Jones and Brehm (1970). In their study, subjects read a summary of a supposed court case. Half of the subjects were explicitly informed "that it was clear from the complete transcript that this was definitely not an open-and-shut-case"; the other half were not so informed. Subjects then read a summary of the prosecution's arguments that did or did not include an additional paragraph briefly mentioning some of the defense witnesses and their testimony. The major dependent measure was subjects' ratings of the guilt or innocence of the defendant in the case.

When subjects were told that the case was definitely not open-and-shut, this should have established for them the freedom to believe that the defendant was innocent *and* the freedom to believe that the defendant was guilty. These subjects were aware that there were two legitimate sides to the issue. Subjects who were not so informed presumably knew that there were two formal sides to the issue (every trial having both a prosecution and defense), but they had no reason to believe that it was legitimate and feasible to believe in either side. This differential establishment of attitudinal freedoms should have affected subjects' responses to the communications they read. Subjects in the aware (of both sides) condition should have regarded the one-sided communication (in which only the prosecution's side was presented) as threatening their freedom to believe that the defendant was innocent. Subjects in the unaware condition had not had this freedom so firmly established and, therefore, should not have experienced any threat to a meaningful freedom from the one-sided communication. Based on this reasoning, Jones and Brehm predicted that subjects in the two awareness conditions would not differ in their responses to the two-sided communication (in which there was some mention of defense testimony as well as a summary of the prosecution's arguments), but that subjects in the aware condition should be less persuaded by the one-sided communication than subjects in the unaware condition and should, therefore, perceive the defendant as less guilty.

The data from this study supported these theoretical predictions. Although the one-sided communication was (unexpectedly) more convincing overall, there was a significant interaction between awareness and type of communication. As can be seen from the means displayed in Table 2.1, aware and unaware subjects did not differ when they read a two-sided communication. When, however, they read the one-sided communication, aware subjects believed the defendant to be less guilty than unaware subjects. An attempt to persuade can be a threat to freedom, and thus create reactance, only when it is directed toward a previously established attitudinal freedom.

The role of awareness of having a freedom also was examined by Hass and Linder (1972) in one of three experiments investigating counterargument availability and message structure. In their third experiment this series, Hass and Linder used a modified version of the

TABLE 2.1
Perceptions of Guilt and Innocence[a]

	Communication	
	One-sided	Two-sided
Unaware	7.53[b]	5.39
Aware	6.68	5.95

[a] From Jones, R. A. & Brehm, J. W. Persuasiveness of one- and two-sided communications as a function of awareness there are two sides. *Journal of Experimental Social Psychology*, 1970, 6, 47–56, Table 2, p. 53.

[b] The higher the number, the greater the perception of guilt and acceptance of the advocated position.

Jones and Brehm paradigm. Subjects were made aware or unaware of the two sides to the issue by either receiving or not receiving a summary of the testimony of defense witnesses. As in the Jones and Brehm experiment, it was assumed that subjects in the aware condition would have the freedoms to accept or reject either side of the case more firmly established than subjects in the unaware condition. All subjects then received a supposed prosecutor's summary. For some subjects, this summary was one-sided and contained only the prosecutor's arguments. For others, the prosecutor's arguments were presented along with a reference to the defense witnesses' testimony. This testimony was not directly disputed but was simply acknowledged by the prosecutor, who concluded that it was not sufficient to outweigh the case for the prosecution. Location of this acknowledgment was varied. For some subjects, it was placed at the beginning of the summary; for others, at the end. All subjects then rated their impressions of the defendent's guilt or innocence.

The results obtained by Hass and Linder are displayed in Table 2.2. There was a significant interaction between awareness and message structure. For unaware subjects, early acknowledgement of counterarguments led to less persuasion than no acknowledgement at all. For aware subjects, the opposite pattern was obtained; early acknowledgement of counterarguments led to more persuasion than no acknowledgement at all. For all subjects, late acknowledgement produced intermediate levels of persuasion that did not differ significantly from the persuasion produced by no acknowledgement.

In examining these results, it should be noted first that the one-sided communication is essentially a replication of the one-sided condition of Jones and Brehm, and that the results duplicate their findings. When confronted with a one-sided communication, aware subjects were persuaded less than unaware subjects. Second, it is apparent that ordering

TABLE 2.2
Perceptions of Guilt and Innocence[a]

	Communication		
	One-sided no acknowledgment	Two-sided initial acknowledgment	Two-sided late acknowledgment
Unaware (counterarguments not provided)	7.12[b]	5.80	6.76
Aware (counterarguments provided)	5.68	7.00	6.12

[a] From Hass, R. G. & Linder, D. E. Counterargument availability and effects of message structure on persuasion. *Journal of Personality and Social Psychology*, 1972, *23*, 219–233, Table 3, p. 229. Copyright 1972 by the American Psychological Association. Reprinted by permission.

[b] The higher the number, the greater the perception of guilt and acceptance of the advocated postion.

of the acknowledgement of the other side is also important. (In the Jones and Brehm study, counterargument acknowledgement was placed around the middle of the prosecutor's summary.) For subjects who are aware, one must acknowledge the existence of the other side (and thus acknowledge their freedom to believe in this other side) early in the communication in order to effectively reduce reactance arousal. If acknowledgement comes late, after considerable time is spent trying to persuade them to believe one side, acknowledging their freedom appears less effective. For subjects who are not so aware that there are two legitimate sides to the issue and for whom the freedom to believe either side is less firmly established, early acknowledgement of the other side is counterproductive. Why this should be so is not entirely clear, although Hass and Linder (1972) suggest that such an acknowledgement may disclose "more fully the persuasive (freedom-reducing) intent of the communication [p. 232]."

The two studies by Jones and Brehm, and Hass and Linder, are the only two experiments in the reactance literature to attempt the direct manipulation of awareness of freedom on an attitudinal issue. More typically in reactance research, both the freedom and the subject's awareness of it are created by experimenter fiat. Subjects are told, for example, "You will be free to choose between these two alternatives," establishing the freedoms to have and not to have each of the alternatives. In contrast, subjects in the no freedom condition are told that one of the two alternatives will be assigned to them.

In a study by Nezlek and Brehm (1975), a rather unusual way of creating a freedom was demonstrated. As part of a supposed investigation of physiological reactions to intellectual tasks, subjects were instructed to count backwards from 100 to 0. Some subjects were allowed to do this without interruption. Others were frequently interrupted and insulted (i.e., told they were not going fast enough, told they should try harder because their data were useless). Nezlek and Brehm hypothesized that gratuitous aggression on the part of the experimenter should create the freedom for subjects to counteraggress. This freedom could then be threatened by not allowing the subject the opportunity to aggress against the experimenter. Accordingly, subjects were told they were to administer a guessing task to the experimenter and half of them were also told that they could shock the experimenter for wrong guesses. The other half were not told anything about shock and were simply instructed to tell the experimenter when he made an error. Before any subject had an opportunity to aggress, subjects were asked to rate how much they liked or disliked the experimenter. The data (displayed in Table 2.3) were consistent with the experimental predictions. While subjects in the insult condition disliked the experimenter more than those in the no-insult condition, there was also a significant interaction between insult and opportunity to counteraggress. Insulted subjects liked the experimenter more when they anticipated an opportunity to hurt him; when they, in other words, had their freedom to counteraggress preserved. Subjects who were not insulted tended to like the experimenter less ($p < .07$) when they anticipated being able to shock him.

Competence to Exercise the Freedom

In addition to knowledge that a freedom exists, reactance arousal depends on the person's believing that he or she has the ability necessary to exercise that freedom. A hypothetical freedom that one believes one cannot exercise is less than hollow; in reactance theory, it is no freedom at all.

The most direct examination of this issue was conducted by Wicklund and Brehm (1968). In their study, male subjects were administered a supposed test of social judgment ability and then were told that they were either high or low in this ability. While engaged in making judgments about two supposed job applicants, subjects received a social influence attempt, ostensibly from another subject. Some subjects received a communication that clearly threatened their freedom to rate the job applicants as they wished ("There is no question about

TABLE 2.3
Mean Liking for the Experimenter (Insulter)[a]

	Opportunity to counteraggress	No opportunity to counteraggress
No insult	1.93[b]	3.43
Insult	.43	− 1.36

[a] From Nezlek, J. & Brehm J. W. Hostility as a function of the opportunity to counteraggress. *Journal of Personality*, 1975, *43*, 421–433, Table 1, p. 426. Copyright 1975 by Duke University Press.

[b] Maximum liking = + 5; maximum disliking = − 5.

it; _____ is the best."); others received a communication that simply stated the other subject's supposed opinion about the applicants. Wicklund and Brehm had predicted that the freedom-threatening communication should produce more reactance than the statement of preference and that this difference should be greater for subjects who believed themselves competent to judge the job applicants. While only the two main effects (for competence and threat) were statistically reliable, the pattern of the results (see Table 2.4) supports their reasoning. The only significant difference between high threat and low threat conditions was for high competence subjects; furthermore, the negative attitude change obtained for high competence subjects who received the high threat communication was significantly different from the attitude change (–.20) displayed by high competence control subjects who never received a communication.

Perceived competence has also been suggested by Regan and Brehm (1972; also reported in Brehm, 1966) to account for sex differences they obtained in a study of buying behavior. To describe a complicated procedure very briefly, subjects were supermarket shoppers in a moderate-

TABLE 2.4
Mean Attitude Change[a]

	High threat	Low threat
High competence	− 2.37[b]	.07
Low competence	.76	2.14

[a] From Wicklund, R. A. & Brehm, J. W. Attitude change as a function of felt competence and threat to attitudinal freedom. *Journal of Experimental Social Psychology*, 1968, *4*, 64–75, Table 2, p. 71.

[b] A negative number indicates movement away from the position advocated by the communicator.

sized southern city. Control subjects purchased items as usual. Experimental subjects received either a high pressure written message to buy a certain brand of bread or a low pressure message. In addition, subjects were given either 25¢ (the purchase price of bread in the good ol' days!) or 35¢. For male shoppers, there was no evidence of a reactance effect. As can be seen in Table 2.5, high verbal pressure led to greater buying of the designated item than low pressure which, in turn, led to greater buying than in the control condition, and amount of money had no effect. For female shoppers, however, there was evidence of a reactance effect. While all of the experimental manipulations increased buying over control levels, the greatest level of conformity to the persuasive communication was obtained in the condition where the *least* pressure was exerted. More female shoppers who received the low pressure message and 25¢ bought the designated bread than those who received low pressure and 35¢, high pressure and 35¢, or (marginally, $p < .15$) high pressure and 25¢. In discussing their results, Regan and Brehm proposed that females in this study felt more competent to choose among different types of bread and that this perceived competence more firmly established their freedoms to reject the advocated bread and to buy non-advocated brands.

TABLE 2.5
Percentages of Compliance (Buying Brand X) Among Shoppers[a]

	Male shoppers	
	Monday	Tuesday
Control (normal buying)	16.7%	11.1%
	With 25¢	With 35¢
Low verbal pressure	37.5%	45%
High verbal pressure	73.3%	77.8%
	Female shoppers	
	Monday	Tuesday
Control (normal buying)	23.6%	17.9%
	With 25¢	With 35¢
Low verbal pressure	70%	40%
High verbal pressure	51.3%	40%

[a] From an experiment by Regan and Brehm reported in Brehm, J. W., *A theory of psychological reactance*, New York: Academic Press, 1966, Tables XVII and XVIII, pp. 88–89.

This sex difference was replicated by McGillis and Brehm (1975) in their replication and extension of the Regan and Brehm supermarket study. Considering only the threat conditions of their study (see Chapter 5 for a more complete description of this experiment), they found a significant reduction in buying behavior for high threat ("You will buy only [brand name]") as compared to low threat ("Please try [brand name]"), but only for female shoppers. Unfortunately for the sake of experimental and theoretical clarity, another replication of Regan and Brehm by Gilbert and Peterson (1971) did not obtain a sex difference, although the latter investigators did find the lowest level of purchasing in the condition where highest pressure was exerted (i.e., high verbal pressure + 35¢).

The Regan and Brehm hypothesis that people with different experiential backgrounds may perceive themselves as differentially competent in certain situations can be extended to any number of populations. Perceived competence should be increased for any group of individuals who have had frequent and successful opportunities to discriminate among particular objects. Goldman and Wallis (1979) investigated this more general possibility by having students who either were or were not majoring in art role-play the selection of one painting from a group of four. All of the paintings were described as costing $30. For two of the paintings, it was noted that the buyer would have to pay money, either the full purchase price or half of the purchase price because of a bonus available to buyers. Bonuses were such for the other two paintings that buyers would not have to pay any money in order to obtain them. Comparing art to non-art majors and paintings costing money versus those that were free, there was a significant interaction (see Table 2.6). Art majors tended to prefer the paintings that cost money, while non-art majors tended to prefer the ones that were free. Goldman and Wallis proposed that the cost attached to two of the pictures constituted a threat to subjects' freedom to select these pictures, but that this freedom was meaningful only for those students

TABLE 2.6
Percentage of Subjects Saying They Would Purchase Paintings[a]

	Paintings that would cost money (%)	Paintings that would not cost money (%)
Art majors	60	40
Non-art majors	35	65

[a] Data from Goldman and Wallis, 1979.

who viewed themselves as competent in evaluating artistic productions.

It should be noted that none of the individual studies we have described is without flaw. Wicklund and Brehm failed to obtain the predicted interaction. The sex difference findings in the supermarket studies range from a post-hoc explanation through replication through failure to replicate. Alternative explanations involving the implied greater value of the costly pictures are certainly possible for the Goldman and Wallis study. Taken as a whole, however, these studies provide reasonably good support for the theoretical logic. Reactance arises from a threat to freedom, and to possess a freedom, one must perceive oneself to be competent to exercise it. If one does not perceive oneself as competent, reactance against a threat to that freedom will be minimal or nonexistent.

The Strength with Which a Freedom Is Held

When one considers that feelings of competency in regard to exercising a freedom can vary throughout the range from feeling incompetent to feeling extremely competent, it becomes apparent that the subjective impression of having a freedom is not all or none. The impression of having a freedom can vary from strong doubt to total conviction. This point is most obvious, perhaps, in regard to control over outcomes through the use of intellectual and physical skills. Accordingly, the first mention of this point as a theoretical amendment to reactance theory occurred in Wortman and Brehm's (1975) discussion of how people respond to uncontrollable outcomes. Their discussion suggested that, depending on an individual's experience with the type of task, the expectation of being able to control the outcome (be successful at the task) can vary from weak to strong. The stronger is the expectation of control (freedom), the more resistant it should be to disconfirmation. Thus, when the individual is unsure about his or her control over the outcome, failure will relatively quickly lead to becoming convinced that one does not, after all, have control over the outcome. On the other hand, when the individual is firmly convinced that he or she can perform the task and thereby control the outcome, extensive failure is necessary to convince the person otherwise. Because failure constitutes a threat to the individual's expectation of control (freedom), it arouses reactance. As is apparent from the preceding discussion, more reactance can be aroused in regard to a firm expectation of control than in regard to a weak one because the threat to control (amount of failure) can become much greater for the former than the latter before the expectation of control is given up.

Variation in the strength with which a freedom is held applies to other kinds of freedoms besides those associated with abilities. Carpenters, for example, can be firmly convinced that they have the freedom to take care of their tools however they wish, but have doubts about their freedom to give orders to their peers on the job. Quite clearly, more reactance would be aroused by a threat to the former freedom than to the latter.

Absolute versus Conditional Freedoms

While all specific behavioral freedoms share the properties of knowledge and competence, some freedoms will be more widely available than others. These more widely available freedoms can be called absolute freedoms; they are available now and in the future, in all situations. Absolute freedoms are probably confined to internal processes. For example, we have the freedom to think some things (though not necessarily all) any time we want. Many freedoms, especially overt acts, are not absolute, but are conditional on the context. A person may, for instance, feel free to smoke in a bar, but not in a movie. The freedom to watch TV may exist for a specific individual only after household chores are completed. Conditional freedoms are no less free than absolute ones; they are more limited in scope.

These limits impose important restrictions on the possibilities for reactance arousal. Take, for example, the situation of being free to watch TV only after doing one's chores. Since the freedom to watch TV does not exist prior to finishing up chores, the injunction "You must not watch TV now" delivered before the chores were done could not pose a threat to freedom. Being told "You must not watch TV after you finish your chores," however, would pose a threat, as would "You must not watch TV now" if the latter statement were made to the person after his or her chores were completed. Both of these statements would threaten a freedom even if the person felt no particular inclination to watch TV. Once the necessary contextual conditions are met (or the person anticipates meeting them), the freedom is established and can be threatened regardless of whether the person actually intends to engage in the behavior.

These distinctions are more than an exercise in Talmudic logic. They represent important psychological differences that must be taken into account if one is to apply the theory properly. It is absolutely necessary that the exact freedom and the exact threat to freedom be clearly specified. A great deal of theoretical and empirical confusion can be avoided by careful specification of what is the threat and what is the freedom.

At this point, it may be helpful to emphasize that all of the foregoing discussion of knowledge, competence, strength of belief in a freedom, and the absolute or conditional properties of a freedom should be firmly anchored to a vantage point somewhere inside the individual's head. For the theory, freedoms are the creatures of subjective reality. If a person thinks he or she has the freedom to do X, and the ability to exercise this freedom, and perceives the conditions of the freedom's existence to be met, then this freedom exists for this person. It is theoretically irrelevant whether this freedom exists according to some more objective criteria. The subjective perception of freedom is the necessary and sufficient prerequisite for a freedom to exist. This statement does not mean that there will be no significant consequences for a person who perceives a freedom to exist even though physical reality does not permit the freedom and/or other people do not view the person as having this freedom. Such consequences may well ensue, but they do not affect the theoretically necessary properties of behavioral freedoms.

The subjective framework on which reactance theory is based has two important theoretical implications. First, viewing freedoms as subjective realities implies that there will be considerable variation in people's beliefs concerning their existing freedoms. These beliefs will be influenced by personal life experiences, cultural patterns, and various characteristics of the social and physical environment. Thus although the perception of behavioral freedoms is posited to be a universal phenomenon, the content of this perception is expected to be specific to the individual and his or her situation.

Second, the subjective foundation of freedoms can create an apparent paradox. Unless there is an established freedom, forces operating on the individual cannot arouse reactance and consequent opposition to those forces. Opposition to external control is thus presumed to occur only when that control intrudes upon territory the person regards as free. As Mugny (1978) states it, "When his freedom is the most threatened, because he is not given the freedom of choice, rather than recover his freedom, he accepts his subjugation [p. 8]." Reactance theory does not expect people always to be motivated to oppose control over their behavior. Instead, it tries to specify those conditions under which this opposition is most likely to occur, and opposition is not expected to occur unless there was perceived freedom to begin with.

Perceived Freedom and Choice

Since reactance theory holds that freedoms are defined internally and subjectively, a great deal of research (e.g., Kruglanski & Cohen, 1973, 1974; Trope, 1978; Trope & Burnstein, 1977) in which observers attribute freedom or choice to an observed other cannot be utilized within the framework of the theory. Attributions of freedom to others are of interest in their own right, but research on this topic cannot tell us directly about how an individual comes to perceive the existence of his or her own behavioral freedoms.

There are, however, two other research perspectives on perceived freedom and choice that seem more relevant to reactance. The first of these is Steiner's (1970) model of perceived freedom. Although most of the research on this theory has used observer subjects' attributing freedom to a target person (and thus will not be examined here), Steiner's theoretical model clearly addresses self-attributions of freedom as well.

Steiner distinguishes between two types of freedom: outcome freedom and decision freedom. The person who has outcome freedom is defined as having a high probability of obtaining desired outcomes; there should, therefore, be greater perceived freedom with positive outcomes than with negative ones. For decision freedom, the person selects the outcomes he or she will seek and the means to use in seeking them. More specifically, Steiner states that "perceived decision freedom is greatest when expected gains are approximately equal [p. 195]."

The second theoretical perspective of interest involves Harvey's (1976) application of Mills' certainty model to perceived choice. This application is directly related to the ambiguity inherent in Steiner's "approximately equal" hypothesis. In this phrase, it is unclear whether Steiner means to stress the "approximately" or the "equal." Harvey and his colleagues have avoided such ambiguity in their approach. They reason that in order for perceived choice to be high, choice alternatives must be differentially attractive *and* there must be the possibility that the unchosen alternative will lead to a more desirable outcome than the initially preferred object. The choice situation that best fits these conditions is that in which there is a small difference in attractiveness between choice alternatives.

Studies on subject's attribution of choice to themselves by Harvey and Johnson (1973) and Jellison and Harvey (1973) supported their prediction that perceived choice would be greater with a small difference in attractiveness as compared to either a large difference or identical attractiveness. Later research by Harvey and Harris (1975) suggested that this relationship may hold only for positive outcomes and, supporting Steiner's view of outcome freedom, found that positive outcomes led to greater perceived choice than negative outcomes.

If we can make a small translation in Steiner's model and substitute "slightly different" for "approximately equal," then Steiner and Harvey et al. can be seen to have proposed the same conditions for maximization of perceived freedom and choice. It is not clear, however, that these would be the same conditions that would be proposed by reactance theory. All three theoretical models deal with perceptions of own freedom and choice, but they deal with this issue at different levels. Steiner and Harvey et al. are concerned with perceived amounts of general freedom–choice. Reactance theory is concerned with specific freedoms.

For example, reactance theory posits that in a free choice situation with three alternatives, the individual would perceive himself or herself to have the freedoms to take each option and to reject each. Although the freedom to take the most attractive alternative would be seen as the most important freedom, the freedoms to take the other two do exist and could be threatened. It is not clear whether Steiner would view the freedoms to have the relatively unattractive second and third alternatives as each representing an outcome freedom.

More generally, there is simply a lack of fit between Steiner's and Harvey et al.'s outcome categories and reactance theory. Negative potential outcomes, like positive ones, can be the source of important freedoms. What is important about a potential negative outcome is the freedom to avoid it, and a choice situation made up of only negative alternatives, therefore, contains the possibility for arousal of reactance if one or more of these avoidance freedoms is threatened or eliminated. Similarly, if one has a choice between a positive and a negative alternative, the elimination of the positive alternative would arouse reactance not only because of the loss of the freedom to have the positive alternative but also because of the loss of the freedom to avoid the negative. In addition, as discussed by Wicklund (1974), reactance theory does not regard individuals as seeking only to accumulate positive outcomes. Reactance can be aroused by forcing a desirable object on a person as well as by eliminating access to it. The freedom to reject the desirable object may be less important than the freedom to obtain it (and therefore the reactance aroused may be less in the former case than in the latter). Nevertheless, both freedoms do exist and can be threatened.

How much reactance would be generated by identical levels of attractiveness is a somewhat more complicated issue. If the attractiveness of the two items is identical because the two items are the same, then no reactance should be aroused. Both items fulfill the same needs, and no freedom is threatened by the loss of one of them. But if the items are indeed different, even though they begin with identical levels of perceived attractiveness, then reactance arousal upon the loss of one should be great. The amount of reactance, in this case, is proportional to the absolute attractiveness of the lost alternative, and any importance that might be attached to the freedom to reject the remaining alternative.

Finally, let us consider the case in which a decision involves two attractive alternatives, A and B, and let us suppose that A is considerably more attractive than B. If we hold the attractiveness of A constant and increase the attractiveness of B, decision freedom or perceived choice, according to Steiner and Harvey *et al.*, will first increase as the two alternatives become nearly equal in attractiveness and then decrease as B becomes clearly more attractive than A. However, in terms of reactance theory, if the individual were to lose the freedom to have alternative B, the amount of reactance arousal would be a direct function of the attractiveness of B, regardless of B's attractiveness relative to A. Quite clearly, decision freedom or perceived choice as conceived by Steiner or Harvey *et al.* would not predict the amount of reactance that would be predicted by reactance theory to occur if B were eliminated from the person's choice. (For further discussion of reactance arousal during choice, see Chapter 8).

This review of the literature on perceived freedom and choice, concentrating especially on the work of Steiner and Harvey *et al.*, suggests that our understanding of the conditions under which individuals perceive themselves to be free (i.e., to have a freedom) is still limited and beset by many unresolved issues. Reactance theory can always argue that the existence of freedom is an assumption that need not be tested and can use face-valid manipulations of freedom in laboratory research. However, there is no doubt that the theory would be considerably enriched by a more detailed conceptualization of the situational variables affecting one's perception of freedom.

Desire for Freedom

In a way, reactance theory assumes a conservative stance on people's desire for freedom. The theory assumes that individuals believe they have specific behavioral freedoms and proposes that if a freedom is threatened, the motive to reassert the freedom will be aroused. Thus people are regarded as motivated to protect that which they already possess. The theory does not assume any particular motive for people to perceive themselves as possessing behavioral freedoms. That they come to have this perception is all that is necessary for the theory. Why this perception comes about is unknown and is not addressed theoretically. Perhaps people do have specific behavioral freedoms and the theoretical assumption mirrors reality. Perhaps people are motivated to believe they have freedoms, regardless of what actually exists. Perhaps the organism is "wired" such that the perception of behavioral freedoms is functional. The possibilities are myriad, and interesting, but not essential to the theory. Moreover, the theory makes no assumptions about any motive to expand or maximize the number of freedoms one possesses.

Indeed, as demonstrated in a study by Brehm and Rozen (1971), the theory sees the expansion of freedom as an inherently complex process. In this experiment, female undergraduate students participated in a supposed study of consumer preference. Over a series of six sessions, subjects rated and tasted three unfamiliar (Argentinian) desserts. Half the subjects were given the freedom to choose which dessert they would taste in a given session: the other half were assigned a dessert. This assignment was yoked to the choice of each high freedom subject. For example, if a high freedom subject chose to taste her most attractive dessert, the corresponding low freedom subject was assigned to taste the dessert that *she* had rated as most attractive. At the last session, an additional item was introduced into the array. This fourth alternative was a familiar dessert that was perceived as more attactive than any of the three Argentinian desserts.[1] Subjects were asked to proceed as usual at this sixth session, but this time they were to rate four alternatives and they could choose (high freedom) or be assigned (low freedom) one of the four alternatives to taste.

These experimental procedures were designed to create the psychological conditions that exist when a person has his or her behavioral freedoms expanded. Over the course of the previous sessions, high freedom condition subjects had firmly established and repeatedly exercised their freedom to choose to taste any of the Argentinian desserts.

---

[1] The fourth alternative was either pound cake or cherry cheesecake. It was intended that the cheesecake be perceived as more attractive than the pound cake and that it therefore constitute a stronger threat to the freedom to taste any of the Argentinian desserts. Although the attractiveness ratings of these two items were in the predicted direction, there was no significant difference between them, and they did not have any differential effects on subjects' ratings of the Argentinian desserts. The attempt to vary magnitude of threat was, thus, unsuccessful. Both new desserts were, however, rated as more attractive than any of the three "old"dessert items.

When the highly attractive new alternative was introduced, subjects were motivated to taste it and this motivation threatened their freedom to taste any of the old choice alternatives. Since the old alternatives also differed in attractiveness for each subject, the most important freedom that was threatened was the freedom to taste that Argentinian dessert that, overall, each subject had regarded as the most attractive of the three. Low freedom subjects, however, had established no freedoms and could not have any freedoms threatened by the introduction of the new choice alternative. Since the low freedom condition is identical to the high freedom condition except for the establishment of freedom, the ratings of low freedom subjects provide an appropriate comparison against which to assess experimental effects on high freedom subjects.

Based on this kind of analysis, Brehm and Rozen predicted that reactance arousal would be maximized for high freedom subjects on their final ratings of their previously most preferred alternative. Reactance was expected to be manifested in an increase in attractiveness of this item. For the most attractive "old" alternative, then, the change in ratings from the average of the first five sessions to the sixth should be more positive for high freedom subjects than for subjects in the low freedom condition.

Brehm and Rozen's results were consistent with their prediction (see Table 2.7). For low freedom subjects, changes in attractiveness ratings after the new alternative was introduced tended to be negative, and were most negative for the alternative that was previously seen as most attractive. For high freedom subjects, the opposite pattern was obtained with the most positive change in attractiveness ratings obtained for the alternative previously regarded as most attractive. The interaction between freedom condition and the most versus the least attractive

TABLE 2.7
Changes in Attractiveness When the New Alternative Was Introduced[a]

	Old alternative[b]		
	Most attractive	Middle attractive	Least attractive
Low freedom	− 1.96	− .71	− .08
High freedom	+ .33	− .26	− .74

[a] From Brehm, J. W. & Rozen, E. Attractiveness of old alternatives when a new attractive alternative is introduced. *Journal of Personality and Social Psychology*, 1971, *20*, 261–266, Table 1, p. 264. Copyright 1971 by the American Psychological Association. Reprinted by permission.
[b] Based on average ratings for the first five sessions.

old items was significant as was each of the individual comparisons between the most and least attractive alternatives within each level of freedom.

These data suggest, then, that no simple statements about one's desire for freedom are possible from a reactance theory point of view. Since freedoms are always seen as specific entities, they may conflict and collide. New freedoms can threaten old ones; any particular freedom may be incompatible with any other particular freedom. In the Brehm and Rozen study, high freedom subjects were, no doubt, pleased to have the opportunity to taste a new attractive dessert; they also, however, showed some regret at losing the chance to taste their most attractive old one.

From this perspective, comments such as those by Gergen (1978) represent a serious misreading of the theory. Gergen asserts that reactance has disregarded "broad cultural patterns." He bases this assertion on the observation that there are "numerous instances in which people have readily relinquished their freedom and have pressed toward increasing controls over their own behavior [Gergen, 1978, p. 511]."

We would take issue with this statement. First, reactance does not ignore "broad cultural patterns." Cultural patterns will affect almost all manifestations of the theoretical variables. Most important, perhaps, cultural patterns will contribute heavily to the specific freedoms that individuals within a given context perceive themselves to possess.

Second, reactance theory cannot address the issue of relinquishing *freedom*; it can speak only to defending or not defending specific freedoms. In point of fact, as the theory notes, people relinquish freedoms every day. They do so every time they make a choice between alternatives. What the theory points out is that there is an internal, counteracting cost for exercising one freedom at the expense of another. The motivation to have the foregone alternative is increased and this alternative is seen as more desirable than it was. The behavioral consequences of such reactance arousal will vary widely depending on the situation. If it is very strong, the person may try to revoke his or her decision and regain the relinquished freedom. If it is not very strong, the only consequence will likely be some increased internal tension and discomfort. This latter set of circumstances probably provides the best description of what happened to the high freedom subjects in the Brehm and Rozen study. Their positive evaluation of the most attractive old alternative was slightly enhanced, but the vast majority of them (24 out of 27 subjects) still chose to taste the new attractive dessert.

Whether people (or rats–Voss and Homzie, 1970; or pigeons–Catania,

1975) have some intrinsic desire for freedom and choice or, on the other hand, desire to escape the unpleasant aspects of personal freedom (Fromm, 1941) are interesting issues, but ones that lie outside the purview of reactance theory. The theory, instead, takes a minimal and conservative position: People are assumed to perceive themselves as having specific behavioral freedoms and, under specific conditions designated by the theory, can be motivated to reassert a specific freedom that is eliminated or threatened with elimination.

Attribution in the Service of Freedom Enchancement

Even within this minimal and conservative framework, however, behavior can become quite complex. If, for example, an individual perceives that a certain action might constitute a threat to a perceived freedom, this individual might avoid engaging in that action. Such avoidance could be seen as reflecting some intrinsic motive to be free (or, at least, to perceive oneself as a free agent). Within the framework provided by reactance theory, however, avoidance would still be considered a defensive, reactive maneuver. Threat is anticipated, a freedom is threatened by implication if not in fact, and the threatening behavior/situation is thus avoided.

The capacity of anticipated threats to threaten freedoms by implication offers an acceptable theoretical foundation for application of the theory to research on the actor–observer difference in causal attributions. As the actor–observer difference was initially proposed by Jones and Nisbett (1972) and Nisbett, Caputo, Legant and Marecek (1973), reactance was seen as one possible explanatory mechanism.

Brehm (1966) has written at some length on the "reactance" motive, or man's desire to see himself as free and able to control events that are important to him. Such a motive is probably best served when the individual perceives himself to act in accordance with the demands and opportunities of each new situation. . . . On the other hand, the individual's sense of freedom should be enhanced to the extent that he sees others to possess broad behavioral dispositions. The more predictable the behavior of others, the more the individual can perceive the social environment to be stable and understandable and therefore controllable [Nisbett et al., 1973, pp. 163–164].

Reviewing the research evidence on the actor–observer difference, Monson and Snyder (1977) stated that while there is some evidence that under certain conditions actors report more freedom than observers, a general identification of situational causality with actor freedom is not warranted: "It is simply that perceptions of freedoms are not inherent in either situational or dispositional attributions; actors will construct whatever self-perceptions will maximize their sense of behavioral freedom and self-determination relative to that of other individuals [p. 103]." Furthermore, Wolosin, Esser and Fine (1975) have pointed out that the world of causality is not divided into the two parts of dispositional versus situational attributions. Attributions to more specific internal causes, such as self-directed decisions, as opposed to more general internal traits may offer the greatest implications of behavioral freedom.

In the midst of all this, we would like to preserve the baby for reactance theory, but throw out some of the bathwater. We must disavow attributions to the "reactance motive" when it is defined as "man's desire to see himself as free." As has been stated, no such motive is assumed. On the other hand, if one type of causal attribution is perceived as a potential threat to freedom, it would be consistent with the theory for this type of attribution to be avoided and attributions that have fewer implied threats to freedom to be adopted.

Research and theory on the avoidance of predictability can be treated in a similar fashion. For example, Miller (1975) found that observers generalized from a sample of an actor's behavior more than did the actual actors. This finding may reflect, at least in part, actor subjects' anticipation of threat to their future behavioral freedoms if they made generalized predictions about their future behavior. Recent work by Snyder and his colleagues (e.g., Snyder & Wicklund, 1981), in which they propose that people sometimes behave inconsistently so as to promote ambiguous causal attributions by others and thus decrease predictability by others, could also involve avoidance of anticipated threats to future behaviors.

THREATS AND ELIMINATIONS

Once a specific freedom has been established, it becomes possible to speak of threats to or eliminations of that freedom. In this section we will describe the various types of threats and eliminations that occur. Such a taxonomy is perhaps not essential for the theory, but it does serve to help define the domain addressed by the theory. First, however, we must examine how threats occur.

What Constitutes a Threat to Freedom

Given that a person believes he or she has a specific freedom, any force on the individual that makes it more difficult for him or her to exercise the freedom constitutes a threat to it. Thus, any kind of attempted social influence, any kind of impersonal event, and any behavior on the part of the individual holding the freedom (including his or her preferences) that work against exercising the freedom can be defined as threats. Obvious examples of social influence attempts that will be seen as threats are commands, persuasion, attempts to bribe for compliance or threaten with punishment for noncompliance, and communication of consensus information. Examples of impersonal events that threaten freedoms are the passage of restrictive laws, the occurrence of shortages in materials and products, and accidents of a social or natural origin, as when an earthquake devastates the city where one had planned to vacation. Threats from one's own behavior occur when preferences or decisions interfere with exercise of a freedom (as when one alternative must be rejected in order to obtain another).

The above examples seem clear enough, but certain potential ambiguities should be noted. Can pure information threaten a freedom? Consider the case of a woman who is trying to decide which of two cars to buy. Having familiarized herself with the available literature on the two cars, our customer prefers the features of Car A over those of Car B. Upon talking to several acquaintances, however, she discovers that the local service department for Car A has a much poorer reputation than that for Car B. This information clearly makes it more difficult for the individual to exercise her freedom to acquire Car A and should constitute a threat to that freedom. If good service is of high importance to this individual, her preference may now switch to Car B. In this instance, those specific freedoms that would have been satisfied only by Car A (e.g., appearance, comfort, handling quality) now are threatened and reactance will be aroused.

A second potential ambiguity is raised by the inclusion of impersonal events as threats to freedom. For example, does the individual who takes a vacation at a resort for swimming and sunning have a freedom threatened by cloudy, rainy weather? The problem in this case centers on the expectation that the individual had in regard to the weather. Quite clearly, the freedom to sun oneself depends on the weather where one plans to do it, and one would not go to a traditionally rainy area to exercise that freedom. Nor can one have a firm freedom to sun oneself in a location where the chances of sun are no better than moderate. A person who went to such a place would have at best only a weak freedom to bask in the sun, and a cloudy day would produce little or no reactance. Only if the individual went to a place that was essentially always sunny would there be a firm freedom that would be threatened by clouds and, thus, would there be significant arousal of reactance.

Sources of Reactance Arousal

The original statement of reactance theory (Brehm, 1966) distinguished between social and nonsocial sources of threats to freedom, and between personal and impersonal threats. These distinctions are not inherent in the theory and will not be emphasized in the present volume. They have some heuristic value in applying the theory to the analysis of various kinds of situations, however, and so they will be discussed briefly here.

Threats to and eliminations of freedom can first be classified in terms of the location of the source. Sources of threat can be internal or external. Internal threats are those we impose on ourselves when, for example, we make a decision and choose one choice alternative while rejecting others. External threats come from a variety of sources, which can be classified in terms of two theoretically independent dimensions.

The first dimension is that of impersonal versus personal abrogations of freedom. This dimension was originally (Brehm, 1966) defined by the perceptions of the individual whose freedom is threatened. In the case of impersonal threats, "an individual cannot easily perceive [the threat] as having been directed at himself" and "is unlikely to impute motives for it" [Brehm, 1966, p. 17]." Personal threats, in contrast, are perceived as intentional. When a person is confronted with a personal threat, "he can perceive or easily imagine that [it] was intentionally aimed at him [Brehm, 1966, p 38]."

This distinction between personal and impersonal threats was viewed as theoretically meaningful because of the differential inferences about the future that each implied. Because a personal threat involves perceived intent to influence one's own free behavior, the possibility that future threats to future freedoms will occur is increased. As we have noted before and will discuss in more detail elsewhere (Chapter 3), implied threats to future freedoms will increase reactance arousal. Impersonal threats, however, because they are not perceived as directed specifically at the person, may not imply threats to future freedoms and may, therefore, create less reactance arousal than personal threats.

It is important to note that this comparison of personal and impersonal threats in terms of threats to future freedoms makes the assumption that the person is more likely to have continued contact with the source of a personal threat than with the source of an impersonal one. This assumption is not always appropriate. Although personal threats would seem more likely to arise from sources with which one has extended contact (i.e., to threaten my freedom, the source will typically have to know *me*), they could conceivably come from a source with which an individual has one and only one interaction. Moreover, it would seem distinctly possible that an impersonal threat could be received from a source with which one interacts frequently. Perhaps the best example of such threats comes from one's interactions with large organizations. The government, the phone company, and one's employer threaten one's freedoms all the time. These organizations can threaten one's freedoms quite impersonally (nothing being directed at any individual person), but when a threat to freedom is received from such a source, there often are important implications for future freedoms.

These considerations suggest that the dimension of personal versus impersonal freedom is too theoretically complex to be very useful. Instead, one should examine the freedom in terms of the more specific variables involved. Does the person expect to have future interactions with the source? If so, implications for threats to future freedoms are heightened and reactance arousal should be increased.

The other dimension on which external threats can be categorized is that of social versus nonsocial threats. Consideration of this dimension points out the important theoretical postulate that threats to freedom can come from social or nonsocial sources. This perspective has been questioned by some theorists. For example, Heilman and Toffler (1976) propose what is essentially an impression management version of reactance theory. In their view, the presence of a social agent is indispensible for reactance effects (i.e., reassertion of the freedom) to occur if not for reactance arousal (see Chapter 10 for an extended discussion of impression management interpretations of reactance theory). Mugny and Doise (1979) speak of catching a "glimpse" ("*entrevior au travers*") of a social source behind any apparently nonsocial one and thus imply that a social agent is necessary for reactance arousal.[2]

This issue is a rather difficult one for reactance theory and, at some level, will probably never be resolved unequivocally. It is a matter of how much of a "glimpse" actually suffices to constitute a perceived social source. To illustrate the problem, let us take a few studies and examine the "socialness" of the agent involved. Some studies, such as those by Sensenig and Brehm (1968), Worchel and Brehm (1971), and Pallak and Heller (1971), use an experimental paradigm in which one person threatens the freedom of another, and here there is no question

---

[2] See also Chapter 8 for a discussion of Brounstein, Ostrove, and Mills' (1979) contention that reactance effects stemming from self-imposed threats to freedom occurring during decision making depend on there being a public statement of predecision preference.

that the source is a social one. Similarly, we can agree that the attitude change studies (see Chapter 6), in which a persuasive communication is heard or read by subjects, clearly involve a social source of threat. In terms of who "receives" the subsequent attempt by the subject to restore freedom by opposing the influence that has been brought to bear, none of the preceding studies had the subject express directly to the threatening agent. In all of them, however, the experimenter did collect the subjects' opinions (though the opinion measures may have been described as anonymous) and, to this extent, the behavioral expression of reactance arousal did take place in a social setting.

In other studies, the threatening agent seems distinctly less social in nature. Brehm, Stires, Sensenig, and Shaban (1966) told subjects that a potential choice alternative had failed to arrive in shipment. Brehm and Hammock (in Brehm, 1966) presented children with two pieces of candy placed either close to or far away from them on a table. Brehm and Weinraub (1977) presented two-year-olds with toys that were either behind a barrier or not. In the supermarket studies (Gilbert & Peterson, 1971; McGillis & Brehm, 1975; Regan & Brehm 1972), shoppers received a card with verbal and monetary inducements on it. All of these studies were intended to create threats from nonsocial agents. Depending, however, on how slight a glimpse one is willing to settle for, some kind of social agent may have been perceived.

Subjects in the Brehm et al. (1966) study may have, for example, seen the experimenter as responsible for the failure in shipment or may not have believed the shipment story. Children in the Brehm and Hammock, and Brehm and Weinraub studies may have perceived the threat to come from the experimenter's placement of the objects rather than from the distance or the barrier, as intended. Shoppers in the supermarket may have perceived either bread company executives or advertising agency employees as threatening their freedom to choose the brand of their choice. Moreover, in the first two studies, the experimenter collected subjects' ratings or watched subjects choose. In the Brehm and Weinraub study, subjects' behavior was observed from behind a one-way mirror, whereas in the supermarket studies, unobtrusive experimental assistants observed shoppers' purchases. In these last two instances, then, it is hard to believe that expressed oposition to the barrier or to the high pressure sales tactic was designed to impress the possible social agent who possibly was perceived as the source of the threat. There were, however, mothers present when 2-year-olds played with toys, and check-out clerks were present when shoppers bought bread, so the reactance motivated behavior did take place in a social context.

It is simply difficult to know how far to take all of this. In order to obtain reactance effects that could not be—in any way, shape, or form—attributed to either a social source of threat or a social recipient of the freedom restoring behavior, one would somehow have to engineer a situation where the subject could not perceive that the threat was social nor that his or her response was observed. Such a study has not yet been done. What we do have is a variety of situations in which the social quality of the source of a threat varies. Reactance effects have been obtained across this range. This suggests to us that neither the source nor the behavioral situation need be social in character for reactance effects to occur.

SUMMARY

A freedom is defined as a belief that one can engage in a particular behavior. Freedoms include what one does, how one does it, or when one does it. A person can come to hold a freedom through experience, formal or informal agreement, observation of how others behave, custom, law, etc. In addition to knowing that a certain behavior can be engaged in, (by, for example, formal agreement), an individual must have the requisite ability in order to have a meaningful freedom. In addition, like a belief, a freedom has the status of an expectancy and can be held with more or less strength. Freedoms also can be absolute, in the sense that one always has them (e.g., the freedom to have fantasies), or they may be conditional, in the sense that they are held only under certain conditions. Experimental evidence supporting the contention that reactance is aroused only when a person holds a freedom and only when the individual feels competent to exercise that freedom was reviewed.

The relationship between freedom as conceived by reactance theory and perceived freedom or choice in current theories of perceived freedom or choice was discussed. Current theories of perceived choice or freedom are concerned with a generalized notion rather than with specific freedoms, and they therefore have little relevance to reactance theory. It was also stressed that although reactance is conceived as a motivational state, there is no assumption in the theory that individuals are motivated to have or gain freedom, only that they are motivated to restore freedoms that are threatened or eliminated.

A threat to freedom is the perception that some event has increased the difficulty of exercising the freedom in question. The source of threats can be external, as when one is subjected to social pressure or when a choice alternative is taken away, or the source can be internal, as when one must choose between two alternatives and thereby eliminate the freedom to have one of them. Additional ways to categorize threats and eliminations were also discussed, with particular attention to whether or not the source of a threat needs to be social in nature to arouse reactance.

CHAPTER 3

Determinants of the Magnitude of Reactance: Characteristics of the Freedom

Formally, reactance has the status of an intervening, hypothetical variable. It is the motivational state that is hypothesized to occur when a freedom is eliminated or threatened with elimination. We cannot measure reactance directly, but hypothesizing its existence allows us to predict a variety of behavioral effects. Because it is cumbersome to have to spell out these connections every time an empirical investigation is described, we will frequently refer to reactance as having been increased or decreased when what we really should say is that the behavioral effects were such that they allow us to make the inference that reactance was increased or decreased. This kind of shorthand is often used when discussing theories involving intervening constructs, and we hope that it will not confuse the reader.

One other caution to the reader may help prevent the following discussion of the theory from creating unnecessary confusion. Reactance is conceived to be a counterforce motivating the person to reassert or restore the threatened or eliminated freedom. It exists only in the context of other forces motivating the person to give up the freedom and comply with the threat or elimination. One general methodological strategy followed by many studies of reactance is to increase the magnitude of reactance such that the reactance forces will be stronger than the compliance forces. When this is done successfully, a true boomerang effect is obtained. That is, negative change away from the position or behavior being advocated for the person is significantly greater than either whatever has happened in a no-influence control group or than the positive change that has occurred in the group where reactance arousal was not maximized. Sometimes, however, only reduced compliance is obtained. The change in the direction of the position or behavior being advocated is less in the strong reactance condition than in the one where reactance arousal is expected to be weak, but it may not differ from or may even be more positive than change in a no-influence control condition. Boomerang effects represent the best evidence for reactance theory, but obtaining reduced compliance (presuming there are no feasible alternative explanations for this reduction) also supports the theory. It is not always possible to intensify the magnitude of reactance arousal such that it overwhelms the existing forces motivating compliance, but neither is it theoretically necessary. As will be seen, the reactance literature contains both boomerang effects and reduced compliance. We believe that both kinds of findings, taken as a whole, provide considerable empirical support for the theoretical model. A more detailed consideration of the conditions under which one may expect boomerang effects as opposed to reduced positive influence is provided in Chapter 4.

Importance of Freedom

Reactance theory is based on two major elements: freedoms and threats. The determinants of the magnitude of reactance are also based on these two major elements. One determinant is the importance of the freedom. In the original presentation of the theory, importance of freedom was defined as an interactive product: "The importance of a given [behavioral freedom] is a direct funtion of the unique instrumental value which the behavior has for the satisfaction of needs, multiplied by the actual or potential maximum magnitude of the need [Brehm, 1966, pp. 4–5]."

This definition points out the crucial issue of whether the free behavior is perceived as having unique instrumental value or not. If it is, then importance of the freedom will vary as a direct function of the magnitude of the need. If it is not perceived as having unique instrumental value, then importance of the freedom will be psychologically insignificant regardless of the magnitude of the need. Unique instrumental value refers to whether or not a given behavior is the only way to satisfy a given need. For a freedom to be important, then, the minimum prerequisites are that the free behavior be perceived as potentially need-satisfying and that no other free behavior be perceived as available that would satisfy this exact same need. "Exact same need" as used here is a critical qualifying statement. In essence, it restricts the class of nonuniquely satisfying behaviors to identical behaviors. If, for example, an individual is choosing between two cars identical in every regard, and one is suddenly the focus of another buyer's attentions, the person should not experience reactance arousal. Car B does not uniquely satisfy any needs since it is identical to Car A; the importance of the freedom is thus psychologically trivial even though the person desperately needs a car; and a threat to an insignificant freedom arouses no reactance. If, on the other hand, the individual is choosing between two cars that are equally attractive and that differ only in color, another buyer's interest in the red car will arouse reactance. Car B does uniquely satisfy the need to have a red car since only it is red; the importance of freedom will be a direct function of how strong one's need is to have a red car; and the reactance aroused will be a direct function of how important the freedom is to the individual.

The second component in the interactive determination of importance of freedom is the magnitude of one's need. As stated in the initial definition quoted above, both actual and potential levels of need intensity have to be considered. A need may be of relatively low magnitude in a specific situation, but if the need has a potentially high magnitude in another situation, the importance of the freedom may be greater than one would expect if only the present level of the need were considered. This reasoning suggests a certain asymmetry in predictions about importance of freedoms. Presuming unique instrumental value to be present, a currently high magnitude of need will always imply an important freedom. Similarly, if a need has only a low potential maximum intensity, then current levels cannot be high nor can the freedom involved be very important. When, however, a need is currently at a low level of intensity, but potential level of need is high, importance of the behavioral freedom will depend on a variety of factors such as how salient the high potential of the need is (e.g., if the intense need state was experienced recently, salience should be high) and whether the current threat implies additional threats in the future when the need state might again be intense. Consider, for example, a teenager who frequently attends late movies. If on a given occasion the teenager's parents bar attendance at a late movie, and the movie is not of much interest to the teenager anyway, one might be tempted to expect little arousal of reactance. But because the teenager is aware that a subsequent late movie might be of great interest, the potential need for the activity of seeing late movies is high, the importance of the freedom is high, and a great deal of reactance could be expected to occur.

In keeping with the subjective orientation of reactance theory, all of the factors underlying importance of freedom operate from within the individual's point of view. Others may see two behaviors as identical, but if the individual sees them as differing, then each behavioral freedom has unique instrumental value for that person. Similarly, others may believe that the individual does not have a very strong need, but if the individual feels the need to be intense, then the importance of the behavioral freedom will be high. This subjective orientation does not mean, however, that we cannot predict and manipulate importance of freedom for other people. In fact, manipulation of importance of freedom in experimental studies has been relatively simple, and a few examples will be described to illustrate this.

Conditions of high importance of freedom have been created by telling subjects that their performance on the experimental task would indicate important aspects of their personality (Burton in Brehm, 1966), was a measure of their intelligence (Wicklund, Robin & Robin in Wicklund, 1974), was for an important scientific project (Brehm & Cole, 1966), and, if accurate, would be rewarded with a fairly large sum of money ($10; Brehm & Mann, 1975). Low importance of freedom comparison conditions have been created, respectively, by informing subjects that the present experiment was only for collection of preliminary data, the task measured nothing of psychological significance, the data were for a student friend and of no consequence, and the potential reward for accuracy was fairly small ($2). It would seem obvious that the importance of task-related behavioral freedoms should be increased in the former set of conditions relative to the latter set, and the results of these experiments indicated that this was so.

These manipulations of importance of freedom basically amount to the experimenter's telling the subject that the behavior in the experiment is important or that it is not, and this has been by far the most typical way in which importance of freedom has been varied in reactance research. More subtle manipulations are possible, if seldom used. For example, in a study by Worchel (1972), viewing films served to make the freedom to behave in the way depicted in the film more important. After watching an aggressive film, children at a summer camp were more likely to oppose a communication urging them to choose a nonaggressive activity than those who had seen a nonaggressive film or no movie at all. Similarly, campers who had seen a nonaggressive film were more likely to oppose a communication advocating their choice of an aggressive activity than those who had seen the aggressive film or had not seen a film (see Chapter 11 for details of this study).

Importance of freedom can also vary as a function of naturally occurring factors such as social status, age, and gender. An illustration of a possible connection between gender and freedom importance is provided in a study by Davis and Martin (1978). Using the Brock pleasure machine, male and female subjects who believed they were participating in a learning experiment were given an opportunity to provide pleasurable vibrations to an opposite sex partner. The partner was either a date or a stranger and was either responsive (saying things like "great" after receiving vibrations) or not. Obtaining a significant triple interaction with a trend for responsiveness to inhibit pleasuring when female subjects were paired with strangers, Davis and Martin hypothesized that the freedom not to use higher (and thus more intimate) levels was more important for females interacting with strangers.

Such a natural covariation of subject characteristics with importance of freedom has also been suggested by Linder and Worchel (1970). In their study of the effects on opinions of effortfully drawing a conclusion from sets of syllogistic statements, significant attitude change away from anti-smoking conclusions was obtained only for smokers in the low effort condition. This condition, where 5 of the 7 conclusions were drawn by the experimenter, was seen by Linder and Worchel as pressuring subjects to adopt opinions against smoking more than the high or medium effort conditions, in which subjects had to draw more conclusions for themselves. Presumably, the boomerang attitude change obtained in the low effort condition occurred only for smokers because the freedom to disagree with anti-smoking statements was more important for them than for nonsmokers.

All of the studies described above varied importance of freedom by varying magnitude of need. There is no reason to believe that unique instrumental value was affected. Unique instrumental value was, however, explicitly varied in a study by Brehm and Weinraub (1977). This experiment will be more fully described in Chapter 11, but two conditions are directly relevant to our present dicussion. In this study, 2-year-old children were confronted with two toys; one of these was placed behind a transparent barrier, the other beside the barrier. In the two conditions in which relatively large barriers were used (.66 m high as compared to a small barrier .33 m in height), two different sets of toys were used. For the different toys condition, the two toys were similar in size and color, but differed in shape. For the identical toys condition, two identical toys were used, with the toys used in this condition counterbalanced across the two toys used in the different toys condition.

Brehm and Weinraub expected that only where the two toys were different would the freedom to have the toy behind the barrier be sufficiently important enough for the barrier to create reactance. They, therefore, predicted that preference for the barricaded toy should be obtained only in the different toys condition and not in the identical toys condition. For male subjects, although not for females, this prediction was confirmed.

The multiplicative definition of freedom importance has generally been accepted and each of its components has received empirical support. However, there has been an alternative theoretical formulation that should be discussed. Citing an unpublished paper by Wicklund, West (1975) suggested that unique instrumental value may not be necessary for a behavioral freedom to be important. Furthermore, West questioned whether the behavioral freedom had to be at all attractive. In previous theoretical considerations, a minimal level of attractiveness had been assumed to be necessary in order to indicate that the freedom was capable of satisfying a need. West does not seem to be denying that the behavior has to satisfy a need, but apparently he does not think that it has to do a very good job at it. Instead of the multiplicative relationship between unique instrumental value and magnitude of need, West proposed that repeated prior exercise of a behavioral freedom can in and of itself create sufficient importance of that freedom. Closely considered, West's proposal does not directly contradict the original need–value formulation of importance. Rather, it addresses that class of behavioral freedoms that on the basis of the need–value formulation would not be expected to be important enough to serve as the basis of reactance arousal.

The only available evidence on the capability of prior exercise in and of itself to establish an important freedom comes from West's (1975) study of student attitudes toward a cafeteria. Subjects in this study were 27 female dormitory residents who, on the basis of pretest responses, had a clearly negative opinion of the food served in the cafeteria. A week after the pretest measures had been taken, subjects in the experimental condition were informed that the cafeteria was to be closed for at least two weeks. Control subjects were either informed that carbonated beverages would not be available in the cafeteria for a few days or given an announcement of a movie. The pretest attitude survey was then readministered. When compared to the two control conditions combined (the two did not differ from each other), experimental subjects showed significantly more positive change in their attitudes toward the cafeteria's food.

West notes that there was an alternative cafeteria "with nearly identical food and architecture" close by and argues from this that the target cafeteria could not have uniquely satisfied significant motives. In his discussion of his findings, however, he acknowledges "that the satisfaction of other important motives (e.g., social motives) may have been eliminated by the closing of the cafeteria (West, 1975, p. 7)." A number of factors, then, make it difficult to determine whether the present study was an adequate test of the prior exercise hypothesis. First, is "nearly identical" equivalent to "identical"? The toys used in Brehm and Weinraub were nearly identical, and yet the difference between them was enough to generate reactance arousal for male subjects. It just is not clear how much similarity between any two given items or behaviors is sufficient to cause these items or behaviors to be perceived as identical. West obviously thought the two cafeterias were identical; we do not know whether his subjects did or not.

Second, what will happen if the setting of an important freedom (e.g., getting together with one's friends for dinner) is eliminated and one is then asked to evaluate an unimportant but related freedom (i.e., eating the cafeteria food)? Will the elimination of the setting that made it possible to exercise the important freedom increase the attractiveness of that setting and of all its features? These are interesting questions that have not been investigated and that are relevant to West's theoretical formulation.

Both of these issues suggest that the hypothesis that repeated prior exercise of a free behavior can in and of itself create freedom importance has not yet been adequately tested. Field experiments can provide important evidence for the generality and strength of a theoretical formulation; however, they are probably not the best place to try out a new theoretical idea. The repeated prior exercise hypothesis needs to be examined further and in a setting where questions such as the ones noted above can be more adequately resolved.[1]

A different formulation of the relationship between expectation of freedom and importance has been suggested by Dickenberger (1979). She distinguished between the freedom to do something and the free-

---

[1] In a personal communication, West has suggested another interpretation of his study, namely, that repeated exercise of a behavior may produce "mindlessness" (Chanowitz & Langer, 1980), which in turn tends to make the activity relatively unattractive. A threat to the freedom to perform that behavior would then instigate "mindfulness," consequent increased attraction of the behavior, and, presumably, increased importance of the freedom to perform it.

dom from something (an outcome) or someone. In regard to the second type of freedom, she hypothesized that the expectancy of freedom is determined by the frequency with which one's freedoms have been threatened in the past, and the proportion of these times that freedoms have been successfully restored. Further, Dickenberger hypothesized that the importance of the freedom-from will be an inverted U-shaped function of the expectancy. When the expected probability that one has a freedom (from) is 0 or 1, the importance of the freedom will be 0, and when the expected probability is .5, importance will be at maximum. In this formulation, then, importance, rather than being independent of expectancy of freedom, is directly dependent on it. While Dickenberger provides some correlational evidence in support of this formulation, we feel that it is too early to judge the merit of this approach.

Number and Proportion of Freedoms Threatened

At a given point in time, a person may have several important freedoms. On a particular evening, for example, there could be six different movies that are of interest to a movie buff, and a threat to the freedom to see any one of these movies would arouse reactance in our movie fan. It is also possible, however, that there could simultaneously be threats to the freedoms to see two or more of these six movies. More reactance should be aroused by threats to several freedoms than to one, and, in general, the magnitude of reactance should be a direct function of the number of freedoms threatened.

Independently of the number of freedoms threatened, the proportion of freedoms that is threatened will also affect the magnitude of reactance. If a moviegoer discovers that a particular movie will not be shown because of equipment failure, the amount of reactance aroused will be greater if that movie was one of only two that he or she was considering than if it was one of ten. In the former case, 50% of the person's freedoms are lost; in the latter case, 10%.

It will be noted that where a specified number of freedoms is available, a variation in the number threatened produces a covariation in the proportion threatened. If two out of ten freedoms are threatened rather than one, we have also increased the proportion of freedoms threatened from 10% to 20%. Hence, to test the proposition that the magnitude of reactance is a direct function of the number of freedoms threatened, proportion would have to be held constant by covarying the total number of freedoms. One such test has been carried out, and will be described at the end of this section. In addition, two studies have examined the effect on reactance of the proportion of freedoms threatened, though the second of these confounds proportion with number.

An early study by Brehm, McQuown, and Shaban (reported in Brehm, 1966) had subjects rate six movies. Since these movies were all different from one another and were of varying attractiveness to the subjects, it was presumed that each movie had unique instrumental value for the satisfaction of different needs. Choice condition subjects were told they could choose one movie to watch from among either six or three. No choice condition subjects were told they would be assigned one to watch from a set of six or three. Later, subjects in these four conditions were told that one movie (the second most attractive one for each subject) had not arrived in shipment. A control group of subjects, who expected to choose one movie from a set of three, was not informed of any elimination. All subjects then rerated all six movies.

Results from the four elimination groups provide the major test of the experimental hypothesis. For choice condition subjects, two sets of freedoms were created, one containing three freedoms and the other six. When one alternative was eliminated, either 33% of the freedoms or 17% had been taken away. Reactance arousal should, therefore, be greater in the first condition than in the second. For no choice subjects, freedoms have not been established and reactance arousal should not differ as a function of the proportion of alternatives eliminated. The results of this study generally provided support for the theoretical hypothesis. While the pattern of mean rating changes in desire to see the second-ranked alternative conformed to experimental predictions, the differences obtained were not statistically reliable. A frequency count of the direction of rating changes obtained stronger results. As displayed in Table 3.1, more subjects in the choice–high proportion condition became more favorable toward the previously second-ranked movie than in the choice–low proportion condition, the no choice–high proportion condition, or (marginally, $p = .10$) the no elimination control condition.

A different perspective on proportion of freedoms was taken by Wicklund, Slattum, and Solomon (1970). These investigators proposed that when a sequential array is presented to an individual, threats to freedom should be maximum early in the sequence. That is, if an individual expects to examine some set of choice alternatives one-by-one and can only select one from the array, pressure to take any one threatens the freedoms to take any of the others. Thus, if six objects are in an array, pressure to take the first object threatens the freedoms to have objects two through six, and 83% of the total number of freedoms is threatened. If, however, three objects have already been examined

TABLE 3.1

Percentage of Subjects Rating the Eliminated (Second-Ranked) Alternative Higher After It Had Been Eliminated[a]

Experimental condition	Percentage of subjects
Expect to choose	
One out of three (16)[b]	56
One out of six (19)	11
Expect to be assigned	
One out of three (13)	23
One out of six (11)	9
No elimination control–	
Expect to choose	
One out of three (18)	28

[a] From an experiment by Brehm, McQuown, & Shaban reported in Brehm, J. W. *A theory of psychological reactance*, New York: Academic Press, 1966, Table VIII, p. 35.

[b] Condition Ns.

and not chosen and then pressure is exerted on the person to take the fourth object, only the freedoms to choose the fifth and sixth objects are threatened, 33 % (2 out of 6) of the total number of freedoms.[2]

The results in the Wicklund *et al.* experiment were consistent with this reasoning. Female subjects expected to examine six pairs of sunglasses, choose one to model, and, if they wished, buy the chosen pair for half price. Half of the subjects were led to believe that the experimenter had a financial interest in any purchase that was made. This belief was induced in order to heighten subjects' perceptions of the experimenter's intent to persuade and, thereby, increase the magnitude of threat to freedom (see Chapter 4 for further discussion of perceived intent). The other half of the subjects were told that the experimenter did not care whether they purchased a pair of sunglasses or not. Subjects then examined the six pairs of sunglasses, the experimenter making some complimentary remark about each pair; each pair of glasses was rated as subjects worked through the set of six.

[2] This analysis assumes that people view a threat to any one freedom relative to the entire set of existing freedoms. It is possible, however, that any given threat to the freedom to reject a given alternative is viewed only in terms of the alternatives that have yet to be examined. In this case, urging someone to take the fourth alternative would threaten two freedoms (i.e., to take the fifth or sixth alternatives) out of a set of three total freedoms, and thus pose a threat to 67 % of the existing freedoms. From either perspective, threats posed early will threaten a larger proportion of freedoms than threats posed later.

Following the ratings, subjects were permitted to examine all the sunglasses again and to choose a pair to model.

It was expected that subjects in the condition where experimenter intent to persuade had been strongly implied (high implication) would experience the most reactance arousal in response to the compliments when early alternatives were being examined. One way to test this hypothesis is to take the difference between ratings for the first and sixth alternatives and compare this difference between high and low implication conditions. Since reactance arousal should decrease attractiveness of the item being examined, the sixth item should be more attractive than the first if early threats to freedom create more reactance than threats to later items in the sequence under conditions of high general reactance arousal (i.e., when experimenter intent to persuade is made salient). The predicted difference between the two experimental conditions was obtained, such that high implication subjects tended to rate the sixth alternative more favorably than the first ($M = 3.9$), while low implication subjects evidenced little difference ($M = -.70$). Furthermore, significantly fewer subjects in the high implication condition than in the low implication condition chose the item examined first or second.

The two studies just described differ on two dimensions in the way in which they examined proportion of freedoms threatened. First, Brehm et al. kept constant the number of freedoms eliminated (one item) and varied the proportion of freedoms eliminated (one out of six, 17%, versus one out of three, 33%). Wicklund et al. varied both the number of freedoms and the proportion of freedoms threatened by the social influence attempt (social influence on the first item threatening the freedoms to have the remaining *five* items, 83% of the total number of freedoms; social influence on the second item threatening the freedoms to have the remaining *four* items, 67% of the total number of freedoms, etc.). Second, Brehm et al. eliminated one item, and thus eliminated the freedoms to have that item and to reject the other alternatives. Wicklund et al. urged alternatives on subjects, and, thereby, threatened the freedoms to reject the advocated alternative and to have any of the other ones.

The comparison between these two studies points out a possible source of confusion when assessing how the magnitude of reactance will be determined by the proportion of freedoms eliminated or threatened with elimination. In the Brehm et al. study, where subjects were faced with an elimination of freedom, reactance arousal was greater for the small array of freedoms (3 movies) than for the large array of freedoms (6 movies). In the Wicklund et al. study, where subjects were urged to choose one item rather than the remaining ones, reactance arousal was greater when the size of the (remaining) array was large (five items) than when it was small (no remaining items). This comparison shows that one must carefully consider the *proportion* of freedoms threatened and not be misled by component elements such as the size of the array of freedoms.

As noted earlier, the size of the array of freedoms must be covaried with the number of freedoms threatened in order to ascertain the effect of variation in number of threatened freedoms. In this way, the proportion of freedoms threatened can be held constant. For example, if 50% of available freedoms are threatened, and, in one case four freedoms are available while in the other there are eight, two freedoms would be threatened in the first case and four in the second. This kind of design was used in a study by Grabitz-Gniech, Auslitz, and Grabitz (1975).

These investigators first constructed a set of 12 modern art prints that were rated about equally attractive. Then, in an initial experimental session, subjects, male and female students, were asked to rate the attractiveness of each of the 12 prints or a subset of 6 prints, and were told that they would be able to choose any 1 for themselves for their participation. They were also informed that a shipment of the prints was expected to arrive within a few days, and they were scheduled to return to make their selections within 4 to 6 days. At the second session, subjects were informed that due to an error in shipment some of the prints would not be available for choice. The prints eliminated were always those that the subject had rated in the middle—i.e., neither the most nor least attractive prints were eliminated. At this point, the proportion of freedoms eliminated was varied: either 33% or 67% of each subject's choice alternatives were eliminated. Thus, for subjects who expected to chose 1 of 6 prints, either 2 or 4 were eliminated, while for subjects who expected to choose 1 of 12 prints, either 4 or 8 were eliminated. Once subjects knew which prints were eliminated, they were asked to rerate all 6 or 12 prints. It was expected, of course, that eliminated prints would tend to be rated more attractive after elimination than before, and that this increase in attractiveness would be a direct function of both the number and proportion of freedoms eliminated.

The results of this experiment failed to support the theoretical expectations for either number or proportion of freedoms threatened. Although there was a trend in the expected direction for proportion of freedoms eliminated ($p < .25$), lending weak additional support to the research cited previously, there was a significant ($p < .05$) effect of number of freedoms in the opposite direction to prediction. Subjects who had 6 alternatives to choose from and had either 2 or 4 eliminated raised their ratings of the eliminated alternatives; subjects who had 12 alternatives to choose from and had either 4 or 8 eliminated lowered their ratings of the eliminated alternatives. Why this reversal of theoretical expectation occurred is not clear. Grabitz-Gniech, Auslitz, and Grabitz speculated, however, that when there are many choice alternatives, they are no longer seen as a set of differentiated freedoms, and elimination of one or more becomes meaningless. In any case, this reversal of the theoretically expected effect of number of freedoms threatened strongly suggests the need for further investigation.

Implications for Future Freedoms:
Increasing Reactance Arousal

In the studies described above, different sets of freedoms existed for subjects in the present. It is possible, however, to consider sets of freedoms as they exist across time. Mr. Jones, for instance, may have only one freedom today, but if he anticipates another related one tomorrow and another one the day after, he may perceive himself as having a set of three freedoms. This extended vision of freedoms can have radically different effects on reactance arousal depending on the perceived target of the threat.

Let us consider first what happens when people have similar sets of freedoms, and the threat to one freedom either implies, or does not imply, threat to the other freedoms in the set. In this situation, the size of the array is kept constant, and the number of alternatives threatened is varied. However, the set of freedoms is not composed of a set of alternatives all present at the same time, but of anticipated free behaviors in the future.

The first experimental investigation of this kind of situation was conducted by Brehm and Sensenig (1966). Male and female high school students participated in a supposed experiment on impression formation. Subjects were told they would be given two pictures and then would decide with which picture they could do a better job of getting an accurate impression of the person pictured. Subjects anticipated looking at five separate pairs of pictures. In addition to choosing one picture from each pair for themselves, subjects were also led to believe that they would choose a picture for a supposed other subject in another room. All subjects then received a note that they believed was from this other subject. Subjects in the control and high implications conditions expected to receive a note prior to selecting a picture from each of the five pairs; subjects in the low implications condition only expected to receive a note prior to selecting a picture from the first pair. The note used in the control condition merely contained a statement of the other subject's preference for himself or herself ("I prefer 1–A [1–B]"). Notes in the implications conditions, however, threatened the subject's own choice ("I think we should both do 1–A [1–B]".). Which picture subjects chose on the first pair of pictures constituted the major dependent measure, with subjects in the high implications condition expected to display the most reactance and conform least to the position advocated in the note.

The results from this experiment were actually rather weak. While there was a significant difference in influence between the control condition and the combined implications conditions (respectively, 73% versus 43% of subjects conforming with the note), there was no significant difference between the high and low implications conditions (respectively, 40% versus 47%). Moreover, what difference there was between these two conditions was accounted for entirely by female subjects. Male subjects showed a slight difference in the opposite (and theoretically deviant) direction.

In a subsequent study, Sensenig and Brehm (1968) suggested that the manipulation of threat used in their first study was weak and, therefore, provided a poor situation in which to test their hypothesis about implied threats. Rather than use choices between unfamiliar and, presumably, unimportant items, they decided to reexamine their hypothesis as it might apply to threats to preexisting attitudes. It was thought that preexisting attitudes would provide important freedoms and that any threat to an important attitudinal freedom should, therefore, be sufficiently reactance arousing to allow for a more adequate examination of the experimental hypothesis. They also decided to employ only female subjects.

Two subjects participated in each experimental session. After completing an attitudinal pre-measure eliciting their opinions on 15 issues of current importance, they were told that they would write five short essays on 5 different issues, selected from those on the questionnaire. Subjects were also told that they would both be required to write in support of the same side of the issue either for only the first essay (low implied threat condition) or for all five essays (high implied threat and control conditions).

As a supposed way to make sure that subjects did write on the same side for one or five essays, subjects were told that one of them would make this decision, but that the decision maker could ask the other person about her preference. Subjects then drew slips to see who would be the decision maker, but each subject actually received a slip indicting that the other subject would make the decision. After being placed in separate rooms, subjects received a supposed note from the other subject. All notes assigned the subject to write on the side of the issue she had favored on the pre-measure. Implied threat condition subjects received a freedom-eliminating note ("I've decided that we will both agree [disagree] with this position"); control subjects received a freedom-reassuring note ("I'd prefer to agree [disagree] with this if it's all right with you"). Subjects were then asked to indicate their "actual feelings" about the attitudinal issue that was to be the focus of the first essay.

The results of this study indicated that only subjects in the high implied threat condition experienced significant amounts of reactance arousal. These subjects showed more negative attitude change (away from the attitude-consistent position urged by the communication) than either subjects in the low implied threat condition (respectively, -4.17 versus $-.27$) or those in the control condition ($+1.37$). The latter two conditions did not differ from each other. These findings provide strong support for the theoretical hypothesis. All subjects presumably viewed themselves as having a set of five freedoms (i.e., the freedom to write on a given side for each essay), and all subjects in the experimental conditions received the identical threat. For subjects in the high implied threat condition, this threat implied potential threats to all five freedoms and thus it would be possible for 100% of their freedoms to be eliminated. Subjects in the low implied threat condition, however, knew that only the side of the first essay was to be determined by their partner, and, thus, that only 20% of their freedoms could be eliminated. The data suggest that the latter circumstances created at most only a trivial amount of reactance arousal, whereas the former created reactance arousal that was sufficient to change subjects' attitudes away from the position that was advocated by the communication *and* that they initially preferred.

Implications for Future Freedoms:
Decreasing Reactance Arousal

If it is possible to increase reactance arousal by implied threats to future freedoms, it should also be possible to decrease reactance arousal by creating future freedoms. Research by Bushcamp (1976) examined this possibility. Using the Sensenig and Brehm procedure, he had some subjects expect to write one essay, while others expected to write two. Subjects who expected to write only one were told that they would have to write on the same side as their partners. Subjects who expected to write two were told they would have to write on the same side as their partners for only the first essay. The Sensenig and Brehm decision-maker procedures were then used and all subjects thought their partners had been selected as the decision-maker. Subjects received either a freedom-eliminating or freedom-reassuring communication. (Bushcamp also attempted to vary the importance of the second attitude issue, but this variation had no significant effect on the results and will not be discussed further). A no choice–no elimination control group was included in the design to provide a baseline comparison group.

The major procedural difference between Bushcamp's study and that by Sensenig and Brehm is that Bushcamp varied the size of the array of freedoms and kept the threat constant, whereas Sensenig and Brehm kept the size of the array constant and varied the implications of the threat. The proportion of freedoms threatened in the Sensenig and Brehm research ranged from 1/5 to (potentially at least) 5/5; this range was 1/2 to 1/1 in the Bushcamp study. Moreover, the focus of the two investigations was quite different. Sensenig and Brehm wanted to examine whether increasing the proportion of freedoms threatened (by implication) would increase reactance arousal; Bushcamp attempted to demonstrate that decreasing the proportion of freedoms threatened would decrease reactance arousal. The two studies also differed in the way they operationalized the condition in which most reactance was expected. Sensenig and Brehm used implied threat to future freedoms; Bushcamp used a direct threat to the only existing freedom.

Let us consider Bushcamp's data in three segments. First, subjects in those conditions where the non-freedom-eliminating note was received as well as those in the no choice–no elimination group showed little attitude change (means ranging from -1.14 to $+.33$). Second, subjects who received a freedom-threatening note and expected to write only one essay showed considerable negative attitude change (-5.50). This result is consistent with the negative attitude change displayed by subjects in Sensenig and Brehm's high implications condition. Finally, in the condition similar to Sensenig and Brehm's low implications condition, Bushcamp's subjects who received the high threat note but expected to have free choice on the second essay showed the most positive attitude change of any group in the study $(+1.58)$.[3]

[3] While Bushcamp does not specify the sex of the subjects in his experiment, his use of the masculine personal pronoun suggests that at least some of the subjects were male. Thus, where Bushcamp obtains results similar to those obtained by Sensenig and Brehm, the cross-sex generality of these results can be inferred. In addition, Heller, Pallak, and

Decreasing reactance arousal by increasing the number of available freedoms may also have been involved in a study by Wellins and McGinnies (1977). These investigators predicted that subjects who were given the opportunity to counterargue while or directly after listening to a counterattitudinal persuasive communication would listen to this message longer than subjects who had no such opportunity.[4] Although their results were not especially strong (e.g., differences at the .05 level usually being obtained only when one-tailed tests were used), the overall pattern obtained in the course of three experiments was consistent with the predicted effect. Unfortunately, however, the procedures used by Wellins and McGinnies do not allow one to rule out explanations other than reactance. For example, subjects given the opportunity to make counterarguments may have felt they needed to listen more closely (and thus longer) to do an effective job.

In examining the notion of decreasing reactance arousal by increasing perceived available freedoms, it is critical to attend to the timing of the introduction. The proportion of freedoms hypothesis assumes that people first perceive what freedoms are available, then receive a threat to freedom, and that the reactance aroused by this threat is a function of the proportion of freedoms threatened. This sequence of events is what appears to occur in the Sensenig and Brehm paradigm. To decrease reactance arousal in terms of this paradigm, one would decrease the proportion of freedoms that was threatened. Another type of paradigm, however, may be involved in the Wellins and McGinnies study. Here, apparently, subjects were first told they would hear a communication advocating a position with which they disagreed; only after this were they informed that they would have the opportunity to counterargue. This sequence raises the possibility that reactance was aroused simply by anticipating hearing a counterattitudinal communication and that when the opportunity to counterargue was introduced, it reduced reactance by reestablishing the subject's freedom to disagree with the communication. While both paradigms provide

---

Picek (1973) replicated part of Sensenig and Brehm's results (i.e., high implied threat versus control) with both male and female subjects.

[4] Making the opportunity to counterargue available should reduce reactance arousal and increase positive attitude change as well as listening time. If, however, individuals are allowed actually to generate counterarguments, these counterarguments would tend to reduce positive attitude change. Since Wellins and McGinnies allowed their subjects to generate counterarguments, it is not surprising that these subjects showed less positive attitude change than subjects who were not allowed to counterague.

ways to reduce reactance and expressions thereof, the underlying theoretical explanations are quite different.

Relative Importance of the Freedoms

The preceding discussion of number and proportion of freedoms was based on the assumption that the importance of the various freedoms was held relatively constant. There will be times, however, when people perceive themselves to have an array of related freedoms that differ in importance. In such cases, the magnitude of reactance aroused should be a function of the relative importance of the threatened freedom as compared to the importance of the other available freedoms. Perhaps the clearest example of such an instance would involve a free choice situation. Consider a person confronting three choice alternatives who knows that he or she can have only one. In one scenario, all three alternatives represent moderately important free behaviors. In another, two alternatives are moderately important, but one is very important. The next step is to suppose that a moderately important behavior is threatened in each. Reactance arousal should be greater in the former case than in the latter as the continued availability of the very important freedom in the latter situation acts to reduce reactance in response to a threat to a less important freedom. In more concrete terms, "When one's choice alternatives are an orange, an apple, and a pear, he should experience a noticeable degree of reactance when someone swipes the apple; but when the choice alternatives are an orange, an apple and an automobile, one will not care much about the loss of the apple [Brehm, 1966, pp. 5–6]."

It should be noted that both the proportion of freedoms principle and the relative importance of freedoms principle can hold only for freedoms that the person sees as *related*. The freedoms must constitute a set such that a threat to any one is seen in the context of the availability of the others. It would not be very helpful, for example, if we took a woman standing at a fruit stand who watches the last apple disappear, and reminded her that she still has her automobile. For this individual, the freedom to have an automobile is irrelevant to the freedoms to have any of several fruits. The other individual mentioned in Brehm's (1966) example, however, has for some reason conceived of his set of freedoms as including both fruits and an automobile; his response to the disappearing apple is thus moderated by thoughts of the still available automobile.

Although little can be said about the principles by which freedoms are grouped together, some guidelines should be noted. Whenever a decision is to be made, the explicit alternatives under consideration represent a group of freedoms. Similarly, when a person periodically exercises a particular freedom, such as having dinner out, present and future instances of that practice constitute a group of freedoms. Other groupings combine kinds of freedoms, such as political, economic, or social. It is apparent as well that what freedoms are grouped together will sometimes be determined by the character of the threat to freedom. Threats that are rationalized or justified will implicitly or explicitly define what freedom or freedoms are included. If gasoline stations are prohibited from providing gas on Sundays, then drivers can anticipate the probable nature and number of the freedoms that have been eliminated. These freedoms should thus be grouped together and should constitute a relatively limited and clearly delimited set of freedoms. On the other hand, completely arbitrary and unjustified threats to freedom can have the effect of grouping widely disparate freedoms. If the head of a business firm announces that gum chewing will no longer be allowed during business hours, then employees are likely to wonder if there are any non-business activities (e.g., smoking, social conversation, having a soft drink) that will not eventually be prohibited.

SUMMARY

A freedom is important to a person when it has unique instrumental value for the satisfaction of one or more important needs. A freedom that would uniquely satisfy an important need will be important either when the need is currently of high magnitude or when the person is aware that the need could, and sometimes will, be of high magnitude. Evidence supporting the proposition that the magnitude of reactance is a direct function of the importance of a threatened freedom was reviewed. This evidence included support for the contention that a freedom, to be important, must have unique instrumental value. The question of whether or not freedoms must have some minimal level of importance in order for threats to arouse reactance was also discussed.

When there is a threat to freedom, the magnitude of reactance is theoretically a direct function of the number of freedoms threatened. In addition, when people believe themselves to have a set of freedoms, as when they have several alternatives from which to choose, the magnitude of reactance is a direct function of the proportion of those freedoms that is subject to threat. A review of relevant evidence found support for the propostion that reactance varies with the proportion of threatened freedoms. However, the only test of the effect of the number of freedoms threatened or eliminated produced a reversal from theoretical expectations.

When there is a threat to a particular freedom, there also can be an implied threat to future freedoms. As implications for future freedoms increase, so should the magnitude of reactance that is aroused. Conversely, decreasing implications for future freedoms and/or creating future freedoms that are not involved in the present threat should reduce the magnitude of reactance. Evidence supporting these propositions was reviewed, and it was noted that one needs to distinguish theoretically between reductions brought about by reducing the proportion of freedoms threatened by implication and those resulting from freedom restoration.

Finally, it was noted that the magnitude of reactance aroused by a threat should increase with the *relative* importance of the freedom threatened. For example, when a person loses a moderately attractive choice alternative out of a set of alternatives, the presence in the set of a highly attractive alternative reduces the relative importance of the freedom to choose the moderately attractive alternative. Thus, reactance aroused by this loss would be less than if all other alternatives were only moderately attractive. This hypothesis, however, has not yet been investigated empirically.

CHAPTER 4

Determinants of the Magnitude of Reactance: Characteristics of the Threat

In order to produce reactance, there must be a freedom and a threat to that freedom. The preceding chapter has focused on the characteristics of the freedom that affect the magnitude of reactance. This chapter will examine the characteristics of threat that affect the magnitude of reactance.

The Effects of Small and Large Forces Against Exercising a Freedom

As was noted in Chapter 1, an event that increases the perceived difficulty of exercising a freedom constitutes a threat to that freedom. The greater is the increase in perceived difficulty of exercising a freedom, the greater is the perceived threat. Thus, in general, the greater are the forces acting against exercising a freedom, the greater will be the perceived threat to that freedom. With very small and very large forces, however, the possibility of special effects must be considered. Let us look first at very small forces.

Threshholds

Although the central notion of reactance theory concerns the motivational consequences of having freedoms threatened, it is important to understand the relationship between forces that impinge on the individual and the perception of threats. At least two interesting questions may be asked about this relationship. (a) Is it possible for forces to be so small that they are not perceived as threats? Is there, in other words, a threshold for the perception of threat? This question is interesting because of the possibility that two or more subthreshold forces, none of which by themselves would cause the perception of threat, when combined could result in a perceived threat to freedom. There has been no explicit attempt to study this question; however, evidence to be reviewed later appears to be consistent with the assumption that subthreshhold forces can combine to create a threat to freedom. (b) Is it possible for a force, though too small to create a perceived threat to freedom, nevertheless to have a positive influence effect? Do individuals accept minimal influence forces without perceiving them as threats? The original formulation of reactance theory (Brehm, 1966) is inconsistent with this possibility, but evidence to be reviewed later suggests that this possibility does exist.

Elimination of Freedom

As the force against exercising a freedom becomes relatively great, the perception of threat changes to the perception that the freedom has been eliminated. This change occurs where the perceived magnitude of the force outweighs the perceived importance of the freedom: The cost of resisting the force becomes greater than the cost of not exercising the freedom. The point at which a threat turns into an elimination of freedom is the point at which the magnitude of reactance is greatest. Additional force (and perceived threat) beyond that point has no effect on the magnitude of reactance. Two crucial theoretical issues are raised by this conceptualization of the elimination of freedom.

First, where a freedom is one that is recurrently exercised, elimination of it on a particular occasion will not necessarily eliminate it for all occasions. An individual who feels free to smoke marijuana where doing so is illegal will acknowledge that his or her freedom has been eliminated when a police officer happens to be nearby. But, knowing that the police officer will not always be around, the individual will not give up the freedom. Because the freedom is not given up, reactance is aroused by the elimination and will persist until the freedom is restored (see Chapter 5 for further discussion of this issue).

On the other hand, some eliminations of freedom will be seen as irrevocable. Perhaps the marijuana smoker finds that marijuana is simply unavailable. Or, perhaps the same individual when faced with the threat of life imprisonment if caught smoking will feel that the potential punishment is so severe that he or she would not take the risk under any circumstances.

The second crucial issue, then, involves what happens to those individuals who come to view their freedoms as irrevocably eliminated. Does the person stay highly motivated to restore a freedom that is impossible to restore? The original formulation of the theory (Brehm, 1966) had little to say about this issue, but research conducted after this initial publication offered the possibility for a more cogent theoretical perspective. During this time, a great deal of research was conducted on "learned helplessness" (Seligman, 1975). This research examined how organisms respond to uncontrollable outcomes, and found, in general, that extended experience with uncontrollable outcomes produces passivity. Because uncontrollability following the expectation of control can be equated to the elimination of a freedom, it became apparent that reactance, which theoretically should occur with the initial experience of an uncontrollable outcome, must dissipate with extended inability to control. Clearly, some modification of reactance theory was necessary to account for the dissipation of reactance over time when a freedom had been eliminated.

In the present volume, we will consider this issue at two different levels. First, in this chapter we will discuss the Wortman and Brehm (1975) model that attempts to integrate reactance and helplessness. This model reformulates, to some extent, the determinants of the magnitude of threat and, as such, is an integral part of reactance theory as it exists today. Second, we wish to consider the broader implications of the various theoretical perspectives on control that have received so much attention in recent years. These perspectives include reactance and learned helplessness, but are not limited to these models. This broader consideration will raise a number of possibilities for future developments in reactance theory and, accordingly, this chapter has been placed after our examination of the current status of the theory.

The Wortman and Brehm integrative model of reactance and helplessness relies in part on the theoretical relationship between the importance of a freedom and the amount of threat to that freedom as codeterminants of the magnitude of reactance. Once this relationship has been spelled out, we will be able to see more clearly what has been added by the Wortman and Brehm model.

The Interactive Effects of Force and Importance of Freedom

As noted earlier, any force acting against the exercise of a freedom constitutes a threat to that freedom. The greater the force, the greater is the threat. The amount of reactance aroused by a threat, however, does not necessarily increase as a direct function of the amount of force or threat, because the amount of reactance that can be aroused in regard to any given freedom is limited by the importance of that freedom. Only small amounts of reactance can be created in regard to freedoms of low importance no matter how great the threat to freedom. Therefore, forces not to exercise a freedom of low importance generally will result in positive influence (that is, in not exercising the freedom). In contrast, threats to relatively important freedoms will arouse a great deal of reactance and can result in negative influence, that is, in exercising the threatened freedom despite the force against doing so. Nevertheless, even with freedoms of high importance, the force against exercising the freedom can be so great that positive influence will result. Only in those rare instances in which a freedom is more important than most other aspects of life or even than life itself is the magnitude of reactance so great that no amount of force will produce positive influence. These relationships between force and the importance of freedom, and their net effects on behavior are depicted in Figure 4.1.

In addition to the interactive effects described above, the figure indicates that there are regions of force within which the resultant

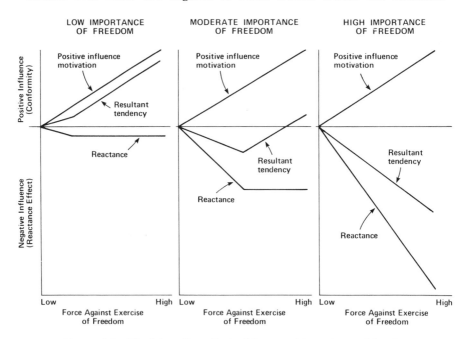

Figure 4-1. The interactive effects of force and importance of freedom.

behavior is a reduction of positive influence that would be produced in the absence of reactance. Where the freedom is of relatively low importance, *only* reduced amounts of positive influence are produced. Freedoms of moderate importance will produce boomerang, or negative, influence up to a certain strength of force, beyond which they, too, produce reduced amounts of positive influence. And, as noted above, freedoms of extremely high importance will produce increasingly strong negative influence effects as force increases.

The Wortman and Brehm Model

The Wortman and Brehm integrative model of reactance and helplessness hinges on a definition of freedom that, although implicit in previous theoretical writings, had not been emphasized. In this model, freedom is defined as the expectation of control. To have a freedom necessarily implies one's control over a behavioral outcome. Thus, if you have a choice, you have the freedom to choose and the freedom to reject an object or behavior, and you have control over whether you end up with or without it. "Expecting control" is thus theoretically equivalent to "having a freedom."

In effect, Wortman and Brehm also postulate that uncontrollable outcomes can be theoretically equivalent to eliminations of freedom. To lose a freedom, to have it eliminated, is to cease to have control over the behavioral outcome of interest. When, therefore, the individual perceives that he or she has a freedom (expects to control a behavioral outcome), reactance arousal will result if the individual has this freedom eliminated (finds the outcome to be uncontrollable). The magnitude of reactance aroused will be determined by characteristics of the freedom (i.e., importance, number or proportion eliminated, relative importance compared with other available freedoms). Threats that pose the possibility of eliminating the freedom (making the outcome uncontrollable) will also induce reactance, and here reactance arousal will be a joint function of the characteristics of the freedom and the magnitude of the threat. It should be clear from this theoretical summary that except for the use of some new language ("expectation of control"; "uncontrollable outcomes"), this aspect of the Wortman and Brehm model is identical to the original reactance formulation.

Although little emphasis was placed on the point, the initial statement of the theory did acknowledge that at some point in time—perhaps after repeated eliminations of a particular freedom or an unequivocal one-time elimination—the freedom would cease to exist and reactance would dissipate. Wortman and Brehm translated this notion into the language of control. They proposed that when an individual *becomes convinced* that an outcome he or she originally expected to control has become uncontrollable, reactance arousal will cease. Exactly how a person is to become convinced is not clear, although presumably characteristics of the freedom and the threat will influence how quickly one becomes convinced. The more firmly held the freedom (the stronger and more confident the expectation of control), the more evidence it should take to become convinced. Conversely, conviction should be hastened by frequency and irrevocableness of the elimination.

It is at this juncture that Wortman and Brehm integrate the learned helplessness model with reactance theory. Not only will reactance cease, but helplessness will ensue. Moreover, the magnitude of helplessness will be a direct function of the factors that would have determined the magnitude of reactance. In particular, elimination of an important freedom, prior to conviction that the freedom has actually been irrevocably lost, should lead to greater reactance and, after conviction, to greater helplessness than would an elimination of a less important freedom. We might also expect the elimination of a greater proportion of freedoms and of freedoms whose relative importance is great to lead to higher levels of both reactance and helplessness.

The behavioral effects of reactance motivation will be discussed at length in the next chapter. However, it is necessary for the present consideration to outline briefly the typical behavioral consequences of reactance and helplessness. When reactance is aroused, the motivation to engage in the behavior that has been eliminated or threatened with elimination is increased relative to this motivation for people who have never perceived themselves as having the freedom or those for whom the freedom was never threatened or eliminated. Typically, reactance motivation finds its expression in behavior that runs counter to the social influence, the persuasive communication, the physical barrier, or one's own preferences prior to a choice. In helplessness, the motivation to engage in the eliminated behavior is decreased[1] relative to the motivational level of people for whom the freedom was never eliminated (i.e., the usual control group in helplessness research—individuals who never received helplessness training), or, presumably, relative to the level for those for whom the freedom never existed. Typically, behavioral effects of the state of learned helplessness in-

---

[1] Wortman and Brehm state that it is not clear what happens to motivation during the helpless state. Is it decreased to very low levels, or does a counter motive not to respond come into play?

clude failure to escape from aversive stimuli and other performance decrements.

Eliminations of freedom, then, cannot be seen as simply maximal cases of magnitude of threat and reactance arousal. Initially, they do generate maximum reactance arousal, but once the freedom is unequivocally eliminated, reactance arousal will cease. And, once again, we might note that the subjective perspective is paramount. The individual's perception of whether a freedom is or is not unequivocally eliminated is what will determine whether reactance or helplessness ensues.

In the following pages, we will consider the empirical evidence on two questions that stem from the preceding theoretical considerations. First, we examine the empirical evidence for the proposition that, up to the point at which a freedom is unequivocally eliminated, increased magnitude of threat leads to increased reactance arousal. Second, we discuss the available data bearing on the Wortman and Brehm integrative model.

Magnitude of Threat and Perceived Intent to Persuade

There has been considerable research demonstrating the relationship between magnitude of threat and reactance arousal. Persuasive communications that demand compliance (e.g., you must believe X, there is no question about it) have been found to produce attitudinal shifts away from the position urged by the communication (e.g., M. Brehm in Brehm, 1966; Snyder & Wicklund, 1976; Worchel & Brehm, 1970). A more powerful and authoritative communicator (i.e., a professor) was found in a study by M. Brehm and J. Brehm (reported in Brehm, 1966) to produce less compliance with the advocated position than a less powerful one (i.e., a high school student); a large barrier to produce more preference for a toy than a small one (S. Brehm & Weinraub, 1977); and a supposedly more accurate prediction of a person's behavior to produce less behavioral conformity than a less accurate one (Hannah, Hannah, & Wattie, 1975; Rozen, 1970).

Additional evidence on this point comes from a wide assortment of studies in which perceived intent to persuade has reduced compliance. In terms of the theory, perceived persuasive intent acts to increase magnitude of threat. When a person views another as intending to influence his or her behavior, the person is clearly aware of being pressured to comply. When intent to persuade is not perceived, the person may regard the other as simply supplying information and since little pressure to comply is experienced, little reactance should be produced. If, for example, a salesperson tells you how great some consumer item is, and you know that he or she is on commission, there should be considerably more threat posed to your freedom not to buy this item than if you know the salesperson does not benefit directly from any purchase you make. This kind of variation in perceived intent to persuade was, in fact, exactly that used to create high versus low threats to freedom in the Wicklund, Slattum, and Solomon (1970) study described previously in Chapter Three.

The relationship between intent to persuade and reactance arousal also has been investigated by Hass and Grady (1975). In this study, subjects were given one of three types of forewarning about an upcoming persuasive communication: both the topic and position of the communication were described, only the topic was described, or only the persuasive intent of the speaker was noted. The persuasive communication was heard by subjects either immediately or 10 minutes after reading one of the types of forewarning messages, and subjects then expressed their opinions on the issue involved in the communication. As displayed in Table 4.1, when subjects heard either the topic forewarning or the forewarning that mentioned both topic and position, attitude change was less positive (i.e., less in the direction of the position advocated by the communication) after a 10-min delay between the forewarning and presentation of the communication. The authors interpreted this result to indicate the influence of counterarguments that subjects, if they had time, would generate. For the persuasive intent condition, however, time had no effect. Regardless of the time between forewarning and persuasive attempt, attitude change in this condition

TABLE 4.1
Mean Attitude Change[a]

Type of forewarning	Delay	
	No delay	10-min delay
Topic and position	8.40[b]	3.20
Topic only	8.85	3.58
Persuasive intent	2.17	3.15
No forewarning control	8.20	

[a] From Hass, R. G. & Grady, K. Temporal delay, type of forewarning, and resistance to influence. *Journal of Experimental Social Psychology*, 1975, *11*, 459–469, Table 1, p. 463.

[b] The higher the number, the greater the attitude change in the direction advocated by the communicator.

was less positive than in the no-forewarning control condition. Hass and Grady (1975) suggest that this finding reflected the action of "a more general topic-independent resistive state, such as psychological reactance [p. 467]."

A study by Frankel and Morris (1976) provides another example of the impact of perceived intent to persuade. In this experiment, subjects read about a supposed plagiarism case being tried before an appropriate college committee. When an unidentified witness cited two mitigating circumstances for the defendant's actions, the lowest penalty was recommended. When, however, subjects read that the defendant himself cited these same two mitigating circumstances, thus implying an intent to persuade, the harshest penalty was recommended. A second study by the authors confirmed the pattern of results for defendant testimony even when the credibility of his testimony was explicitly assured.

Finally, a study by Friedland (1976) might be mentioned in this context. Friedland's subjects participated in a gambling game with a supposed other subject. The game was either cooperative (the subject's winnings would determine whether both won a prize) or competitive (only one of the pair could win the prize), and the supposed partner was described as either superior or inferior to the subject in a task-related ability. Friedland found that compliance with the partner's requested task behavior increased with increasing severity of threat (i.e., increasing monetary penalties) in three of the experimental conditions. For subjects in the competitive condition who interacted with an inferior partner, however, there was no relationship between severity of threat and compliance. Friedland reported that these subjects also had significantly stronger perceptions of the partner as solely interested in controlling their behavior.

We presume that some reactance arousal was present in the three experimental conditions in which compliance increased with increasing severity of threat, but that the motives for compliance were considerably stronger. On the other hand, increasingly strong reactance arousal may account for the failure of subjects in the competitive–inferior condition to conform more when even very strong threats were used. Our major interest in the present discussion, though, is with the self-reported perceptions of partner interest. It would appear that subjects in the competitive–inferior condition viewed their partner's influence attempts as being without reasonable justifications (such as, "We're working together," or "He knows this kind of stuff better than I") and that this lack of legitimacy led them, instead, to perceive his behavior as a naked play for power. While it is not possible to know in what temporal sequence perceptions and resistance to influence occurred, it is consistent with reactance theory's emphasis on the role of perceived intent to influence that they covaried.

If perceived intent to influence can increase reactance arousal, decreased intent to influence should reduce this arousal and increase compliance. A study by Zillman (1972) may bear upon this possibility. Subjects in this study were given different transcripts of a supposed trial. The transcripts were written so as to provide subjects with either a positive, negative, or neutral initial attitude towards the defendant's guilt. Subjects then read a supposed summation by the defense. Half the subjects read a summation in which statements ("Johnny was a peaceful boy") were used; the other half read a summation in which the statement form was transformed into the agreement–question form ("Johnny was a peaceful boy, wasn't he?"). Subsequent recommendations for length of incarceration were a function of initial attitude (the more favorable, the more lenient the recommendation) and the rhetorical form used in the summation. The question form produced more lenient recommendations than the statement form. Zillman suggested (though he apparently provided no measure of this in the study) that the increase in persuasion obtained when the question form was used might reflect impressions of "minimal intent to persuade" created by this rhetorical form.

Another area in which perceived intent to persuade may be important is that of the experimental situation itself. Rosnow and Davis (1977) have proposed a curvilinear model of demand characteristics in experimental settings. Increasing clarity of experimental demand is postulated to increase both reception of these demands and resistance to them. Rosnow and Davis suggest that initially greater reception of the demand will lead to increased compliance with it, but that at some point reactance forces will exceed the receptivity gains and compliance will decrease. It would seem likely that one frequent characteristic of experimental demand, from the subject's point of view, is that the experimenter intends to influence his or her behavior.

As far as we know, there has been no empirical demonstration of the Rosnow and Davis curvilinear model. There is, however, some support for the notion that increased perceptions by subjects of the experimenter's intent to influence can reduce subjects' compliance. Whether this effect is better viewed as reflecting the last part of a curvilinear model or whether a linear formulation (i.e., increasing demand leading to decreasing compliance) is implicated cannot be determined without a more direct test of the two models.

That awareness of demand characteristics can reduce compliance was indicated in a study by Turner and Simons (1974). Subjects in this experiment met a supposed other student who appeared to have just completed the experiment. This confederate–subject either gave subjects no prior information about the upcoming experiment, told them that some deception was involved, or said, "I bet [the experimenter] thinks those guns. . . .will make you change your reaction [p. 343]." High versus low evaluation apprehension was also manipulated; subjects were told that the experimental results either would indicate "psychological maladjustment" or were for a pretest control group. All subjects then received seven shocks from (another) confederate to anger them, and, in the guise of evaluating their partners' work, were able to deliver shocks to the confederate. For all subjects, except for a no weapon control group, a pistol and a shotgun were located near the shock machine. The data from this study indicated that aggression was affected by both perceived demand and evaluation apprehension. High levels of information about the purpose of the study and of evaluation apprehension reduced the number of shocks that subjects delivered to their partners.

Additional evidence on how perceived intent to influence by an experimenter can affect subjects' responses comes from a study by Kohn and Barnes (1977). These investigators were able to find little evidence for reactance in response to a persuasive communication. What evidence they did find, however, was limited to males who were suspicious of the experimenter's intent. For this particular experiment, then, perceived intent to influence on the part of the experimenter (who was not the supposed writer of the communication) appeared to have been necessary in order to arouse detectable levels of reactance arousal in male subjects.

Another example of the importance of perceived intent to influence is provided by Carver's (1977) study of the relationship between reactance arousal and objective self awareness (OSA). Objective self awareness (Duval & Wicklund, 1972; Wicklund, 1975) is that state hypothesized to exist when one views oneself as an object and focuses on the self. It is contrasted with a state of self awareness in which the person focuses on the environment and does not direct attention to the self. Although these two states are seen as mutually exclusive, awareness can fluctuate easily from one to the other. Studies of OSA have increased the amount of time spent in the OSA state by using various reminders of the self. Subjects in typical OSA experiments have looked at themselves in mirrors, heard their own voices on a tape-recorder, or been aware of being observed by others.

Carver (1977) used the presence of a mirror to enhance OSA. In

Carver's first experiment, subjects who participated in the experiment while facing a mirror (supposedly left in the experimental room for another experiment) reported perceiving greater attempted influence from a freedom-threatening communication (i.e., "You have no choice but to agree with me") than subjects who were not confronted with a mirror. In his second experiment, Carver used an experimental paradigm modeled after that used by Snyder and Wicklund (1976). Subjects were or were not exposed to a mirror, and a persuasive communication was read that either did or did not threaten subjects' freedom to reject the position advocated in the communication. The major dependent measure was the amount of attitude change obtained relative to an opinion pre-measure.

As Carver had predicted, increased OSA led to more reactance arousal when the high threat note was received than in the comparison no mirror condition (see Table 4.2). Indeed, the only indication of an actual boomerang effect was obtained in the high threat–mirror condition; all three other conditions evidenced attitude change toward the position of the communicator. It should be noted that since other reactance studies (including that by Snyder and Wicklund) were not conducted in front of a mirror, the absence of any apparent reactance in the high threat–no mirror condition (either a boomerang or reduced compliance) is somewhat surprising and may suggest that the experimental manipulations (other than the mirror) were rather weak. When, however, the mirror was provided, OSA presumably increased, perception of the high threat communicator's attempt to influence presumably increased, and sufficient reactance was aroused to induce attitude change away from the position advocated in the communication.[2]

Perhaps the most complex examination of the role of intent to persuade in relation to reactance arousal was conducted by Heller, Pallak, and Picek (1973). These investigators assumed that perceived intent to persuade would, by itself, create reactance arousal, but that such arousal would be "discounted" if the influence agent's behavior was innocuous and clearly *not* freedom threatening. In such a situation, Heller *et al.* predicted that reactance effects would be "attenuated."

Subjects in this experiment participated in pairs consisting of one subject and one confederate. After subjects completed a supposed departmental survey of attitudes, the experimenter explained that they

[2] While Carver's first experiment seems to suggest that OSA enhances reactance effects by increasing perceived intent to influence, other theoretical explanations of the relationship between OSA and reactance are possible. See Carver (1978) for consideration of these other possibilities.

TABLE 4.2
Mean Opinion Change[b]

	Threat to attitudinal freedom	
	High	Low
Mirror present: high OSA	$-.25^{b}$	.45
Mirror not present: low OSA	.50	.32

[a] From Carver, C. S. Self-awareness, perception of threat, and the expression of reactance through attitude change. *Journal of Personality*, 1977, 45, 501–512, Table 2, p. 506. Copyright 1977 by Duke University Press. Reprinted by permission.

[b] The more negative the number, the greater the attitude change away from the position advocated by the communication.

would be writing five essays on five different topics. Examples of various topics were given, including one (on establishing nuclear power plants near populated areas) that had been included in the previous survey, and that would be the target issue for the later experimental manipulations. When the experimenter mentioned this particular issue, the confederate stated either that he or she had decided to persuade as many people as possible about it (high intent), that he or she was not really interested in the issue (low intent), or said nothing at all.

From this point on, the experimental procedure was similar to that used by Sensenig and Brehm (1968). Subjects were told that it was important that they and their partners write on the same side of the five issues and that to accomplish this, one of them would be randomly chosen as the "deciding partner." It was noted that this person could consult with his or her partner if he or she wished. In fact, the confederate was always designated as the deciding partner. After the confederate was ostensibly taken to a separate cubicle, subjects received either a high threat ("you must") or low threat ("if it's alright with you") communication advocating the position on the nuclear power plant issue that was consistent with the subject's attitude expressed on the earlier attitude survey. In a no threat condition, subjects were told they could write on the side of the issue that they preferred, no deciding partner was mentioned nor selected, and no communication from the partner was received. Subjects were then asked to indicate their present attitude toward the establishment of nuclear power plants, and to answer some manipulation check questions, including one on the extent to which the partner was perceived as wanting to influence their opinions.

The data from this experiment are displayed in Table 4.3. Looking

TABLE 4.3
Mean Attitude Change and Perception of Intent[a]

Intent condition	Threat condition		
	High	Low	No
High			
Attitude change	− 9.00[b]	1.00	− 7.81
Intent	39.75[c]	23.50	38.88
Low			
Attitude change	.25	1.25	− .75
Intent	15.19	13.38	16.81
No			
Attitude change	− 4.44	3.63	− .88
Intent	15.13	9.06	9.31

[a] From Heller, J. F., Pallak, M. S., & Picek, J. M. The interactive effects of intent and threat on boomerang attitude change. *Journal of Personality and Social Psychology,* 1973, *26,* 273–279, Table 1, p. 276. Copyright 1973 by the American Psychological Association. Reprinted by permission.

[b] Negative change indicates change away from the position advocated by the confederate's note.

[c] The higher the score, the more the subject perceived that the partner wanted to influence his or her opinion.

first at the no intent conditions where subjects received no information about their partners' intentions, the high threat condition produced significantly more negative attitude change (from pre- to post-test) than low threat. These results replicate those of Sensenig and Brehm. Second, among subjects in the no threat conditions, those in the high intent condition showed more negative attitude change than those in the low intent condition. Heller *et al.* interpret this negative change as a reactance effect. However, given that the intent manipulation was designed to indicate motivation to persuade *without any information* being given about the attitude position of the confederate, this interpretation is questionable. It seems more likely that subjects confronted with another person who had recently discussed the issue and had a high intent to persuade would have felt relatively inexpert and uncommitted, and that this feeling would have led them to take a more neutral position on the issue.

In terms of Heller *et al.*'s major theoretical concern, the cells of greatest interest are those in the 2 × 2 design where both threat and intent are varied. Here, it can be seen from Table 4.3, the combination of high intent and high threat produced substantial negative attitude change (although this change was not significantly different from that found in the high intent–no threat condition), whereas high intent that was accompanied by low threat behavior produced slightly positive attitude change. The difference between high and low threat under high intent conditions was significant. Moreover, the high intent–high threat condition produced significantly more negative attitude change than that obtained in the low intent–high threat condition.

Heller *et al.* interpreted this pattern of findings in accordance with the correspondent inference theory of Jones and Davis (1965), and suggested that reactance effects depend on the target individual's being able to make correspondent (i.e., congruent) inferences based on the influence agent's motivation *and* behavior. When these two inferences are not correspondent (as in the conditions of high intent–low threat and low intent–high threat), reactance effects should be reduced (or even eliminated). Presumably, this comes about because the reactance that is aroused (either by the threat or the perceived intent) is "discounted."

Although we find the results of Heller *et al.*'s study very interesting, we would interpret them somewhat differently. First, as we have suggested, persuasive communications that occur in the absence of perceived intent to persuade simply may not be perceived as threats to attitudinal freedom. Usually, relatively coercive communications will imply intent to persuade, and reactance arousal (such as in Heller *et al.*'s no intent–high threat condition) should occur. It would be possible, however, to demonstrate lack of intent and if this is done (as in Heller *et al.*'s low intent– high threat condition), we would expect reactance to be less—not because it is discounted, but because less of it is aroused. Second, at least two possible mechanisms could underlie the lack of reactance effects in the high intent–low threat condition. Subjects could have changed their perceptions of the influence agent's intent; in fact, perceived intent was significantly less in the high intent–low threat condition than in the high intent–high threat condition. However, it is not clear when this change might have occurred. Perhaps, as Heller *et al.* seem to suggest, reactance is first aroused by the perceived intent, then subjects discount or distort the influence agent's motivation, and then there is little effort made to restore freedom by changing one's opinion away from the position advocated by the influence agent. On the other hand, it is possible that the low threat communication changed subjects' perceptions of intent, this in turn reduced the threat to freedom and resulted in less reactance.

Summation of Threats: Single Freedoms

Perceived intent to influence appears to increase the magnitude of threat by making it clear that a threat to freedom does, in fact, exist. Threats, however, do not necessarily come in packages of one. In any given situation, there may be more than one threat to a given freedom. Furthermore, there may be multiple threats to multiple freedoms. In this section, we will consider the case where one freedom is multiply threatened. In the next section, we will discuss the more complex theoretical issue of the possible effects on reactance arousal of having more than one freedom threatened by more than one threat.

Theoretically speaking, the effects of more than one threat to one freedom should be quite straightforward. These effects should summate. The reactance aroused by multiple threats together should be greater than the reactance aroused by any single one. There is some question about whether the summated effect would simply be additive or whether, instead, it might be multiplicative (see Wicklund, 1974, for a discussion of this issue). One supposes that the timing of the threats might be important here. If two threats were received virtually simultaneously, an additive effect might be expected. If, on the other hand, one threat was received and then after a meaningful amount of time had elapsed another threat was received, the initial threat (as suggested by Wicklund) might sensitize the person to future threats. The reactance arousal produced by the second threat might, then, be greater than would be expected by merely adding together the reactance arousal produced by each threat in isolation.

In the present discussion, we will not attempt to distinguish between an additive and multiplicative effect. Such a distinction is, as we have said, theoretically possible, but it is difficult to document empirically. Instead, we will focus on the sheer variety of instances in which summated reactance effects appear. Some of the studies described below were designed to investigate reactance; others were not and, for these, the reactance interpretation is strictly post hoc. Sometimes the summated effects are greater than reactance effects produced by each threat in isolation. At other times, only the combined threats suffice to produce detectable reactance effects. Taken as a whole, the studies described below provide rather compelling evidence for the potency of multiple threats to a given freedom.

Monetary and Verbal Inducements

Both monetary rewards and verbal persuasion exert pressure on an individual to comply with an influence attempt; both can therefore arouse reactance. One might expect that if both strong monetary and strong verbal inducements are brought to bear on a single behavior, the individual would experience considerable reactance. Two studies suggest that this might be the case.

In their replication of the Regan and Brehm (1972) supermarket study, Gilbert and Peterson (1971) provided shoppers with either a high or low pressure verbal inducement to buy a certain bread, and with either the purchase price of the bread (25¢) or with more money than was needed for the purchase (35¢). Although the results were marginal (p = .10), the lowest percentage of shoppers complied with the promotional inducements when both verbal and monetary pressures were high (see Table 4.4). It should be mentioned that in the original experiment by Regan and Brehm, increasing either verbal or monetary pressure tended to reduce compliance for female shoppers, but the combination of the two pressures did not produce the lowest amount of buyer compliance. (A third version of the supermarket study, by McGillis and Brehm (1975), did not vary monetary inducement).

Doob and Zabrack (1971) also investigated the possible summative effects of monetary and verbal inducements. Subjects were selected randomly from the Toronto phone directory and sent a questionnarie that they were asked to fill out. Along with the questionnaire, subjects received either a freedom-threatening statement urging them to complete the questionnaire or a polite request. Cross-cutting this manipulation, money (10¢ in the first two experiments; 20¢ in the third) was or was not included. In the course of three experiments using these procedures, Doob and Zabrack were unable to demonstrate a reactance effect on compliance with the request. In all three, when money was included, more people completed the questionnaire. Interestingly, however, in their third experiment—where the most money was included ("to insure prompt return") and the strongest wording of the freedom-threatening demand was used—11% of the subjects in the high threat–money included condition returned a blank questionnaire (in the stamped envelope that was provided to all subjects) *and* the money. None of the subjects in the other three conditions returned a blank questionnaire. This finding suggests that subjects were unable directly

TABLE 4.4
Percentage of Shoppers Purchasing the Advertised Item[a]

	Verbal message	
Monetary inducement	Low pressure (%)	High pressure (%)
25¢	47.5	60
35¢	52.5	30

[a] From Gilbert & Peterson, 1971. Reprinted by permission.

to express their reactance arousal by simply keeping the money and not filling out the questionnaire. Instead, they chose this rather indirect way that, presumably, reduced reactance and avoided guilt.

Attractiveness of the Communicator

We usually think of attractiveness of the communicator as a factor increasing compliance. Precisely because communicator attractiveness does motivate the person to comply, however, it should also increase reactance. Under some circumstances, then, high attractiveness of the communicator should reduce compliance. This point was demonstrated in a study by Brehm and Mann (1975), who found that when the importance of attitudinal freedom was high, attractive influence agents led to less compliance than unattractive ones. When, however, the importance of the threatened freedom was low, the attractive influence agents obtained more compliance than the unattractive ones.

Communicator attractiveness apparently can also combine with other threats to create a summated reactance effect. In a study by Dickenberger and Grabitz-Gniech (1972), subjects were either high or low on need for approval (as measured by a median split on the Marlowe–Crowne Social Desirability Scale). Attractive versus unattractive pairs were created by telling half the subjects that, according to a questionnaire they had completed, "both partners fit excellently together" and expressing, to the other half, "regret that a good partner could not be found for scheduling reasons." During the experiment, the partner (who was actually an experimental confederate) tried to influence the subject to go along with her and refuse to answer one type of experimental question. A significant interaction was obtained between subject type and partner attractiveness on subjects' question-answering behavior after the partner had left the room. When either the internal pressure (need for social approval) or the external pressure (partner attractiveness) was high, subjects complied with the influence attempt. When, however, both were high as well as when both were low, subjects reacted against the partner's directives. These data suggest that the partner's influence attempt was strong and, perhaps, somewhat inappropriate. Without any significant motives inducing compliance, subjects opposed the partner's attempt to coerce their behavior. Significant motives (high need for approval, high partner attractiveness) in isolation served to induce compliance, but when both were present, reactance was aroused and opposition to influence occurred. This pattern is also consistent with the possibility, mentioned earlier, that small forces can produce positive influence while large forces are perceived as threats to freedom.

Instruction, Modeling, and Role Playing

Like communicator attractiveness, instuctions to do something, observing someone else do it, and role-playing the desired behavior are all ways that are frequently used to increase engagement in the behavior. And, as pressures toward compliance, they can all arouse reactance. Two studies by Staub provide a good illustration of this point and demonstrate the summated reactance effects that can be produced by these factors acting in combination.

Staub (1971) investigated the use of role-playing and instruction in promoting prosocial behavior among kindergarten children. Two types of reactance effects are of interest in this study. First, there was a main effect for instruction (i.e., the experimenter pointed out the positive consequences of helping) on helping: providing instructions reduced subsequent helping to an adult. Second, various summative effects were obtained. On a measure of helping another child in distress, girls tended to be less helpful when role-playing and instruction were combined than when either factor alone was present or when neither was present. For boys on this measure, role-playing combined with instruction led to the greatest level of helping. On a measure of generalized prosocial behavior (sharing with another child), however, boys tended to help less when role-playing and instruction were combined than when either factor was present alone. Girl's sharing behavior was unaffected by treatment conditions.

A possible summation effect was also obtained in a later study by Staub (1972). In the second of two experiments reported in this paper, only seventh-grade boys participated. On an immediate measure, both persuasion and modeling increased the target behavior (delayed gratification), regardless of whether these factors were presented singly or together. Two weeks later, however, on a delayed posttest, persuasion and modeling treatments produced more delay of gratification compared to the control group (who had listened to a neutral speech) only when these treatments had been presented in isolation. Those subjects who had received both persuasion and modeling showed levels of delay of gratification not significantly different from those of the control group.

The results of these two studies are obviously quite complex. One must consider the sex of the subject, the type of behavior being measured, and the time of the measurement. There is, also, fairly little evidence in either study of strong reactance effects where compliance is reduced significantly below baseline levels. Overall, though, these two studies do support the contention that though there may be many situations in which two things are better than one, two types of persuasive influence can often be worse.

A study by Aletky and Carlin (1975) indicates that naturally occurring variables such as gender may play a role in facilitating summation reactance effects. In this study, male and female subjects were instructed to grip a dynamometer as part of the experimental task. After an initial squeeze, half the subjects received no other information; the other half were told that successful performance was an indicator of good health. In addition, subjects were or were not given a placebo (inert jelly applied to the forearm) that was described as relieving muscle fatigue. Subjects then gripped the dynamometer again.

It is easiest to discuss the results of this study by considering each sex separately. The authors assumed that females would not be particularly motivated to perform well on the dynamometer in the absence of any other information. This assumption seems borne out by the decrement in grip strength found for female subjects who received no motivating information (see Table 4.5). The authors also assumed that females would be motivated to demonstrate good health and that, once this motivation was present, a placebo should increase performance even more. The improvement in performance for female subjects who received motivating information, and especially those who received the placebo, is consistent with this reasoning.

For males, however, the experimental conditions should have created a different situation. It was assumed that males would be motivated to do well on the task even in the absence of motivating information about good health. A desire to display muscular strength should, by itself, increase effortful performance. Moreover, the presence of a placebo should lead to even more improvement. The authors,

TABLE 4.5
Mean Change in Level of Dynamometer Grip[a]

	Female		Male	
	Motivational information		Motivational information	
	Absent	Present	Absent	Present
No placebo	− 2.0	2.2	− 3.5	5.0
Placebo	− 2.0	3.7	3.8	− 9.0

[a] From Aletky, P. J. & Carlin, A. S. Sex differences and placebo effects: Motivation as an intervening variable. *Journal of Consulting and Clinical Psychology*, 1975, *43*, 278, Table 1, p. 278. Copyright 1975 by the American Psychological Association. Reprinted by permission.

thus, expected that male subjects in the no motivating information condition who received a placebo would show increased strength of grip on the second trial, and this prediction was confirmed. It is not clear, however, why male subjects in the no motivating information condition who did not receive a placebo showed a rather substantial decrement in performance. In the motivating information–no placebo condition, male subjects were expected to be even more motivated; the motives to display both strength and good health were present. A substantial improvement in strength of grip was obtained in this condition. Finally, when all the facilitating factors were added together (motive to look strong, motive to look healthy, and presence of placebo), male subjects displayed a large *decrement* in performance. It seems possible that male subjects in this condition felt under a great deal of pressure from both internal and external sources. This felt pressure may well have aroused significant reactance, which could be reduced by performing poorly on the second trial. It is also possible that increased anxiety led to the obtained performance decrement, but the simplicity of the task would seem to work against this interpretation.

Sexual Arousal and Urinary Acid Phosphate

Theoretically, it is reasonable to expect that reactance arousal could have physiological effects as well as cognitive and behavioral ones. At least in some situations, reactance arousal might well be accompanied by general physiological arousal. The possibility that more specific physiological effects might also be produced is suggested by Barclay's (1971) study of sexual arousal.

In this study, male subjects were given either correct information about the effects of the experiment or incorrect information. In the correct information condition, subjects were told that the experiment was a study of sexual stimulation on the production of urinary acid phosphate and that this production was expected to increase for subjects who watched a pornographic film and became sexually aroused. It was stated that no increase was expected for subjects who watched a neutral film. Subjects who received incorrect information were told that the study involved "the effect on imagery of viewing a film of sexual content" and that the Thematic Apperception Test would be administered after subjects watched either a sexual or neutral film. The notion that subjects who watched the sexual film would become sexually aroused was not mentioned in this condition. All subjects then watched one of the two films. Prior to experimental instructions and after the film, subjects provided a urine sample.

TABLE 4.6
Changes in Levels of Urinary Acid Phosphate[a]

	Information about experiment	
	Correct	Incorrect
Sexually experienced and inexperienced subjects		
Pornographic film	− .26	3.77
Neutral film	7.75	− 1.50
Sexually experienced subjects only		
Pornographic film	− .56	7.65
Neutral film	10.90	− 2.65

[a] From Barclay, A. M. Information as a defensive control of sexual arousal. *Journal of Personality and Social Psychology*, 1971, *17*, 244–249, Tables 2 and 3, pp. 247 and 248. Copyright 1971 by the American Psychological Association. Reprinted by permission.

The major dependent variable in this study was the change in level of urinary acid phosphate. Analysis of these data obtained a significant interaction between information received by the subject and film watched. For subjects who had watched the neutral film and had received incorrect information about the study, a slight decline in acid phosphate was found (see Table 4.6). An increased level of acid phosphate was found for subjects who had watched the pornographic film and had received incorrect information, and for those who watched the neutral film and received correct information. In regard to the latter finding, Barclay suggested that these subjects, who knew others were watching a sexually arousing film, were becoming sexually aroused by their own fantasies. For subjects who watched the pornographic film and had been correctly informed (and, thus, had been explicity told that watching the sexually arousing film should cause them to become sexually aroused and, therefore, to produce higher acid phosphate levels), there was a slight decrease in acid phosphate from before the film to after.

The above interaction was subsumed by a marginally significant interaction involving sexual experience (i.e., whether subjects reported that they had had sexual intercourse or not). Inexperienced subjects had little reaction to the experimental conditions. With experienced subjects, however, the interaction described was even stronger (see Table 4.6).

Barclay's findings show a typical summation pattern. Two variables, each of which alone produces compliance, together reduce compliance. Presumably, subjects who were told that they would become aroused and who were placed in an arousing situation successfully avoided becoming sexually aroused. That this pattern was stronger for experienced than for inexperienced subjects is also consistent with reactance theory. It would be expected that experienced subjects would more firmly hold the freedoms to become aroused and not to become aroused than inexperienced subjects.

Summation Effects: Different Freedoms

In his 1974 book, Wicklund proposed "a hydraulic principle" in reactance arousal. He stated, "When a freedom cannot be regained directly the motivation resulting from that freedom will push over into a second freedom [p. 86]." The situation addressed by Wicklund involves a reactance summation effect that would accrue when each of two freedoms has been threatened by different threats. For example, if reactance has been aroused in a teacher because she has just discovered that she will not have a choice about which courses to teach after all, also being told that coffee will no longer be allowed in the teacher's lounge may create an unusually strong reactance response. The reactance from the first threat to freedom may add to the reactance aroused by the second threat and result in a stronger response to the second threat than would normally have occurred. Before discussing the two experiments Wicklund cites in support of this proposition, let us make a couple of theoretical distinctions critical for this topic.

It is necessary to consider this type of multiple threat situation in terms of the proportion of freedoms principle described earlier. This principle as originally stated, and tested, referred to the impact of a single threat on a freedom embedded within an array of other freedoms. However, there is no reason why cases of multiple threats to multiple freedoms could not be viewed the same way. If a person has six choice alternatives and four of them are taken away, each by a different event or person, then a greater proportion of freedoms is eliminated than if only one choice alternative is removed, and greater reactance will be aroused.

It is doubtful, however, that Wicklund had this particular theoretical principle in mind when he discussed the possibility of a hydraulic principle. Although he never states this directly, Wicklund seems to assume that the different threats to different freedoms occur at different times.[3] If such threats were widely separated in time, one could still argue that

---

[3] Wicklund does state that the threats involved will occur in "fairly close proximity." This statement is made, however, in the context of pointing out that the reactance aroused by the first threat must still be present when the second occurs, and that, if too much time elapses between the two threats, this initial reactance may dissipate.

the proportion of freedoms principle was involved, but this would seem to require more stretching of the principle than is probably desirable.

We will take the liberty, then, of slightly modifying Wicklund's proposal. It seems to us that in order to investigate the possibility that there is a hydraulic principle in reactance arousal, certain minimal criteria must be met. There must be at least two different threats, each to one of at least two different freedoms. The threats must be separated in time, although it is also necessary to assume that there is some underlying connection between the two threats or freedoms. Without such a connection, there would seem little reason to expect the person to summate the arousal for the two threats. Finally, we presume, as does Wicklund, that for some reason, no reduction is possible for the reactance aroused by the first threat and that this arousal, therefore, remains psychologically potent.

Unfortunately, neither of the two studies cited by Wicklund appears to meet these criteria. Both studies involve the combining of a threat to personal space with other aspects of an interpersonal situation. In the first study (Albert & Dabbs, 1970), which was designed to test the relationship between physical distance and persuasion, subjects heard a persuasive communication by a speaker who sat very close, moderately close, or far away, and who was either hostile or friendly to the subject. Persuasiveness of this communication decreased as a function of both coming closer and being hostile. As one would expect from our previous discussion of summation effects when one freedom is threatened, the greatest amount of reactance (a marginally, $p < .10$, significant change away from the speaker's position) occurred in the condition where closeness and hostility were combined.

While this study does, then, provide another example of a summation effect, it is difficult to see it as a test of a hydraulic principle. Given that all threats occurred virtually simultaneously, it would seem more likely that either subjects felt a large proportion of their freedoms were threatened (i.e., freedom to maintain personal space; freedom to accept or reject the position advocated by the speaker; freedom to have a civilized interaction during their participation in the experiment), or perceived all of the threats as threatening their attitudinal freedom. After all, a stereotyped image of an overly forceful persuader is of a person who sits close to you and is aggressive and hostile in his or her delivery.

Similar problems in interpretation arise in regard to the second study cited by Wicklund. Here (Liberman and Wicklund reported in Wicklund, 1974), female subjects expected to participate in an interview. During this interaction, the interviewer positioned herself either close to the subject or far away. Of the questions in the interview, 10 were highly personal, and 10 were quite impersonal. As expected, the number of personal questions answered by subjects was a function of an interaction between physical distance and type of question, with considerably more refusals to answer occurring with personal questions asked by the close interviewer (see Table 4.7).

Besides being a doubtful test of a hydraulic principle, it is not even clear that a summation effect was obtained in this experiment. It is assumed by Wicklund that the freedom not to answer a personal question is more important than the freedom not to answer an impersonal one, and, thus, that the asking of a personal question constitutes a threat to an important freedom. Since, however, there was no difference between mean number of items not answered for personal versus impersonal questions when the interviewer was far away, it was not demonstrated that asking a personal question, in and of itself, posed a threat to freedom. Being close while asking questions did seem to pose a clear threat to freedom; fewer personal as well as impersonal questions were answered when the interviewer was close. Only one threat was thus demonstrated and the reactance produced by this threat was, as one would expect, greater when a more important freedom was at stake.

Although these two studies do not seem serviceable as tests of a possible hydraulic principle, there is more recent research that does appear to offer support for this notion. It is important to emphasize that none of these studies was designed to test for reactance effects and, thus, that the following interpretations are unabashedly post hoc. It should also be pointed out that all of these studies appeared after the publication of Wicklund's book.

Christensen (1977) reported two studies on the "negative subject" in experimental settings. Using a verbal conditioning paradigm (and, as is

TABLE 4.7
Mean Number of Questions Not Answered[a]

Interviewer distance	Type of question	
	Personal	Impersonal
Close	1.79	.95
Far	.29	.24

[a] From an experiment by Liberman & Wicklund reported in Wicklund, R. *Freedom and reactance*, Hillsdale, N.J.: Erlbaum, 1974, Table 17, p. 89. Reprinted by permission.

typically the case, including only subjects who were aware of the conditioning contingencies in the data analyses), Christensen exposed subjects to a variety of experiences prior to and during conditioning. In his first study, three experimental conditions were created. All subjects in these conditions were given verbal reinforcement for "he" or "she" sentences. For one-third of the subjects, this was the only experimental manipulation. Another one-third received instructions prior to the experiment that the experiment might involve manipulation of their behavior. The final one-third received information about possible manipulation and a prior attempt to influence (i.e., they participated in a supposedly separate study in which demand characteristics were blatant). Only subjects in the last experimental situation failed to condition during reinforced trials.

In a second study, all experimental subjects again received verbal reinforcement during conditioning trials. The one-third who received only reinforcement conditioned as did the one-third who had had a prior nonmanipulative experience. For the one-third of subjects who had had a prior manipulative experience, however, there was again little evidence of conditioning to reinforcement, and no significant increase in the target sentences was obtained. Christensen concluded that previous exposure to attempted influence was the critical variable in resisting conditioning.

These data are quite consistent with a hydraulic principle. Subjects experienced a threat to a freedom in the first experiment (i.e., a blatant attempt to control their behavior in the experiment) and then were confronted with a quite different threat to a quite different freedom in the second experiment (i.e., an attempt to elicit more "he" and "she" sentences through the use of verbal reinforcement). Compared to subjects who experienced only the single threat of reinforcement, subjects who had experienced both threats showed more opposition to influence (i.e., less conditioning). There is, however, one serious problem in interpreting Christensen's data in terms of hydraulic reactance arousal. It is not clear whether subjects had the opportunity to reduce reactance arousal in the first experiment by resisting the influence attempt made there. If they did not, then the data fit a hydraulic model rather well. If they did, then it is possible that rather than "carrying over" their reactance arousal from the first experiment to the second, subjects were sensitized by the first experiment to any threats to freedom that might occur in experimental settings. One would expect that such sensitization would lead these subjects to perceive greater intent to influence on the part of the second experimenter than subjects who had experienced no prior influence attempt.

It should also be noted that these data are consistent with a self-presentational perspective. Christensen appears to endorse this interpretation, and comments that "subjects want to look good, but looking good does not always mean going along with the experimenter [p. 398]." Interestingly, however, in both of Christensen's studies, the two different experiments were conducted by two different experimenters. If subjects were trying to "look good," it is not clear for whom they were doing so. It seems just as plausible that having experienced a threat to freedom in the first experiment, the reactance aroused there (or the sensitization) affected subject's responses to the subsequent conditioning experiment.

The other studies that provide support for some type of hydraulic principle in reactance arousal are found in the more recent literature on learned helplessness. In order to understand how the methodological procedures that support the hydraulic model principle came to be used in helplessness studies, a brief history of helplessness research will be provided.

The learned helplessness model (Seligman, 1972; 1975) was initially proposed to account for the effects of uncontrollable electric shock on animal's subsequent difficulties in avoidance learning. It was observed that dogs that had received uncontrollable shocks failed to escape from later shocks that were, in fact, escapable by crossing a barrier. Animals that had not received uncontrollable shocks usually learned in just a few trials to avoid the shock completely. In contrast, the animals that had been exposed to uncontrollable shocks would passively accept the shocks. Seligman proposed that helpless animals have learned that their behavior and their outcomes are noncontingent—that their behavioral responses do not effect control over the shock. The incentive for initiating instrumental responses is, therefore, diminished.

Although the evidence for the learned helplessness model is rather good for animals, attempts to apply this model to human behaviors have run into several problems (see Wortman & Brehm, 1976, for a review). One methodological problem, in particular, is of interest for the present discussion. Early helplessness studies on humans (e.g., Hiroto, 1974; Hiroto & Seligman, 1975; Thornton & Jacobs, 1971) applied the research paradigm used with animals without substantial modification for human consumption. Typically, the same experimenter was used to give both the training (experience with uncontrollable aversive outcomes) and test (experience with controllable outcomes) tasks. The same room might be used and the tasks were often quite similar. The results of many of these studies supported the helplessness model, but the lack of differentiation between training and test experiences raises concern about how much generalization is really involved (see Cole & Coyne, 1977) and makes several alternative explanations quite feasible (e.g., anger at the experimenter, disbelieving the experimenter's instructions that the test task was controllable).

To deal with this issue, recent studies have begun to take more care to separate the training and test tasks. With this separation, however, several experiments (Hanusa & Schulz, 1977; Roth & Bootzin, 1974; Wortman, Panciera, Shusterman, & Hibscher, 1976) that were designed to produce performance decrements on the test task have, instead, obtained improvement in performance. These findings have a variety of implications for the learned helplessness model (as well as for its subsequent attributional reformulation by Abramson, Seligman, & Teasdale, 1978) that need more detailed consideration than would be appropriate here. The facilitation effects that were obtained have, however, two direct implications for reactance theory. First, these findings contributed to the theoretical consideration that reactance and helplessness might be related effects. The Wortman and Brehm integrative model that stemmed from this consideration has been decribed previously and will be discussed in more detail in the immediately following section. Second, the obtained facilitation effects, at least in a general sense, may provide support for the operation of a hydraulic principle in reactance arousal.

This support comes from the fact that these studies fulfill all our criteria noted earlier. There is an initial elimination of freedom and no restoration of freedom is possible. Subjects presumably expect to be able to succeed on tasks presented in an experiment and they fail miserably if they are so unfortunate as to be in the helpless conditions. Then there is another threat to another freedom. Upon entering the "second experiment," subjects are confronted with another task that threatens their freedom to perform well. If we can assume that the two tasks (that are usually similar in format, but different in content) eliminate or threaten different specific behavioral freedoms, then the improved performance on the second task (relative to performance by a group that never experienced helplessness training) certainly suggests that reactance arousal has carried over from the first to the second situation.

Much beyond this suggestion, however, it would be somewhat foolhardy to go. These studies on learned helplessness were not designed to test for a hydraulic principle in reactance, nor, indeed, for anything having to do with reactance. Furthermore, the facilitation effects were unexpected and all explanations of them are *post hoc* and speculative.

Reactance and Helplessness:
The Wortman and Brehm Integrative Model

The facilitation effects obtained in the learned helplessness studies we have been discussing are consistent with the Wortman and Brehm model, but they cannot be viewed as providing particularly strong support. Besides not being designed to test the model and not predicting the facilitation effects that were obtained, these studies, at best, provide support for only one-half of a two-part model. A more convincing demonstration of the utility of the integrative model would require obtaining both facilitation and helplessness within the same experimental paradigm. At the time of this writing, four studies have obtained results that meet this requirement and that support the general model.[4]

A study by Roth and Kubal (1975), though designed independently of the Wortman and Brehm model, provided the first experimental test of the formulation. In this study, subjects went through a typical learned helplessness experimental paradigm, with contingent or noncontingent reinforcement (i.e., accurate or random information on the correctness of their responses on each trial) being received in the course of working on soluble concept formation tasks. Subjects received either contingent feedback on one problem (50 trials), noncontingent on one problem (50 trials), or noncontingent on three problems (50, 40 and 30 trials, respectively). Prior to working on the task, subjects either were informed that the concept formation problem[s] they would be working on offered "really good" prediction of success in college or were given no information about the task's predictive validity. The test situation came immediately after the training experience. It was presented as a completely different experiment (different room, different experimenter), and consisted of a second type of concept formation problem. Measures of ability and persistence constituted the major dependent variables. A no training control group also participated in the test task and can be considered as a baseline comparison group.

[4] A fifth study, by Shaban and Welling (reported in Glass & Singer, 1972), was cited by Wortman and Brehm in support of their theoretical model. Although the results of this study can be interpreted within the model's framework, possible alternative explanations (noted by Wortman & Brehm) introduce considerable ambiguity. In addition, a recent study by Baum, Aiello, and Calesnick (1978) that claims to fit the model will not be discussed. These investigators found interesting and rather complex evidence of helplessness among dormitory residents given prolonged experience (seven weeks) with a relatively uncontrollable dormitory situation, as well as considerable amounts of hostility and dissatisfaction after shorter exposure, but there was no evidence of reactance effects. Since subjects first participated after one week of residence, it may be that an earlier testing would have provided the baseline against which both facilitation and helplessness could have been demonstrated.

TABLE 4.8
Measures of Helplessness[a]

	Training experience			
	No training control	Contingent feedback	Helplessness training	"Double" helplessness training
Number of problems solved				
Low importance		2.89	4.56	3.67
	3.33			
High importance		3.44	4.11	2.00
Number of requests for a new problem				
Low importance		1.22	.22	1.00
	.78			
High importance		.89	.56	2.56

[a] From Roth, S. & Kubal, L. Effects of noncontingent reinforcement on tasks of differing importance: Facilitation and helplessness. *Journal of Personality and Social Psychology*, 1975, *32*, 680–691, Table 1, p. 686. Copyright 1975 by the American Psychological Association. Reprinted by permission.

Data for the two major dependent measures are presented in Table 4.8. Number of problems solved was viewed as a measure of ability, whereas subjects who made *more* requests for new problems, thereby indicating that they were giving up on a previous problem, were viewed as *less* persistent. Before examining these data, it is important to be clear about what the Wortman and Brehm model would predict. First, increasing amounts of helplessness training should create the expected curvilinear relationship. Relatively small amounts should pose a threat but not an irrevocable elimination to the expected freedom to solve problems. Reactance should be aroused and should motivate subjects to restore their freedom by doing well on a similar task. As helplessness training is prolonged, however, the subject's freedom to perform well (at least on this type of task in an experimental situation) should be irrevocably eliminated and helplessness should ensue. Helpless subjects should perform less well and be less persistent than the baseline control group, while subjects experiencing reactance arousal should perform better and be more persistent.

Second, we need to consider the possible effects of varying importance of freedom by telling half of the subjects that their performance will predict an important outcome. When a person perceives a freedom as important, he or she should be reluctant to admit that the freedom has been irrevocably lost. This reluctance should prolong the reactance part of the curve. In addition, importance of the freedom will increase the magnitude of both the reactance and helplessness effects. Thus, even though importance of freedom will, by prolonging the reactance phase, change the shape of the curve, the reactance or helplessness coming from a threat to or elimination of an important freedom should always be equal to or greater than the reactance or helplessness coming from a threat to or elimination of an unimportant freedom. These relationships are diagrammed in Figure 4.2.

The data from the Roth and Kubal study provide partial support for these theoretical contentions. Comparing across groups that had received either contingent or noncontingent feedback in the training phase, significant quadratic trends were obtained for the low and high importance of freedom conditions on number of problems solved, and for the high importance of freedom condition on number of requests for a new problem. A marginally significant ($p < .115$) quadratic trend was found for the low importance of freedom condition on the latter measure. Table 4.9 summarizes the effects obtained when nonorthogonal contrasts between the helplessness conditions and the no training control group were performed.

These analyses indicate that although the predicted general shape of the curve was obtained (or was at least marginally significant) for both

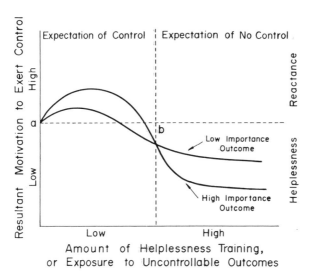

Figure 4-2. Effects of control, outcome importance, and amount of helplessness training.

TABLE 4.9
Summary of Nonorthogonal Contrasts[a]

	No training control versus:	
	Helplessness training	"Double" helplessness training
Number of problems solved		
Theoretical prediction	HT > NTC	NTC > DHT
Findings		
Low importance	Obtained	Not obtained
High importance	Not obtained	Obtained
Number of requests for a new problem		
Theoretical prediction	NTC > HT	DHT > NTC
Findings		
Low importance	Not obtained	Not obtained
High importance	Not obtained	Obtained

[a] Data from Roth & Kubal, 1975.

importance groups for both measures, there was no clear effect for the importance of freedom variable. One would have expected that both reactance and helplessness effects would be greater for high importance subjects. Instead, while only high importance of freedom subjects showed any significant helplessness effects, only the low importance of freedom condition showed a significant facilitation effect (and that was found only on the problems-solved measure). The rather fragmented effect of importance of freedom on the present results should be placed in context. Two questions were asked that were designed to be checks on the manipulation of importance of freedom; on neither one was there a significant difference between high and low importance of freedom conditions. It is possible, then, that some of the erratic effect of this variable on the behavioral measures is attributable to a weak manipulation of the variable. A more powerful manipulation might obtain results more consistent with the theoretical model.

In the Roth and Kubal study, noncontingent feedback was confounded with the aversiveness of repeated failure. Noncontingent feedback on concept formation problems makes it impossible for subjects to solve the problem(s) presented. This confound, present in all helplessness studies that utilize concept formation tasks in the training phase, is distinctly at odds with the procedures of the animal studies (e.g., Seligman & Maier, 1967) where amount of aversive stimulation is equivalent for animals receiving either helplessness (i.e., uncontrollable shock) or nonhelplessness (i.e., controllable shock) training. The Wortman and Brehm model is in agreement with Seligman's formulation on this point. It is not aversiveness per se that produces helplessness or reactance, it is the perception that a freedom has been threatened or eliminated. To use a rather violent example, one can be beaten to a pulp and still perceive the freedom to win the fight. And, one can be barely scratched, and completely give up hope.

Separation of the two variables of aversiveness and control was achieved in a study by Brehm and Bryant (1976). Subjects in this experiment were told that they were participating in the final phases of the creation of a "revolutionary, new personality test." The validity of the test was strongly emphasized, and it can be inferred that all subjects regarded their freedom to respond to the test as important. Subjects were told that there would be two parts of the test. They would answer the first set of questions and then receive written evaluation feedback from a "prominent research psychiatrist." Feedback was also expected after the second part was completed though none was actually given.

The first part of the test consisted of twenty items that offered an A and B alternative for action in a variety of topical situations. Subjects were told to express their preference for A or B by selecting a button from a 13-button panel in front of them on which a 13-point bipolar scale was printed. At the end of the first part, subjects received feedback (actually prepared in advance) from the supposed psychiatrist. Three types of feedback were used. Congruent feedback consisted of presumably face-valid comments on the subject's preference (for A or B) that interpreted this preference in terms of various personality dimensions such as honesty, altruism, trustworthiness, and conformity. Oppositional feedback interpreted subjects' preferences along the line of the same types of personality dimensions, but opposite to the common-sense interpretation provided in congruent feedback. Uncorrelated feedback interpreted subjects' preferences in terms of personality dimensions totally unrelated to the content matter of the test item (see Table 4.10).

Although this study was not conducted to investigate the Wortman and Brehm model, it shares an underlying assumption with that model and can thus be examined within the framework of the model. Brehm and Bryant assumed that oppositional feedback would threaten a subject's freedom to present herself to the psychiatrist as she desired. This threat should not, however, be perceived as an irrevocable elimination of freedom. Even though the interpretations should usually be per-

TABLE 4.10
Types of Feedback[a]

Sample item
Your best friend has told you a very intimate secret. Your friend has asked you not to tell this secret to anyone else. The next day you are with some other friends and they start talking about your best friend. You feel a great desire to tell your friend's secret. What do you decide?

A. Tell your friend's secret
B. Keep silent about the secret

Congruent feedback
A. The strength of your choice for A indicates that you are more concerned about your immediate pleasures than you are about the possible discomfort of others.
B. The strength of your choice for B indicates that you believe that interpersonal trust depends upon people's keeping their promises.

Oppositional feedback
A. The strength of your choice for A indicates that you are aware that you sometimes fail to keep promises; this awareness tends to make you highly trustworthy.
B. The strength of your choice for B indicates that you wish to emphasize your interpersonal loyalty; this emphasis indicates your difficulty in being loyal to others.

Uncorrelated feedback
A/B The strength of your choice for A (or B) indicates that you frequently manifest phobias, i.e., things that others are not afraid of (heights, closed spaces); thus you restrict considerable portions of your life in order to avoid contact with these feared situations.

---

[a] Adapted from Brehm, S. S. & Bryant, F. Effects of feedback on self-expressive decision making. *Journal of Personality*, 1976, 44, 133–148. Copyright 1976 by Duke University Press.

ceived by subjects as "wrong," these interpretations do deal with a personality dimension related to the subject's response. Uncorrelated feedback, on the other hand, should eliminate the subject's freedom to present herself to the psychiatrist as she desired. Being totally unrelated to her response, it should give the subject no room to hope to control the impression she would create. It was expected, then, that oppositional condition subjects would try harder to create their desired impression on the second half of the test, whereas subjects in the uncorrelated condition would give up and not try. To test this hypothesis, the major dependent measure consisted of the change in the extremity of subjects' preferences (regardless of A or B direction) from Part I to Part II (another set of situational problems was used for the second part of the test).

The results of the study were consistent with the experimental prediction and thus provide support for the Wortman and Brehm integrative model. After feedback, subjects in the congruent condition changed very little in the extremity of their ratings. Compared to these subjects, subjects in the oppositional condition became more extreme, and subjects who received uncorrelated feedback became less extreme. The relative independence of these effects from aversiveness per se is demonstrated by the lack of relationship between negativity of evaluation received and changes in self-presentation extremity. The greatest number of negative feedback statements was received by subjects in the oppositional condition, the next greatest by uncorrelated condition subjects, and the least by congruent condition subjects. Thus, the most helpless response was produced by subjects receiving a moderate number of negative evaluations, and the most freedom-restoring behavior came from those subjects who received the greatest number of negative statements. Subjects who received the greatest number of positive evaluations showed little change. It is difficult to see how the pattern of results that was obtained could be predicted on the basis of the negativity of the evaluations received by subjects.

A confound between aversiveness and control is primarily a problem for interpreting helplessness effects. It cannot stand as a potential alternative explanation for the quadratic trends obtained by Roth and Kubal. Another confound in the Roth and Kubal study, however, could be potentially more troublesome for the Wortman and Brehm model. It is possible that attempts to restore one's freedom, especially if the attempts involve relatively strenuous physical or mental effort, can occur only if one is not fatigued. If one is tired, one may still be motivated but unable. In this regard, it is interesting that on a questionnaire that Roth and Kubal administered directly after the training task, there was a tendency for increased helplessness training to lead to increased reports of fatigue. The linear trend for this effect was significant only for high importance condition subjects, though the same basic pattern was obtained for low importance condition subjects. Furthermore, across all experimental groups, the most fatigue was reported by the only condition (high importance–"double" helplessness training) in which significant helplessness effects were obtained on the behavioral measures. The Brehm and Bryant study is not subject to this alternative interpretation. All subjects experienced the same amount of work (and it was not particularly great for any of them) during the initial part of the experiment.[5]

[5] Success in controlling for this alternative explanation is also suggested by the lack of significant differences on a fatigue rating included in a mood questionnaire administered by Brehm and Bryant. It should be noted, however, that this rating was obtained after the second part of the experiment. Roth and Kubal also re-administered their

Two experiments by Pittman and Pittman (1979; Pittman & Pittman, 1980) round out the evidence on reactance and helplessness. The manipulation of helplessness was carried out in the same way in both studies. All subjects first worked on a practice concept formation problem. Subjects assigned to the control (no helplessness) condition then simply guessed the correct responses to six additional concept formation problems, each of which consisted of ten trials, without receiving feedback about whether or not their guesses were correct. Subjects in the low helplessness condition also guessed without feedback on the first four problems, and then received noncontingent feedback (implying and leading to failure) on the last two problems. Subjects in the high helplessness condition received noncontingent feedback on all six problems. On completion of the concept formation task, all subjects reported to a second room where a second experimenter asked them to participate in the establishment of norms for an anagram task. They were informed that they might be able to find a pattern in the anagrams that would aid solution, and they were asked to solve, one by one, twenty five-letter anagrams in which the pattern of letter scrambling was constant. The performance measures were the number of trials till three anagrams in a row were solved within 15 sec, the number of anagrams not solved within 100 sec, and the mean response latency for all twenty anagrams.

In the first of these two experiments, subjects were selected according to their score on the Internal–External Locus of Control Scale (Rotter, 1966). Pittman and Pittman reasoned that those persons who scored high on internality would have a firmer expectation of control than would those who scored high on externality, and would consequently show a more pronounced reactance effect to the experience of helplessness (see Chapter 9 for discussion of the relationship between reactance and the I–E scale). This prediction was supported by the results. On the mean number of trials till anagrams were quickly solved, high internals exposed to low helplessness performed better than did no treatment internals. In contrast, high externals showed a decrement in performance from the low helplessness treatment compared to the no treatment control subjects. Also in support of the Wortman and Brehm model, both internals and externals exposed to high helplessness showed deficits in performance compared to their no treatment controls, and internals revealed a greater deficit than did externals. The other two performance measures obtained a similar pattern of results.

The second experiment by Pittman and Pittman (1980) used unse-

---

fatigue item after the second part (test task) of their experiment. Here, no linear trends were significant, although the highest absolute level of fatigue was still reported by subjects in the high importance–"double" helplessness training condition.

lected subjects and examined the effects of helplessness treatments on information processing. The performance measures on anagrams solution were consistent with the results for high internals in the previous study. Low helplessness produced better performance, high helplessness worse, compared to no treatment controls. In addition, mood measures in both experiments indicated that the conditions that produced improved performance also produced relatively high feelings of hostility, while the conditions that produced lowered performance also produced relatively high feelings of depression. The pattern of mood measures in both studies tended to rule out the possibility that performance deficits in the high helplessness condition were due either to hostility or anxiety.

Taken together, these four experiments provide reasonably good support for the Wortman and Brehm model. The predicted nonmonotonic relationship between the magnitude of threat (helplessness treatment) and tendencies to re-exert control or to give up have been obtained, and alternative explanations in terms of fatigue, hostility, or anxiety have been ruled out by design and by mood data.

The Wortman and Brehm prediction of an interaction between amount of threat (helplessness experience) and importance of freedom was tested directly only in the Roth and Kubal experiment, and it was not confirmed by the results. The manipulation of importance in that study was apparently weak, however, and may not have provided an adequate test. In contrast, the reasoning by Pittman and Pittman that high internals would have greater expectations of control (and perhaps would feel that control was more important) than high externals, was supported by the predicted interaction between threat and locus of control. Internals performed better than externals in response to low threat, and worse than externals in response to high threat. There is at least some support, then, for the hypothesized interaction between amount of threat and importance (or firmness of expectation) of freedom.[6]

Reactance Arousal by Implication

Until now, our discussion of the determinants of the magnitude of reactance has focused exclusively on threats to or eliminations of

[6] A recent unpublished paper by Seta and Seta (1980) reports an experiment in which these investigators found that the attractiveness of a low value goal was increased by a small amount of failure whereas the attractiveness of a high value goal was increased only by a large amount of failure. This effect was interpreted as inconsistent with reactance theory but as consistent with an intrapersonal equity model. It was further proposed that the equity model can account for both the enhancement and helplessness effects found in human helplessness research.

freedom received directly by the person. Theoretically, however, threats do not have to be direct. The original presentation of the theory clearly recognized the possibility of indirect threats to freedom: "If the loss of a free behavior to an observed person could just as well happen to oneself, then one's own free behavior is threatened [Brehm, 1966, p. 7]."

A study by Andreoli, Worchel, and Folger (1974) investigated the possibility of reactance arousal as a function of threat to another's freedom. Female subjects participated in this study in small groups of four and five. Under the guise of studying group discussion techniques, they were told that two discussions would be held and that two of them would participate in the discussion while the others observed. Subjects were then taken to separate listening cubicles where they all learned that they would listen to the first session. They also were informed at this time that they would participate in the next discussion as a discussant. Their partner for this upcoming session was designated as subject A or B (who also were supposedly the participants in the first discussion session) or subject D (who subjects thought was an observer for the first session). All subjects then heard a supposed interaction (actually pre-recorded) between subject A and the experimenter. Subject B was presented as having left the room briefly. In this interaction, A either threatened ("It's obvious we are going to have to talk about . . . ") or did not threaten ("I'd prefer . . . , but we haven't decided yet") B's freedom to participate in the selection of the topic for discussion. For those subjects who heard A threaten B's freedom, the experimenter either accepted the threat ("All right") or restored B's freedom ("We'll just wait for B to come back and make sure you both want that one"). In all cases, the discussion topic urged by the supposed subject A was the one actual subjects had previously ranked as the one they preferred most. After hearing the tape, subjects rated how much they would like to discuss each of the topics.

To summarize the variables presented in this study, subjects observed either no threat to freedom, a threat to freedom without restoration by a third party, or a threat to freedom followed by restoration of freedom. They expected to interact in a subsequent session with either the threatener, the person whose freedom had been threatened, or a neutral party. If reactance can be aroused by observing a threat to someone else's freedom, subjects who observed such a threat should evidence more reactance (i.e., less subsequent preference for the advocated topic) than subjects who did not observe a threat or subjects who observed freedom restored. Furthermore, while all subjects were similar to the person whose freedom was threatened in that all were subjects in the same experiment and anticipated participating in the second discussion, the strength of the implied threat presumably would have been greater for those who expected to interact with the threatener than for those who expected to interact with either the person threatened or the observer.

The first prediction was confirmed by the results of the study by Andreoli et al. Subjects who observed a threat rated their initially preferred topic less favorably after hearing the tape than did subjects who had heard no threat or those who had heard freedom restored (see Table 4.11). There was, however, no significant interaction between threat condition and expected interaction partner, and Andreoli et al. concluded that the expected partner had no effect on reactance arousal. Inspection of these data, however, reveals a trend for reactance arousal in the threat condition to be greater for those subjects who expected to interact with the threatener. Using the MS error term from the overall analysis for a test of the theoretical prediction, we find that subjects who heard the threat to freedom and expected to interact with the threatener (subject A) rated the advocated topic significantly less favorably (t [94] = 2.23, $p < .05$) than subjects who heard the threat and expected to interact with a neutral party (subject D). Subjects who heard the threat and expected to interact with the threatened party (subject B) gave favorability ratings in between those of the other

TABLE 4.11
Subjects' Mean Ratings of Initially Preferred Discussion Topic after Overhearing the Interaction between Subject A and the Experimenter[a]

	Expected interaction partner		
	Subject A	Subject B	Subject D
Threat	9.00[b]	7.82	6.27
No threat	2.27	3.17	3.18
Freedom restored	3.09	3.62	3.00

[a] From Andreoli, V. A., Worchel, S., & Folger, R. Implied threat to behavioral freedom. Journal of Personality and Social Psychology, 1974, 30, 765–771, Table 1, p. 769. Copyright 1974 by the American Psychological Association. Reprinted by permission.

[b] Responses are answers to the question, "Please indicate how much you would like to discuss each of the following topics in your first discussion," 1 = very much; 31 = not at all.

two conditions, and these ratings were not significantly different from the ratings in either of the two other conditions.[7]

SUMMARY

A freedom is threatened whenever an event increases the perceived difficulty of exercising that freedom. It is possible, however, that events or forces of small magnitude may not by themselves create a perceived threat though when combined, they do. This idea is supported by a fair amount of evidence in the literature.

Events of great magnitude, on the other hand, can create so much difficulty for exercising a freedom that the freedom is effectively eliminated. Although the elimination of a freedom initially should arouse reactance just as does a threat, consideration of the research on learned helplessness has led to a reconsideration of what happens when freedoms are eliminated. It seems likely that when a person becomes convinced that a freedom has been eliminated, the freedom is given up and reactance dissipates.

In between very small and very large forces, the effects of reactance aroused by threats to freedom will vary with the importance of the freedom. Because freedoms of low importance give rise to little reactance when threatened, forces to give up freedoms of low importance will tend to result in overt compliance. Where freedoms of moderate to high importance are involved, however, the magnitude of reactance can be greater than the force to give up the freedom, resulting in considerable resistance to compliance and even in boomerang effects. Very high forces to give up the freedom will still result in compliance. Only if the importance of a freedom is extremely great—perhaps as great as the importance of life itself—will great forces fail to produce compliance.

A review of the research on threats to freedom reveals a wide variety of ways in which freedoms can be threatened. Threats have been shown to reduce attitude change from a persuasive communication, especially where the threat involves a perception that the com-

---

[7] People's sensitivity to reactance arousal in others has also been demonstrated in a study by Worchel, Insko, Andreoli, and Drachman (1974). In this study, observer subjects attributed attitudes to the actor that opposed the activity that the actor was required to engage in. Since these subjects were explicitly told they would only observe the experiment, there is little reason to believe that they themselves experienced any reactance arousal. They did, however, apparently infer such arousal on the part of the individual they observed.

municator intends to influence the recipient of a communication. Perceived intent to influence has also been shown to reduce other kinds of influence such as the induction of aggession.

Various kinds of forces, singly and together, have been found to act as threats to freedom. Among these are verbal and monetary inducements to behave in a particular way, the attractiveness of a would-be influence agent, instruction, modeling, and role-playing. In addition, sex roles can act on the individual (in conjunction with other pressures) to reduce compliance with appropriate sex role behavior.

It is possible that different threats to different freedoms enhance the magnitude of reactance such that the response to any one threat is magnified by the presence of the other threats. This increase in reactance from previous threats to different freedoms would presumably depend on a moderate degree of temporal proximity and would occur only when reactance from the initial threat is not reduced prior to the occurrence of a second threat. The clear evidence for this view was found to be meagre but supportive. However, if research on human helplessness can be interpreted as presenting subjects with threats to separate freedoms to perform well, the enhancement effects frequently obtained in this research paradigm can be interpreted as further support for the notion that reactance from different threats to separate freedoms can cumulate.

Research on the Wortman and Brehm integrative model of reactance and learned helplessness was extensively reviewed. Four studies were described that, taken together, provide reasonably good support for a nonmonotonic relationship between the magnitude of threat and tendencies to re-exert control or to give up. The Wortman and Brehm prediction of an interaction between amount of threat and importance of freedom in producing reactance and helplessness has also received some empirical support.

Although the perception of threat to freedom will most typically occur because of forces applied directly on the individual, a threat may also be perceived by implication. Implied threats will occur when people have freedoms that they observe to be threatened or eliminated for other people who are much like themselves. Only one experiment has examined this proposition, but it produced fairly strong supporting evidence.

CHAPTER 5

Effects of Reactance

Reactance is defined as a motivational state and as such is assumed to have energizing and behavior-directing properties. Because the theory stipulates conditions under which there will be behavioral attempts to restore freedom or there will be changes in the subjective evaluation of potential outcomes, it easily lends itself to test by the measurement of behavior or the use of rating scales. Unlike the concept of cognitive dissonance (see Kiesler & Pallak, 1976; Wicklund & Brehm, 1976), reactance has not been examined in regard to its energizing properties. It nevertheless presumably has these qualitites and would produce, for example, physiological evidence of arousal, latent learning, and interactive effects with weak versus strong habits. Studies of such effects would be particularly informative where a freedom has been eliminated with the consequence that direct behavioral effects of reactance are not possible. To the best of our knowledge, however, no attempts have been made to examine these manifestations of the energizing properties of reactance.

Direct Restoration of Freedom

As a motivational state directed toward the reestablishment of behavioral freedoms that have been threatened or eliminated, the most obvious manifestation of reactance arousal would be direct behavioral efforts to restore the freedom. There are, however, a number of factors that might limit direct restoration.

First, as we have seen, an irrevocable elimination, though initially it would arouse reactance, would be expected eventually to produce helplessness. In other cases, however, where the person is not certain that the freedom is truly lost, reactance will be aroused, but direct behavioral restoration of freedom may still not be attempted. For example, if one expected to choose between apples and oranges and then learned that the local supermarket was out of apples for the day, it is unlikely that one would perceive the freedom to obtain apples as irrevocably eliminated. One knows that apples are available in other stores, and that this store will have apples in the future. A person's motivation to obtain apples would be increased and one might express this motivation by direct restorative efforts, such as going to another store, but one might not. In cases such as this where the likelihood of direct behavioral attempts at restoration is uncertain, better indicators of the motivational state might be feelings and desires rather than overt behavior. Later in this chapter, we will consider a variety of possible subjective responses that can be generated by reactance arousal.

Even in situations in which direct restorative attempts are likely (situations where there is a threat to, but not elimination of, freedom), direct reestablishment of freedom may still be restricted. One restricting factor will be the costs associated with any direct attempt at reestablishment. Even if success is probable, the costs to the person may be sufficiently high to deter direct restoration. Many such costs are possible, depending on the specific situation. For example, if one's freedom is threatened by another person who has control of a number of important outcomes and this other person were to know of any direct restorative attempts, the cost of punishment by this individual for attempting to reestablish one's freedom will act as a deterrent (see Chapter 7 for a further discussion of social power and reactance). Costs can also be internal. A study by Feldman-Summers (1977), for instance, indicates that if freedom restoration would result in one's being responsible for a negative outcome to another person, direct attempts at freedom restoration are reduced. In this case, it is presumed that this kind of perceived responsibility would violate one's view of oneself as a beneficent, not malevolent, person and that the cost of this violation of one's self-image is too high a price to pay.

Another factor that should affect direct restoration attempts is the ease and likelihood of some other mode of freedom restoration. As pointed out by Götz-Marchand, Götz, and Irle (1974) in regard to dissonance reduction, reduction of reactance arousal may be most likely to occur by means of the first mode presented, even if this mode is indirect rather than direct. At other times, however, sequence of presentation of modes of freedom restoration will not determine which mode the person uses. This relative lack of importance for sequence, under some conditions, was demonstrated in a study by Brehm and Cole (1966) on the effects of receiving a favor.

Subjects in this experiment expected to provide first-impression ratings for either an important project or a relatively unimportant one. It was thought that the belief that the project was important would create a more important freedom to be objective (and, therefore, accurate) about the person subjects were to rate. This person, presented as another subject but actually an experimental confederate, unexpectedly performed a favor for half of the subjects (i.e., brought cokes and wouldn't accept any offered payment). It is important to note that the confederate was out of the room when the experimenter described the experiment to the subject. Thus, the favor occurred before the confederate had an opportunity to find out that he would be rated by the subject, and, therefore, the favor could not be perceived by subjects as a blatant attempt at ingratiation for an ulterior purpose.

Even though, in this experimental design, the favor cannot be seen as an attempt by the confederate to secure favorable ratings, the favor does act to pressure the subject to feel positively toward the confederate and, thus, to rate him favorably on the first impression ratings. This pressure to reciprocate the favor in some way threatens subjects' freedoms to be objective, and this threat should arouse more reactance when the freedom is important than when it is not.

The question of interest for the present discussion is how this reactance would be expressed. The first opportunity that subjects had to express reactance was on the first-impression ratings, which followed soon after the experimenter had explained the study to the confederate. It would have been possible for those subjects for whom reactance arousal was high to restore freedom by rating the confederate relatively unfavorably. Restricting the use of this mode of freedom restoration, however, were subjects' desires to be objective and accurate in their ratings—and this desire should have been greatest in the same condition (high importance of freedom) where reactance aroused by the favor was greatest. Apparently, in the present experiment, the desire for accuracy was greater than the need to restore freedom immediately. Experimental conditions had little effect on the first-impression ratings that were obtained (see, however, discussion later in this chapter of a study by Worchel, Andreoli, & Archer, 1976).

After the first-impression ratings were completed, subjects were confronted with an unexpected opportunity to help the confederate. This opportunity would seem especially appropriate for freedom restoration. Subjects could decide whether or not to reciprocate the favor they had received, and this decision could be made without any restrictions imposed by experimental instructions to be objective and accurate. Not surprisingly, then, rather dramatic effects of reactance arousal were obtained on this measure. When subjects had not received a favor from the confederate, 53% of them helped him. When subjects had received the favor, but the importance of their freedom to be objective was low, 93% helped. For subjects whose importance of freedom to be objective was high, however, receiving a favor resulted in only 13% of them helping the confederate.

These data are not cited in order to argue that sequence of mode of presentation of freedom restoration is unimportant. No doubt, there will be times when that sequence is quite important. The Brehm and Cole study does indicate, though, that any mode of freedom restoration may be more or less desirable, and that if an initially presented mode is undesirable, it can be passed over.

The complexity of the determinants of direct restorative attempts— and the number of restrictive factors that can inhibit direct restoration—does not mean that empirical documentation of direct restorative action is missing. In fact, there are many such findings. For example, boomerang attitude change has been obtained in the theoretically expected conditions by a number of investigators (e.g., Albert & Dabbs, 1970; Brehm & Mann, 1975; Bushcamp, 1976; Feldman-Summers, 1977; Heller, Pallak & Picek, 1973; Pallak & Heller, 1971; Sensenig & Brehm, 1968). Moreover, such diverse behaviors as decrements in gripping a dynamometer (Aletky & Carlin, 1975), increment in extremity of self-presentation (Brehm & Bryant, 1976), toy preference (Brehm & Weinraub, 1977), refusals to answer questions (Liberman & Wicklund, reported in Wicklund, 1974) decreased choice of sunglasses (Wicklund, Slattum, & Solomon, 1970), and differential movie preference (Worchel, 1972) have occurred as direct attempts to restore a threatened freedom. (These studies are described in more detail in other sections of this book). In general, then, the empirical evidence for direct restoration as a function of reactance arousal is substantial and compelling.

Although the motivational state of reactance is directed toward action that will restore freedom, freedom can be restored without any action on the part of the individual. For example, an external agent can act on behalf of the person whose freedom has been threatened so as to directly restore the threatened freedom. The first of two experiments reported by Worchel and Brehm (1971) demonstrated this type of direct restoration of freedom by another person. Each subject believed himself to be in a three-person group and was told that the group was to decide which of two case studies (A or B) to work on. Unknown to the subject, the other two members were experimental confederates. When, prior to any group discussion of the two cases, one of the confederates demanded that the group work on a particular case, subjects indicated a desire to work on the opposite case, demonstrating the expected reactance effect. However, when the first confederate's demand was followed by the second confederate's protesting that he had not yet made up his mind about which case was better, thus restoring the group's (and subject's) freedom to choose, subjects indicated a preference for the demanded alternative. Thus, when the subject's freedom was restored by the second confederate, no evidence of reactance was found in the subject's preference.

A series of experiments by Schwarz (1980) also examined the conditions under which direct restoration of freedom by another individual reduces reactance. Following suggestions by Frey, Kumpf, Ochsmann, Röst-Schaude, and Sauer (1976) and Grabitz-Gniech and Grabitz (1973), Schwarz hypothesized that for a restoration of freedom to reduce reactance, it must be perceived as under the control of (potentially caused by) the person experiencing the reactance. It is not necessary that the person have caused the restoration, only that the restoration lead the person to believe that he or she *could* have restored the freedom.

To test this hypothesis, Schwarz led subjects to believe that they were participating in consumer research about new popular music groups, and that for participation, each would be able to choose one of the four phonograph albums that were being evaluated in the study. Subjects were run one or two at a time, along with a confederate who played the role of a subject. At the beginning of the experimental session, the experimenter explained that his normal experimental room was being used for another study and that they would therefore have to work in a different room. The subjects were given initial information about the four albums and, on that basis, were asked to rate them on attractiveness. The experimenter then "discovered" that the boxes containing two of the four records had been left in the original experimental room, where they were now locked up, and would be unavailable as choices. Subjects were informed which two records were unavailable. This procedure, then, constituted the elimination of freedom. Subjects were then given some additional, promotional-type information about the four albums and asked to rate the albums again.

The design involved four different conditions. One was an elimination of freedom without restoration, described above. A second involved no elimination of freedom (all records were available for choice). The third and fourth conditions implemented a restoration of freedom after freedom was eliminated. The third condition restored freedom without giving subjects the impression that they had control. This was done by having the experimenter receive a telephone call from the other investigator, saying that the experimenter should come and get the two boxes of records left in the original research room. The fourth condition restored freedom in a way designed to give subjects the impression that they themselves could have done it. When the experimenter announced that two records would not be available because they were locked in the other experimental room, the confederate asked if something could not be done about it. The experimenter then ostensibly called a janitor to have him unlock the room. This procedure had been found in a pilot project to give subjects the impression that they themselves could have restored the freedom.

Increased attraction of the eliminated records, compared to change in attraction of the noneliminated records, was used as an index of reactance. Comparisons of the different conditions indicated that the elimination aroused reactance, that restoration of freedom reduced reactance, and that reactance was reduced by the same amount whether or not subjects had the impression that they could have restored the freedom. This latter finding suggests that a feeling of personal control over restoration is not necessary to reduce reactance; what is necessary is simply that the freedom be restored.

Unlike earlier research, the restoration of freedom in the above experiment reduced the reactance effect but did not eliminate it. In order to examine why the reactance effect was not eliminated, Schwarz carried out two further studies, only the second of which need be reported here. Schwarz hypothesized two possible reasons for the partial reduction of reactance effects. First, unlike earlier research, the restoration of freedom was delayed a few minutes after the elimination of freedom, and consequently, the measurement of the reactance effect was also delayed relative to the no elimination and no restoration conditions; thus, the time of measurement could account for the partial restoration effect. Second, cognitive processes may follow the arousal of reactance such that what the individual first remembers are the positive characteristics of the eliminated alternatives and the negative characteristics of the noneliminated alternatives. Thus, even if reactance were totally reduced by the restoration of freedom, there might be residual cognitive change that would enhance the relative attractiveness of the alternatives that had been temporarily eliminated.

To test these hypotheses, Schwarz used a procedure similar to that of the experiment described earlier. Five conditions were created: (a) No elimination of freedom; (b) elimination and immediate restoration of freedom; (c) elimination and delayed restoration of freedom; (d) elimination of freedom and immediate dependent measure; and (e) elimination of freedom and delayed dependent measure. The latter two condtions, without restoration of freedom, allow one to see if there is some decrement in reactance effects over time (4 min after elimination). The condition of elimination and delayed restoration of freedom allows one to see if there is a replication of the partial reduction of reactance effects. The reactance effects in question, of course, are the relative increases in attractiveness of the eliminated alternatives as compared to changes in the attractiveness of the noneliminated alternatives.

In order to examine cognitive processes associated with reactance arousal and restoration of freedom, subjects were asked to list attributes that first came to mind about the four different music groups, and then to indicate whether each attribute was positive or negative. Schwarz constructed an index for each type of alternative (eliminated or not) that consisted of the number of positive attributes listed before any negative attribute was mentioned, relative to the total number of attributes listed. In other words, this index indicates the propensity of subjects to think first of positive attributes, and allows one to see if reactance produces greater accessibility of positive attributes for those alternatives that are eliminated.

The results on the ratings of the alternatives indicated that (a) immediate restoration of freedom completely eliminated the reactance effect; (b) delayed restoration of freedom partially reduced the reactance effect; and (c) delay of measurement in nonrestoration conditions had no effect on the magnitude of the reactance effect. Thus, delay of restoration does indeed only partially reduce reactance effects, and this partial reduction cannot be accounted for by the amount of time that passes between the elimination of freedom and the measurement of the effect. This pattern of results is consistent with the idea that some sort of cognitive processing, due to reactance, tends to produce persistence in the evaluational changes of the alternatives. However, all that Schwarz found on the recall of attributes measure was that in the two no-restoration conditions combined compared to the no elimination *and* delayed restoration conditions, there was significantly less first recall of positive attributes for the *noneliminated* alternatives. This pattern of attribute recall clearly does not explain why delay of restoration only partially reduces the reactance effect on attractiveness of the eliminated alternatives. What Schwarz had anticipated, and what would have provided an explanation of the partial reduction of reactance effects, was increased first recall of positive attributes of the *eliminated* alternatives in the delayed restoration condition compared to other conditions. Such differential recall of positive attributes could presumably account for why the eliminated alternatives remain relatively attractive even after freedom is restored. Schwarz concluded, and we agree, that there was thus no evidence to support the notion of a cognitively produced persistence effect, even though there were some cognitive effects apparently due to reactance. The significance of such cognitive effects in reactance processes is not clear and can be determined only by further analysis and research.

In sum, the following conclusions may be drawn from Schwarz' research. For restoration of freedom to reduce reactance, it is not necessary that the individual believe he or she had control over the restoration. However, delayed restoration only partially reduces reactance effects, and in the present research, there was no evidence that the persistence of reactance effects after delayed restoration was due to biased cognitive processing of information about eliminated and non-eliminated alternatives. Why delayed restoration of freedom produces only a partial reduction in reactance effects thus remains a mystery.

Indirect Restoration: Restoration by Implication

Just as reactance can be aroused by implication, so can it be reduced. In the Andreoli, Worchel, and Folger (1974) study described in Chapter 4, both the threat and the restoration were by implication. Subjects who overheard the threat to another person *and* restoration of this other person's freedom did not differ in their ratings of the advocated topic of discussion from subjects who had not heard any threat.

Other examples of freedom restoration by implication are provided in studies by Worchel and Brehm (1971) and McGillis and Brehm (1975). In the second of two studies reported by Worchel and Brehm, each subject anticipated making an individual choice between two human relations cases that they would try to solve. Subjects participated in three-person groups, with the other two supposed subjects actually being experimental confederates. Prior to rating the two case studies, subjects either heard no comments from the confederates (no threat condition), heard one say, "Well, I think it's obvious that we'll work on task A/B" (threat condition), or heard the threat followed by a statement from the other confederate, "Wait just a minute. I really haven't made up my mind about the two tasks yet" (restoration of freedom condition). These procedures created a direct threat to the subject's freedom (the first confederate's "we" presumably referring to all three people present) and an indirect restoration of freedom (the second confederate never specifically mentioning the subject and there being no group decision involved.

Since only subjects in the threat condition should be in a continuing state of reactance arousal, opposition to the first confederate's influence attempt was expected to be greatest in that condition. The data strongly supported this prediction. Subjects in the no threat condition showed no strong preference for one case over another. In the threat condition, 83% of the subjects preferred the case *not* advocated by the first confederate, while in the restoration condition, 83% of the subjects preferred the case advocated by the confederate. This latter result provides good evidence of the creation by strong influence attempts of motives both to comply and to resist. Once the person's freedom was restored and the motive to resist influence reduced, the still existing motive to comply had a powerful effect on behavior.

The effects of restoration by implication were also explored in a field study by McGillis and Brehm (1975). Using the Regan and Brehm (1972) supermarket study paradigm, McGillis and Brehm provided customers with the amount of money necessary to buy the brand of bread being promoted. Along with the money, customers were given high threat instructions ("you will buy *only* . . .") or low threat ("please try . . ."). For some customers, freedom to purchase the bread of their choice was restored in the following manner. A middle-aged, casually dressed woman would approach the bread stall as a customer did, and then in front of the customer, she would say, "I don't feel that I have to buy this (brand name being promoted) bread." She then selected a specific alternative kind of bread.

The findings from this study were quite similar to those obtained by Regan and Brehm. All shoppers exposed to the promotional campaign bought more of the designated item than shoppers not so exposed. For female shoppers only, however, the low threat promotion produced more purchases of the target item than did the high threat one.

The restoration manipulation greatly increased the level of purchases of the designated brand. Although less than 1% of the shoppers in the baseline conditions purchased this item and (overall) 16% of the shoppers in the threat conditions purchased it, 74% of the shoppers in the restoration condition bought this item. Moreover, restoration effects were obtained for both sexes, suggesting the possibility that the threat conditions had aroused reactance in male shoppers as well as females. The very few subjects in the restoration condition relative to threat conditions (35 versus almost 500 in *each* of the other two) and the possibility that the restoration statement by the supposed other shopper could have itself produced reactance caution against over-interpretation of these data. However, the dramatic increase in compliance obtained through the use of freedom restoration by implication in this applied study is perfectly consistent with similar effects obtained by Worchel and Brehm in their laboratory research.

Although there are other viable ways to restore freedom indirectly (e.g., by manifesting reactance on a freedom-relevant behavior other than the one directly threatened), restoration by virtue of other people's behavior has received by far the most attention. This attention may stem from the possible ramifications of this idea. For example, Mugny (1978) suggests that the confederate who restored his own freedom in the Worchel and Brehm study and, thus, reduced subjects' reactance can be viewed as analogous to those few members of a powerless group who are allowed to succeed by those who actually control the society. Restoration of freedom by implication of another person's acts could then serve the purpose of disguising the power of some people over others. Through the use of such "fronts," powerful people could reduce the opposition to their power from less advantaged individuals. After all, Archie Bunker (of TV's "All in the Family") was against "excessive" taxation of the rich because he did not want anyone to take away his freedom to become a millionaire--and he could point to some examples of people "no better" than he who did become millionaires as proof that this freedom did exist.

Another possible ramification of freedom restoration by implication from another's behavior is that individuals who are motivationally aroused but feel unable to restore freedom directly might seek out others who do act in a freedom-restoring way. This seeking out could presumably occur in both reality and fantasy. Since restoring freedom may often involve going against the dictates of society, a motive for vicarious freedom restoration might be a factor in the continual fascination that outlaws and desperados have for so many law-abiding citizens.

Subjective Responses

Attractiveness of the Threatened or Eliminated Outcome

Regardless of the behavioral consequences that result from reactance arousal, the arousal of psychological reactance always should be accompanied by a host of subjective reactions. The most obvious subjective reaction involves the individual's evaluation of the threatened outcome. Desire for this outcome should increase, and its attractiveness should be enhanced. This proposition has received strong support in a variety of studies. For example, when a communication is censored (see Chapter 6 for a more detailed discussion), desire to hear that communication increases. Reactance arousal has been found to enhance the attractiveness of items as diverse as records (Brehm, Stires, Sensenig, & Shaban, 1966), toys (Brehm, in press; Hammock & Brehm, 1966), cookies (Worchel, Lee, & Adewole, 1975), Argentinian desserts (Brehm & Rozen, 1971), and members of the opposite sex (Pennebaker, Dyer, Caulkins, Litowitz, Ackreman, Anderson, & McGraw, 1979; Wicklund & Ogden, cited in Wicklund, 1974).

It should be noted that this increased attractiveness is not always absolute, that is, relative to no change at all. Various factors such as regression to the mean and the use of items relatively low in attractiveness to avoid frustration (see discussion below) act to make it difficult to obtain absolute increases in attractiveness. However, relative to the appropriate comparison group (such as one in which subjects do not have the freedom of choosing the item, or one in which the freedom exists but is not threatened or eliminated) in which reactance is not aroused, reactance arousal has been shown to produce a clear and consistently documented increment in *relative* attractiveness.

As noted above, many reactance experiments take the precaution of guarding against the alternative explanation of frustration. An example of how this is done is provided in a study by Hammock and Brehm (1966) that has recently been replicated by Brehm (in press). In this experimental paradigm, children were led to expect to either choose or be assigned one gift item from a set of two taken out of a larger array. The items that were chosen for the set were those that were initially ranked third and fourth in subjects' rankings of the entire array. In the first study of two reported by Hammock and Brehm, as well as in Brehm's recent replication, all subjects were given their third-ranked alternative, and none of the subjects was allowed to choose. This procedure guards against frustration in two ways. The items used to create the set did not include the subject's favorites (i.e., those ranked first or second). Moreover, within the set of two, the most preferred (the third-ranked) was given to the child and the least preferred (the fourth-ranked) was not given.

Reactance theory would predict that, relative to children who never expected to have a choice, subjects who did expect to choose but who were not allowed to do so should increase their preference for the eliminated object (fourth-ranked) and decrease their preference for the

TABLE 5.1
Mean Ranking Changes

	No choice condition		Choice condition	
	Eliminated, ranked fourth	Gift, ranked third	Eliminated, ranked fourth	Gift ranked third
Hammock & Brehm, 1966[a]	− .43	.00	.23	− 1.23
Brehm, in press[b]				
Males	− .97	− .66	− .08	− 1.50
Females	.13	− .97	− .82	− 1.00

[a] From Hammock, T. & Brehm, J. W. The attractiveness of choice alternatives when freedom to choose is eliminated by a social agent. *Journal of Personality*, 1966, *34*, 546–554, Table 1, p. 550. Copyright 1966 by the Duke University Press.

[b] From Brehm, S. S. Psychological reactance and the attractiveness of unobtainable objects: Sex differences in children's responses to an elimination of freedom. *Sex Roles*, in press. Copyright pending by Plenum Publishing Corp.

obtained object (third-ranked). Both studies (see Table 5.1) confirmed this prediction (in Brehm's study, only for male children), but neither study found any indication of absolute, significantly different from-zero, increase in attractiveness of the eliminated object.

This methodology, then, makes a trade. Frustration is convincingly ruled out, since highly desired objects are not eliminated. Supporting this contention, when Brehm (in press) gave subjects a chance to choose a gift for themselves from among the entire array, all the children chose either their first- or second-ranked alternative. The price for this theoretical clarity, however, is that reactance effects may be less than dramatic (see Chapter 11 for more details of these studies).

Hostility

Another type of subjective reaction brought about by reactance arousal is hostility toward the agent who has threatened the behavioral freedom. This kind of hostility must be distinguished from the hostility that will accompany aggressive instrumental action aimed at restoring freedom. For example, if someone threatens the freedom to have a specific choice alternative by taking it away, a person can act aggressively and grab it back, and probably feel pretty hostile while doing so. On the other hand, what if in the same situation, the person cannot act aggressively to restore freedom? Will the individual still feel hostility even though no instrumental aggressive act is possible? And, will this hostility be expressed in behaviors that in no way will serve to restore freedom?

These questions were addressed in a study by Worchel (1974). Male subjects were told by the experimenter to expect one of the following three events: that they would have a choice among three items, that they would receive the most attractive of the three items, or that they would be assigned one of the three items. All subjects were then assigned one of the items by an "experimental assistant"; subjects received either their first, second or third most attractive alternative. At this point, subjects were given an unexpected opportunity to display hostility toward the assistant. They were asked to evaluate whether or not the assistant should be hired on a more permanent basis to assist with the experimenter's research.

Results from this study (displayed in Table 5.2) strongly supported the hypothesis that reactance arousal could be accompanied by noninstrumental hostility and, furthermore, suggested the major importance of threat to freedom in inducing hostility. Subjects who expected to be assigned an item showed no differences in hostility as a function of item received. Thus, simple frustration (being deprived of one's most attractive alternative) did not increase hostility relative to that experienced by individuals who were deprived of less attractive items. Subjects who expected to receive their most attractive alternative showed an increase in hostility only when they received the least attractive alternative. Frustrated expectations, therefore, do appear to increase hostility, but only when there is a considerable disconfirmation of the expectancy. For subjects who expected to be able to choose, hostility increased as the attractiveness of the alternative they received decreased. Furthermore, choice condition subjects displayed signifi-

TABLE 5.2
Mean Hostility Scores[a]

	Attractiveness of alternative received		
Expected method of item assignment	Most attractive	Second most attractive	Least attractive
Expect choice	13.57[b]	17.07	22.21
Expect most attractive	10.50	10.00	14.36
Expect assignment	11.40	9.50	10.50

[a] From Worchel, 1971. Reprinted by permission.

[b] Ratings made on the question, "Everything considered, do you think this person would make a good experimenter and should be considered for the job of research assistant?" 1 = very definitely yes; 31 = very definitely no.

cantly more hostility than expectancy condition subjects for all choice alternatives. Reactance arousal was the single most powerful determinant of hostility in Worchel's study.

Having stated this, we should note that reactance arousal will not necessarily be accompanied by feelings of hostility. The exact characteristics of the threat to freedom will have a strong impact on whether or not hostility toward the agent is felt. There may typically be a feeling of disturbance, or discomfort, when reactance is aroused, but whether these feelings will include hostility to the agent will depend on such factors as the perceived legitimacy of the threat, the freedom the agent had about making the threat, the intent of the agent, etc.

Self-Direction

One further subjective response to reactance arousal should be mentioned. In the original presentation of the theory, it was noted that, "While there is no assumption that a person will necessarily be aware of reactance, it should be true that when he is, he will feel an increased amount of self-direction in regard to his own behavior [Brehm, 1966, p. 9]."

This proposal might seem at first glance to be paradoxical. After all, a person experiencing reactance has just had a freedom threatened or eliminated. He or she is in danger of (at least momentarily) or already has lost control over an important behavioral outcome. How could such a person feel more self-direction? Actually, there is no paradox. There is a great deal of difference between self-direction and control. The point being made here is that, as with any motivational state, when reactance is aroused, the organism is propelled toward a goal. Motivational arousal has the virtue of ordering our priorities. It suddenly becomes clear what we want. Whether we will get it is another issue altogether.

Denial of Threat

As Worchel and Andreoli (1976) point out, the individual who has had reactance aroused may frequently find himself or herself in a disturbing and uncomfortable position. If, on the one hand, he or she attempts to restore the threatened freedom directly, this may well involve antisocial or counternormative actions. If, on the other hand, the person complies with the freedom-threatening directive, he or she has relinquished an important freedom. Given such a dilemma, it would be expected that in some situations, the best response to reactance arousal would be to try to make the threat go away by denying that it ever occurred.

Direct denial of reality, however, may be somewhat difficult. How can we pretend that certain words were not spoken or certain actions were not taken? The work by Worchel and his associates suggests more subtle, and probably more likely, ways in which a person can effectively deny the threat without having to grossly distort reality.

Two studies by Worchel and his colleagues (Worchel & Andreoli, 1974; Worchel, Andreoli, & Archer, 1976) addressed this issue through their examination of attributional processes. In the Worchel and Andreoli study, female subjects either anticipated interacting with a supposed other subject in an upcoming experimental task, or did not expect to interact. This task was described (out of the hearing of the other supposed subject) as either competitive or cooperative. When the other subject, actually a confederate, arrived, she acted in either a friendly or hostile manner toward the subject. Then, either subjects were told that a supposed personality test had predicted the confederate's behavior or nothing was said about what might have caused the confederate's behavior. The major dependent measure consisted of subjects' responses to a questionnaire asking them to attribute the confederate's behavior to either dispositional or situational causes.

Worchel and Andreoli predicted that reactance arousal should be greatest in those conditions in which the anticipated interaction conflicted with the confederate's behavior. Subjects anticipating a cooperative interaction should value their freedom to act cooperatively with the confederate, and this freedom would be threatened by the confederate's hostile behavior. Conversely, subjects anticipating a competitive interaction should value their freedom to behave competitively, and this freedom would be threatened by the confederate's friendly behavior. The subject is thereby caught in the dilemma of either giving up an important freedom or not reciprocating the confederate's behavior. However, this dilemma is present only if the confederate's behavior is perceived as meaningful for the anticipated interpersonal interaction. If the behavior can be viewed as having been caused by the situation and, therefore, as not reflecting anything specific about the confederate, then implications for the upcoming interaction will be reduced and the subject can simply act as she wishes in this interaction without basing her action on reactance or compliance. Worchel and Andreoli, therefore, predicted that subjects who were not told anything by the experimenter about what might have caused the confederate's behavior would be most likely to make situational causal attributions for this behavior when they were in the cooperative–hostile and competitive–friendly conditions. This prediction was confirmed as shown in the data displayed in Table 5.3.

Subjects who had been told that the confederate's behavior reflected her personality were unable to use this method of denying the threat, and there were no between condition differences in their attributions. For these subjects, reactance arousal presumably was still present. Worchel and Andreoli measured the subjective effects of this arousal by having subjects evaluate the confederate on a number of questions. As expected, the most derogation was obtained for the friendly confederate when subjects anticipated a competitive interaction and for the hostile confederate when subjects anticipated a cooperative interaction. However, this pattern of results was obtained only for subjects who had been forced to make a dispositional attribution. For those subjects who had been allowed to make situational attributions, derogation was considerably lower in these conditions since the threat had been effectively denied. (See Table 5.4)

A second study by these investigators (Worchel, Andreoli, & Archer, 1976) further elaborated the use of attributional processes to deny a threat to freedom. Using a modification of the Brehm and Cole (1966) experimental paradigm (described earlier in this chapter), Worchel et al. varied importance of freedom by telling subjects in the high importance condition that their ratings of another person on a supposed "Whitman Scale" predicted their "social sensitivity and intelligence," and that accurate ratings could result in a $10 prize. For low importance subjects, the ratings were described as a pretest. This manipulation of the importance of the freedom to be accurate and objective on

TABLE 5.3
Means of Attribution Questions[a]

Locus of causality	Confederate's behavior	Type of future interaction anticipated		
		Cooperative	None	Competitive
Free attribution	Friendly	11.75[b]	16.42	6.58
	Hostile	7.17	18.25	14.08
Forced attribution	Friendly	25.25	25.42	25.75
	Hostile	25.25	23.25	24.42

[a] From Worchel, S. & Andreoli, V. A. Attribution of causality as a means of restoring freedom. *Journal of Personality and Social Psychology*, 1974, 29, 237–245, Table 1, p. 240. Copyright 1974 by the American Psychological Association. Reprinted by permission.

[b] 1 = situational; 31 = dispositional.

TABLE 5.4
Means of Derogation of the Confederate[a]

Locus of causality	Confederate's behavior	Type of future interaction anticipated		
		Cooperative	None	Competitive
Free attribution	Friendly	43.00[b]	41.33	50.92
	Hostile	84.42	109.33	97.75
Forced attribution	Friendly	63.17	37.67	76.00
	Hostile	124.25	102.33	108.67

[a] See Table 5.3, Footnote a, Table 3, p. 242.

[b] The lower the number, the more positive the evaluation.

their ratings was conveyed to subjects prior to the time when the experimental confederate (presented as another subject) entered the room, and the experimental procedures were designed to give the clear impression that the confederate did not know the purpose of the ratings.

All subjects then received a favor from the confederate, who won some money on an experimental task and spontaneously split it with the subject. After this, the experimenter explained that the sharing behavior of the confederate was related to the Whitman Scale. It was stated that the first part of the scale (self-ratings that had been completed by the subject and the confederate) could sometimes predict an individual's sharing behavior. The experimenter presented one of the following causal explanations for the confederate's behavior: The situation was responsible (all subjects in this situation shared, regardless of their scores on the scale); the recipient was responsible ("she was the type of person that most people would want to share with in any situation"); the favor-doer was responsible ("she was the type of person that would be motivated to share with anyone in any situation"); or the unique interaction between the two was responsible ("there must be something special about the relationship between the two subjects that caused the sharing"). A control condition was also run in which no mention was made of personality test predictions of sharing. After rating each other on the second part of the scale, subjects were given a sorting task. The confederate was given more sheets of paper to sort and sorted so that all subjects had an opportunity to help.

Contrary to the Brehm and Cole study where little difference between experimental conditions was produced on the ratings of the confederate, the rating scale data and the help-offered data were quite similar in the Worchel et al. study[1]. Subjects for whom the freedom to be objective (and thus not obligated to the other subject) was important and for whom the attribution of favor-doing was to the unique interaction between themselves and the other subject rated the confederate as least attractive and were least likely to help (see Table 5.5 for helping data.)[2] For our purposes, the most important aspect of these results is the way in which the other types of attributions were able to reduce the amount of reactance aroused. Again, through attributional sleight of hand (though this time by the experimenter rather than by the subjects themselves), what would have been a threat to freedom was defined away (see Chapter 7 for further discussion of the Worchel et al., 1976, study).

Preservation of Other Freedoms

There will be occasions, however, when none of the remedies for reactance arousal will work. Neither direct restoration nor indirect restoration will be available, and it will not be possible to deny the threat. What then happens to this arousal? One effect that could occur is that the person could become motivated to preserve future freedoms. This motivation could then act to produce enhanced reactance arousal

---

[1] Although the Worchel et al. study had many elements in common with the Brehm and Cole experiment, there were significant procedural differences, and female subjects rather than males participated. It is not clear what differences between the two studies might have determined the presence versus absence of reactance effects on the first-impression ratings.

[2] This finding appears to contradict that obtained by Worchel and Andreoli (1974). In that study, attribution to the unique character of the confederate (i.e., her personality) created reactance, whereas in the present study reactance arousal was greatest when the causal attribution was to the unique interaction. Worchel et al. (1976) note this apparent discrepancy and point out that while the unique interaction created the most reactance when the freedom was important, attributions to the favor-doer appeared to create the next highest level. Presumably, then, attributions to either the favor-doer or the unique interaction create more of a possibility that future threats will occur and, thus, a greater number of freedoms is threatened by implication.

Another apparent contradiction with previous work is Worchel et al.'s (1976) failure to obtain a difference between importance conditions when no attribution was made for the subjects. Since Brehm and Cole (1966) did not give their subjects attributions, these two conditions would appear to be the most direct replication of the earlier research. Worchel et al. discuss this apparent discrepancy and argue that the very unexpected nature of the favor in the Brehm and Cole study may have led subjects to make an attribution either to the unique character of the actor or to the unique interaction. Moreover, they suggest that the more unexpected nature of the favor in the Brehm and Cole study than of the one they used may have created greater overall levels of reactance arousal.

TABLE 5.5
Percentage of Subjects Helping the Confederate[a]

		Attribution			
	Situation (%)	Unique recipient (%)	Unique favor-doer (%)	Unique interaction (%)	No attribution (%)
High importance of freedom	50	50	42	17	58
Low importance of freedom	58	58	67	75	58

[a] From Worchel, S., Andreoli, V., & Archer, R. When is a favor a threat to freedom: The effects of attribution and importance of freedom on reciprocity. *Journal of Personality*, 1976, 44, 294–310, Table 2, p. 306. Copyright 1976 by Duke University Press. Reprinted by permission.

if another freedom were threatened. Such a motive and subsequent increases in reactance could be involved in the possible hydraulic reactance effects discussed previously in Chapter 4. A motive to preserve freedom might also lead the person to avoid potential threats to freedom. Some suggestion of such avoidance has been found in the research on commitment that will be discussed in Chapter 6.

SUMMARY

Reactance, as a motivational state, has two direct effects: It impels attempts to regain lost or threatened freedoms, and it magnifies motivation toward the threatened or lost behaviors and/or their intended outcomes, making them subjectively more attractive. A considerable body of experimental evidence illustrating both effects was reviewed. It has also been demonstrated that an external agent (e.g., another person) can restore freedom by acting *directly* on behalf of the person whose freedom has been threatened.

Just as reactance can be aroused by implication, so it can be reduced. Theoretically, there are two ways in which freedom can be restored by implication. First, people whose freedom has been threatened can attempt to restore their freedom, not by directly exercising the threatened freedom, but by exercising another freedom that would imply that they continue to have the one that was threatened. This proposition has not, however, received empirical examination. Second, an individual whose freedom has been threatened can have it restored by an external agent who, by restoring his or her own freedom, restores the person's freedom *by implication*. Experimental tests were described supporting this kind of implied restoration of freedom.

Because the direct exercise of a threatened freedom would frequently be antisocial or antinormative in nature, an individual might seek to avoid direct restoration. Although indirect restoration of freedom, as noted above, would be one possible way of avoiding antisocial behavior, it is also possible that a person would simply seek to deny that any threat to his or her freedom had occurred. Theoretically, such denial would be most likely to occur where there was some ambiguity about the threat. Studies that were designed to test this line of reasoning have found supportive evidence.

PART II

Selected Topics

CHAPTER 6

Persuasion and Attitude Change

Social psychological theories have traditionally concerned themselves, at least in part, with the process of persuasion and attitude change. Reactance theory is no exception to this tradition. Somewhat unexpectedly, however, the topic of attitude change has been a rather difficult one for the theory. What seemed a simple extension of theoretical principles has turned into an increasingly complex theoretical problem that has not yet been adequately resolved. In this chapter, we shall discuss the theoretical and empirical history of this issue and offer an alternative theoretical perspective. We shall also discuss a number of more specific topics related to reactance and attitude change: commitment, "sleeper" effects, and censorship.

Before examining the theoretical issues involved in applying reactance theory to attitude change processes, we need to have a working definition of attitudes. For the purpose of the present discussion, we adopt a definition similar to those proposed by Rosenberg (1960) and Jones and Gerard (1967). This definition holds that attitudes are evaluative beliefs that serve to promote an underlying set of values. On a more operational level, attitudes are beliefs that subjects typically possess prior to participating in an experiment, and the objects of these beliefs are typically not present in the laboratory. It is possible, however, to make an object present in the laboratory relevant to the subject's attitudes by presenting the subject with attitudinally relevant objects (e.g. descriptions of supposed but actually ficticious political candidates who advocate specified political values and goals). In such instances, preferences for the laboratory stimuli can serve as a measure of subjects' attitudes.

One of the distinctive characteristics of attitudes is that, for so much of the time at least, they are all "in the head." At some point, we may find ourselves in situations where we need to act on what we believe, but there are many occasions in daily life where our more important attitudes (e.g., political, religious, racial, sexual) are not directly expressed in our overt behavior. Moreover, there are many potential attitude issues on which one may not have any position at all. Every opinion poll contains a "don't know" or "haven't decided" option, and, for many issues, the number of people endorsing this option is sizeable.

Attitudinal Freedoms

In reactance theory terms, the first two freedoms that can be distinguished for any attitude issue is the freedom to take a position (*any* position) versus the freedom not to take one. If a person feels unable to discriminate among different positions *and* if he or she believes that the psychological implications of taking any position would be significant, then the most important freedom for this person would be the freedom not to take a position. Urging any position on this person could threaten this freedom, and the person would try to reestablish freedom by clinging to the least committed stance available. Thus, while urging a "pro" position on the person would create reactance, there is no reason to expect boomerang attitude change (i.e., the person's changing his or her position toward "con") since adopting the "con" position is just as much a threat to the freedom not to take any position as is adopting the "pro" position.

The above discussion addresses that instance where the person anticipates possibly significant psychological consequences from adopting any position. It would be possible, of course, for a person to be unable to distinguish among positions and not anticipate possibly significant psychological consequences from adopting one. In this case, the freedom not to take a position is unimportant. For this person, there will be little or no reactance aroused by a persuasive communication advocating a given position. Instead, the person should be easily swayed.

Both types of individuals described above are characterized by initially neutral opinions, and we would not expect either type to react to a persuasive communication by moving in the direction opposite to that advocated. Both types of individuals, therefore, would be inappropriate subjects for reactance studies in which attitude change away from the communicator's position is the predicted effect. This reasoning, first mentioned in Brehm (1966), has led most subsequent attitudinal research on reactance processes to delete subjects who have initially neutral attitudes, to preselect only subjects who have a position on the issue at hand, or to use opinion issues on which virtually everyone has a position. From a methodological standpoint, some kind of information concerning initial attitudes prior to the experimental procedures is vital if we are to be certain that the appropriate psychological conditions for reactance effects have been created.

Restricting our attention to those people who have taken a position on the issue is an important initial step, but this restriction by no means eliminates all the complexities involved. Next, we must consider what exact position has been taken. For example, has the person taken the position reflected in the second statement of a 7-point scale, or is the person's position better described by a latitude of acceptance including the first, second, and third statements on the scale? Since the freedoms involved are defined by the person's position, any ambiguity about the position taken will interfere with our ability to predict his or her behavior.

In terms of our example, if the person's position is described by only the second statement, then advocating that he or she adopt, for example, the third position on the scale threatens the freedom to *maintain* his or her initial position (as well as the freedom to reject the position being advocated). If, however, the person's position includes the third statement, then urging that statement on the person threatens the person's freedom to *reject* his or her initial position (as well as the freedom to adopt the other positions). Depending on the person's initial position, the same communication can threaten different freedoms, and the resultant motivation to restore freedom will necessarily be different.

Reactance theory research, unfortunately, has not paid much attention to the need for specifying the person's exact position. Typically, subjects are simply classified as pro or con on a given issue and then exposed to a communication that supports their side of the issue or advocates the other side. The assumption has been that it is the side that is psychologically important, not the exact position on that side. This assumption probably works reasonably well with counter-attitudinal communications. Regardless of exactly how an individual feels about Y, he or she is sure that Y is believed rather than not-Y. It is not clear, however, that this assumption works as well for attitude-consistent communications. It may be that in some cases what was designed to be an attitude-consistent communication was, in fact, perceived by some subjects to be discrepant with their initial attitudes.

Such perceptions, even if they occurred for only a few subjects, could be expected to introduce considerable noise in the system and make it more difficult to obtain the predicted reactance effects. Interestingly, however, this has not proved to be the case. Reactance effects have been repeatedly demonstrated to be more reliable for attitude-consistent communications than for counter-attitudinal ones. These findings suggest that although failing to determine more precisely the exact characteristics of the subject's initial attitude probably has increased error variance, this increased error has not been enough to obscure the predicted effects.

Another issue of theoretical concern is how firmly the person has adopted his or her position. Strength of belief will directly determine the importance and availability of attitudinal freedoms. To illustrate this point, let us consider a person who, on a single attitude dimension, believes X and rejects Y, and let us vary the strength of this person's belief in X. If the belief is of moderate strength, we have the following set of freedoms and their particular levels of importance.

Freedom to accept (maintain) X	Moderately important
Freedom to reject X	Slightly important
Freedom to accept Y	Slightly important
Freedom to reject Y	Moderately important

Threats to these freedoms should produce the following amounts of reactance arousal.

Counter-attitudinal threats: "Don't believe X"; "Believe Y"	
Threat to freedom to accept X	Moderate reactance
Threat to freedom to reject Y	Moderate reactance

Attitude-consistent threats: "Believe X"; "Don't believe Y"	
Threat to freedom to reject X	Slight reactance
Threat to freedom to accept Y	Slight reactance

What if, however, the person has a very strong belief in X? In this case, the importance of the freedoms and the level of reactance resulting from a threat to freedom should be as follows.

Freedom to accept (maintain) X	Very important
Freedom to reject X	Not important
Freedom to accept Y	Not important
Freedom to reject Y	Very important

Counter-attitudinal threats

Threat to freedom to accept X	Great reactance
Threat to freedom to reject Y	Great reactance

Attitude-consistent threats

Threat to freedom to reject X	No reactance
Threat to freedom to adopt Y	No reactance

It could be said of the person who has an extremely strong belief in favor of X that he or she no longer has the freedom to reject X nor the freedom to accept Y.

From these examples, two theoretical principles can be derived. First, the importance of freedom and, thus, the magnitude of reactance aroused by a threat to attitudinal freedom is a direct function of the intensity with which that attitudinal position is held. The more strongly a person holds an attitudinal position, the more reactance will be aroused by a threat to that position. Second, counter-attitudinal communications should create more reactance than attitude-consistent communications. Or, more generally, since discrepant communications with increasing discrepancy will become more and more counter-attitudinal, the greater the discrepancy between an initial attitude and the position being advocated, the greater the reactance aroused.

No research has been conducted on the first principle in which intensity is viewed as determining importance of freedom. This is consistent with the more general lack of interest shown by reactance researchers in the specific characteristics of people's attitudes. There has been, however, considerable research on the discrepancy hypothesis and, as one would say in beginning a good story, this is where all the trouble started.

Effects of Discrepancy on Reactance

The first study to test the discrepancy hypothesis was conducted by Brehm and Krasin (reported in Brehm, 1966). Women students from a single college dormitory were contacted on two different days by the same experimenter. On the first day, subjects filled out a 12-item opinion questionnaire about their attitudes toward various topical issues. Prior to the second interaction, a questionnaire was prepared for each subject with a position marked for each of the items except the sixth and twelfth. Some marked positions agreed with the subject's; others differed by 1, 2, or 3 points, always in the direction of the opposite end of the 10-point scale. Discrepancy size was varied, so that the same item did not always have the same size discrepancy for all subjects.

On the second contact with the subject, the experimenter told her that the marked questionnaire was from another student in another university. All subjects were asked to predict the other student's responses on the two unmarked items and then to fill in their own opinions on the questionnaire. Subjects in the high threat to freedom condition were told, "We are sure you will be greatly influenced by the opinions stated, and that your answers this time will tend towards those of the student." Nothing was said in the low threat condition about subjects' opinions being influenced.

Brehm and Krasin predicted that for low threat subjects, greater discrepancy would lead to greater persuasion when subjects gave their own opinions on the questionnaire. In the high threat condition, however, where intent to influence was clearly stated, greater discrepancy should arouse greater reactance and lead to less persuasion. The data from this experiment were consistent with the prediction and with the general discrepancy hypothesis (see Table 6.1). The interaction between threat condition and discrepancy sizes 1 and 3 was significant. Going from discrepancies of 1 to 3 points, low threat subjects became more positive, whereas high threat subjects became more negative.

Unfortunately, there are a variety of methodological problems with this study. First, all discrepancies were based on initial position and were toward the opposite end of the scale. Thus, in order to count as "reactance," a subject had to move toward (or become more extreme than) her own initial position. Moving in the direction of your own initial response is the type of reactance effect typically associated with counter-attitudinal communications.

In this study, however, both counter-attitudinal and attitude-consistent discrepancies were presented. In terms of sides of the issue, only subjects whose initial opinion on a given item tended toward the middle of the scale (points 4, 5, 6, and 7) were exposed to a position

TABLE 6.1
Mean Opinion Change as a Function of Threat and Discrepancy[a]

	Discrepancy size			
	0	1	2	3
Low threat	−.22[b]	.15	.50	.57
High threat	−.17	.07	.00	−.13

[a] From an experiment by Brehm & Krasin reported in Brehm, J. W. *A theory of psychological reactance*, New York: Academic Press, 1966, Table XIX, p. 108.

[b] A minus sign indicates movement away from the position of the other person. Only minus change is possible where the discrepancy size is zero.

that clearly took the other side. This procedure meant that some subjects were receiving attitude-consistent information for a given discrepancy size, whereas, with the same discrepancy size, others were receiving counter-attitudinal information.

Second, subjects with neutral opinions were not deleted. Thus, the only subjects getting counter-attitudinal information were also subjects who, as we have described earlier, are least appropriate for a test of the hypothesis. Additionally, high threat condition subjects may have perceived intent to persuade as varying with discrepancy size. Since intent to persuade was clearly stated, these subjects may have thought that the items with the large discrepancies were the ones on which there was most concern that the subject be influenced. If this occurred, the decreasing persuasion obtained for high threat condition subjects could have been a function, not of increasing discrepancy, but of increasing perceived magnitude of the intent to persuade.

These methodological difficulties make it difficult to assess the Brehm and Krasin experiment. The data were as predicted and therefore generate support for the discrepancy principle. However, the procedures used in the study create considerable interpretive ambiguity.

Prior Exercise of Freedom

As it turns out, the results of a subsequent and much better designed study by Worchel and Brehm (1970) suggest that the results of the Brehm and Krasin study may have been artifactual. In the experiment by Worchel and Brehm, only one attitude issue was used: whether or not the Communist party should be treated as an equal political party in the U.S. On an initial premeasure, the distribution of opinion was bimodal, and all subjects participating in the experiment had at least a moderately strong initial opinion. Some subjects read a speech advocating treating the Communist party like any other U. S. political party, while others read a speech favoring government regulation. For half the subjects, high threat to attitudinal freedom was created by sprinkling the speech they read with comments such as "you must believe" and "you have no choice but to believe this." For low threat condition subjects, these comments were not included. After reading the speech, subjects filled out a questionnaire that included an item on the relevant attitude issue.

Initial analyses of the data indicated that whether or not subjects initially favored treating the Communist party equally in the U.S. did not affect the results. Attitude change was then assessed in terms of threat condition and of whether subjects read a speech that agreed or disagreed with their initial attitude. The percentage of subjects who changed away from the communication's advocated position, changed toward this position, or did not change from their intitial attitude is displayed in Table 6.2.

Two significant effects are particularly important for the present discussion. First, among subjects who read a communication with which they initially agreed, high threat subjects showed less positive attitude change than low threat subjects. Further, high threat subjects in the agree condition showed less positive attitude change than high threat subjects in the disagree condition, who, indeed, evidenced very little negative attitude change. These results are obviously not consistent with a discrepancy hypothesis. The only evidence for attitude change away from the communicator's position was found for high threat subjects who received an attitude-*consistent* communication.

One possible methodological problem in regard to these results should be noted. Regression toward the mean works to promote negative attitude change among subjects who initially agree with the communication, but it works to promote positive change among subjects who initially disagree with the communication. That is, boomerang change away from the communicator is manifested by agree subjects' moving toward the opposite end of the scale, whereas disagree subjects have to become more extreme on a position on which they are already moderately extreme. Regression to the mean, however, cannot account for the significant low threat versus high threat difference found for agree subjects.

TABLE 6.2
Percentage of Subjects Moving Toward or Away from the Advocated Position[a]

	Toward (%)	No change (%)	Away (%)
Initial disagreement			
Low threat (15)[b]	80	13	7
High threat (20)	80	5	15
Initial agreement			
Low threat (18)	56	22	22
High threat (20)	20	15	65

[a] From Worchel, S. & Brehm, J. W. Effects of threats to attitudinal freedom as a function of agreement with the communicator. *Journal of Personality and Social Psychology*, 1970, 14, 18–22, Table 2, p. 20. Copyright 1970 by the American Psychological Association. Reprinted by permission.
[b] Condition Ns.

In discussing these results, Worchel and Brehm (1970) suggest that perhaps disagree subjects were not motivated to oppose counterattitudinal communications because, by already being in disagreement, they had already demonstrated their freedom. The investigators were uncertain, however, about whether such a prior exercise of attitudinal freedom would affect reactance arousal or reactance reduction.

The notion of prior demonstration of freedom has been discussed extensively by Wicklund (1974), and his proposals are two-fold. First, he hypothesizes that Worchel and Brehm's subjects may not have differed in reactance arousal as a function of initial agreement or disagreement. This hypothesis stems from Wicklund's view that the discrepancy principle is based on the information possessed by the person, and that "the further a person is from a communicator, the more 'contrary communication' information he might be presumed to have [p. 54]."

From Wicklund's perspective, it is how much information one has that is inconsistent with the communication that determines the importance of the freedom to reject the communication. Discrepancy of position advocated only acts as a carrier variable in that, for positions highly discrepant from one's own, one usually has a great deal of information inconsistent with that position. Information, however, may be forgotten: "Therefore, it would be possible that two people of widely divergent opinions actually possess no differential information about the issue, simply because they have forgotten it all [Wicklund, 1974, p. 54]." For Wicklund, if information is forgotten, discrepancy of position will have no effect on importance of freedom and, thus, no effect on reactance arousal.

The second part of Wicklund's proposal agrees with the idea put forth by Worchel and Brehm (1970) that subjects "initially in disagreement were already demonstrating their freedom to disagree, and because of this they had no motivation to demonstrate that they could be different from the communicator [p. 55]." Wicklund is somewhat unclear about the exact mechanisms underlying this prior demonstration effect, but a later paper by Snyder and Wicklund (1976) is more explicit. Snyder and Wicklund state that prior exercise of a freedom "operates to prevent the onset of reactance in the face of an actual threat [p. 128]." Their reasoning appears to be that having observed oneself exercise the freedom in the past, one is more secure about having the freedom. This security should reduce the perceived magnitude of threat and, thus, the magnitude of reactance arousal.

Wicklund's solution to the theoretical problem raised by Worchel and Brehm's results is both ingenious and complex. There are, however, some aspects of this solution that seem less than compelling. In discussing these aspects, it is necessary to focus separately on each of the two components in Wicklund's model.

First, there is Wicklund's proposal that differential information is crucial to the effect of discrepancy on importance of freedom. This proposal must be examined carefully. We have no difficulty accepting the notion that the more information a person has that is consistent with the position urged by an advocate, the less important it will be to disagree with the communicator. With additional information in support of the advocated position, the person is likely to become more confident about that position and more committed to it. The freedom to reject this position is, thereby, rendered of little or no importance. Conversely, with relatively little information that is consistent with a communication, confidence may be weaker and the freedom to reject the position should be more important. Reactance arousal should thus be less when one possesses more information consistent with the position being advocated. This proposition makes good theoretical sense, and a study by Ferris and Wicklund (reported in Wicklund, 1974) provides empirical support for it.

We do not, however, view the effect of discrepancy as being totally subsumed by how much consistent or inconsistent information one possesses. As we have stated previously, strength of belief should determine importance of the freedoms involved regarding any attitudinal issue, and necessarily, the freedom to reject a position in which one believes will be less important than the freedom to reject a position in which one does not believe. Less discrepant (more attitude-consistent) communications will, thus, threaten less important freedoms than will more discrepant (counter-attitudinal) communications.

As long as a person perceives himself or herself as being competent to hold a position, the freedom to hold that position is important regardless of the amount of information the person can generate in its defense. Now, if, at some point, the person tries to generate supporting information and cannot, then this may impair his or her confidence and the freedom to hold that position may become less important. We think it unlikely, however, that every time a person takes a position or responds to a persuasive communication, he or she searches the relevant memory banks to see what information is available. People probably do forget the information that led them to adopt a position they have taken, but they probably are not aware of having forgotten it.

Moreover, even if people do forget information, they do not forget it all. In the Worchel and Brehm (1970) study, it is quite implausible that subjects (Duke University undergraduates in the late 1960s) had forgotten everything they knew about the Communist party and were thus equivalent in information regardless of attitudinal position. There seems no real reason to question that subjects who read an agreeing communication had more information consistent with the communication than subjects who read a disagreeing communication. There seems no real reason, therefore, to question that more reactance should have been aroused by the more discrepant *and* more information-inconsistent, counter-attitudinal communication.

The second part of Wicklund's proposal views subjects in the disagree condition as having engaged in a prior demonstration of their freedom that "prevents the onset of reactance." In discussing the prior demonstration of freedom proposal, it is important to distinguish between the process itself and the use of this process to explain the Worchel and Brehm results. Two studies by Snyder and Wicklund (1976) provide reasonably compelling evidence that prior demonstration of a freedom *can* reduce reactance.

In the following, we will consider only that portion of Snyder and Wicklund's results that is directly relevant to prior demonstration. Their procedure had subjects favoring a supposed candidate for appointment to a (fictitious) Marijuana Study Commission receive or not receive an opportunity to write an essay opposing that candidate. All subjects were then exposed to a persuasive communication arguing in favor of the candidate they supported. The high threat communication was loaded with the usual freedom-threatening phrases ("the only reasonable choice"; "there is no question"; "you have no choice"), whereas the low threat communication was not. Opinions about the candidates were then measured. In both studies, the same pattern of results was obtained. Subjects given the opportunity to write against their candidate did not differ as a function of threat; subjects not given the opportunity to write the counter-attitudinal essay showed more reactance in the high threat condition than in the low threat condition (see Table 6.3).

Thus it does appear that a prior demonstration of freedom can significantly reduce reactance. This reduction may well operate through increased security about the freedom which, in turn, reduces the perceived magnitude of threat. In this latter regard, it is unfortunate that in neither study by Snyder and Wicklund were subjects' perceptions of threat obtained.

A Theoretical Alternative to the Prior Exercise Principle

It is not so clear, however, that prior exercise of freedom can account for the results obtained by Worchel and Brehm (1970). One wonders, for instance, when and how the prior exercise was effected. In the Worchel and Brehm study, the premeasure of attitudes was obtained two

TABLE 6.3
Mean Opinion Change[a]

	High threat	Low threat
Experiment I		
No prior exercise	− .50[b]	1.14
Prior exercise	.67	.55
Experiment II		
No prior exercise	− .83	− .21
Prior exercise	− .15	− .26

[a] From Snyder, M. L. & Wicklund, R. A. Prior exercise of freedom and reactance. *Journal of Experimental Social Psychology*, 1976, *12*, 120–130, Tables 1 and 2, pp. 124 and 127.

[b] A negative number indicates attitude change away from the position advocated in the communication and initially held by the subjects.

weeks before the study in a mass-testing session with other introductory psychology students. There was, thus, no opportunity for subjects overtly to exercise their freedom prior to reading the persuasive communication. It is important, however, to note that *covert* exercise of a prior attitudinal freedom is always continually possible. Perhaps as long as one knows that one believes not-X when urged to believe X, this knowledge in and of itself is sufficient to constitute a prior exercise of freedom.

Another area in which there are questions about the prior exercise explanation for the Worchel and Brehm study involves evidence that magnitude of threat was reduced for subjects receiving the high threat counter-attitudinal persuasive communication. In that study, agree subjects (receiving the attitude-consistent communication) did not differ from disagree subjects (receiving the counter-attitudinal communication) on various evaluations of the communicator: expertise, sincerity, intent to persuade, prominence, bias. Although there was no direct measure of the threat presented by the communication, this complete absence of differences in evaluations of the communicator suggests the possiblity that agree and disagree subjects may not have differed in their perceptions of threat. If prior exercise of freedom does operate to reduce magnitude of threat, different perceptions of threat would be expected.

If one has trouble using the prior demonstration principle to account for the Worchel and Brehm results, then one should consider the possibility that the results themselves are unreliable. This, however, is most unlikely since Wicklund and his colleagues have reported two replications of the effect (Ferris & Wicklund reported in Wicklund, 1974; Experiment I in Snyder & Wicklund, 1976).[1] Rather than dismiss the results, then, it may be more appropriate to (a) recognize the problems involved with applying the prior exercise explanation, as we have done, and (b) consider an alternative theoretical perspective.

From this alternative perspective, it is crucial to distinguish between the arousal of reactance and its subsequent reduction. In terms of arousal, this alternative approach would follow both the original theoretical statement and Wicklund's proposal about the information base. The greater the discrepancy between one's initial position and the freedom-threatening communication, the greater should be the reactance aroused. Also, the greater the amount of information that one possesses that is discrepant with the communication, the greater should be the reactance aroused. Usually, of course, these principles will covary: Counter-attitudinal communications are more discrepant with initial position, and one has more information inconsistent with such communications.

Let us next consider how individuals who have received a freedom-threatening counter-attitudinal communication might reestablish their freedom. Actually, reestablishment would be very easy. If a person believes X and the freedom to believe this is threatened by someone else telling the person to believe Y, subsequent endorsement of *any* position on the X side immediately reestablishes the freedom to believe X. Confronted with a motive to comply as well as a motive to resist, the

---

[1] Studies by other investigators have sometimes appeared to support Worchel and Brehm (1970), and sometimes not. Rozen (1970) reports more reactance when subjects were predicted to choose an initially preferred item than when subjects were predicted to select the other alternative. These data are consistent with the previously cited research. Kohn and Barnes (1977) report a failure to replicate Worchel and Brehm, but the high level of subjects' suspiciousness in this study (46%) and the investigators' failure to verify the actual initial attitudes of their subjects make their data difficult to interpret. Zillman and Cantor (1974) obtained reactance against a counter-attitudinal speech using "rhetorical concession," while this rhetorical style led to increased persuasion for attitude-consistent subjects. These data, however, differ considerably from the main effect of persuasiveness obtained with "rhetorical elicitation of agreement" in an earlier study (Zillman, 1972). Until the psychological differences created by these two presentational styles are more fully understood, it is difficult to compare either study with Worchel and Brehm.

There is some suggestion, however, that when one departs from a paradigm in which an opinion or preference established prior to the experiment provides the dependent variable, verbal behaviors that are inconsistent with an individual's beliefs or expectations may create more reactance than verbal behaviors that are consistent with such beliefs. For example, Stivers and Brehm (1980) found that (simulated) therapists' communications that disagreed with subjects' more important freedom concerning personal responsibility aroused more reactance than therapists' communications that

person can satisfy both motives simultaneously. He or she can comply by moving toward the counter-attitudinal position, but can resist by staying on his or her initial side. Given this state of affairs, it may be difficult to create strong enough reactance to propel one's attitude further away from the communicator's position. Psychologically, except in cases of extreme threat or a strong commitment (see "Commitment," in this chapter) to one's initial position, it just is not necessary.

Individuals confronted with an attitude-consistent communication do not have so obvious a compromise solution available to them. If one's position is urged upon one by a freedom-threatening communication, the only way to reestablish freedom is to move away from the position advocated by the communication and, thus, away from one's initial position. However, if the communication advocates a position on the same side of the issue, but not coincident with that of the individual, a compromise response would be available. For example, individuals who favor a moderate position on the issue and who are confronted with a persuasive communication advocating an extreme position on the same side could evidence both persuasion and reactance by moving toward the position advocated by the communication *but* still remaining in the moderate range. This view of attitude-change processes and reactance arousal is predicated on attending more carefully to the person's exact position on the issue than, as we noted earlier, has been done in previous reactance research.

In contrasting the prior demonstration principle with this alternative compromise principle, there is, then, one area of disagreement. The prior exercise principle stipulates that reactance arousal is "pre-

---

agreed with subjects' more important freedom (see Chapter 13 for more details of this study). Also, Worchel (1972) found that children at summer camp opposed a communication advocating choice of a certain camp activity more when they had had a chance to see a movie on this activity than when they had seen a different movie or no movie at all (see Chapter 11 for more details of this study). In this study, viewing the film presumably made the freedom to engage in the film-related activity more important. It is also possible, however, that the film led the children to expect to engage in a film-related activity and, thus, that the communication advocating another activity went against the children's expectations. Finally, in a study by Worchel and Andreoli (1974) that was described earlier in Chapter 5, confederate behavior at odds with subjects' expectations for the type of interaction they would have with the confederate led to more reactance than confederate behavior that was consistent with these expectations. These studies raise the possibility that when important freedoms and expectancies are involved, behavior that is more discrepant with these freedoms and expectancies will arouse more reactance. Perhaps, then, the attitudinal research reviewed in this chapter has failed to utilize attitudes that are sufficiently important, and this failure has obscured the reactance that could be aroused by counter-attitudinal communications (see also later discussion in this chapter on commitment to an attitudinal position).

vented," whereas the compromise principle holds that reactance is aroused. The question, in other words, is whether or not an attitude-discrepant "freedom-threatening" communication arouses reactance. This question could be examined by cross-cutting high and low threat counter-attitudinal communications with importance of the issue. If a high threat communication, compared to a low threat communication, produced relatively less positive change for a high importance issue than for a low importance one, then this would support the proposition that reactance is indeed aroused and the compromise explanation would be upheld. Such research, as well as that on commitment, should help evaluate the prior exercise and compromise principles.

COMMITMENT

In our example earlier in this chapter of the individual who believed strongly in a specific attitudinal position, it was stated that this individual has lost the freedom to reject the position he or she has adopted as well as the freedom to accept other attitudinal positions. This self-imposed elimination of freedom can be considered the result of a strong commitment (Kiesler, 1971) to a specific attitudinal position. Prior to that commitment, as the individual foresees his or her approaching loss of freedom, there should be reactance arousal, and the person should be motivated to avoid the loss of freedom that commitment would bring. Increasing preference for a certain attitudinal position will threaten the freedoms to reject that position and adopt others, and the person, thereby, should become motivated to adopt other positions and reject the preferred one. This type of self-imposed threat to freedom should occur prior to making any kind of firm decision, regardless of whether the decision to be made concerns attitudes, objects, or behaviors. We discuss more generally the processes involved in predecisional reactance arousal in Chapter 8. For now, our interest is in what happens after the person has become committed to a specific attitudinal position.[2]

Once an unequivocal commitment is made and the freedoms to reject that position and adopt other positions are lost, reactance arousal would appear to be restricted to two types of threat to freedom. First, the commitment itself can threaten future freedoms. Although the person cannot reject the position to which he or she is committed, it is possible to protect other freedoms from being lost. Studies by Kiesler,

---

[2] Commitment has also been studied in regard to future interaction with another person. This type of commitment is discussed in Chapter 7.

Roth, and Pallak (1974) and Sullivan and Pallak (1976) suggest that committed individuals will prefer behaviors that allow for the most restrictive definition of their commitment and will avoid behaviors that elaborate "attitudinal implications of their beliefs." It would seem then that although committed individuals do not try to forsake their commitment, they do try to narrow the range of that commitment as much as possible, thereby preserving other related freedoms.

The second kind of threat to freedom that should arouse reactance in people who have made a strong commitment is freedom-threatening advocacy of the counter-attitudinal position. These people do have the freedom to reject other positions, and if these positions are urged strongly upon them, they should reject them strongly. Attitude-consistent advocacy, however, should not arouse reactance, nor should subsequent "freedom restoration" that occurs after a strongly worded, attitude-consistent communication have any effect on committed individuals' attitudinal positions.

These hypotheses were investigated in studies by Sullivan and Pallak (1976) and Pallak and Sullivan (1979). In both studies, the same general procedures (fashioned after Sensenig and Brehm, 1968) were followed. Subjects participated in pairs in a supposed study on communication processes. After completing a multi-item pretest questionnaire that contained the crucial attitude issue (i.e., opinion about a university tuition increase), subjects made an audio tape arguing against a tuition increase; since subjects were against such an increase, this tape was consistent with their initial attitudes. Public commitment subjects were told to include their name and address on the tape; private commitment subjects were told not to identify themselves. It was assumed that the public commitment condition created a stronger commitment than the private commitment condition.

Following the tape-recording, subjects anticipated writing three essays. They were told they would both have to write the essays on the same side of the issue and that one of them would be the "deciding partner." This person could, however, consult with the other subject if she wished. Subjects drew lots, which were prearranged so that each subject believed that the other was the deciding partner, and went to separate cubicles. On the first essay, subjects were told they would be writing either for or against (a) a tuition decrease, (b) a tuition increase, or (c) tuition loans for students. Subjects then received either a high threat ("I've decided that you must write the first essay in favor of a tuition decrease") or low threat ("If it's all right with you, I'd prefer . . . ") attitude-consistent communication from the partner.

Subjects then filled out a supposed background questionnaire in which they were asked again to express their opinion about a tuition increase. At this point, the experimenter announced that the experiment was running late, and there would be time for only one essay. In the Sullivan and Pallak study, subjects were asked to circle the essay topic and side of this topic that they wanted to write on, and were informed that the experimenter would tell the deciding partner about their preference. In the Pallak and Sullivan study, freedom was restored when subjects were explicitly told to disregard the partner's note and make their own choice. Subjects' essay choices constituted the primary dependent measure.

Both of these studies obtained evidence of differential reactance arousal as a function of commitment. In the Sullivan and Pallak study, there was no difference as a function of threat in public commitment subjects' choices of the essay advocated by the partner. For private commitment subjects, however, the typical reactance effect was obtained, such that more subjects receiving the low threat communication chose this essay topic than those receiving the high threat communication (see Table 6.4).

In the Pallak and Sullivan study, attitude change scores taken from a comparison of the premeasure with the background questionnaire given prior to the restoration of freedom showed this same pattern, subjects in the private commitment–high threat condition displaying a clear absence of positive attitude change. Subjects' compliance after freedom was restored indicated that restoration did not affect strongly committed subjects. Private commitment subjects, who had differed as a function of threat on attitude change, did not differ as a function of threat after freedom was restored (see Table 6.5). Public commitment subjects, who had not differed on attitude change as a function of threat, also did not differ as a function of threat after freedom-restorative actions by the experimenter.

TABLE 6.4
Percentage of Subjects Choosing the Essay Topic Advocated by the Partner[a]

	High threat (%)	Low threat (%)
Public commitment	41.67	25.00
Private commitment	.00	41.67

[a] From Sullivan, J. J. & Pallak, M. S. The effect of commitment and reactance on action-taking. *Personality and Social Psychology Bulletin*, 1976, 2, 179–182, Table 1, p. 181. Copyright 1976 by Sage Publications, Inc. Reprinted by permission.

TABLE 6.5

The Effect of Commitment and Threat on Attitude Change (Pre-Restoration of Freedom) and on Compliance (Post-Restoration)[a]

	Attitude change		Compliance	
	High threat	Low threat	High threat	Low threat
Public commitment	9.93[b]	7.14	57.14%[c]	57.14%
Private commitment	−.57	8.86	28.57%	28.57%

[a] From Pallak, M. S. & Sullivan, J. J. The effect of commitment, threat and restoration of freedom on attitude-change and action taking. *Personality and Social Psychology Bulletin*, 1979, 5, 307–310, Table 1, p. 309. Copyright 1979 by Sage Publications, Inc. Reprinted by permission.

[b] Positive attitude change indicates change favorable to position advocated by the communication.

[c] Percentage indicates proportion of subjects who chose the essay advocated by the communication.

Although these data are consistent with Pallak and Sullivan's theoretical predictions, it is unfortunate that they did not include a no-restoration control group to ensure that, in the absence of both strong commitment and freedom restoration, the essay choice measure could detect differential response to threat. It should be remembered, however, that this same essay choice measure was used by Sullivan and Pallak and, in their study, the measure did obtain reliable high versus low threat differences for private commitment subjects.

It is also regrettable that neither of the two studies we have described included counter-attitudinal advocacy conditions. As we have discussed at length previously, there has been considerable difficulty in obtaining a reactance effect for freedom-threatening, counter-attitudinal advocacy conditions. Interestingly, however, highly committed subjects may be the best population with which to get these effects. Counter-attitudinal advocacy, if strongly worded enough, should create strong reactance arousal for highly committed subjects which should be detectable (relative to low threat or less committed subjects) in terms of either less attitude change toward the counter-attitudinal position or actual boomerang change away from this position. A study in which commitment, threat, and counter-attitudinal versus attitude-consistent advocacy are varied would seem essential to support our previous contentions about reactance arousal from counter-attitudinal communications and to document more fully the differential reactance responses of committed and uncommitted individuals.

Fortunately, a study fulfilling these requirements has recently been reported by Schwarz, Frey, and Kumpf (1980). These investigators asked German high school students who were in favor of mandatory social service for women to write an essay in support of their own view (high commitment) or in support of an unrelated issue (low commitment). Subjects were then asked to read a "letter to the editor" from a (ficticious) German newspaper; the letter either supported or opposed mandatory social service for women. In addition, half of the letters concluded that "everyone will have to decide for himself what his position is to be" (low threat), while the other half concluded, "I am firmly convinced that each and every reader will concur with me. There is no alternative!" (high threat). Control group subjects wrote the irrelevant essay and received a communication on an irrelevant topic. Subsequent to reading the communication, subjects filled out a questionnaire that measured their attitude on the issue as well as various manipulation effects. Results on the latter questions confirmed that the difference between low and high threat communications was perceived as intended.

Postexperimental attitudes on the issue are displayed in Table 6.6. As is apparent, they reveal a significant three-way interaction in the form that our theorizing would predict. Among subjects receiving a supportive communication, acceptance of the advocated position was greatest for those who were highly committed and who received a high threat communication. There is a nonsignificant trend for low commitment subjects to show less agreement with the advocated position when they

TABLE 6.6

Postexperimental Attitudes as a Function of Commitment, Reception of a Supporting or Opposing Communication, and Threat to Freedom[a,b]

	Position of communication			
	Supporting		Opposing	
	High threat	Low threat	High threat	Low threat
High commitment	6.6	$5.3^{a,b}$	5.9^{b}	$5.4^{a,b}$
Low commitment	4.9^{a}	$5.4^{a,b}$	$5.4^{a,b}$	4.2
Control group		$5.3^{a,b}$		

[a] From Schwarz, N., Frey, D., & Kumpf, M. Interactive effects of writing and reading a persuasive essay on attitude change and selective exposure. *Journal of Experimental Social Psychology*, 1980, 16, 1–17, Table 2, p. 10.

[b] Attitude scores could range from 1 to 7, high scores being consistent with subjects' initial position. Means not sharing the same superscript differ at p less than .05 by the Newman-Keuls test.

received a high threat communication than when they received a low threat communication. In contrast, among subjects receiving an opposing communication, acceptance of the advocated position was least (though nonsignificantly) for high commitment subjects who received the high threat communication, and greatest for low commitment subjects who received the low threat communication. However, only among low commitment subjects was a significant reduction in acceptance produced by high threat compared to low. Thus, although these data fall quite clearly into the pattern predicted, the specific reactance effects were weak. It is possible that stronger effects would have been obtained with an issue of greater importance and/or a threat of greater magnitude. In any case, the data obtained by Schwarz et al. are sufficiently encouraging to indicate that further research on the interaction among commitment, supporting or opposing communications, and threat would be worthwhile.

SLEEPER EFFECTS

Attitude change does not always take place immediately. Sometimes there are "sleeper" effects: What looked like an ineffective message turns out, at a later time, to elicit persuasion. Reactance theory offers a useful framework in which to consider these effects. Because the theory assumes that any persuasive communication creates two kinds of forces—those leading toward positive change and those leading toward resistance—it predicts that by taking away the resisting forces, positive change would be obtained. Studies by Worchel and Brehm (1971) and McGillis and Brehm (1975) in which large increments (over baseline levels) of positive change have been obtained when a threat to freedom was followed by a restoration of freedom have supported this hypothesis. These studies manipulated restoration of freedom as a between condition variable. To document a sleeper effect, it is necessary to show a change from ineffective to effective persuasion across time for the same individuals. This kind of delayed persuasiveness was demonstrated in a study by Brehm and Mann (1975).

Subjects in Brehm and Mann's experiment participated in small groups in a supposed study of group decision-making processes. Some of the subjects were told that individual decisions on the material being presented were highly important because there would be a $10 prize for accurate decisions. Others were told that the individual accuracy prize was $2 and, presumably for them, their individual decisions were less important. All subjects were told that the group would receive a

$15 participation fee that they could divide among themselves as they wished.

Half the subjects participated in highly attractive groups, in which the group members were presented as liking them a lot; the others participated in relatively unattractive groups, in which the group members had been presented as not liking them very much. Subjects were then led to believe that they deviated in opinion from the rest of their group, and group pressure (including a bribe involving giving them more than their share of the $15 group fee) was exerted to make them change their opinion.

Subjects were next given an opportunity to express publicly (i.e., on a measure that supposedly would be shown to other group members) and privately their opinion on the issue being discussed by the group. After this, the experimenter gave the group a chance to vote on how they wished to distribute the $15 participation fee. Subjects were then given a final private opportunity to express their opinion. They were told that their responses on this measure would not be shown to the group and would be used to determine whether or not they had won the individual accuracy prize.

Brehm and Mann had predicted that subjects who believed their individual decisions to be highly important and who were in a highly attractive group would experience the most reactance. Their freedom to make an individual decision was highly important and the pressure from the attractive group was difficult to ignore, and thus highly reactance arousing. This prediction was confirmed for the first two (public and private) opinion measures. The high importance–high attraction subjects showed the least amount of positive attitude change of any of the four experimental groups (see Table 6.7). Indeed, subjects in this condition tended to boomerang, moving in the direction opposite to that advocated.

The final measure offered an opportunity for delayed influence. Here, since the $15 had already been distributed (although subjects did not know what this distribution would consist of), previous threat to freedom from group influence was rendered obsolete and subjects' freedom was restored. One would expect, then, that the influence pressure associated with inducing reactance would be associated with inducing positive change once freedom was restored. There was a marginal trend ($p < .20$) in this direction, with subjects in high attractiveness groups tending to show more positive attitude change than subjects in low attractiveness groups.

In showing positive attitude change on the final, private measure, subjects in the high attractiveness–high importance condition demon-

TABLE 6.7
Mean Opinion Change From Initial Opinion[a]

	Before restoration		After restoration
	Public	Private	Private
Low importance of freedom			
Low attractiveness of the group	3.70[b]	2.39	1.31
High attractiveness of the group	8.62	6.38	3.77
High importance of freedom			
Low attractiveness of the group	5.61	3.69	1.15
High attractiveness of the group	−2.31	−2.85	4.92

[a] From Brehm, J. W. & Mann, M. Effects of importance of freedom and attraction to group members on influence produced by group pressure. *Journal of Personality and Social Psychology,* 1975, *31,* 816–824, Table 1, p. 820. Copyright 1975 by the American Psychological Association. Reprinted by permission.

[b] Positive numbers indicate opinion change in the direction advocated by other members of the group.

strated a dramatic switch from their prior position. Although subjects in the other three conditions tended to decline in positive attitude change from the first private measure to the last, subjects in the high attractiveness–high importance condition moved from negative change (relative to initial pre-threat levels) to positive influence. In fact, this group of subjects, who had displayed the most reactance prior to restoration of freedom, showed the most positive change (though not reliably so) after restoration.

It is important to note that the reason why this group displayed strong positive change is not necessarily clear. Brehm and Mann assumed that the positive change simply represented the true positive influence from the group position on the opinion issue once reactance had been removed. An interesting alternative interpretation is suggested by Gruder, Cook, Hennigan, Flay, Alessis, and Halamaj (1978).

These investigators hypothesized that a crucial determinant of sleeper effects may be the presence or absence of a discounting cue in the persuasive communication. Such a cue is expected to suppress attitude change immediately but, after time, may be forgotten (or disassociated from the message content). When the discounting cue is eliminated, the person should respond only to the content of the message and persuasion should be effected. This line of reasoning is clearly similar to the reactance analysis, except that a more informational approach rather than a motivational one is taken.

Gruder *et al.* list the following criteria for determining whether delayed attitude change should be considered a sleeper effect.

1. For people who receive only the content of the message, there should be immediate positive attitude change.
2. For people who receive message content and a discounting cue, there should be no immediate positive attitude change.
3. The positive attitude change by the message-only group at delayed measurement should be greater than that by the message plus discounting cue group at immediate measurement.
4. The message plus discounting cue group should equal the positive attitude change of the message-only group at delayed measurement.

It should be noted that these criteria do point to there being a significant increase in positive attitude change from immediate to delayed measurement for individuals exposed to the discounting cue. These criteria do not, however, predict that discounting cue messages might produce *more* positive attitude change at the delayed measurement than that produced at that time in the message-only group.

Two studies are reported by Gruder *et al.* In the first, supportive but somewhat weak evidence of a sleeper effect was obtained on one of the two attitudinal issues they investigated. In the second, Gruder *et al.* added reactance to the mix and more compelling evidence was obtained. Specifically, in addition to no message, message only, and message with discounting cue (a note from a supposed editor saying the conclusion was false) conditions, the second experiment also included a second type of discounting cue (a note from the editor that restated the conclusion and said it was false), a reactance condition ("you must believe" inserted in the persuasive communication), and two reactance and discounting cue conditions in which the reactance phrase was paired with each discounting cue.

In discussing their data, Gruder *et al.* concluded that only the two combined reactance and discounting cue conditions met all their criteria for an "absolute sleeper effect." Furthermore, in the reactance only and one of the two combined conditions, there were marginal trends ($p < .11$) for these groups to show more positive attitude change at the delayed measurement than was shown by the message-only group.

Taken as a whole, the Gruder et al. studies provide striking evidence of the role of reactance in sleeper effects. Indeed, their data suggest that reactance motivation may be a necessary component if a reliable sleeper effect is to be obtained. The authors also provide a possible explanation for why reactance conditions in their study (and that by Brehm and Mann) may have eventually produced increased positive attitude change that tended to exceed baseline comparison groups.

Gruder et al. report that subjects in the reactance conditions in their second study reported significantly greater interest and involvement with the persuasive communication than subjects in the message only condition. It may well be, then, that when reactance is aroused, the person's attention to and consideration of the message is enhanced. This attentional enhancement has no particular effect immediately, but later when freedom has been restored or the threat has been reduced by the passage of time, enhanced attention facilitates persuasion. This reasoning suggests the intriguing possibility that for maximum persuasiveness in the long run, a persuasive communication should first threaten attitudinal freedom and then have that freedom restored—either directly, or indirectly by the passage of time or change in situation.

CENSORSHIP

Our discussion in the preceding sections has indicated the variety and complexity of reactance effects that are induced by persuasive communications. In the real world, however, not all persuasive communications are heard; sometimes they are censored and removed from the public domain. If a person believes that he or she has the freedom to hear a persuasive communication and this freedom is denied by an act of censorship, reactance should be aroused. The desire to hear the communication should be increased. Moreover, especially if the censorship cannot be overridden at the present time, individuals may restore their attitudinal freedom by moving their attitudes in the direction that the communication would have taken had they been allowed to hear it.

Empirical support has been garnered for both of these hypotheses. An early study by Wicklund and Brehm (reported in Wicklund, 1974) found that more junior high school students who were told that an expected speech was cancelled by a member of the school board moved toward the speaker's position than did those who were told the speech was cancelled due to the speaker's illness.

Ashmore, Ramchandra, and Jones (1971) also examined the effects of censorship. Subjects in their no communication control group were simply asked for their position on the attitude issue at hand (police on campus). Other subjects were told that the experimenter had expected to play a speech for them, but that the college dean had forbidden him to play it for college undergraduates. This speech was presented as either consistent or inconsistent with the subjects' own beliefs (as determined by a premeasure). Subjects' initial opinions were evenly distributed between the two sides of the issue and did not influence subsequent attitude change. Censorship did, however, have an effect on later attitudes. Subjects who heard their own position censored became more extreme in their opinion (M = 1.75), while subjects who heard the other position censored moved opposite to their initial position (M = − 2.00). The difference between own position and other position was significant, and each censorship condition differed marginally from the no censorship control group (M = − .17).

Although these studies amply document the existence of a reactance response to censorship, they leave at least one question of interest unanswered. Perhaps the obtained effects depend on having the censorship carried out by a negatively evaluated agent. Would censorship by an attractive, positively evaluated source have the same effect?

This question has been addressed in two studies by Worchel and his colleagues. In the first study, (Worchel & Arnold, 1973), subjects in three censorship conditions were told that the experimenter had planned to play a taped speech, but was prevented from doing so by one of three sources. These sources were identified by pretesting as positively evaluated by students (YM–YWCA) or negatively evaluated (John Birch Society). The third censorship source was the neutral one of a broken tape-recorder. Two other experimental groups were also told about the censorship by the positive or negative source, but the experimenter told these subjects she had decided to play the tape anyway. Two control groups were included in the design; one in which subjects were told nothing about the tape or censorship (no censor–expect not to hear) and one in which subjects were told they would hear the tape and nothing about censorship was mentioned (no censor–expect to hear). Subjects (except those in the no censor–expect not to hear condition) were asked how much they desired to hear the speech, and all subjects were asked for their opinions about the issue that would have been discussed in the speech.

The results of this study indicated that the value of the source did not

TABLE 6.8
Mean Responses to Desire to Hear the Communication[a]

| | Censor | | | |
	Positive	Negative	Neutral	None
Expect not to hear	4.46[b]	3.28	4.73	Question not asked
Expect to hear	8.95	6.27	Condition not run	8.57

[a] From Worchel, S. & Arnold, S. E. The effects of censorship and attractiveness of the censor on attitude change. *Journal of Experimental Social Psychology*, 1973, 9, 365–377, Table 1, p. 371.
[b] 1 = very much; 21 = not at all.

affect reactance arousal. Subjects who thought the tape was censored by *any* source reported significantly greater desire to hear the tape than subjects who did expect to hear the tape, and there was no difference in reported motivation among the censored groups (see Table 6.8). The attitudinal data were more complex (see Table 6.9), but still basically supported the reactance theory predictions. Considering only subjects who did not expect to hear the tape, subjects in all three censorship conditions favored the position that would have been advocated by the speaker more than those subjects who were not informed of any censorship, and there was no difference among censorship groups.[3] For subjects who did expect to hear the tape, evidence of the effect of source was obtained. Subjects who learned that a positively evaluated

[3] These results do conflict somewhat with those obtained by Wicklund and Brehm. Wicklund and Brehm did not include a no censor control group, and this makes interpretation of their results somewhat ambiguous. It is clear, however, that the school board member's censorship caused a greater number of the students to move toward the speaker's position (71%) than did the speaker's illness (50%). In this experiment, then, source of the censorship did affect attitude change, whereas comparable source differences in the Worchel and Arnold study (campus groups versus a broken tape-recorder) did not affect attitude change. The difference between these two studies may have involved the greater implications for future freedom posed for junior high school students by actions of members of the school board. Certainly, there are more potential threats to these individual's future freedoms from a school board member censoring a speech than from a speaker becoming ill. On the other hand, subjects in the Worchel and Arnold study may not have perceived there to be many implications for future threats from either the campus groups or the broken tape-recorder. In this regard, it is of interest to note that there is a trend within Worchel and Arnold's data for the most reactance to be aroused by the negative source and the least by the neutral source. These data suggest the possibility of differential implications for future threats for these subjects, albeit at a low level.

TABLE 6.9
Means of Subjects' Attitudes on "Police on Campus" Issue[a]

	Censor			
	Positive	Negative	Neutral	None
Expect not to hear	6.88[b]	5.53	7.39	9.38
Expect to hear	12.67	5.38	Condition not run	8.95

[a] See Table 6.8, Footnote a, Table 2, p. 372.

[b] Responses to the statement, "Police should never be allowed on university campuses": 1 = strongly agree; 21 = strongly disagree.

group had tried to censor the tape agreed less with the expected speaker's position than did subjects in the no censorship group, whereas subjects who learned that a negatively evaluated group had tried to censor the speech become more in favor of the speaker's position. Thus, source of the censorship affected subjects' attitudes only if their freedom to hear the speech had been restored.

This general pattern of results was replicated in a study by Worchel, Arnold, and Baker (1975) in which agreement or disagreement with the position advocated was varied as well as expertise of the censor. In this study, all subjects (except for two control groups who expected to hear the speech and were told nothing about a censor) were told that the experimenter had been prevented from playing a speech. Subjects were told that the speaker would speak either in favor of a position they supported or against a position they supported (two different attitudinal issues were used), that the censor was the YM–YWCA or the John Birch Society, and either that the censor was expert on this issue or no information was provided about the speaker's expertise.

Significant three-way interactions were obtained on measures of both desire to hear the speech and attitudes. Only subjects in the condition in which an attractive and qualified source censored a position with which they disagreed showed less desire to hear the speech than the appropriate control group; subjects in all other censorship conditions displayed increased desire to hear the speech. Attitudinal data closely paralleled the reported motivation findings. Subjects in seven out of the eight censorship conditions moved toward the speaker's position; only subjects who had been told that the attractive, qualified source had censored a speech with which they disagreed failed to show positive attitude change.

There is, therefore, considerable evidence demonstrating reactance arousal in response to censorship, and the Worchel, Arnold, and Baker (1975) study provides rather dramatic evidence of how robust this effect can be. One exception to this overall consistency, however, should be mentioned. In a study by Sloan, Love, and Ostrom (1974), subjects were exposed to heckling of a speaker while they attempted to listen to a speech. The authors had predicted that the heckling would increase subjects' agreement with the speaker. No such general effect was obtained and, instead, attitude change was a complex function of initial attitude, heckling, and which of two speeches subjects heard.

Negative results are always difficult to interpret. One could argue that the threat posed by the hecklers was not of sufficient magnitude to arouse reactance. Given the strong nature of the heckling employed (e.g., "Shoot a few more students, Dick"; "Bullshit!") this seems unlikely. It is also possible to suggest that the freedom to hear the speech was not very important. If this variable is interpreted in terms of attitudinal position, we would then have trouble explaining how Worchel and Arnold (1973) obtained strong censorship effects on an attitudinal issue on which subjects were neutral (see no censor conditions in Table 6.9; also stated to be so by Worchel, Arnold, & Baker, 1975). If, however, this variable is interpreted strictly in terms of the freedom to hear the speech, then a possible explanation does arise. Sloane *et al.* used two old speeches (one by Nixon and one by Muskie). It is possible that since the students knew these speeches were "old hat" and may, in fact, have already heard them (or, at least, about them), the freedom to hear the speech was not very important.

SUMMARY

The application of reactance theory to the understanding of attitude change is somewhat complex. In general, the freedoms involved are to take no position on an issue, to take a particular "pro" position, to take a particular "con" position, and to take a neutral position. The importance of these various freedoms will tend to vary with how much information the individual possesses in regard to the issue. Having little or no information makes the freedom not to take a position important, whereas having information makes the freedoms to hold a particular position and reject other positions important. In general, there will be a relationship between the extremity of an individual's position and the importance of the freedom to hold that position and to reject deviant positions.

Threats to attitudinal positions take two forms: They assert that a person must hold a counter-attitudinal position, or they assert that a person must hold an attitude-consistent position. Theoretically, the more discrepant is the advocated position from the one held by the person, the more reactance should be aroused. Thus, counter-attitudinal advocacy should arouse more reactance than attitude-consistent advocacy.

A review of the experimental evidence of freedom threatening communications revealed that, in contrast to the expectation that counter-attitudinal communications would produce large reactance (boomerang) effects, only attitude-consistent communications did so. The fact that counter-attitudinal communications have not produced the theoretically expected strong reactance effects has been explained by appeal to "prior exercise of freedom." Supposedly, by virtue of holding or expressing a counter-attitudinal position, a person has already demonstrated that he or she has the freedom to hold that position and is thus relatively impervious to counter-attitudinal threats. That prior exercise of an attitudinal freedom reduces reactance effects from attitude-consistent persuasive communications has been demonstrated experimentally. However, while prior exercise reduces the effects of threats in arousing reactance, it is not the only factor that can account for why reactance effects are stronger for attitude-consistent than for counter-attitudinal threatening communications.

An alternative explanation derives from considering how freedom can be restored by attitude change. People who receive a counter-attitudinal threat can restore freedom by remaining on the same side of the issue (opposite to the side they are told to adopt) and still show some compliance by moving slightly in the direction of the advocated position, thus satisfying both compliance and reactance motives at the same time. People who receive an attitude-consistent communication have a more difficult problem: In order to resore freedom, they must change toward the other side. Thus, restoration of freedom requires boomerang change to attitude-consistent communications but not to attitude-inconsistent communications.

Evidence was also reviewed indicating that commitment to an attitudinal position has an important effect on reactance processes. In general, once someone has become strongly committed to a given attitudinal position, the freedom to reject that position no longer exists. Thus, high threat persuasive communications advocating an attitude-consistent position to which the person is committed should not arouse reactance. This hypothesis has been confirmed in three studies. Moreover, strong commitment to an attitudinal position should provide a condition under which there will be a strong reactance (boomerang) effect to counter-attitudinal communications. The single study that has examined this possibility obtained weak but supportive results.

Sleeper effects, in which the persuasive effect of a communication shows up only after the passage of time, are predictable when the persuasive communication threatens freedom. The relevant research has demonstrated rather clearly that sleeper effects can occur when persuasive attempts threaten freedom, and even suggests that reactance arousal may be a necessary condition.

Finally, research on the effects of censorship was described. This research has been quite uniform in finding strong reactance arousal as a function of direct censorship. There is some question, however, about whether more indirect forms of censorship (such as heckling) will produce reactance arousal and consequent attitude change in the direction of the position being censored.

CHAPTER 7

Social Relationships: Social Power, Close Interpersonal Relationships, and Helping

In this chapter, we shall consider three of the more *social* psychological processes to which reactance theory is relevant. We begin with an analysis of the rather complex relationship between the social power of influence agents and reactance arousal. Although much of this discussion is, by necessity, theoretical, the results of a number of studies are consistent with the theoretical perspective that we take. In the second section, we describe the relationship between reactance and close interpersonal relationships. This is an area of potentially great interest in terms of the theory, but one that has received relatively little research. Finally, we close with a rather extended, though still highly selective, review of the relationship between reactance arousal and helping.

SOCIAL POWER

Social power is a complex concept from the point of view of reactance theory. An individual with high social power may have the ability to produce a variety of motives that operate in the direction of positive influence. Credibility, expertise, and prestige are among the characteristics that may be possessed by an individual with high social power. In addition, however, high social power frequently means the ability to reward or punish those with less power (French & Raven, 1959), and this ability carries with it the possibility that those with less power will be compelled to comply with a request or order regardless of how they privately feel about the behavior in question. The ability to reward or punish particular behaviors depends, in turn, on the ability to survey the target behaviors; the power that derives from the ability to reward or punish is severely limited where surveillance of the target behavior is difficult or impossible.

Influence Attempts Where Observation Is Not Possible

In order to examine the effects of social power on reactance arousal, let us first consider the simplest case, where the power of the social agent does not include the ability to observe the target behavior and the opportunity to punish noncompliance is, thereby, precluded. Under these circumstances, social power can be considered simply as one form of influence and, in general, as the magnitude of influence pressure increases, threat to freedom and consequent reactance arousal should increase and positive influence should decrease. Two studies in the literature offer support for this "simplest case" prediction.

An early study by M. Brehm and J.W. Brehm (reported in Brehm, 1966) provided college students with low or high threat communications from either a supposed high school student or a supposed professor. The low threat communication merely advocated a given opinion; the high threat communication ended with a coercive statement indicating that the students "must agree" with the persuasive argument they were reading. For the communication from the high school student, movement toward the position advocated by the communicator was uniformly high and did not differ significantly as a function of low versus high threat (71% versus 86%). In response to the communication from the professor, however, significantly more subjects moved toward the communicator's position when threat was low (62%) than when threat was high (40%). Thus, the combined effect of the two sources of pressure (the wording of the communication and the social power of the communicator) produced the least positive influence.

Pennebaker and Sanders (1976) conducted a clever field study to examine reactance effects of social power where surveillance was unlikely. Placards were placed in the stalls of male restrooms in university buildings. The signs displayed either a high threat ("Do NOT write on the walls!") or low threat ("Please, do not write on the walls") injunction against graffiti. The signs were attributed to either a powerful influence agent ("J.R. Buck, Chief of Security") or a less powerful agent ("J.R. Buck, Grounds Committeeman"). The dependent measure was the mean number of graffiti written on the placard (virtually all the graffiti being found to be written there) per 2-hr intervals. Two significant main effects were obtained. Graffiti production was elevated under high threat and under high authority. Although the interaction was not significant, the general pattern of results is quite consistent with that found by Brehm and Brehm. The difference between the low and high threat conditions for low authority was minimal (.33 versus .58). Under conditions of high authority, this difference was considerably larger (.63 versus 1.24), and the largest mean number of graffiti per 2-hr period occurred when a high authority figure prohibited writing on the walls.

These experiments demonstrate that agents with social power generate influence pressure, and consequent reactance effects, even in the absence of any ability to observe and retaliate for noncompliant behavior. Social power in these instances is presumably equivalent to the characteristics of credibility, expertise, and prestige. As we have noted, however, social power also frequently includes the ability to reward or punish the target individual for compliance or noncompliance with the influence attempt, and this ability rests on the probability of the target's behavior being observed by the social influence agent. These considerations will make our analysis more complex.

Influence Attempts Where Observation Is Possible

First, it is necessary to enlarge on the general statement we have made that increasing influence pressure will lead to increasing reactance and decreasing positive influence. A more detailed and complex portrayal of the role of influence pressure (i.e., magnitude of threat) was presented in Chapter 4 (see Figure 4.1). In that analysis, it was pointed out that the importance of the freedom being threatened by the influence attempt sets critical limiting conditions on the arousal of reactance. First, where freedoms of little importance are threatened by influence pressure, even small amounts of pressure will tend to produce positive influence effects. As this pressure increases, reactance arousal will increasingly reduce this positive influence, though the maximum reactance arousal that is possible will be small. Beyond the point of maximum reactance arousal, increasing influence pressure will result in increasing compliance with the pressure.

The effect of influence pressure on freedoms of moderate to high importance is initially quite different. Here, small to moderate pressure to give up the freedom should result in boomerang effects (i.e., behavior opposite to that advocated by the influence attempt) because the magnitude of reactance arousal will be greater than the magnitude of the motive(s) favoring positive influence. High amounts of influence pressure, however, will produce positive influence motives of greater magnitude than that of reactance, and positive influence, reduced by the maximum amount of reactance aroused, will occur. Finally, only where the importance of the freedom in question is extremely high will influence pressure fail to produce compliance regardless of its magnitude.

However, it should now be emphasized that the perceived ability of an agent with social power to observe the target behavior and, thereby, to punish noncompliance will qualify any existing influence pressure. With the magnitude of promised reward or threatened punishment held constant, the pressure on the individual to comply should be a direct function of the probability of noncompliance being discovered. This increased pressure will, in turn, create forces toward compliance as well as forces toward reactance.

In summary, increases in the pressure to comply will increase the magnitude of reactance and the amount of consequent noncompliance *except when the circumstances are as follows:*

1. The importance of the freedom is low. Here, noncompliance should not occur regardless of the characteristics of the social agent applying pressure.

2. The social power of the agent, *even in the absence of an opportunity to observe,* is very high, and the importance of the freedom is *not* extremely high. In such instances, as noted in the foregoing analysis, compliance reduced by the maximum amount of reactance arousal should occur.

3. The increase in the pressure to comply involves a high probability that a powerful social agent will be able to observe the target behavior and, by inference at least, will be able to punish noncompliance or reward compliance. When freedoms of moderate importance are threatened by the influence attempts of such a social agent and punishments or rewards controlled by the social agent are important to

the target person, overt compliance should occur—even though, covertly, reactance has been aroused. In regard to the latter point, such covert reactance arousal would not occur for any substantial amount of time if the overall social power of the influence agent was such that the target person's freedom was irrevocably eliminated.

In support of this analysis, let us first examine a number of studies where noncompliance has been obtained while the social influence agent was present and, thus, could observe the target individual's behavior. It will be recalled (see Chapter 6) that in the experiment by Brehm and Mann (1975), group members who deviated from the group norm were explicitly offered a reward if they would conform. These individuals evidenced nonconformity *both* publicly and privately when the freedom to decide for themselves was made very important *and* when the pressure to conform came from a highly attractive group. In this case, we assume that the importance of the freedom was sufficiently high that even the high social power of the attractive group, along with the ability of this group to observe and punish noncompliance, was not sufficient to produce compliance, covertly or overtly.

Using a Sherif paradigm and an experimental confederate, Moscovici and Neve (1971) found that 92% of their subjects moved away from the confederate's position when the confederate was present. Presumably, the confederate's presence created pressure on subjects to conform and this pressure was resisted. When, however, the confederate left the room and pressure was thus reduced, 83% of the subjects complied with the influence attempt. This latter finding illustrates the strength of the motive to comply once the motive to resist has been reduced (see also Chapter 5).

Bickman and Rosenbaum (1977) also found the presence of a peer to enhance opposition. In this study of crime reporting, female shoppers who were discouraged by a (confederate) bystander from reporting an observed incident of shoplifting were more likely to report the crime if the bystander stayed than if she left. (It should be noted that in this study, no effect for surveillance was found when bystanders encouraged reporting. Presumably, the freedom to report a crime is more important than the freedom not to, and threat to the former freedom created greater reactance.)

In a study by Organ (1974), the presence or absence of a superior's surveillance of a subordinate was examined. Subjects (male business majors) were led to believe that they would be assigned to roles either as the president or as branch managers of a simulated business concern; actually, all subjects were assigned to play the role of branch managers. Subjects were told that the president could determine how to pay subjects acting as branch managers for their participation. They either expected or did not expect that the president would see a copy of their responses to experimental materials, and they either received or did not receive a highly flattering compliment from the president. On a measure of deviation from the president's recommendations, there was a marginally significant ($p < .08$) interaction between surveillance and receiving a compliment. For those subjects who did not expect the president to see their work, receiving the compliment tended ($p < .10$) to increase their compliance with the recommendations. For those subjects who did expect the president to see their work, however, receiving a compliment significantly decreased compliance.

In none of these studies, then, was surveillance by the influence agent(s) sufficient to suppress overt opposition to the influence attempt. Moreover, in all of these studies except that of Brehm and Mann (1975) where surveillance had no effect, surveillance increased reactance. These results provide reasonable support for our contention that surveillance will increase influence pressure that will increase reactance unless the freedom is of low importance. In addition, surveillance should increase opposition to the influence attempt (or, at least, decrease compliance with it), unless the possible rewards and punishments controlled by the influence agent are important to the target person. Further support for this analysis can be obtained from examining studies where surveillance decreased opposition to influence. Four studies in the existing literature appear to demonstrate instances of the effect that, for convenience, we will call reactance suppression. It is important to note that by this term, we mean suppression of direct restorative action, not suppression of the motivational state itself.

In a study by Grabitz-Gniech (1971), subjects evaluated four paintings in an initial session and expected to evaluate them again in another session. At this time, however, they were informed that one painting (the third most attractive) was not available. The reason for the unavailability of this item was failure to arrive in shipment (as in Brehm et al., 1966) or "stylistic incompatibility." This latter rationale was conveyed by having two other supposed subjects (actually confederates) designate the target alternative as incompatible with the others. By having the confederates state their opinions first, subjects were induced to agree with this judgment.

Change scores in attractiveness ratings of the eliminated alternative indicated that, although this alternative increased in attractiveness when it was eliminated due to a failure to arrive in shipment, it decreased in attractiveness when it was eliminated due to stylistic incompatibility. The procedures used in this study make a number of alternative explanations for the results possible. The decrease in attractiveness for the incompatible alternative could have resulted from dissonance reduction, since subjects did agree to the elimination. Furthermore, agreeing to have the choice alternative eliminated may have meant that subjects perceived the freedom to have this picture as having been irrevocably given up. On the other hand, it is possible that subjects who went along with the group experienced reactance arousal and increased desire for the picture, but suppressed the behavioral consequences of this motivational state. Behavioral suppression in these circumstances might have been motivated by avoidance of potential censure from the group (although it is not clear whether subjects thought the group might get to know about their ratings).

Another study by Grabitz-Gniech (Dickenberger & Grabitz-Gniech, 1972) is also suggestive of a suppression effect. In this study, subjects were given two opportunities to comply with an influence attempt by a supposed other subject. The first opportunity occurred directly after the influence attempt while the other subject was present. Here, compliance was obtained. Later, however, when the other subject had left the room, subjects displayed opposition to the influence attempt.

These results are particularly interesting since they reverse the previously described findings of Moscovici and Neve (1971), Bickman and Rosenbaum (1977), and Organ (1974). In these studies, presence of the influence agent led to resistance to the influence attempt, but in the Dickenberger and Grabitz-Gniech study, surveillance led to conformity. This difference, according to our model, could be a function of the potential cost of noncompliance. Subjects in the Dickenberger and Grabitz-Gniech study may have perceived this cost to be quite high. The confederate had expressed herself in no uncertain terms ("I think [these] questions are absolutely stupid"), and subjects may have thought they would be subject to the same kind of abuse if they did not comply. There is no indication from the procedures of the other three studies that subjects could have anticipated such a cost for noncompliance. Furthermore, at least in the Bickman and Rosenbaum, and Organ studies, the behavioral freedom that was threatened (to report a crime; to make up one's own mind on a career-relevant task) may have been considerably more important than the freedom in the Dickenberger and Grabitz-Gniech study to answer a series of "everyday questions." It should also be noted in regard to the study by Dickenberger and Grabitz-Gniech that the subsequent direct restoration of freedom after the confederate left the room (and the potential cost for noncompliance was eliminated) essentially eliminates the theoretical possibility that the previous compliance in the confederate's presence entailed an irrevocable loss of the freedom.

Two studies reported in a paper by Heilman (1976) provide extremely pertinent evidence for reactance suppression. In the first study, subjects were asked to sign an attitude-consistent petition. Directly before signing, subjects (pedestrians en route to or from a supermarket) were exposed to a communication asking them not to sign. This communication was supposedly either from a high power official ("a top level federal official") or a low power one ("a local Concerned Citizens Association official"). The communication stated the official's opposition to the petition (low pressure), stated his opposition and added a direct influence attempt ("He has said that people absolutely should not be allowed to distribute or sign such petitions") to pressure subjects not to sign (high pressure), or (retaliation condition) added a threat of retaliation ("He also said that careful note will be taken of all who do sign") to the high pressure communication. The dependent measure was the proportion of subjects in each experimental condition who signed the petition.

Heilman's results (see Table 7.1) were consistent with the theoretical analysis described earlier. For the low power official, increasing threat led to increasing opposition. For the high power official, however, a curvilinear function was created by the increasing intensity of threat. High pressure increased opposition over low pressure, but the retalia-

TABLE 7.1
Percentage of Subjects Signing the Petition[a]

	Low pressure (%)	High pressure (%)	High pressure and retaliation (%)
Experiment I			
Low power official	52	72	88
High power official	57	77	18
Experiment II			
Anonymous	78	84	88
Non-anonymous	62	84	30

[a] From Heilman, M. E. Oppositional behavior as a function of influence attempt intensity and retaliation threat. *Journal of Personality and Social Psychology*, 1976, *33*, 574–578, Tables 1 and 2, pp. 576 and 577. Copyright 1976 by the American Psychological Association. Reprinted by permission.

tion condition reduced opposition relative to both high and low pressure conditions. We assume that although reactance arousal should have been maximized in the high power–retaliation condition, the potential cost for signing the petition was too high for subjects to risk. Moreover, given that the high pressure and retaliation messages were identical except for the threat of retaliation and subjects in the high pressure condition displayed considerable opposition, it is unlikely that subjects in the retaliation condition perceived themselves to have lost the freedom to sign the petition.

The results of a second study conducted by Heilman are also consistent with the present model. Again, supermarket shoppers served as subjects and were asked to sign an attitude-consistent petition. The same three types of messages were used, and all were attributed to the high power (federal) official. In this study, however, the type of petition signing that was requested was varied. Some subjects were asked to provide the same kind of information that subjects in the first study had been asked for: their signature and their address. Other subjects were asked merely to give a vague indication of where they lived and were told explicitly that "signatures are not necessary."

The non-anonymous condition was designed as a replication of Experiment I, and the results were quite similar. Opposition to the communication increased from low pressure to high and fell off dramatically when retaliation was threatened. Among anonymous subjects, Heilman had expected a linear trend for opposition as a function of threat. Although the overall pattern was consistent with this prediction, there were no significant differences between conditions. As Heilman (1976) notes, "Apparently, anonymity sharply reduced subjects' general reluctance to sign petitions, . . . obscuring any differential effects of the experimental manipulations (p. 577)." In spite of this flattening out of anonymous subjects' responses, however, the critical difference between anonymous and non-anonymous subjects when retaliation was threatened was significant (see Table 7.1), with greater opposition (i.e., more endorsement of the petition) occurring in the anonymous condition.

The implication of these data for the present analysis is clear. Anonymity reduced the power of the influence agent to punish noncompliance and, thereby, reduced the potential cost of opposition. With this cost reduced, it was not necessary to suppress the behavioral consequences of the motivational state.

While the proposed theoretical model of the effects of social power on direct freedom restoration describes the theoretical components of the successful use of power to suppress opposition, it can also be used to generate suggestions about how that success could be imperiled. First, of course, there must be recognition of the existence of the freedom vis-à-vis the influence agent and, second, the threat to this freedom posed by the influence agent must be perceived. Third, as reactance arousal is heightened in the face of prohibitive social power, indirect expressions of that arousal are more likely to take place than direct attempts to reestablish freedom. If, however, any given freedom can be established as sufficiently important, then no influence agent, no matter how powerful, could prevent the direct expression of opposition.

Translating these steps into the real world of social and political confrontation, we find many parallels. Increasing recognition of one's freedoms and the threats posed to these freedoms are exactly some of the psychological functions fulfilled by various prerevolutionary speakers and writers. Consciousness-raising efforts seek to establish people's awareness of their specific behavioral freedoms. The phase of indirect reactance reduction would appear to parallel the various acts of sabotage that, while less than a direct confrontation with the agents of social power, communicate an unmistakable signal of discontent and opposition. Once at least some individuals become convinced that a given freedom is of supreme importance, direct confrontation will take place, even if the cost of that confrontation is life itself. The history of revolution (both political and religious) suggests that, at first, only a few people judge a freedom worth dying for, but that the deaths of martyrs serve as models to help others recognize the freedom and its importance.

Reactance theory is not a sociopolitical theory, and neither are we expert in this area. There are, however, obvious parallels between what the theory says about individual psychological functioning and what can be observed in the larger social context, and we have briefly described these parallels here.

CLOSE INTERPERSONAL RELATIONSHIPS

Reactance theory has been applied to two stages of close interpersonal relationships; when the relationship is being formed and after a commitment to the relationship has been made. In this section, we shall examine the theoretical ramifications and empirical research relevant to both types of social interaction.

"Hard to Get"

For reactance theory, attractive people are like any other attractive objects. If an individual feels attracted to another person and perceives the freedom to form a relationship with that person, then anything that makes it difficult to form the relationship should increase the motivation of the individual who desires the relationship and, thereby, increase the attractiveness of the target person. Basically, two types of difficulties can arise and serve as barriers to the formation of the relationship: There may be personal barriers, created by some aspects of the target person, or there may be external barriers, created by various social and environmental obstacles to the relationship.

One kind of personal barrier that has been studied involves the target person's willingness to date other people. Unfortunately, the overall thrust of this research suggests that the "hard to get" effect is surprisingly hard to get. Walster, Walster, Piliavin, and Schmidt (1973) summarized a series of experiments designed to examine the "hard to get" phenomenon. These investigators suggested that a woman who plays hard to get with a male suitor might be seen as more attractive because (a) dissonance created by the effort involved could be reduced by perceiving the woman as more attractive; (b) the frustration created by the hard to get woman would add to the drive state created by her attractiveness; (c) people may have learned that elusive goals tend to be more valuable; and (d) the frustration and consequent physiological arousal with which one may respond to the hard to get woman could be relabeled as passionate love. Nevertheless, five experiments that were designed to reveal the increased attractiveness of a hard to get woman all failed to obtain the expected effect. In a sixth experiment, Walster *et al.* found that a woman who selectively preferred one male suitor (i.e., the subject) to others was liked more than one who indiscriminately liked all suitors or one who indiscriminately indicated minimal enthusiasm for all suitors.

However, in none of these experiments did it appear that the suitor had a clearly established freedom to obtain the woman before she played hard to get. As will be seen in the research to be discussed shortly, the introduction of an external barrier *after* a freedom has been established does increase attractiveness of a target person. Theoretically, then, the book is not closed on the "hard to get" phenomenon. We would expect that if a suitor's freedom to establish contact with a desired individual is first clearly established, the latter's playing hard to get will arouse reactance and increase his or her attractiveness to the suitor.

Research findings are considerably more consistent with the theory when external barriers have been studied. Driscoll, Davis, and Lipetz (1972) examined the external barrier of parental interference. Through the use of questionnaires and interviews repeated across time, they found that reported parental interference and reported romantic love were significantly correlated for both married and unmarried couples, although the correlation was higher for the unmarried couples. The special importance of external barriers in the precommitment stage was illustrated by the higher correlation for unmarried couples and by the finding that only for unmarried couples was there a nearly significant (p = .06) correlation between reported changes in parental interference and changes in romantic love.

A laboratory study by Wicklund and Ogden (reported in Wicklund, 1974) used physical unavailability to increase attractiveness of a member of the opposite sex. Female subjects were led to expect to rate five men, after reading questionnaires supposedly completed by them, and then to meet one of them and talk with him. Just before the ratings, subjects were told either that they could choose one man to talk with or that one would be assigned to them. After the initial ratings were completed, the experimenter announced that one of the men would not show up and one would be late in coming to the session. Attractiveness of the men described as late and absent was systematically varied through all levels of initial attractiveness. After subjects had been told about the absent and late arrivals, they were asked to read over the questionnaires again and to rerate the attractiveness of the five men. The difference in attractiveness between the first and second ratings constituted the major dependent measure.

The results of this study indicate that, as long as one expects to have the freedom to interact with any one of a group of individuals, sheer unavailability of members of this group can affect attractiveness. When subjects expected to be able to choose with whom they would talk, increased attractiveness was found for both the absent (M = + 10.00) and late (M = + 8.28) males. For no choice subjects, however, both the absent (M = − 4.56) and the late (M = − 6.56) males decreased in attractiveness. The difference between the choice and no choice conditions was marginal in the absent condition (p < .07) and significant in the late condition.

Contrary to expectation, there was no difference among choice subjects in attractiveness ratings for the absent versus the late male. Wicklund (1974) comments on this:

When the study was designed it was thought that a threat of elimination would probably produce less reactance than an elimination, but apparently the psychological impact of the two conditions was about equivalent. This may have been because the degree of lateness was not specified, and subjects could have ruled the late man out as well as the absent one [p. 115].

The third study in which an external barrier was used as an obstacle to forming a relationship is a field experiment by Pennebaker, Dyer, Caulkins, Litowitz, Ackreman, Anderson, and McGraw (1979). Male and female clients of three drinking establishments located "within walking distance of a respectable Southern university" were asked to rate the attractiveness of members of the opposite sex as well as of the same sex present in the bar. Attractiveness ratings were obtained at three different times during the evening. The experimenters had reasoned that the freedom to meet a member of the opposite sex would be threatened as the closing time of the bar got closer, and that "the girls" (as well as the boys) should "get prettier at closing time." The freedom to meet members of the same sex should also be threatened by closing time, but this freedom, presumably, would not be as important and so less reactance should be aroused. The results of the Pennebaker *et al.* study supported these hypotheses. There was a significant interaction between time of measurement and sex (opposite versus same) of target. Members of the opposite sex were rated as more attractive as closing time approached, while ratings of same sex individuals did not vary significantly over time.

Committed Relationships

There has been little discussion of the applicability of a reactance theory analysis to understanding the complex dynamics of an ongoing, committed relationship. In this section, we will begin to rectify this situation. Committed relationships offer a rich arena for reactance effects. The complexity of the interplay among theoretical variables found in committed relationships can be demonstrated by the following outline of some of the major psychological effects of being committed to another person.

In the following postulates, we take the perspective of Person X, who is committed to Person Y. We will then consider only the effects that Y's actions can have on X's motivation and behavior.

1. Commitment to the relationship enhances the power of Person Y to reward and punish Person X (see previous analysis of social power in this chapter).
    a. The importance for X of getting along with Y is increased by commitment, and motives to comply with Y's influence are increased.

    b. As motives to comply are increased, the magnitude of per-
       ceived threat to a freedom is also increased.
2. A committed relationship typically involves a wide variety of
   behavioral dimensions.
    a. Person X will have many freedoms that could be affected by
       Person Y.
    b. A threat by Y to one of X's freedoms can easily imply threats to
       other freedoms that X holds vis-à-vis Y.
3. A committed relationship typically involves future as well as present behaviors.
    a. If Person X currently holds a freedom vis-à-vis Person Y, it is
       likely that X will expect to have that freedom on future occa-
       sions as well.
    b. If a present freedom of X is threatened by Y, X may well
       perceive that future exercise of that same freedom is also
       threatened.

This outline suggests the potency of committed relationships for the
arousal of reactance. Because commitment enhances the perception of
threat from influence pressure, and because many present and future
freedoms can easily be threatened by implication, even small influence
pressures are capable of arousing great reactance. On the other hand,
commitment also produces greater pressures toward positive influence,
based on the person's need and desire to get along with the other person.
In general, then, commitment to an interpersonal relationship should
dramatize the conflict between positive influence tendencies and reactance.

Unfortunately, for all this theorizing, there have been only two studies
specifically designed to examine the relationship between commitment
to another person and reactance arousal. We will inspect these experiments within the theoretical framework we have proposed and explicate the relationship between the variables operationalized in each
study and those we see as important theoretically. It is necessary to
note at the outset, however, that the interpersonal commitment created
in the following experiments is, at best, but a pale shadow of commitment as it exists in actual, ongoing relationships.

In their 1971 study, Pallak and Heller used a modified version of the
Sensenig and Brehm (1968) procedures to vary both interpersonal commitment and threat to freedom. Subjects participated in pairs and were
told that they would have to write on the same side of five issues. Supposedly one partner would be the deciding partner, with the right to
decide which side would be written on and with the right to consult his

or her partner about this decision. Actually, all subjects were led to believe that their partners had been chosen by lot to make the decisions. High commitment subjects were told they would be involved in three additional, future sessions with the same partners; low commitment subjects were told they would participate in the three later sessions with other partners. All subjects were told they would be doing different tasks in the future sessions (i.e., tasks not connected with the essay-writing of the first session).

Subjects then received a high threat or low threat communication, supposedly from their partners. This communication advocated writing the first essay on the side with which the subject initially agreed and was phrased in either a freedom-threatening manner ("I've decided that we will both agree [disagree] with this first topic. You must write your essay in favor of [against] lowering the voting age.") or a nonthreatening manner ("I'd prefer to agree [disagree] with this first topic. If that's all right with you, go ahead and write your essay in favor of [against] lowering the voting age").

The major dependent variable was subjects' attitude change from a pretest measure of opinion to a post-communication opinion item. A significant interaction between commitment and threat was obtained (see Table 7.2). For low commitment subjects, the high threat note produced more negative attitude change (away from the position advocated in the note) than the low threat note. For high commitment subjects, however, there was no significant difference between high and low threat, although there was a trend for high threat subjects to show more positive attitude change than low threat subjects.

TABLE 7.2
Opinion Change and Evaluations of the Partner[a]

	High threat		Low threat	
	High commitment	Low commitment	High commitment	Low commitment
Opinion change	3.86^b	-5.86	.06	1.24
Liking of partner	24.64^c	25.86	33.53	30.29
Partner competence	29.86^c	39.65	38.00	40.65

[a] From Pallak, M. S. & Heller, J. F. Interactive effects of commitment to future interaction and threat to attitudinal freedom. *Journal of Personality and Social Psychology*, 1971, 17, 325–331, Table 1, p. 328. Copyright 1971 by the American Psychological Association. Reprinted by permission.

[b] Positive change indicates change in the direction advocated by the communication; negative change indicates change away from the position advocated.

[c] The higher the number, the more positive the evaluation of the partner.

Although these data offer clear support for Pallak and Heller's prediction that commitment to future interaction would decrease reactance effects, the procedures used in the study raise several important theoretical issues. First, we would presume that the commitment to work in additional sessions with the partner would increase this person's potential power; however, there is no reason to believe that the person's potential social power would prohibit the subject's direct attempts to restore freedom. Simply working for a time with someone should not give that person any necessary power to punish noncompliance. Moreover, it is not clear whether subjects thought their partners would ever see the opinion questionnaire they filled out after receiving the note. We would expect then that subjects' anticipation of future interaction would make getting along more important, but also that the pressure to get along and comply would increase reactance arousal and that the cost of noncompliance was not prohibitively high.

Second, all subjects expected to write five essays and have the partner decide for all five of them. Thus, for high threat subjects, a number of future threats to freedom could be anticipated. The effect of commitment on anticipation of future events, however, is unclear. Subjects knew only that the additional sessions would not involve essay-writing; they did not know what would be involved. High commitment–high threat subjects may have focused on future freedoms that would be available in these future sessions, or they may have focused on the possibility of future threats.

Third, it does seem fairly certain that the opinion issue on which subjects anticipated writing the first essay was not of critical importance to them. Posttest means of importance of their opinion ranged from 41.64 to 64.50 on a 91-point scale. Furthermore, in the first election after the voting age was lowered (and conducted after this study had been completed), only a small proportion of 18–21-year-olds actually voted (1972: 48.3%—lowest proportion of any eligible age group).

It would appear, then, that this experiment provided high commitment subjects with a threat to, at best, a moderately important attitudinal freedom; created a relatively important need to get along with the other person; and did not establish clearly the ability of the influence agent to either observe or punish noncompliance. Under these circumstances, the importance of the need to get along may well have been greater than the importance of the opinion freedom involved. Furthermore, although the lack of punishment-based social power should have allowed subjects to express opposition, it also may have led (even in the high threat condition) to only moderate perceived influence pressure. Reactance arousal should not, then, have been particularly strong, but the pressures toward positive influence may have been relatively great. On the other hand, when the need to get along with the other person was not present, subjects (in the low commitment condition) did manifest efforts to restore the attitudinal freedom that had been threatened.

Interestingly, there are some data from the Pallak and Heller study that suggest that the compliance of high commitment-high threat subjects was not achieved without some cost to the relationship (see Table 7.2). Regardless of commitment condition, partners who sent the high threat note were liked less than partners who sent the low threat communication. Moreover, high commitment-high threat subjects perceived their partners as less competent than did subjects in the other three conditions. Thus, although commitment to future interaction served to induce compliance with attitudinal influence, it did not eliminate negative reactions to the freedom-threatening agent and may even have increased such reactions. If the individuals in this study actually had had a chance to interact, these reactions might have been critically important for the tenor of future interactions between the two individuals.

An experiment that examined possible reactance effects as a function of *both* anticipated and actual interaction with a person who has threatened freedoms was carried out by Dickenberger (1979). This experiment also examined the effects of repeated threats to freedoms where subjects expected future interaction with the threatener or with someone else. Finally, this experiment tested how people respond to a threat to freedom after they are exposed to earlier threats that they did or did not have an opportunity to restore.

In the experimental procedure, subjects in four conditions anticipated participating in two studies that were to be run by the same experimenter or by different experimenters. Two additional groups were run in which there was no anticipation of a second study. In the first study, subjects were asked to evaluate, one by one, three sets of three oil paintings. A threat to evaluational freedom was instituted by the experimenter's making positive remarks about a particular painting. In one set of conditions, there was a threat to freedom in each set of paintings. In another set of conditions, there was a threat to freedom only in the third and last set of paintings. Crosscutting this manipulation of amount of threat was a manipulation of who the subject expected to run the second study in which he or she was to participate: either the same experimenter or a different one. Thus, this part of the design was a 2 (single threat or repeated threats) by 2 (same experimenter versus different).

In the two conditions in which subjects did not anticipate participation in a second study, all subjects were exposed to repeated threats, and the opportunity to express reactance was manipulated. Subjects were supposed to rate each painting on a questionnaire, and subjects in one condition were allowed to do so. However, in the other condition, the experimenter said that the senior investigator had forgotten to include rating questionnaires for all of the pictures. Subjects in this condition found that there was no questionnaire for the threatened paintings in the first two sets, thus preventing the expression of reactance in the first two sets but not in the third.

The dependent variable for all of the above conditions was the rating of the threatened paintings. Because the threat consisted of a positive statement about the painting, reactance would be shown by a relatively low rating.

The subjects who expected to participate in a second study were asked to fill out a questionnaire on a variety of unimportant and uninteresting topics. The experimenter was the same or different, as subjects had been led to expect. The questionnaire allowed responses of "yes," "no," or "don't know," and in order to arouse reactance, the experimenter requested that all subjects use the "don't know" category as little as possible. The measure of reactance, in this case, was the extent to which the "don't know" category was used.

This complex design permitted Dickenberger to test a number of hypotheses. Her first hypothesis was that subjects who had been prevented from expressing reactance to threats on the first two sets of paintings would show more reactance on the third set than those who had been able to express reactance on each set. As hypothesized, the mean rating (standard score) for the former group $(-.62)$ was reliably less than that for the latter $(.45)$.

The second hypothesis was that repeated threats to freedom would produce more reactance (more negative ratings) than a single threat to freedom. There was a small trend in this direction, but it was not sufficiently reliable to support the hypothesis.

Dickenberger's third hypothesis was that those who anticipated participation in a second study with the same experimenter would show more reactance on the third set of paintings than would those who anticipated a different experimenter. The respective mean ratings for the two conditions, $-.23$ and $.32$, were reliably different and thus support this hypothesis. Although the interaction between expected same and different experimenters and the number of threats was not significant, individual comparisons of cell means indicated that the effect due to experimenters was significant in the repeated threat condition and not in the single threat condition. Thus, the effect of repeated threats appeared to depend on anticipation of future interaction. The combination of repeated threats and anticipation of dealing with the same experimenter in a second study produced the greatest, though not a significantly greater, amount of reactance.

The last hypothesis was that in the second study, those subjects who were exposed to the experimenter who had already threatened their freedom would show more reactance than would those exposed to a new experimenter. This hypothesis was tested by comparing the mean frequencies with which the "don't know" category was used, high frequencies indicating more reactance. The means were significantly different but in the direction opposite to that predicted. Those exposed to the same experimenter complied more than those exposed to a different experimenter. Dickenberger's explanation of this reversal is that subjects exposed to the same experimenter had already restored their freedom in regard to that person (in the first study) and, consequently, the probability of having that general interpersonal freedom was high, making the importance of the specifically threatened freedom low. Our interpretation differs somewhat from hers. We would agree that the prior restoration of freedom vis-à-vis the same experimenter could plausibly produce less reactance. However, we would argue that (a) two specific behavioral freedoms were involved in the two studies and (b) reactance was reduced because the experimenter's threat was reduced, not because the second freedom was made less important. Although the exact mechanism for the latter effect is not clear, possible factors could include a reduction in the experimenter's power, prestige, and/or credibility that ensued after subjects restored their freedom in response to the initial threat.

In summary, Dickenberger's experiment makes a number of points relevant to reactance processes. First, when there is a threat to freedom that has been preceded by prior threats from the same person, reactance is greater if there has been no opportunity to respond to those prior threats than if there has been such opportunity. This suggests that the effect of a threat is enhanced by the prior existence of reactance, but it leaves unanswered the question of whether or not the threats must come from the same source or, perhaps, must involve similar freedoms. On the other hand, when it was possible to respond to each threat (from the same experimenter), the number of threats (three versus one) had no effect on the magnitude of reactance. This finding, too, suggests that it is the existence or nonexistence of reactance at the time that a threat occurs that is important. As long as individuals could respond to the repeated threats, number of threats had no effect.

Second, when people anticipate further interaction with the person who threatens freedom, as opposed to interaction with a different person, more reactance is aroused. This effect was significant where there were repeated threats but not where there was only one threat. Thus, commitment to future interaction with the threatener *can* result in relatively great reactance. This conclusion is in direct contrast to the results of the Pallak and Heller (1971) study, described previously. As we noted in the discussion of that study, their conditions may not have been optimal for maximizing reactance effects from commitment. The Dickenberger experiment shows that with repeated threats to freedom, when we might expect reactance effects to be greater, commitment to future interaction with the threatener does indeed result in stronger reactance effects.

Finally, Dickenberger's experiment found that a threat to a different kind of freedom in a new situation results in more compliance when delivered by a prior threatener of freedom than by a person who had not delivered prior threats. Because all prior threatened freedoms could be restored, this finding can be interpreted as evidence that the opportunity for prior restoration of freedom reduces the effect of later threats from the same person. As has been discussed previously, both restoration of (a single) freedom (Chapter 5) and prior exercise of freedom (Chapter 6) tend to reduce reactance effects. All these findings appear to illustrate the same rule, namely, that knowing that one does indeed have the freedom mitigates the perception of threat, and, therefore, reduces reactance arousal.

This discussion, we hope, will serve to point out the need to consider a host of contextual variables when examining reactance processes in committed relationships. It is not possible to say simply that commitment will increase or decrease reactance arousal. It is necessary to look at the power of the influencing agent, the importance of the threatened freedom, the implications for future freedoms, and subjects' feelings about the agent as well as their direct attempts to restore freedom. All of this suggests, to us, an important and intriguing area for future research.

HELPING

The helping situation is another example of an interpersonal relationship in which both compliance and reactance motives are often simultaneously aroused. There has been considerable research on possible reactance effects that may appear in at least some helping situations. First, we will discuss those characteristics of requests for help that are most likely to arouse reactance.

Importance of the Freedom Not To Help

Helping should be reduced if the request for help threatens an important freedom not to help. This hypothesis has not been studied explicitly, but the effects on helping of the freedom not to be obligated have been examined. It will be remembered that in the Brehm and Cole (1966) study, conditions of high versus low importance of accuracy in first-impression ratings were created. If it is highly important to be accurate in describing your impressions of an individual, it is also highly important not to be obligated to be nice to him or her. A favor from this individual then threatens this freedom and should motivate you not to be nice and, presumably, not to be helpful. In line with this reasoning, subjects who were in the high importance–received a favor condition were less helpful when a later opportunity to help was presented than were subjects in any of the other conditions. Using a slightly modified version of the Brehm and Cole procedures, Worchel, Andreoli, and Archer (1976) also obtained less helping (for unique interaction subjects) when subjects thought that the freedom to be accurate and thus unobligated was important than when subjects thought this freedom was relatively unimportant.[1] (Both these studies have been described in Chapter

[1] Brounstein and Sigall (1977) proposed an ingratiation analysis of the effects obtained by Brehm and Cole (1966) and Worchel et al. (1976). Brounstein and Sigall had an experimental confederate either be highly dependent on the subject's evaluation of his task performance (i.e., the confederate's pay was based on this evaluation) or not dependent (i.e., pay was to be randomly determined). A favor was then performed by the confederate either before or after the dependency of the confederate had been described. Subjects rated how much they liked the confederate; on these ratings, they were told to be as candid as possible. Planned comparisons revealed that there was no difference in liking as a function of dependency when the favor was performed before the dependency conditions were introduced, but that high dependency decreased liking when the favor was performed after the dependency conditions were described.

Two explanations would seem possible for the discrepancy between the Brounstein and Sigall study and those two studies (Brehm and Cole, 1966; Worchel et al., 1976) that obtained decreased helping when the favor occurred before the confederate was aware that subjects needed to make accurate evaluations. Brounstein and Sigall propose that subjects in the Brehm and Cole experiment (and presumably the Worchel et al. study as well) may have assumed that the confederate knew about the subject's need to make accurate evaluations. This is possible, but rather unlikely given that the procedures were specifically designed to make it clear that the confederate did not know.

The second explanation that could account for the discrepancy focuses on Brounstein and Sigall's failure to manipulate importance of the freedom to be unobligated. These investigators imply that all subjects would regard this freedom as important—"The role re-

5.) In some other studies described below, the importance of the freedom not to help also may have varied across experimental conditions.

Pressure to Help

Pressure on people to be helpful can come from a number of sources. The help may be badly needed, the request may be forcefully made, or it may be important for the helper's self-image to be helpful. Reactance theory views pressure to help like any pressure to act in any given way, that is, as creating the dual motives of compliance and resistance. If, however, there is a threshhold for the perception of threat, then at relatively low levels of pressure, the motive to comply with the request and act in the socially valued manner should outweigh reactance arousal. When, on the other hand, the pressure on the person to help becomes sufficiently strong to be perceived as a threat to freedom, reactance arousal should act to reduce the amount of help that is given. A number of studies have found this predicted association between pressure to help and help given.

Dependency

One way to increase pressure on the person to help is to increase the intensity of the need for help. Research by a number of investigators has demonstrated conditions under which high dependency can arouse reactance.

In Jones' (1970) study, subjects were undergraduates who were participating in an experiment for credit in their introductory psychology course. After spending about 30 minutes completing a questionnaire, subjects in the high choice condition were told that the experiment was over and they had earned their experimental credit. It was then mentioned that another experimenter was requesting subjects and that they should read over this request and decide whether they wanted to participate. Low choice subjects were told that 5 minutes' participation in what was termed "a second part of the project" was required in order to earn their experimental credit. Cross-cutting this manipulation of

---

quirements for the subject were described so as to make clear the importance of his behaviors [p. 121]"—but they provide no data on this point. Since Brehm and Cole as well as Worchel *et al.* obtained the predicted reactance effect only when the freedom was important, it would seem crucial to document that it was so perceived. Without such documentation, it is hard to know what to make of Brounstein and Sigall's findings.

choice, Jones varied the number of subjects needed by the supposed second experimenter. Low dependency subjects learned that he needed 10–20 out of the available 700 in the subject pool; high dependency subjects learned he needed 250–300. All subjects were asked to indicate how much time they would devote to the second experiment; it was possible to give from 5 minutes to 4 hours.

The choice manipulation in this study is a rather unusual one. Low choice subjects had no choice about helping for 5 min, but they were free to refuse any help beyond this amount. Once the differential 5 min is accounted for (and this was done in the data analysis by adding a constant of 5 min to all scores for high choice subjects), subjects in both high choice and low choice conditions were free to refuse to volunteer (more) time.

This equivalence may, however, be more logically apparent than psychologically real. Subjects in the low choice condition may have felt that once they had come back for 5-min participation in the second experiment, they might as well stay a while and help the experimenter out. They had the freedom to refuse to stay longer, but this freedom may have been of trivial importance. For high choice subjects, this was not the case. They had to make the decision whether or not to come back for the other experiment, and, since scheduling this would require at least some effort on their part, the freedom not to participate at all should have been fairly important. This analysis suggests that the variable manipulated by subject choice in the Jones study was probably not the existence or nonexistence of the freedom not to help but, rather, the importance of the freedom not to help.

From either theoretical perspective, however, the prediction would be the same. High dependency should increase helping only for low choice subjects. For high choice subjects, the reactance aroused by high dependency should offset any added motive to comply and, therefore, helping under high dependency conditions should be equal to or lower than helping under low dependency conditions. This is the pattern that was obtained (see Table 7.3). There was a marginally significant ($p <$ .06) interaction between choice and dependency. Low choice subjects helped significantly more under high dependency than under low dependency, but high choice subjects did not offer different amounts of help as a function of dependency.

Importance of the freedom not to help may also have been involved in a study by Schaps (1972). Subjects for this field research were 64 shoe salesmen working in their regular jobs. Dependency was varied from high to low by having a customer–confederate appear in a shoe with a broken heel or enter the store without any damaged footwear.

TABLE 7.3
Mean Number of Minutes Volunteered[a]

	High dependency	Low dependency
Low choice	46.7	18.0
High choice[b]	18.3	36.7

[a] From Jones, 1969. Reprinted by permission.

[b] Five minutes were added to the score for each high choice subject.

By having the confederate enter the store when there were many or few other customers, Schaps varied what he termed the "costs" of helping. In terms of reactance theory, these costs translate into the importance of the freedom not to help. When one is busy, the freedom not to help is important. This freedom is considerably less important when one is not taking care of other customers. Using a "service index" (i.e., number of pairs shown, time spent in serving, and number of trips to the stockroom for additional shoes), Schaps found that when salesmen were not busy, high dependency led to more helping than low dependency. When, however, the salesmen were busy, there was no difference between high and low dependency conditions (although, as in Jones' study, there was a trend for helping to be greater in low dependency than in high dependency conditions).

A study by Schwartz (1970) indicated another condition under which high levels of dependency may lead to reactance. Subjects were "community members" who were contacted after they had finished donating blood. These individuals were told that there was a young woman who needed a bone marrow transplant and were asked to join a pool of possible donors. The young woman's need was presented as slight (she might need it), moderate (she needed it), or high (she would die without it). Subjects were also told that there was a high (1/25) or low (1/1000) likelihood that their marrow would match the woman's. The dependent measure of helping ranged from not going to have a blood-test for compatibility (0), willing to have blood tested (1), at least 50–50 chance would donate (2), to willing to be on call for future transplants (3).

As in the study by Jones, there is some ambiguity in the study by Schwartz about the theoretical implications of one of the variables manipulated. The concern in this case is with the likelihood manipulation. On the one hand, it would seem that high likelihood would have created more pressure to volunteer: If there is a good chance that we can do something to help, then it would seem more incumbent on us to act than if it were likely that our actions would be of no avail.

Schwartz, however, explicitly rejects this interpretation, and, indeed, it can also be argued that if the chances of a match are high, it should be easier to get someone else whose marrow would match. This perception should reduce the pressure on any given individual to volunteer. Unfortunately, Schwartz provides no supplementary data that would enable us to have a better idea of how subjects perceived the likelihood manipulation.

From another perspective, however, it seems clear that the high likelihood condition must have created greater reactance arousal than the low likelihood condition. For people who believed that there was a 1/25 chance that their marrow would match that of the young woman, being requested to volunteer for the pool threatens not only their freedom not to volunteer but, potentially, their freedoms not to undergo the various procedures necessary for actual donation. In the low likelihood condition, such implications for future freedoms were not at all likely. The only freedom being threatened was the freedom not to volunteer for the pool; there was very little chance that the donation itself would ever occur.

Schwartz's data were consistent with this latter interpretation. Under conditions of low likelihood, agreeing to volunteer was a positive function of need: the more need, the more help people volunteered. Under high likelihood conditions, however, help was a curvilinear function of need: Moderate need increased the amount of help volunteered, but high need reduced help offered to somewhat below the level offered when the young woman's need was only slight.

The importance of implications for future freedoms, which seems crucial in interpreting Schwartz's study, was also investigated in the study by Jones described previously. Half the subjects in Jones's experiment were told that the second experimenter was running a number of studies in addition to the one for which he was then requesting participation and that he would be likely to try to recruit subjects to be in all of them. The other half were not told of any other experiments. There was a marginally significant main effect ($p < .07$) for subjects in the high implications condition to volunteer less time than in the low implications condition. Unlike Schwartz, however, Jones did not find an interaction between implications and dependency.

Another helping study in which implications for future freedoms may have been involved was conducted by Harris and Meyer (1973). Subjects were Saturday shoppers in a shopping center mall. The experimenter stood next to a sign that indicated either low ("I'd appreciate it"), moderate ("I'll get some points toward my grade in my research methods course"), or high ("If I don't get [them], I'll fail my research methods course") need for signatures. In both the moderate and high dependency conditions, it was specified that 50 signatures were required; no number was mentioned in the low dependency condition. Cross-cutting the dependency manipulation was a variation of threat to freedom that Harris and Meyer conceptualized in terms of "the possibility of future contact with and requests from the Experimenter [p. 240]." In the high threat condition, subjects were asked to sign their names and give their phone numbers; in low threat conditions, subjects were asked to give their names and favorite colors.

Harris and Meyer obtained partial support for the reactance theory predictions. As in the Jones study, there was a significant main effect for the implication threat variable; more individuals signed under low than under high threat. The data for both sexes showed the same general pattern, but only the difference for females was significant. This finding suggests that the freedom not to reveal one's phone number and the associated freedom not to be contacted later by a stranger may, in general, be more important for females than for males.

The effect of implications for future freedom was modified by a significant dependency by threat interaction. High threat reduced helping in the low and moderate dependency conditions, but there was no difference between threat conditions under high dependency. There was also a main effect for dependency, such that greater dependency led to increased helping. These data are not supportive of theoretical predictions. Reactance theory would predict that threat should reduce helping most under conditions of high dependency; instead, this study found that threat reduced helping least under conditions of high dependency.

Interpretation of these data (both the parts that support reactance theory and those that do not) is made distinctly tenuous by the methodology used in this study. The signs displaying the experimental manipulations were varied randomly every 10 min during the two Saturday afternoons on which the study took place. As the authors note, it was not possible to count the number of people who saw the signs and did not help. Statistical analyses, therefore, were based on the assumption of equal numbers of subjects present during each time period. This assumption may or may not have been valid, and it is difficult to know how much confidence one should place in results that are based on it.

Another examination of the interaction between threat and dependency was reported by Henion and Batsell (1976). Subjects were selected randomly from a list of previous blood donors and were contacted by phone. For half the subjects, high need for donors was explicitly mentioned ("our backup supply of your blood type is extremely low"). The other half were simply asked to donate; need was not emphasized. Threat to freedom was varied by telling high freedom subjects, "Of course, we recognize an offer to help by a donor is completely voluntary" and telling low freedom subjects "We certainly do hope you are going to help out."

In discussing the results of this study, two theoretical points should be made clear. First, all subjects had the freedom to choose whether or not to donate. The low freedom message did put more pressure on subjects to comply and thus was a greater threat to their freedom not to agree to donate. It, however, did not in any way eliminate the freedom to refuse. Second, the threat to freedom was actually quite mild. There was no comment in this study that approximated the usual kind of high threat communication (e.g., "you must," "you have no choice") used in reactance research. These points suggest that although reactance arousal, and tendency to refuse to volunteer, should be greater in the low freedom (actually better called high threat) condition than in the high freedom condition, this difference would not be expected to be very great.

The data (displayed in Table 7.4) indicate that the results of this study partially support the reactance theory analysis. There was a marginally significant main effect ($p < .08$) for freedom (or, as we would prefer to call it, threat to freedom) conditions. More subjects whose freedom to refuse to volunteer was not threatened (high freedom) volunteered than did subjects whose freedom to refuse was threatened (low freedom). There was also a main effect for dependency; high dependency generated more agreement to volunteer than low dependency. Reactance theory would predict that high threat to freedom would reduce the difference between high and low dependency, but there is no hint of this interaction and, if anything, the data are in the opposite direction.

Let us now summarize the results of these five studies. In three

TABLE 7.4
Percentages of Subjects Agreeing to Donate[a]

	High dependency (%)	Low dependency (%)
High freedom (low threat)	64	51
Low freedom (high threat)	57	34

[a] Adapted from Henion and Batsell, 1976.

studies (Jones, 1970; Schaps, 1972; Schwartz, 1970), the interaction of dependency and another reactance-relevant variable was as predicted by the theory. For two studies, this was not the case. Harris and Meyer (1973) obtained a significant interaction between dependency and implications for future freedoms, but the pattern of this interaction was opposite to that predicted by the theory. Henion and Batsell (1976) did not obtain a significant interaction between dependency and threat to freedom, and the trend in their results is opposite to that predicted by the theory. At the moment, though, we tend to regard the data supporting the theory as somewhat more compelling than the data not supporting it. The two nonsupporting studies involved a questionable methodological assumption and a very mild threat to freedom. The three supporting studies, though they all contain some ambiguity about how best theoretically to define the operational variables, appear to have been sound methodologically and to have created appropriate psychological conditions for an adequate test of theoretical hypotheses.

Verbal Messages

Though urging people to provide help that is badly needed is perhaps the most obvious way verbally to threaten their freedom not to help, other types of verbal messages can also threaten this freedom. For example, in a second experiment reported by Henion and Batsell, subjects (randomly selected from the same donor list used in the previously described experiment) were asked either to "drop by sometime within the next few days" or to set up a definite appointment. The request for a definite appointment may have threatened subjects' freedoms in two ways. This request may have signaled the strong persuasive intent of the caller, and it could also have threatened subjects' freedoms to do something at the appointment time other than donate blood. In accordance with this reasoning, more subjects (59%) were found to agree to donate blood when an appointment was not requested than when one was requested (34%).[2]

Other kinds of verbal statements have also been found to reduce helping. In the study by Staub (1971) described earlier (Chapter 4), statements by the first experimenter pointing out the positive conse-

---

[2] It should be noted that in both the Henion and Batsell studies, only agreement to donate was affected. Actual compliance rates did not differ as a function of the experimental variables. This lack of effect on actual compliance suggests that both the compliance and reactance motives aroused by the experimental manipulations were rather weak and "washed out" over time.

quences of helping other people reduced the help provided by kinder-garten children to another experimenter.

Stating the obvious can also reduce help. Goodstadt (1971) con-ducted two experiments in which male subjects were induced to like or dislike a same-sex confederate (the confederate acted warmly or coldly toward the subject; subjects were led to believe their opinions were similar to or dissimilar from those of the confederate; and the con-federate acted cooperatively or competitively during an experimental task). After using all these procedures to establish liking or disliking, the experimenter either made no statement, made a mild statement confirming the subject's feelings ("Apparently you like [dislike] _____"), or (in the second experiment only) made a strong statement about the subjects's feelings ("It's very clear that you like [dislike] _____"). Subjects were then given a chance to help the confederate complete the experimental task.

Although there were some minor differences between the results of the two studies (probably as a function of minor differences in the pro-cedures used), the general pattern was similar in both (see Table 7.5). In the no statement conditions, subjects who liked the confederate helped more than subjects who did not like him. Helping was reversed, how-ever, in the statement conditions. In Experiment I, where only a mild statement was used, more subjects who disliked the confederate helped him than subjects who liked him. In Experiment II, where the mild statement was even milder ("we don't put too much weight on mea-sures like this") and the helping was costlier to the subjects, the mild statement led to approximately equal numbers of subjects helping regardless of their feelings toward the confederate. The strong state-ment, however, induced more subjects who disliked the confederate to help him than subjects who liked him.

The results of both experiments suggest that when the experimenter "drove home" the point of subjects' feelings toward the confederate, the subjects' freedoms to be nice (if they disliked him) or not to be nice (if they liked him) were threatened. Freedom could then be established by acting contrary to one's feelings. The pattern of the data in the sec-ond experiment also indicates a difference between the freedom to be nice and the freedom not to be. Even the very mild statement increased helping for subjects who disliked the confederate. Goodstadt (1971) ex-plains this finding by suggesting that "people are probably more sen-sitive about it being known that they dislike another person [p.620]." We would take a different tack and suggest that the freedom to be nice is, in general, probably more important than the freedom not

TABLE 7.5

Percentages of Subjects Who Helped the Confederate[a]

	Confederate liked (%)	Confederate disliked (%)
Experiment I		
No statement	40.0	10.0
Statement	10.0	40.0
Experiment II		
No statement	78.5	42.9
Mild statement	78.5	71.4
Strong statement	28.5	71.4

[a] From Goodstadt, M. Helping and refusal to help. *Journal of Experimental Social Psychology*, 1971, 7, 610–622, Tables 1 and 2, pp. 614 and 618.

to be nice, and that even a mild threat to the former freedom can arouse psychologically significant reactance.

Modeling

The evidence is reasonably compelling that what people say to us can arouse reactance and reduce helping. Research also supports the notion that what other people do can have similar effects. Willis and Goethals (1973) found that having a friend model compliance to a request to donate to a local orphanage decreased male high school students' willingness to donate (relative to conditions in which the friend's opinion was not solicited or the friend's opinion was conveyed by another person). It should be noted that this experiment had considerably heightened the potential for reactance arousal by telling all subjects that previous tests they had completed had established that the friend was a very strong leader while they were very submissive followers.

A study by Fraser and Fujitomi (1972) suggests that modeling may differentially affect helping depending on the person making the request. One Halloween night, experimental confederates made UNICEF requests to 366 residences. All solicitors were either Oriental female adults or Oriental female children. Each solicitor carried with her a glass jar that was either empty, half full of coins, or half full of coins and dollar bills. In this situation, adults were expected to arouse more reactance than children. Adults are more powerful influence agents in general, and, since they are less likely to go trick-or-treating, their perceived intent to obtain UNICEF donations should be greater. Fraser and Fujitomi's data supported this hypothesis. Significantly fewer people donated when the solicitor was an adult (42%) than when the request was made by a child (69%).

Although the modeled prior compliance variable (money in the jar) had no statistically reliable effect, the trend for an interaction between solicitor and modeling conditions was quite apparent. Donations tended to increase with modeled prior compliance when children requested donations and to decrease when adults requested money. The combination of the most powerful influence agent (adult) and the most dramatic evidence of prior compliance (jar half filled with coins and dollar bills) produced the lowest absolute number of people who donated (33%). When a child asked for donations, however, this type of modeled prior compliance led to the largest absolute number of donations (77%).

Internal Pressures

Another source of possible reactance arousal in helping situations comes from internal pressures on the person to help. If a person is altruistically motivated or believes himself or herself to be the type of person who helps others, a request for help will create internal pressures to comply. These pressures threaten the person's freedom not to comply and arouse reactance. It is necessary to realize, however, that the importance of the freedoms to help and not to help will be differentially affected by altruistic motivation and beliefs about oneself. For the person who is altruistic, the freedom to help should be very important and the freedom not to help should not be so important. The importance of the freedom not to help, however, can be increased by situational factors. Having something to do at the time that help is needed, for example, would increase the importance of the freedom not to help.

If one considers only the internal tendency to help, one would simply predict that as the tendency increases, reactance arousal in response to pressure to help would decrease. For individuals who have a high tendency to help, increasing the pressure to help should increase the amount of help given. For individuals who have a low tendency to help, however, the freedom not to help should have greater importance. As the pressure on these individuals to help increases, greater reactance should be aroused and the resultant tendency to help should be relatively less, though helping may still increase with increasing pressure. Of course, an individual who had *no* interest in helping might well place considerable importance on the freedom not to help; such an individual would be expected to show increasing resistance to helping as pressure to help increased.

Individuals with a strong tendency to help would be expected to show reactance effects in response to pressure to help only if (a) the pressure to help were put in such a way that it implied threats to other, important freedoms, or (b) the freedom not to help was very important for situational reasons, as noted above. Unfortunately, there is little research evidence on these issues, and what there is does not provide support for the current analysis.

The study by Willis and Goethals (1973) mentioned earlier examined the relationship between an individual difference measure of social responsibility and reactance arousal. Several days prior to participating in the experiment, subjects completed the Allport, Vernon, and Lindzey (1960) Study of Values scale. Subjects were chosen who were either high or low on the Social Responsibility Subscale. Willis and Goethals hypothesized that people high on social responsibility would regard the freedom to help as very important and the freedom not to help as less important. For people low on social responsibility, the two freedoms should be more equivalent. It was expected, therefore, that as the external threat to the freedom increased in magnitude, subjects low in social responsibility should help less; subjects high on social responsibility were expected to help less only at the most extreme level of threat.

These hypotheses were not confirmed. Increasing threat to freedom did decrease agreement to donate funds to a local orphanage (see Table 7.6), and subjects high on social responsibility did agree to help more

TABLE 7.6
Percentages of Subjects Who Agreed to Donate[a]

	Social responsibility	
	High (%)	Low (%)
High threat (no model and model absent conditions combined)	65	30
Low threat (model present and model present-threat conditions combined)	95	55

[a] Adapted from Willis and Goethals, 1973.

than those low on social responsibility, but there was no significant interaction between magnitude of threat and subject type. Indeed, there was only the barest hint that the difference between high and low social responsibility subjects was less under high threat than under low.

These data, then, do not provide support for either our theoretical analysis nor for Willis and Goethals' specific predictions. Alternative explanations for negative results are, of course, usually legion and numerous ones are possible here: for example, insufficient threat to freedom created in the high threat condition; insufficient sensitivity of the social responsibility subscale as a measure of the importance of subjects' freedoms not to help in this *specific* instance. Since the logic of the theoretical analysis still appears compelling, we hope future research on these issues will provide more definitive evidence.

Internal versus External Locus of Need

One of the major problems in interpreting the helping literature, or at least some parts of it, in terms of reactance theory arises because of the loose fit between many of the experimental variables and the theoretical variables deemed important by the theory. It will not have escaped the diligent reader that a goodly portion of the previous discussion of the conditions under which helping will be reduced has had to focus on defining—or redefining—experimental manipulations in terms of theoretical variables. Nowhere is this problem more evident than in the helping studies that have investigated the differential effects of the attributed locus of the need for help.

A theoretical article by Berkowitz (1973) summarizes the evidence for proposing that if the person's need for help is outside his or her control, reactance arousal to the person's request for help will be reduced. Berkowitz suggests that people's tolerance for reactance is enhanced when the help request is a "proper" one from someone who is not responsible for needing help. When, however, the person's need for help is seen as his or her own fault, "it's as if subjects could succumb to the resentment created by the relatively great demand upon them when this demand wasn't entirely proper [Berkowitz, 1973, p. 313]."

It is not immediately apparent how one is to translate such terms as "tolerance, " "succumb," or "proper" into the language of reactance theory, and we would make a different theoretical argument to account for the findings cited by Berkowitz. Before detailing this alternative approach, however, let us review briefly the evidence in favor of the general proposition that when need is attributed to the person's own responsibility, helping will be reduced relative to when the need is attributed to external factors beyond the person's control.

The initial study examining this hypothesis was conducted by Schopler and Matthews (1965). Undergraduate male subjects participated in groups of four and were told that subjects would be assigned the roles of "director" or "associate" in a study of partnerships. Actually, after being placed in separate booths, all subjects were assigned to the director role. During the puzzle solving task that ensued, all subjects received a series of requests from their supposed associate partner for letters to use in the puzzles. Since subjects were paid for completed words and most of the requests were for letters that could be used by subjects in completing a word, complying with the requests was costly to the subjects. Half the subjects were led to believe that the request was generated by the experimenter ("the experimenter said I had to ask my director for letters"); the other half were led to believe the request was decided on by the other subject himself ("I figure my best bet is asking you"). A clear effect for locus of request was obtained. Help was more likely to be given when the need for help was created by the externally imposed directive of the experimenter.

A study by Berkowitz (1969) varied both the dependency of the person who needed help and the cause of the need. Again subjects participated in groups and, though led to believe that some would be workers and some supervisors, all were told they had been chosen by chance to be supervisors. To create the dependency conditions, subjects were told that the workers (but not the supervisor) were eligible for a prize, which would be given to the worker with the best grade. Grades were described as based 80% (high dependency), 50% (moderate dependency), or 20% (low dependency) on worker productivity. All subjects then read a request (supposedly from a worker) to contribute to a worker's productivity by making some of the designated items (paper pads). This message always said that the supposed worker was falling behind. Half of the subjects were told that the reason was internal ("I took it sort of easy during the first period"), while the other half were given an external cause ("the experimenter gave me the wrong paper").

Productivity data indicated that subjects worked harder to assist the person who needed help because of the experimenter's mistake. Although the interaction between locus of need and dependency was not significant, the means were examined. The only significant difference between external and internal locus occurred under conditions of high dependency. Moreover, there was a trend for helpfulness to increase with increasing dependency when the cause was external and to decrease with increasing dependency when the cause was internal.

Another study examining locus of need was conducted by Horowitz (1968). Subjects expected to make judgments about a stimulus person. This stimulus person was presented as a graduate student who, in addition to serving as the stimulus person for the judgment task, also was conducting his own research and needed subjects to participate. Half the subjects were told they had no choice and had to participate in the stimulus person's research in order to receive their experimental credit. The other half were told they had earned their experimental credit by participating in the judgment task and that it was completely up to them whether or not they participated in the second study.

The manipulation of locus of dependency involved two parts. First, subjects received a personality profile of the stimulus person (supposedly for the judgment task). The externally dependent stimulus person was described as "characteristically independent and strong," while the internally dependent stimulus person was described as "characteristically dependent and weak." Second, the externally dependent stimulus person described his need for subjects as stemming from a new and unforeseen time limit set by his professor. The internally dependent stimulus person said he needed subjects because of "unfortunate planning" and his underestimation of how many subjects he would need. Subjects were then asked how much time they were willing to spend participating in the second experiment; possible options ranged from 0 to 8 hours. Analysis of the (transformed) time-offered data revealed a significant interaction between choice and locus of dependency. Under no choice conditions, subjects offered to spend more time in the second experiment when the cause of the dependency was external. Under choice conditions, however, subjects offered to spend more time when the cause of the dependency was internal.

It is important to note that all three of these studies confound their manipulation of locus of need with other impactful psychological variables. In the Schopler and Matthews study, the internally dependent associate made it clear that he could get the materials he needed from either "a random pool" or from the subject. The externally dependent associate emphatically stated that he had no choice about the matter; getting help from the subject was " the only way" for him to complete his work. Internally dependent associates thus indicated that they had greater resources and were less dependent on the subject than the externally dependent associate. Subjects in this experiment may well have wondered why the internally dependent associate chose to ask them for assistance. With the externally dependent associate, there was no need for this question to arise. An alternative description of the manipulation of locus of need in this study is, then, that when subjects were presented with a request for help, the motive for that request was either clear (externally dependent) or unclear (internally dependent).

The studies by Berkowitz and Horowitz also contain a major confound. In Berkowitz's experiment, the person with an externally caused need for help is presented in a positive light as the victim of another's mistake. The internally dependent person is presented as lazy. This association between evaluation and locus of dependency is even more striking in Horowitz's study. There, the externally dependent person is described as independent and strong, and is, again, the victim—this time of another's unforeseen decision. The internally dependent person, on the other hand, is described as dependent and weak, as well as appearing stupid. For these two studies, it is perfectly possible to translate external versus internal locus of dependency into the good guys versus the bad ones.

This kind of confound between locus of causality and evaluation of the person who needs help is also found in a more recent study by Benson and Catt (1978). The occasion for soliciting help was a door-to-door appeal campaign for the United Way. In the internal locus of need condition, the person asking for contributions stated that, "It's true; most of those who receive this help have themselves to blame, but even so . . . " In the external locus of need condition, the person soliciting funds stated, "You know, most of those who receive this help are innocent victims. No one asks to be crippled or blind or mentally retarded." This seems a very clear example of presenting some good people to help versus some bad ones. In this study, dependency was varied from high ("they need your help desperately") to low ("they could use your support"). Reason for giving was also varied. Some residents were told, "It's really your responsibility to help." Others were informed, "I know it would make you feel good . . . " The dependent measure was the amount of money donated. Although level of dependency had no effect on contributions, external dependency and the feel-good rationale both increased contributions. Additionally, there was a significant interaction between these last two variables, such that the combination of external locus of dependency and a feel-good rationale led to significantly larger contributions than did the other three conditions.

One additional study is relevant to the present discussion. In the Worchel, Andreoli, and Archer (1976) study mentioned previously (Chapter 5), a modified version of the Brehm and Cole (1966) favor-doing paradigm was used. Subjects for whom the freedom to be objective (and thus not obligated to the other subject) was important and for whom the attribution of favor-doing was to the unique interaction between themselves and the other subject rated the confederate as least attractive and were least likely to help (see Table 5.5 for helping data).

The Worchel *et al.* (1976) study is particularly relevant to the present discussion because it suggests a theoretical rationale for why certain causal attributions for the dependency of another person might be more reactance arousing than others. In the Worchel *et al.* study, attributions were clearly made for all conditions (except the no attribution control group) and, in the condition where helping was reduced, no derogation of the needy person was conveyed in the experimental presentation of this person. To the contrary, subjects were led to believe they had a "special" bond with the confederate in the unique interaction condition and, yet, when an important freedom was threatened, considerable reactance was aroused.

The notion of a bond with another person should remind us of the earlier discussion of committed relationships. We pointed out that committed relationships carry implications for future behaviors and that a threat to a present freedom can imply potential threats to future freedoms. We would suggest, then, that even though subjects in the unique interaction condition were not instructed to interact further with the confederate, they may well have perceived some possibility of this happening. In fact, they may have felt pressured to continue the relationship with the confederate. They had received a favor from this person, the experimenter told them they had a "special relationship," and now they had a chance to be helpful in turn.

It would seem quite possible that subjects in the unique interaction condition anticipated that they might get to know the confederate better and interact with her after the experiment was over. When the importance of the freedom to be unobligated was low, these conditions produced highly favorable evaluations and a great deal of helping. When, however, the importance of the freedom was high, the resultant reactance arousal led to relatively unfavorable ratings and little help.

We would propose, then, that locus of need is not, in and of itself, relevant to reactance theory. At times, however, locus of need will serve as a carrier variable for more theoretically relevant variables. In helping situations, the most clearly discernible variable may be implications of future threats to future freedoms. In the Schopler and Matthews study, for example, the ambiguity of the internally dependent associate's behavior may have implied to subjects that this person was capable of all kinds of freedom-threatening behaviors. His request for help was not justified by his situation, and so the determining and limiting causes of his behavior could not be assessed. Similarly, the "you're responsible" rationale in the Benson and Catt study may have reduced helping because it implied that people who gave to this appeal should give to other appeals as well. The "feel good" rationale does not appear to carry this kind of implication. There are many ways to make oneself feel good, and helping out "those less fortunate" is only one.

Moreover, even though the locus of need variable is confounded with evaluations of the other in the Berkowitz and Horowitz studies, implications for future freedoms may have varied as well. A person who is lazy and gets behind, as in the Berkowitz study, is more likely to need further help than is someone who is victimized by a presumably rare mistake. A person who is dependent, as in the Horowitz study, is more likely to need a lot of help. Internal locus of dependency, therefore, may be associated with greater dependency—not greater dependency in terms of amount of help presently needed, but greater dependency in terms of future frequency of needing help. Theoretically, the former kind of dependency creates reactance by making it hard to refuse the request and thus by increasing the magnitude of threat. The latter kind of dependency creates reactance by implying possible threats to future freedoms, and, thus, implicitly, threatens a greater number of freedoms.

It could be that in the real world there is a natural association between being responsible for one's plight and threatening future freedoms not to help. The two, however, are not necessarily associated. For example, if a person expects to be in a given situation with a number of other people for a period of time but have no contact with these people otherwise, a situational attribution for the need for help should threaten more freedoms by implication than personally attributed dependency.

Our present analysis closely parallels that made by Monson and Snyder (1977) in their discussion of the actor-observer difference. As noted previously (see Chapter 2), Monson and Snyder argue that, depending on the circumstances, either a dispositional or a situational attribution could represent a greater threat to freedom. We believe that the same point applies to the relationship between locus of need and the freedom not to help.

Theoretical Issues

The studies cited throughout this chapter would appear to offer ample evidence that some need situations can arouse reactance and reduce the amount of help that is offered. A few cautionary notes are, however, in order. First, reactance cannot and should not be expected to explain all reductions in helping. Sometimes other explanations are considerably more parsimonious. In the Benson and Catt study, for example, the finding that "internal causation" reduced helping relative to "external causation" would appear to have little to do with reactance. Implications for future freedoms would not seem to have differed between the two conditions, but evaluations of the potential recipients of donations differed dramatically. It would be a strange world indeed if blameless victims did not receive more aid than those who are themselves at fault, and no appeal to reactance theory is necessary to explain such findings.

Second, if the theory is to be used to predict or explain the data, the operations must be clearly and explicitly linked to theoretical variables. The freedom must be specified as well as the threat and any related variables, such as implications for future freedoms and magnitude of threat, also need to be clearly defined in terms of the theory.

The Horowitz study provides a good example of what can be learned from careful analysis of experimental operations. It will be remembered that an interaction between locus of need and choice was obtained, and, to assist in the present discussion, these data are presented in Table 7.7. These findings have been viewed as contradicting those (see Table 7.3) obtained by Jones (1970). If, for the moment, we assume that Jones' high dependency condition is analogous to Horowitz's internal locus condition (although dependency in the first is defined in terms of present assistance needed, whereas in the latter study, potential frequency of need is implied), the contradiction becomes apparent. Under high choice, Jones obtained equivalent amounts of helping, while, under choice, Horowitz obtained more help for greater depen-

TABLE 7.7
Amount of Help Given[a]

	Internal locus of need	External locus of need
No choice	3.04[b]	3.77
Choice	4.58	4.11

[a] From Horowitz, I. A. Effect of choice and locus of dependence on helping behavior. *Journal of Personality and Social Psychology*, 1968, *8*, 373–376, Table 2, p. 375. Copyright 1968 by the American Psychological Association. Reprinted by permission.

[b] Help given by endorsing one point on a nine-point scale. 1 = no help; 9 = eight hours of participation in the second experiment. Data are square root transformations of helping scores.

dency. Conversely, under low choice conditions, Jones obtained more help with greater dependency; under no choice conditions, Horowitz obtained less help for more dependency.

This apparent contradiction is especially confusing in that Horowitz's manipulation of no choice seems more powerful and less ambiguous than Jones' manipulation of low choice. As we noted previously, Jones did not really create no choice or even low choice about helping per se. He did create no choice about coming back for a future experiment and, as we have hypothesized, this could have created low importance of the freedom not to help for a substantial period (i.e., more than 5 minutes) of time.

Horowitz, however, instructed subjects that they had either no choice or complete choice about participating in a second experiment. Unfortunately, he then proceeded to eliminate this difference between conditions.

After listening to the tape recording subjects were asked to indicate on a 9-point scale how much help, in terms of spending time in sensory deprivation, they were willing to give. Category 1 gave the subjects the option of not participating in the actual experiment by writing a few comments to help the dependent person improve his request so that it might be more effective. This was essentially a *no-help* category. Subjects in the no-choice condition could of course fulfill their obligations by choosing Category 1. [Horowitz, 1968, p. 375].

We discover, then, that there are no no-choice subjects. All subjects were given the choice of whether or not to help by participating in the second experiment. If we presume that all subjects came to the experiment expecting to participate in only one experiment, then some subjects had their expected freedom to participate in only one more strongly threatened (although *not* irrevocably eliminated) than other subjects, and this should have aroused greater reactance. Furthermore, the more dependent person (internal locus of need) should have aroused greater reactance than the less dependent one (external locus of need). We would expect, therefore, that opposition to providing help would be greater for no choice than for choice subjects and for internal locus subjects than external locus subjects. Moreover, the combination of no choice and internal locus might be expected to generate the most resistance. Horowitz's data on amount of help offered only partially support these reactance theory predictions. Interestingly, however, the number of subjects who endorsed Category 1 and thus refused to help are entirely consistent with this analysis (see Table 7.8).

TABLE 7.8
Percentages of Subjects Who Refused to Help[a]

	Internal locus of need (%)	External locus of need (%)
No choice	43	12
Choice	20	3

[a] Data from Horowitz, 1968.

Reactance to Being Helped

If reactance arousal can be created by requests for help and help thereby reduced, what about those situations in which someone receives help from another? Will receiving help create reactance? And if it does, what might be the attitudinal and behavioral consequences? In this section, we shall briefly describe several studies that we consider especially relevant to this issue. We shall not attempt an exhaustive survey of the literature on recipients' responses to being helped and for a more thorough review refer the reader to other sources (e.g., Fisher, DePaulo, & Nadler, 1981; Gergen, 1974).

First, of course, the experiments by Brehm and Cole (1966) and Worchel, Andreoli, and Archer (1976) demonstrated that when a person is presented with an unexpected favor under conditions where it is important to be unobligated to the favor-doer, the tendency to help the favor-doer on a subsequent task is reduced. These studies have already been discussed in some detail (see Chapter 5).

Two studies by Gergen and his colleagues also suggest that receiving help can, under some circumstances, be viewed unfavorably. Gergen, Ellsworth, Maslach, and Seipel (1975) report that Swedish, American, and Japanese subjects all showed little attraction to a donor who provided them with resources without any stated obligation. Since favors do create some felt obligation to reciprocate, we would suggest that a favor not accompanied by an overtly stated obligation threatens, by implication, numerous freedoms. Without an overtly stated obligation, one does not know what one will be called upon to do to discharge one's obligation.

In another examination of the reciprocity norm, Morse, Gergen, Peele, and van Ryneveld (1977) had subjects receive help that was either expected or not. This help was presented as either violating normative standards or not. Subjects' reciprocity behavior was determined solely by expectations. The unexpected favor led to more reciprocal helping than the expected one. Attractiveness of the helper, however, was determined by the interaction between expectations and normative violations. The helper was rated as least attractive by those subjects who received an unexpected favor that violated normative standards.

It seems reasonable to us to assume that subjects in the unexpected–norm violated condition felt the most obligation to return the favor. The unexpected favor may have suggested to subjects that there was something unique about their interaction with the helper (Worchel, Andreoli, & Archer, 1976), and the favor that violated normative standards should have been perceived as more costly to the helper. While we would expect reactance arousal to be heightened in this condition, we are not particularly surprised that reciprocal helping was not reduced. Normative pressures to reciprocate favors can be very strong, and it sometimes takes very high levels of reactance arousal to act against these pressures. Attraction to another is not, however, subject to these strong normative standards; it is our own business whom we like. The reduction in attractiveness for the helper in the unexpected–norm violated condition is consistent with our hypothesis about reactance arousal in this situation. This reduced attractiveness also implies that if future interactions occurred between these recipients and the helper, the recipients might well be less helpful on future occasions.

An earlier study by Schopler and Thompson (1968) also demonstrated that the effect of a favor depends on the appropriateness of the conditions under which it occurs. Female subjects were presented with a flower in a formal or informal interview, and were subsequently given an opportunity to help the interviewer who had presented the flower. Compared to subjects who received no flower, those who received the flower under appropriate (informal) conditions offered more help, whereas those who received the flower under inappropriate (formal) conditions offered less help. The psychological effects of receiving a favor under inappropriate conditions in this study would appear similar to the unexpected–norm violated condition in the Morse *et al.* study. Subjects may have felt more pressured to reciprocate and, because the formal interviewer's behavior was unexpected, future freedoms may have been threatened by implication.

If there is the possibility that receiving help can threaten freedom and create reactance, then perhaps self-initiated help would be better than other-initiated help. This hypothesis has been explored by Gross and Piliavin and their colleagues. Let us first describe two of their studies relevant to this topic and then discuss the theoretical issues that are raised.

In a study by Broll, Gross, and Piliavin (1974), subjects were instructed to solve what was actually an insoluble problem. Half the subjects were told they could obtain help by requesting it; the other half were offered help every 8 min. The amount of help received (i.e., number of requests or number of acceptances) was the major dependent measure. The data from this study (as well as from three pilot studies cited by the authors) indicated that more help was obtained when help was offered than when it had to be requested.

Piliavin and Gross (1977; also reported in Gross, Wallston, & Piliavin, 1979) investigated the effects of self-initiated versus other-initiated help in the real world. Subjects in their research were women family heads who were new admissions to the Minneapolis Aid to Families with Dependent Children (AFDC). Clients were placed in one of four conditions. Combined services clients received social services and income maintenance supervision from the same worker. Separated services clients received these two types of services from two different workers. How clients obtained services was also varied. Some clients were told they needed to initiate service requests themselves; others were visited by a worker at periodic intervals. It should be noted, however, that the manipulation of this last variable was rather weak. Clients in the client-initiated condition were also sent postcards reminding them of the worker's availability, and clients in the worker-initiated condition were told they could ask for services at any time.

Piliavin and Gross examined the number of requests for new financial and nonfinancial services that occurred during worker–client contacts. Client requests for new services tended to be higher in the combined services condition (requests for new financial services were significantly higher) and in the worker-initiated condition (requests for new nonfinancial services were significantly higher). Clients receiving separated services on a client-initiated basis had the least positive view of the service worker's helpfulness, and clients receiving separated services felt they did not see the social services worker often enough.

In considering both the laboratory research and field project described above, it is crucial to examine the importance of the freedoms involved. In the Broll et al. study, subjects had the freedoms to refuse or accept the offer of help. The freedom to accept help was important because help could enable them to solve the experimental problem. The freedom to reject help, in this context, was of trivial importance. An offer of help, therefore, threatened only an unimportant freedom, and little reactance arousal would be expected. Certainly not enough reactance arousal should have been generated to cause subjects to act against their own interests by refusing help.

In the field study by Piliavin and Gross (1977), a similar analysis can be applied to the worker-initiated versus client-initiated services conditions. When an individual has a great need for assistance (as presumably these women had), the freedom to reject help is trivial—and, at some psychological level, it may not even exist. There is thus no reason to believe that significant reactance arousal would be created by worker-initiated contacts, nor that the clients would attempt to preserve their remaining freedoms by not requesting new services. Moreover, from a practical point of view, it is easier to ask for help when someone shows up on your doorstep, and it may be psychologically easier as well.

Sheer practical utility would also seem the most likely explanation for the advantage that combined services showed over separated ones. In combined services, the single-service worker does become a more powerful figure and one, therefore, more potentially reactance arousing. In order to arouse reactance, however, an important freedom must be threatened. If only the trivial freedom to reject the assistance that one badly needs is threatened, even a very powerful figure will arouse little reactance. Moreover, since it is easier to deal with one individual than with two, it is not surprising that combined services were utilized more and liked more than separated ones.

In conclusion, then, we do think it is possible that offers of help can create reactance. In order to predict the magnitude of this arousal, it is necessary to consider the importance of the freedom that is threatened (as well as the magnitude of the threat). In order to predict the behavioral consequences of any reactance that is aroused, it is necessary to consider the costs to the person of restorative action. Only when significant reactance is aroused in a situation where restoration of freedom would not be too costly would one expect behavioral effects such as refusing to reciprocate the help one had received, refusing to accept the help one was offered, or preserving other freedoms by not asking for any additional assistance.

SUMMARY

The social power of one person over another depends on factors such as prestige, expertness, and trustworthiness, and on the ability of the power figure to reward compliance or punish noncompliance. Because pressure due to any of these factors can increase the difficulty of exercising a freedom, any of them can cause reactance. In order for promises of reward or threats of punishment to be effective, there must also be the ability of the power figure to observe compliance or noncompliance. In contrast, the first three factors—prestige, expertness, and trustworthiness—do not require surveillance of compliance in order to have the capability of threatening freedom. The experimental literature reveals that figures who have authority or prestige do create reactance when they make freedom-threatening statements.

Where a power figure has the ability to survey compliance or noncompliance, whether noncompliance (overt reactance) will occur will depend on the importance of the freedom being threatened and the importance of the rewards and punishments that the influence agent can bring to bear against the target person. When an unimportant freedom is involved, reactance arousal should be minimal and overt opposition should not occur. When, however, a freedom of at least moderate importance is threatened, surveillance accompanied by unimportant rewards and punishments may increase overt opposition, while surveillance accompanied by important rewards and punishments may decrease overt opposition, though still increasing covert reactance arousal. This rather complex analysis of the effects of social power on reactance appears supported by a review of a number of studies in this area.

The formation of a close interpersonal relationship can be partly understood in terms of reactance theory. If one has the freedom to form a close relationship with another, events that increase the difficulty of exercising this freedom will tend to increase one's motivation to do so as well as the perceived attractiveness of the other person. One possible kind of threat to the freedom to form a relationship would be the other's playing "hard to get". Although research on this phenomenon has failed to demonstrate increased attraction when the other plays hard to get, other research, some based explicitly on reactance theory, has found increased attraction when external events interfere with the relationship.

When two people have a close interpersonal relationship, reactance theory suggests a number of important considerations for understanding their relationship. A close relationship implies commitments that affect what freedoms will exist or how important these freedoms will be. A close relationship also implies a broad and continuing relationship, which means that a threat to freedom can easily imply threats to other and future freedoms. Hence, the potential for reactance arousal in a close interpersonal relationship is both narrowed by the commitment and enhanced by the potential for implied threats to freedom. Although there has been no reactance-based research on individuals involved in long-term committed relationships, research in which subjects anticipate future interaction with another person has shown both the reactance-reduction and reactance-enhancement effects of this mild form of commitment to another person.

Another social behavior affected by reactance is the tendency to help another person. Where the freedom not to help is important, pressure to help will threaten that freedom and thereby reduce the consequent amount of help given. Extensive research has shown that help may be reduced by explicit pressure to help, high dependency for help, modeling help, and potential future need for help. Research has also shown that attributions about the helping situation will qualify resistance to giving help.

When a person receives help, reactance arousal will be determined by the importance of the freedom that is threatened and the costs of restorative action. Only when an important freedom is threatened and restorative action would not be too costly would one expect significant reactance effects such as refusing to reciprocate the help one had received, refusing to accept help one was offered, or preserving other freedoms by not asking for additional assistance. These premises appear consistent with both laboratory and applied research in this area.

CHAPTER 8

Reactance and the Decision-Making Process

Although many threats to freedom will come from sources outside the individual, threats to freedom may also be self-imposed. In the Brehm and Rozen (1971) study described earlier (see Chapter 2), the threat to preferring one of the old choice alternatives was created by the person's attraction toward the new alternative. Introducing the new alternative into the environment was necessary to create the threat, but the actual threat to freedom came from an internal source: the person's own motivation to choose the alternative that was most attractive.

The simple act of making a decision between different alternatives is sufficient, theoretically, to arouse reactance. As a person approaches a decision, a preference for a particular alternative and the implied choice of that alternative threaten the freedom to have the other alternative(s), and the freedom to reject the preferred alternative. Because the reactance aroused by these threats is directed toward having the less preferred alternative(s) and rejecting the preferred one, total motivation as well as the consequent attractiveness of the alternatives is modified. Initially less preferred alternatives will become more attractive, while the initially preferred alternative will become less attractive. Indeed, if the alternatives were initially close together in attractiveness, a less attractive one could become more attractive than the one initially preferred.

That people may choose what was intially a nonpreferred alternative has been demonstrated in a number of studies (e.g., Festinger & Walster in Festinger, 1964; Girard, 1977; Rodrigues, 1970). Although these choice reversals are consistent with the reactance theory analysis, none of these studies manipulated variables specific to the theory and, thus, none of them provides specific support of this particular theoretical approach.

More relevant to the present interpretation of prechoice convergence effects are those studies that have used theoretically relevant variables. In the following studies two such variables were involved: magnitude of threat and importance of freedom. We shall discuss each of these variables in turn, along with the empirical examinations that bear on them.

Magnitude of Threat

Two studies by Linder and his colleagues investigated magnitude of threat as a function of time to the decision. Although the results of these two studies were quite similar, the earlier study by Linder and Crane (1970) confounded amount of time until the decision had to be made with amount of information that subjects might expect to obtain about the decision alternatives. In our discussion, therefore, we will describe only the study by Linder, Wortman, and Brehm (1971) in which this confound was eliminated.

Female undergraduate subjects in this study expected to be interviewed by one of two possible interviewers, both described as graduate students in clinical psychology. Subjects were given written descriptions of the two possible interviewers, and they also were told they would have a 3-min chat with them. To create the impression of only a short time remaining until the decision had to be made, half of the subjects expected the chat to take place momentarily. The other half of the subjects were told one of the interviewers was "still tied up," but that the chat could take place in about 7 min. All subjects were then asked to rate how much they would like to be interviewed by each of the two interviewers. It was clear to subjects that these ratings were not equivalent to making a decision, since all subjects expected to talk with the interviewers before making a final choice. A third group of subjects did not expect to be interviewed, but simply read the written materials and rated the interviewers.

In both the Linder and Crane (1970) and Linder et al. (1971) studies, it was hypothesized that the threat posed by an initial preference for one choice alternative should increase as the decision time grew nearer. The greater threat produced by the nearer decision reflects the increasing implications that preferences start to have for overt action. When a decision is a long time off, an initial preference for one alternative threatens the freedom *to prefer* the other alternative, but that's all. When, however, the decision is close at hand, preference for one alternative implies a possible choice of that alternative and threatens both the freedom to prefer the other alternative and the freedom to actually choose that other alternative. Thus, the threat posed by a preference when a decision is about to be made threatens more freedoms (preference and choice) than a preference when a decision is a long way off, and, by implication, threatens a more important freedom (choice as opposed to preference) as well.

The results from the Linder *et al.* study (and from the earlier study by Linder and Crane) were consistent with this hypothesis. Absolute attractiveness differences between the two possible interviewers declined as the time subjects anticipated having before the decision became shorter (see Table 8.1). These findings were replicated by Carver and Scheier (1981) who used the same procedures, but also divided their subjects into high and low private self-consciousness (see Chapter 9 for a more extensive discussion of this individual difference variable). Carver and Scheier obtained a main effect for threat such that high threat (3 min until the decision) subjects rated the two interviewers as closer together in attractiveness than did low threat subjects (10 min until decision time). A marginally significant interaction between threat and private self-consciousness was also obtained and is discussed in Chapter 9.

Importance of Freedom

A study by Wicklund (1970) also examined the effects of magnitude of threat on predecision convergence but used a very different way of

TABLE 8.1
Absolute Value of the Difference between the Ratings of the Two Interviewers[a]

No decision condition	10.9
10 min until the decision	12.8
3 min until the decision	7.4

[a] Data from Linder, Wortman, and Brehm, 1971.

varying threat magnitude. Theoretically, any obstacle that makes it harder for a person to obtain a choice alternative that he or she expects to have the freedom to obtain will constitute a threat to that person's freedom. Obstacles can be physical, psychological, or financial. Wicklund employed a financial barrier and hypothesized that making it more costly to obtain the initially nonpreferred choice alternative should increase prechoice convergence. Wicklund also raised an important theoretical issue concerning the effects of importance of freedom on prechoice convergence, and we shall discuss that issue after describing the procedures used in his study.

Subjects in this study initially rated the attractiveness of eight consumer items. Half of the subjects (aware condition) were told that the experimenter had selected out two of the items and that the subject would choose one of them as his gift for participating. Subjects in the unaware condition were told that two choice items would be selected randomly at the end of the experiment and they would choose their gift from between these two. All subjects were then told that two items (one of which was always the lower rated of the two choice alternatives for aware condition subjects and an equivalently rated item for unaware condition subjects) were subject to a state tax. The amount of this tax was $.75 (high threat) or $.20 (low threat), and subjects were informed that if either of these items was chosen as a gift, they would have to pay the tax. Subjects in the no fee conditions were not informed of any state tax. All subjects then rerated all the items and were allowed to alter their ratings of individual items throughout a 15-min period.

Wicklund hypothesized that the larger the financial barrier (i.e., the fee) attached to the initially nonpreferred alternative, the greater predecisional reactance should be aroused and the greater should be predecisional convergence. This hypothesis, however, applies only to subjects in the aware condition, who knew that one of their choice alternatives had a fee attached to it. Since unaware subjects did not know when they made their ratings what two choice alternatives would be selected for them, the fee poses only a possible, not an actual, threat to decision freedom. Reactance arousal and, therefore, predecision convergence should be considerably less for these subjects than for ones in the aware condition.

The data from this study are quite complex. Wicklund reports attractiveness ratings obtained immediately after the experimental manipulations and at the end of the 15-min rating period. Data are also reported in terms of a discrepancy between the higher and lower rated decision alternatives (i.e., actual choice alternatives for aware subjects; items with ratings yoked to these for unaware subjects) as well as in terms of changes across ratings for the initially lower-rated alternative. Fortunately, there are two theoretical principles that inform us of the most appropriate data for a test of the hypothesis. First, as in the studies by Linder and his associates, reactance effects should be maximized as the time for making the decision draws nearer. Subjects in Wicklund's study were kept informed of the amount of time left in the rating period and presumably expected to make a decision between their two alternatives (either already designated or to be randomly selected) at the end of this period. Final ratings would thus appear more appropriate for a test of the hypothesis than earlier ones.

Second, Wicklund makes a rather compelling case that reactance arousal should affect the ratings of the lower-rated alternative more than those of the initially higher-rated alternative. This argument runs as follows. The preference for the initially higher-rated alternative threatens two freedoms: the freedom to reject this alternative and the freedom to have the other alternative. Since both alternatives are relatively attractive, the importance of the freedom to reject either one of them should not be very important, whereas the importance of the freedom to have either one of them should be fairly great. Thus, the importance of the freedom to have the initially nonpreferred alternative should be greater than the importance of the freedom to reject the initially preferred alternative. We would expect, therefore, that greater reactance arousal should occur in regard to the former freedom and that reactance would be reflected by increased perceived attractiveness of the initially nonpreferred alternative. This line of reasoning suggests that the most appropriate data for a test of the hypothesis would come from changes (from initial to final) in the ratings of the initially nonpreferred alternative.

These data are displayed in Table 8.2. The general pattern is consistent with that predicted by the theory. Attractiveness of the initially nonpreferred alternative increased as a function of barrier strength for aware subjects, but decreased for unaware subjects. While the barrier versus awareness interaction was not significant, the expected difference between aware and unaware subjects is significant in the high fee condition.[1] These results, then, reflect the joint effect of an external threat (the imposed fee) and a self-imposed threat (the implication of preference for choice.)

---

[1] It should also be noted that the no fee condition in which subjects are aware is a conceptual replication of the studies discussed above in which predecisional convergence was demonstrated. The Wicklund study obtained a trend toward convergence in the preference ratings of the choice alternatives, but this effect was not statistically reliable.

TABLE 8.2
**Rating Changes (Final–Initial) of Initially
Nonpreferred Choice Alternative**[a]

	Aware	Unaware
High fee	.40	−11.47
Low fee	−.27	−5.07
No fee	−1.73	.53

[a] From Wicklund, R. A. Prechoice preference reversal as a result of threat to decision freedom. *Journal of Personality and Social Psychology*, 1970, 14, 8–17, Table 2, p. 14. Copyright 1970 by the American Psychological Association. Reprinted by permission.

These results also bear on a more general theoretical issue raised earlier (Chapter 2) concerning the effect of information gain on a preexistent freedom. The question raised was whether or not new information that makes the selection of an alternative more difficult constitutes a threat to freedom. The answer provided by the Wicklund experiment is affirmative; when subjects learned of a fee that was attached to their nonpreferred choice alternative, their evaluation of that alternative was high relative to evaluations by subjects who did not know whether any of their choice alternatives would have a fee attached.

Decisions Involving Multiple Choice Alternatives

In all of the studies described above, there were only two choice alternatives, and the individual could have only one of them. Sometimes, however, we are confronted with a set of choice alternatives that include more than two items, but from which we can still have only one. How would reactance arousal created by predecisional preferences affect our perceptions of the attractiveness of the alternatives in this kind of situation?

When we are confronted with a choice among multiple alternatives, any preference for one of them threatens our freedoms to have any of the rest, as well as the freedom to reject the initially preferred alternative. In the previous instance of a two-alternative situation, we followed Wicklund's proposal that the freedom to have the nonpreferred alternative will be more important than the freedom to reject the initially preferred alternative, and, thus, that reactance will have the effect primarily of increasing the perceived attractiveness of the initially nonpreferred alternative. If all the alternatives were reasonably attractive, this reasoning could be applied to the multiple-alternative situation, and we would expect that the nonpreferred alternatives would all tend to increase in attractiveness in proportion to their initial level of attractiveness. The initial level of attractiveness, of course, determines the importance of the freedom of having that alternative.

In addition, however, the choice of one from among several alternatives can arouse more reactance in regard to the initially preferred alternative. This is because the tendency to choose a single alternative simultaneously threatens the freedoms represented by all of the other alternatives. Thus, in the case of multiple alternatives where only one may be chosen, we can expect that the initially preferred alternative will become less attractive. This effect should occur along with the previously noted tendency for initially less preferred alternatives to increase in attractiveness.

A study by Brehm, Jones, and Smith (1975) examined the effect on attractiveness of multiple alternatives when only one alternative can be chosen. In a series of three studies, college students were asked to rate the attractiveness of twenty different books divided into two lists of ten each. Subjects were informed that for their participation in the ratings, they would later be able to choose one book from one of the lists; they were also informed, before rating any of the books, which of the two lists they would be able to choose from. Half the subjects were allowed to choose from one list and half from the other. In all three studies it was found that the item rated highest on the no-choice list tended to be rated no better than second highest when it was on the choice list. With the data of all three studies combined, it was found that the first and second ranked items on no-choice lists were reversed in ranking when they were choice items by 57% of the subjects. In general, the pattern of ratings from the three studies was as predicted from the analysis just described. The most attractive book under no-choice conditions was clearly less attractive under choice conditions, while there was a slight (nonreliable) tendency for the second-, third-, and fourth-ranked items under no choice conditions to be rated as more attractive under choice conditions.

MILLS' CERTAINTY THEORY

The studies we have described appear to provide good evidence of the usefulness of reactance theory in accounting for predecision reversals; yet they should not be taken to suggest that prechoice convergence appears prior to every decision. The theory does specify that a preference for one alternative will threaten one's freedoms to obtain the other alternative(s), but whether or not sufficient reactance is aroused to produce convergence will depend on numerous specific factors about the decision (such as the attractiveness of the alternatives and the time until the decision has to be made).

Another factor that would counter tendencies toward convergence is described by Mills (1968) in his theory of choice certainty. Mills proposes that people want to be certain that the action they take is the best of all posssible options. If the need for certainty about one's actions is high, then the person would be best served during the predecisional phase by divergence between choice alternatives. Divergence should reduce uncertainty; convergence would increase it. Research by Mills and O'Neal (Mills & O'Neal, 1971; O'Neal, 1971; O'Neal & Mills, 1969) has supported the hypothesis that decision divergence may occur prior to a choice.

From our point of view, there is no need to regard these two theoretical perspectives as competing theories. Rather, both may be applicable. The motive to preserve freedom and the motive to reduce uncertainty would seem psychologically independent and may well be heightened by different circumstances. Up until quite recently, however, there has been no effort to try to specify the different situations in which one motive might be expected to be stronger than another.

Two experiments reported in a paper by Brounstein, Ostrove, and Mills (1979) offer the first empirical evidence on this issue. Brounstein et al. hypothesized that prechoice convergence may have been obtained in the two studies by Linder and his colleagues (as well, presumably, as in the replication by Carver and Scheier) because the prechoice ratings made by subjects in these experiments were perceived by subjects as likely to be seen by the experimenter. "This could have made the subjects feel that expressing a preference for one alternative would commit them to choosing it, for to do otherwise would leave the experimenter with the impression they were inconsistent or flighty. Such an impression should be expected to be stronger, the shorter the time from the preference to the choice [Brounstein et al., 1979, p. 1958]."

Before presenting the data obtained in Brounstein et al.'s studies, we need to consider their hypothesis regarding reactance theory. In none of the studies using the Linder paradigm was any emphasis placed on the experimenters' seeing the subjects' ratings. It could be, however, that subjects assumed that they would see them, since there also was no reason given why they should not. On the other hand, there is little reason to believe that subjects were afraid to change their preference because they worried about the experimenter's impression of them. Subjects had a perfectly legitimate excuse for changing their opinions—they all anticipated obtaining additional information during their talks with the interviewers prior to making a choice. Also, any concerns about being perceived as "flighty" could just as well have led subjects to want to appear decisive and, therefore, to rate the interviewers divergently.

Even though we cannot agree with the exact reasoning of Brounstein et al., there is a possibility that public expression of one's preferences might increase reactance arousal. A public expression is more of a commitment—not only to the experimenter for possible impression management concerns but to oneself. If subjects did assume the experimenter would see the ratings, they may have taken them more seriously, and awareness of their preferences' implications for future action could have become more salient. Moreover, the accuracy of their ratings could have become more important. In this way, subjects' freedoms to choose or reject either interviewer would be more important, and the threat to freedom posed by a preference would be relatively high.

After suggesting that public expression of preference increases reactance arousal, Brounstein et al. go on to hypothesize that private expression of preference will reflect the motive to reduce uncertainty and produce divergence between the choice alternatives. While predecisional divergence had been shown in the studies by Mills and O'Neal cited above, this research had always used a number of evaluative ratings and had never obtained a direct "bold, blatant discrimination, as in the studies by Linder et al [p. 1958]." Interestingly, in these studies, subjects also had given their rankings to the experimenter. Brounstein et al. imply that subjects in the choice uncertainty studies still felt their rankings were private because several dimensions were involved and, presumably, this would make it more difficult for the experimenter to keep track of their preferences.

In their first experiment, Brounstein et al. used a modified version of the Linder et al. procedure. Subjects anticipated either choosing or not between two interviewers, and those in the predecision condition expected about 3 min to elapse between their ratings of the interviewers and their choice. Two distinct departures from the Linder et al. procedures should be noted. First, subjects were not led to expect to have a chance to talk with the two interviewers before choosing. Second, the measure of attractiveness was taken in a very different fashion from that used previously. Subjects were shown an elaborate machine that was supposedly a new measuring device. They were then told it was broken, but the experimenter suggested that the subjects could use their feelings about the two interviewers as a practice trial while the machine was being fixed. Subjects in the public condition turned the dial to the appropriate rating for each interviewer and read the number aloud to the experimenter. Subjects in the private condition were just told to turn the dial. The experimenter sat behind a partition and supposedly could not see what the subject did; in actuality, a dial attached to the subject's dial allowed him to record the subject's response.

As in the Linder *et al.* studies, the dependent variable was the absolute difference between the ratings of the two interviewers. A significant interaction between type of assessment (public vs. private) and decisional phase (predecision vs. no decision) was obtained. Individual comparisons revealed that while subjects in the public condition tended to rate the two interviewers more similarly in the 3-min predecisional condition than in the no decision condition, this difference was not significant (see Table 8.3). In the private condition,

TABLE 8.3
Means of the Absolute Difference in the Ratings of the Interviewers[a]

	Experiment I	
	Decision conditions	
	No decision	Predecision
Public assessment	10.7	7.9
Private assessment	8.1	15.4
	Experiment II	
	Time to choice	
	10 min	3 min
Public assessment		
Information expected	7.1	5.4
Information not expected	9.5	6.6
Private assessment		
Information expected	7.0	7.1
Information not expected	10.0	14.9
Replication conditions	8.4	7.2

[a] From Brounstein, P., Ostrove, N., & Mills, J. Divergence of private evaluations of alternatives prior to a choice. *Journal of Personality and Social Psychology,* 1979, *37,* 1957–1965, Tables 1 and 2, pp. 1960 and 1963. Copyright 1979 by the American Psychological Association. Reprinted by permission.

however, more divergence was obtained in the predecisional condition than in the no decision condition.

In discussing these results, Brounstein et al. note the possible effects that excluding the get-acquainted talks with the interviewers might have had on their results. They hypothesized that, "The freedom to choose the nonpreferred alternative and reject the preferred alternative may be more important when additional information about both of the alternatives is expected [Brounstein et al., 1979, p. 1961]." In other words, when additional information is expected, the possibility of changing one's mind is greater. It is important to note, however, that when the possibility of changing one's mind is relatively great, the threat to freedom posed by a preference is reduced. If one does not anticipate receiving more information about the alternatives, it is more likely that one's preference will be translated into actual choice. Thus, people not anticipating further information should feel psychologically closer to behavioral commitment than people anticipating further information. As we have mentioned previously, the more a preference has implications for actual choice, the greater should be the threat to the freedoms to choose the nonpreferred alternative(s). Thus, contrary to the position of Brounstein et al., it is our view that reactance arousal, and prechoice convergence resulting from such, should be greater when people do not anticipate further information than when people do anticipate obtaining this information.

Although we disagree with Brounstein et al.'s reasoning on reactance effects as a function of expecting information, the absence of a get-acquainted session is of concern. First, this absence does represent a marked deviation from the original experiments by Linder et al., and such a deviation is more worrisome due to Brounstein et al.'s failure to obtain a significant reactance effect among subjects giving public ratings of the choice alternatives. Second, expecting prior information or not should have a strong effect on the likelihood of obtaining a divergence effect. It would be expected that individuals who anticipate receiving information put their decisions "on hold." Since the additional information would make any preference uncertain, it would be inappropriate to try to reduce uncertainty when one knows that additional information will soon be obtained. The additional information itself constitutes an overriding uncertainty. When, however, subjects do not anticipate receiving further information, there is no information outstanding to prevent them from being motivated to reduce uncertainty and from acting on this motivation by increasing the perceived difference between the choice alternatives.

Brounstein et al. examined these issues in a second experiment. The procedure here was very similar to that used in the first study, except for the following. Half the subjects anticipated a get-acquainted chat, while the other half did not. Instead of the no decision condition used in the first experiment, the 3-min condition in the present study was contrasted with a condition in which subjects expected to make their choice about 10 min after rating the interviewers. In addition to the above 2 (public versus private decision) × 2 (expect additional information or not) × 2 (3 min versus 10 min until the decision) design, Brounstein et al. also conducted two replication conditions in which the procedures of Linder et al. (including the questionnaire measure of attractiveness as opposed to the machine-dial ratings used by Brounstein et al.) were duplicated virtually exactly.

The data from the second Brounstein et al. study are displayed in Table 8.3. There was a trend towards greater convergence in the short time to decision condition than in the long time to decision condition for subjects in both public conditions (expect and not expect further information) and for subjects in the replication conditions. None of the individual comparisons was significant, however. For subjects in the private decisions condition, expect or not expect information conditions had a large impact. When subjects expected additional information, there was no difference between the 3-min and 10-min conditions. When, however, no additional information was expected, the decision alternatives were rated more divergently when the decision was near at hand than when it was further away.

Before trying to interpret these data theoretically, let us consider the empirical facts that seem well substantiated. First, the convergence effect seems, while not always strong, quite reliable. Significant convergence effects have been obtained by Linder and Crane, Linder et al., and Carver and Scheier. Nonsignificant trends consistently confirming the theoretical prediction were obtained by Brounstein et al. in their first experiment and under three different conditions (public–information expected; public–information not expected; replication) in their second. Second, divergence of decision alternatives was obtained in both the studies by Brounstein et al. when subjects made a private decision and did not expect further information. Third, the data suggest that the anticipation or not of further information has a major impact on divergence under private conditions and virtually no impact on convergence under public conditions.

Brounstein et al. interpret these data as indicating that reactance theory and uncertainty theory apply to two different domains of choice behavior, reactance theory to "the overt expression of a preference which involves commitment," and uncertainty theory to private evaluations. Our contention would be somewhat different. We would propose that both theories are applicable to both domains, but that they operate as competing motives.

Some circumstances will strengthen one motive more than the other. Public expression of a preference may well increase the importance of making accurate estimates of one's preferences and the implications of the preferences for future action. Reactance arousal should thus be strengthened. With a private expression of preference, reactance arousal would presumably be reduced, and the motive to reduce uncertainty might well be stronger. Some variables should act to increase both motives. Having only a short time before making a choice appears to heighten the strength of both reactance and the motive to reduce uncertainty. Similarly, relative attractiveness of the nonpreferred alternative may well strengthen both motives. Alternatives that are closer together in attractiveness increase both the importance of the freedom to choose the rejected alternative and the amount of uncertainty experienced by the person; both the need to restore freedom and the need to reduce uncertainty would, therefore, be intensified.

Finally, some variables appear to have a significant impact on only one of the motives. The data obtained by Brounstein *et al.* suggest that if the conditions are appropriate for relatively high reactance arousal, whether or not additional information is expected has only a trivial impact on preferences for the choice alternatives (although it should be noted that, as we would predict, the difference between the two time-to-decision conditions tended to be larger in the not-expected condition than in the expected condition). Anticipating future information has, however, significant impact on the motive to reduce uncertainty. When future information is not expected, the combination of private expression and short time until the decision produces a divergence in one's preference evaluations. When, however, future information is expected, these setting conditions are not sufficient to bring about choice divergence.

POSTDECISION REGRET

The above discussion has considered only those convergence and divergence effects that have been obtained during the predecision phase. Convergence and divergence also appear during the postdecision period. Postdecision divergence has been considered in detail by dissonance theorists (see discussion in Wicklund & Brehm, 1976) and certainly seems the predominant effect. Convergence, however, also can occur, as demonstrated by Walster (in Festinger, 1964). Obtaining ratings of the choice alternatives at varying times (between different groups of subjects) after the decision, Walster found that there was a slight trend toward dissonance reduction (divergence of alternatives) on immediate postdecision ratings, a trend toward preference reversal (convergence) at 4 min (not significantly different from zero, but significantly different from the preceding and following measurement periods), significant dissonance reduction at 15 min, and a very slight trend toward dissonance reduction at 90 min.

Festinger (1964) proposed that postdecision convergence can be understood within the framework of dissonance theory. Shortly after making a decision, the person supposedly attends to those elements of the decision that are dissonant. Thus, unattractive aspects of the chosen alternative are salient as are the attractive aspects of the unchosen alternative. The first manifestation of this focus of attention is reflected in decision convergence: The chosen alternative becomes less attractive and the unchosen alternative more attractive. Although examining these dissonant cognitions initially increases dissonance, doing so facilitates change of these cognitions and eventual dissonance reduction through postdecision divergence. This explanation of the regret effect after a decision was examined in a study by Brehm and Wicklund (1970). They reasoned that if Festinger's explanation was correct, making the dissonant elements of the choice more salient should increase regret. Contrary to prediction, however, maximum regret was found to be greater in the no salience than in the salience condition. Similar results have been obtained by other investigators (e.g., Carlsmith, Ebbesen, Lepper, Zanna, Joncas, & Abelson, 1969).

Postdecisional regret also can be understood within the framework of reactance theory. If a person can have only one of the choice alternatives, making the decision eliminates the freedom to have the unchosen one. Since directly before the choice the person possessed the freedoms to have either alternative, this elimination should lead to reactance arousal, and the increased motive to obtain the unchosen alternative should be reflected in increased attractiveness of the unchosen alternative. The freedom not to have the chosen alternative is also eliminated, and reactance arousal should produce decreased perceived attractiveness of this alternative. If, however, the person sticks with his or her decision, the elimination of freedom becomes irrevocable. Once the freedoms to have the unchosen alternative and not to have the chosen one are truly given up, no reactance arousal would be expected and dissonance reduction processes could procede unhampered.

This explanation is perfectly consistent with the theory; unfortunately, however, there are no empirical data to back it up. The dissonance explanation has been called into question by the Brehm and Wicklund experiment, but the reactance explanation has yet to be examined. The procedure necessary for such an examination is quite clear. Theoretically relevant factors (e.g., importance of the freedom, magnitude of threat) should be varied, and regret should be found to increase as a direct function of the increasing strength of these variables.

SUMMARY

When a person has two alternatives to choose from, he or she has the freedoms to accept or reject each of the alternatives. A preference for one of the alternatives threatens the freedom to prefer the other. In addition, the tendency to select an alternative threatens the freedom to reject that alternative and to accept the other. The closer a person is to the decision point, the greater should be this threat to freedoms. One effect of this threat, theoretically, is to make the more attractive alternative appear less attractive and the less attractive alternative appear more attractive, as the decision point is approached. Empirical support for these predictions has been obtained in a number of studies, though in no case has there been a reliable decrease in the attractiveness of the preferred alternative (the freedom to reject this alternative being of very low importance).

Having two attractive choice alternatives, only one of which can be chosen, and then discovering that there is some additional difficulty involved in choosing the less attractive alternative should threaten the freedom to select the less attractive one. Thus, the less attractive alternative should increase in attractiveness during the preselection period, and it should do so in direct proportion to the difficulty of choosing it. This line of reasoning, too, has been supported by research.

Where there are many attractive alternatives, only one of which can be chosen, the tendency to select the most attractive threatens several freedoms (to choose each of the other alternatives) and should arouse considerable reactance. Research has shown that in this case, the most attractive alternative tends to become less attractive during the predecisional phase of choice, and tends to be rated as less attractive than the alternative that was initially rated as second most attractive.

Mills' choice certainty theory predicts that as a person approaches a decision between nearly equally attractive alternatives, the preferred alternative will tend to become more attractive, the nonpreferred less attractive. Recent research was described showing that divergence in the attractiveness of alternatives (uncertainty reduction) tends to occur when ratings are private, whereas convergence (reactance) tends to occur when ratings are public. The relationship between reactance and choice certainty theories was discussed.

Finally, postdecision regret processes were discussed. Although regret has long been considered within the framework of dissonance theory, empirical evidence is inconsistent with this explanatory approach. Regret processes can also be viewed as an expression of reactance. Unfortunately, however, there has been no empirical investigation of the role of reactance arousal in producing postdecision regret.

CHAPTER 9

Individual Differences in Psychological Reactance

Reactance theory comes from a tradition in social psychology that does not emphasize individual differences. Not surprisingly, then, the amount of individual difference research directly bearing on the theory is rather small. In this chapter, we will discuss the relevant empirical literature and comment on the type of individual difference research that might be productive for theoretical development. Another type of individual difference—sex differences—will be discussed in Chapter 12.

CONTROL

In our earlier consideration of the central role of freedom in reactance theory, we pointed out that different life experiences would be expected to have radical effects on individuals' perceptions of what their freedoms are. These life experiences may become codified into general action tendencies that operate as (or, at least, can be viewed as) personality traits. If one type of personality configuration differs from another in perception of freedoms, or threats to freedom, this difference should directly influence the amount of reactance aroused.

Locus of Control

One individual difference variable that might be expected to fit within this general rubric is that of Rotter's (1966) internal versus external locus of control. People high on internal locus of control are described as perceiving reinforcement to be contingent on their own behavior. People high on external locus of control are described as perceiving reinforcement to be contingent on environmental agents (e.g., fate, chance, other people).[1]

These descriptions might lead one to presume that internals would perceive themselves to have more behavioral freedoms than externals, but two studies reported by Harvey, Barnes, Sperry, and Harris (1974) indicate that there is no consistent evidence on this general point. Rather, as Harvey et al. (1974) state, "differences in perceived choice between internals and externals may depend upon characteristics of the choice options (p. 451)." Perhaps, then, the connection between locus of control and reactance theory is more involved with the importance of behavioral freedoms than with the sheer number of freedoms available. A study by Moyer (1978), for example, suggests that although choice had a slight enhancing effect on the performance of internals, the lack of choice had a larger effect in depressing performance. Internals, therefore, may place more importance on the freedoms involved in choices than do externals and experience stronger reactance when these choices are denied. The results of the study by Pittman and Pittman (1979) on the relationship between I–E and the effects of varying amounts of helplessness training (see Chapter 4) are also consistent with this hypothesis. Whatever the exact theoretical link (and this, of course, is one of the major problems with individual difference variables—it is difficult to know what *exactly* is different), there is considerable evidence that reactance arousal is differentially affected by locus of control.

Several studies have shown that internals are more resistant to influence than externals. Using a minimum acquisition criterion, Getter (1966) distinguished among those who conditioned when reinforced *and* when subsequently not reinforced (conditioners), those who condi-

---

[1] Research by Mirels (1970) indicates that the original I–E scale contains two factors: "a belief concerning felt mastery over the course of one's life and a belief concerning the extent to which the individual citizen is deemed capable of exerting an impact on political institutions [p. 226]." The first factor would appear more relevant to the psychological processes addressed by reactance theory. It should be noted, however, that the research efforts reported in the present chapter all used the full-scale I–E rather than any one of its component factors.

tioned only when not reinforced (latent conditioners), those who extinguished when no reinforcement was provided (extinguishers), and those who did not condition at all (nonconditioners). Conditioners had significantly higher I–E scores (i.e., were more external) than any of the other groups. Strickland (1970) also investigated the relationship between I–E and verbal conditioning. Although no relationship was found between conditioning and I–E on her full sample, I–E was related to aware subjects' denial of influence. Internals were more likely to deny influence than externals. Looking more closely at a small subsample of aware subjects who denied being influenced, Strickland found nonconditioners tended to be more ($p < .07$) internal than conditioners.

Responses to persuasive communications have also been found to be affected by subjects' I–E scores. Biondo and MacDonald (1971) obtained significantly less conformity to a persuasive communication for internals than for externals. Ryckman, Rodda, and Sherman (1972) presented subjects with a high-involvement attitudinal issue and a high-prestige communicator who was or was not expert on the issue. Externals showed significantly more persuasion than no influence controls, regardless of the communicator's expertise; internals showed no persuasion relative to the control condition. More influence for externals than for internals was also obtained in a study by Eisenberg (1978). In this study, the experimenter said he was interested "in the *loudest* tones," and externals rated the tones as being louder than internals.

Although this evidence is suggestive, it represents only a crude fit between the theory and locus of control. More compelling evidence of such a fit is provided by findings indicating that the difference between internals and externals on resistance to influence is affected by variables central to reactance theory. In the Biondo and MacDonald study, for instance, degree of influence exerted was varied among none, low ("this . . . appears to be one of the best ever . . .), and high ("I don't see how you have any choice . . . "). There was a significant interaction between I–E and level of influence (as well as the main effect for I–E noted earlier). When no influence was exerted, internals and externals did not differ. Internals conformed less than externals under both low and high levels of influence, but only for internals under high influence did resistance to change approach ($p < .10$) being significantly different from attitude change displayed by internals in the no influence condition. Thus, the best evidence for negative attitude change away from the position advocated by the communicator was obtained when internals received a high-pressure communication that threatened their freedom to disagree.

As has been noted above, Eisenberg's procedure emphasized the experimenter's interest in loud tones for all subjects. In addition, subtle influence condition subjects heard the experimenter say, "How about this one?" for 5 of the 17 tones rated. Overt influence subjects heard the experimenter say, "This tone is louder than the rest. You'll want to give it a higher rating." Besides the main effect for I–E described above, Eisenberg also found a marginally ($p < .07$) significant interaction between I–E and influence condition. Though no significant differences were found between internals and externals for any experimental condition, there was a tendency ($p < .10$) for internals to show less influence than externals in the overt influence condition.

A similar finding had been earlier reported by Ritchie and Phares (1969). In this study of attitude change, internal and external subjects were exposed to a communication coming from either a high prestige or low prestige source. A significant interaction was obtained, with externals conforming more than internals only when the communication had been attributed to a high prestige communicator.

Thus, although the exact pattern of the data differed among the three studies described above, the general theoretical point was consistent. In two of the studies (Eisenberg; Ritchie & Phares), the difference between internals and externals was maximized under conditions of high threat to freedom. In the Biondo and MacDonald study, the greatest amount of negative attitude change was obtained for internals subjected to a high threat influence. These data suggest that the individual differences measured by I–E have their greatest impact in those situations where magnitude of threat to opinion freedom is greatest and where, therefore, reactance arousal should be maximized.[2]

The hypothesis that the difference between internals and externals is enhanced under conditions of high levels of reactance arousal is further strengthened by an early study by Crowne and Liverant (1963). Using an Asch perceptual discrimination conformity paradigm, externals conformed more than internals only when subjects could place monetary bets on their judgments. When no betting was possible, differences in conformity as a function of I–E were not obtained. These results suggest that resistance to influence was enhanced for internals when the freedom not to be influenced was highly important. At lower levels of freedom importance (i.e., when money was not involved), I–E did not differentially affect resistance.

Another important consistency between I–E effects and reactance

---

[2] A dissertation by Gore (1962) had suggested that internals resist only subtle influence, not overt pressure to conform. Both Biondo and MacDonald as well as Eisenberg provide compelling arguments that Gore's data do not allow for this interpretation.

theory variables comes from the two verbal conditioning studies by Getter and Strickland mentioned earlier. It will be remembered that Getter distinguished among subjects who showed different types of conditioning responses. As noted before, conditioners had significantly higher I–E scores. In addition, the group with the lowest I–E score (latent conditioners) was composed of subjects who conditioned only on the unreinforced (extinction) trials. These subjects had I–E scores that were significantly lower than those of either the conditioners or nonconditioners.[3] Thus, in this study, subjects high on internality did not condition when pressure was put on them to do so, but when this pressure was removed, they complied with the experimental demands. This effect is strikingly reminiscent of the sleeper effects (see Chapter 6) found by Brehm and Mann (1975) and Gruder et al. (1978).

Strickland's study also provides some evidence that internals are susceptible to influence once the pressure to conform is removed. She reports that 10 of the 14 subjects who were aware of the experimental contingencies and denied being influenced "were assessed as internal." Of these 10, 7 "showed a rise in the last extinction block."

The studies we have discussed suggest that internals display more reactance arousal than externals: Internals resist influence more, they especially resist influence when threat to freedom is high or importance of freedom is great, and they comply with influence when the threat to freedom is removed. A study by Cherulnik and Citrin (1974), however, suggests that the difference between internals and externals may lie not so much in their propensity to reactance arousal, but in their differential response to different types of threats to freedom.

Using an experimental paradigm modeled after that of Brehm, Stires, Sensenig, and Shaban (1966), Cherulnik and Citrin had extreme internals (scoring 9 or below) and extreme externals (13 or above) initially rate four contemporary posters, all of them shown to be highly attractive in pretesting. Subjects were told they would be given their choice of one of these posters as a gift. Two days later, subjects rerated the posters. At this time, two-thirds of the subjects learned that their third most attractive poster would not be available as a gift. For half of these subjects, the reason given for this unavailability was failure of the poster to arrive in shipment. The other half were told that, on the basis of an inspection of the subject's scholastic and personal school records,

---

[3] Internality also appears associated with extinction. Getter had a small group of subjects ($N = 12$) who conditioned when reinforced, but extinguished when no reinforcement was provided. These subjects had I–E scores that were significantly lower than those of conditioners, but did not significantly differ from either nonconditioners or latent conditioners.

the experimenter had decided that one poster would not be "meaningful" to the subject. All subjects (including those for whom no poster was unavailable) rerated all four posters.

Cherulnik and Citrin predicted an interaction between type of freedom elimination and subject type. Specifically, they reasoned that internals would be most sensitive to losses of free behaviors for which they were responsible, and externals would be most sensitive to losses of behavioral freedoms for which they were not responsible. Internals were expected to show the most reactance arousal (i.e., increased attractiveness of the eliminated alternative) when there was a "personal elimination" (i.e., when the experimenter had deleted the picture because it was not "meaningful" for the subject) and externals when there was an "impersonal elimination" (i.e., when the poster failed to arrive in shipment). These predictions were strongly supported by the data obtained (see Table 9.1). There was a significant interaction between type of elimination of freedom and subject type, with internals becoming more favorable to the eliminated poster under personal elimination and externals becoming more favorable under impersonal elimination.

In some ways, these data are puzzling. The impersonal elimination condition had been used by Brehm *et al.* (1966) with an unselected group of undergraduates, and a reactance effect obtained. Interestingly, however, the comparison between the groups comparable to those used in the Cherulnik and Citrin study (choice–elimination versus choice–no elimination) was only marginally significant ($p < .09$ when two studies were combined). The weak trend for internals in the Cherulnik and Citrin study to show increased attractiveness for the eliminated alternative in the impersonal elimination condition suggests

TABLE 9.1

Mean of Pre-Post Changes in Ratings of Attractiveness of the Eliminated Item[a]

	Impersonal elimination	Personal elimination	No elimination
Internal	2.28	7.39	−1.89
External	11.33	−1.00	−.45

[a] From Cherulnik, P. D. & Citrin, M. M. Individual difference in psychological reactance: The interaction between locus of control and mode of elimination of freedom. *Journal of Personality and Social Psychology*, 1974, *29*, 398–404, Table 2, p. 402. Copyright 1974 by the American Psychological Association. Reprinted by permission.

that just such a weak effect would be obtained without the reduction in variance provided by grouping subjects on the basis of I–E.

The Cherulnik and Citrin study, then, may not conflict with the previous study by Brehm et al., but the *former* study does involve an unfortunate confound among several variables relevant to reactance theory. It would seem clear that the difference between the personal and impersonal eliminations of freedom is more than just the type of elimination or the subject's personal responsibility for that elimination. Surely, more freedoms are threatened by someone going through your records without your permission and deciding what is meaningful for you than by a simple failure of something to arrive in shipment. The number of freedoms threatened, directly and by implication, is greater in the personal condition, and the perceived intent to persuade of the experimenter should be greater. As we have seen before, differences between internals and externals appear to be maximized under conditions of strong threats to freedom. If then, the personal condition is considered a stronger threat to freedom, it is not surprising that internals show more reactance here than do externals, or that internals show more reactance here than when the milder (impersonal) threat was presented. What remains unanswered, though, is the question of why externals showed such strong reactance arousal in response to the impersonal (and, according to our analysis, mild) threat.

A study by Baron and Ganz (1972) would also seem relevant to this issue. In this study, black, male fifth-graders served as subjects. Using Crandall's Intellectual Achievement Responsibility (IAR) Scale, which the authors describe as the most suitable measure of locus of control for children in regard to task performance, subjects were selected who were assessed as internally or externally controlled for both success and failure. Subjects were then asked to perform on an experimental task for which they received intrinsic reinforcement (i.e., they were allowed to see whether their responses were correct or not) or external reinforcement (i.e., the experimenter praised them for success or gently admonished them for failure). A significant interaction between locus of control and type of reinforcement was obtained (see Table 9.2). Internals performed better under intrinsic reinforcement, while externals performed better under extrinsic reinforcement.

Again, it would seem to us that type of reinforcement has been confounded with degree of influence exerted. One could interpret these data as showing that internals conform to task requirements less than externals when overt influence is applied, and less than other internals exposed to no influence conditions. In this case, the apparent task decrement for externals under no influence (intrinsic) conditions could

TABLE 9.2
Mean Number of Correct Responses[a]

	Type of reinforcement	
	Intrinsic	Extrinsic
Internal	21.9	12.2
External	15.9	20.1

[a] From Baron, R. M. & Ganz, R. L. Effects of locus of control and type of feedback on task performance. *Journal of Personality and Social Psychology*, 1972, *21*, 124–130, Table 2, p. 128. Copyright 1972 by the American Psychological Association. Reprinted by permission.

be interpreted as reflecting a low state of motivation that can be enhanced by experimenter praise and admonishment.

We have offered these alternative explanations of the Cherulnik and Citrin, and Baron and Ganz studies not so much because we prefer our explanation to theirs, but because we wanted to try to interpret their data in light of the previously described research on locus of control. It does seem fairly well established that there is some association between being internal and resisting overt external influence (see also discussion of I–E and responses to psychotherapy in Chapter 13). The exact theoretical principles through which this association occurs are not clear. It is also not clear whether this association is general in nature (more internality, more resistance to influence) or whether there is some more specific characteristic of the influence attempt that mediates the responses of internals and externals. All of these issues, of course, suggest possible topics for future research in this area.

Type A Coronary-Prone Behavior Pattern

While Rotter's Internal–External Locus of Control is probably still the most widely used individual difference related to personal control, there are other individual differences related to control. One such individual difference variable that has been the subject of a great deal of recent research is the Type A coronary-prone behavior pattern (CPBP). Type A's are characterized by hard-driving competitiveness and a sense of time urgency, Type B's by more placid and less hurried behavior (Friedman, 1969; Glass, 1977). The former individuals run a substantially greater risk of developing heart disease than the latter (Jenkins, 1976). Glass, Snyder, and Hollis (1974) have suggested that the

Type A behavior pattern may represent efforts by the person to control his (or her, although the vast majority of work on Type A coronary-prone behavior pattern has been conducted with males) behavioral outcomes.

Correlations between the most typically used measure of Type A CPBP (the Jenkins Activity Survey for Health Prediction (JAS); Jenkins, Zyzanski, & Rosenman, 1972) and Rotter's I–E scale are usually positive, but low. (For example, using Glass's 1977 student version of the JAS, a recent study by Smith, 1980, found a significant correlation of .24 with I–E on a group of college students selected for extreme Type A versus Type B scores.) Manuck, Craft, and Gold (1978) have suggested the following distinction between these two individual difference variables: "Specifically, locus of control refers to a generalized *expectancy* for control, or a belief concerning the extent that personal behavior may significantly determine life events . . . , while the Type A behavior pattern suggests a need or *motive* for control [p. 410]."

In a recent examination of the relationship between the Type A CPBP and psychological reactance, Carver (1980) reports three experiments in which male and/or female A's and B's received either a high or low threat communication advocating an attitude-consistent position. In the first experiment, perceived coerciveness was measured. Two main effects were obtained, with A's perceiving more coercion than B's and subjects receiving the high threat communication perceiving more coerciveness than subjects receiving the low threat communication. Even though the interaction was not significant, Carver did examine the individual means. The difference between A's and B's was significant under low threat, but not under high threat. Both males and females participated in this study, and there was no effect of sex of subject.

The second experiment reported by Carver examined the effects of freedom-threatening communications on attitude change in Type A's and B's. In this study, only the threat × trials (pre versus post attitude) and the type × trials interactions were significant. The high threat communication led to less positive attitude change than the low threat, and Type B's showed more positive attitude change than Type A's (see Table 9.3). Again, although the higher order interactions were not significant, Carver examined the individual means, this time in terms of both Type A and gender. Type A males showed no indication of persuasion by the communication, and there was no difference between high and low threat conditions for these subjects. Type B males, however, did show significant positive attitude change as a function of the low threat communication but no opinion change under high threat. Type A females, like their male counterparts, did not show any

TABLE 9.3
Mean Opinion Change[a]

	High threat		Low threat	
Experiment II	Males	Females	Males	Females
Type A	.23	−.45	.14	.00
Type B	.00	.11	1.07	.73
Experiment III (females only)				
Type A		−.47		.28
Type B		.33		.31

[a] From Carver, C. Perceived coercion, resistance to persuasion, and the Type A behavior pattern. *Journal of Research in Personality*, 1980, 14, 467–481, Tables 2 and 3, pp. 475 and 476.

significant attitude change, although there was a nonsignificant trend for them to display negative attitude change (away from the position advocated by the communication) in the high threat condition. Female Type B's showed positive attitude change under low threat, but no attitude change under high threat.

Carver also briefly reports a replication of the above experiment. He states that this replication produced a comparable pattern of results for male subjects. For female subjects, however, Type A's showed reliably greater resistance to the high than the low threat communication (an effect that had been only a nonsignificant trend in the original study), and Type B females showed resistance to the low threat communication but not to the high. Even though there was little evidence of actual boomerang change in these two experiments, Carver interprets lack of attitude change as indicating resistance to the persuasive communication. He suggests, then, that Type A males resist low threat communications more than Type B males, but that both Type A's and B's resist strongly threatening communications. For female subjects, the pattern is less clear and Carver conducted a third experiment to investigate females' attitudinal responses.

In his third experiment, Carver had Type A and Type B female subjects respond to a "female issue" (the stimulus person was a female candidate for a Women's Rights Study Commission). Threat was varied as before. A marginally ($p < .08$) significant interaction between subject type, threat, and trials was obtained (see Table 9.3). Individual comparisons revealed that, again, Type A females resisted influence more in the high threat condition than in the low threat condition. There was, however, no difference in attitude change for Type B females as a function of threat.

Although the bits and pieces of all this are difficult to put together —and perhaps it is somewhat premature to try—there do seem to be some general trends that are worth noting. First, both I–E and Type A CPBP appear related to resistance to influence, but the relationships involved appear quite different in form. Threat to freedom seems to act as a threshold variable for Type A males; they perceive coercion at lower levels than Type B males and react against lower levels of threat. Once aroused, however, reactance appears to stabilize for Type A males, and there is no indication that reactance increases as threat increases. On the other hand, Type B males as well as internals (in general, there being no reported sex differences for I–E effects on responses to influence attempts) appear sensitive to the level of threat, with increasing resistance to influence provoked by increasing levels of threat to freedom. Externals appear to conform to pressure to comply, and there is some evidence (Biondo & MacDonald, 1971; Eisenberg, 1978; Ritchie & Phares, 1969) that conformity increases as threat to freedom increases.

This set of findings is consistent with the notion that I–E and Type A CPBP both relate to personal control but relate in different ways. Although the exact nature of such a difference is not apparent, Manuck et al.'s (1978) distinction may have some application. If internals expect to control, then conceivably, expectations of control could be differentially disconfirmed, and resistance to influence would increase with greater disconfirmation. If Type A's, however, are motivated to control, it is possible that exercising a certain level of control is sufficient regardless of the intensity of the threat. These hypotheses are, of course, quite tentative and speculative, but would appear interesting enough to warrant further investigation.

A second point suggested by Carver's (1980) research is that the behavior of Type A and Type B females seems to lie outside any parsimonious theoretical formulation. Type A females, like their male counterparts, are apparently more sensitive than Type B's to coercion, but there is no evidence that threat to freedom acts as a threshold variable for Type A females. Instead, Type A females respond more like Type B males and internals, increasingly resisting influence as magnitude of threat to freedom increases. Type B females did not respond in any consistent way during Carver's research. In Experiment II, female Type B's resisted high threat influence more than low threat; in the replication of Experiment II, they resisted low threat influence more than high; and in Experiment III, there was no difference in their resistance to influence as a function of threat. Additional research with Type A and B female subjects is clearly needed before any viable theoretical interpretation of these data can be attempted (see Chapter 12 for further discussion of possible sex differences in the Type A coronary-prone behavior pattern).

SELF-CONSCIOUSNESS

Another line of individual difference research with direct relevance to reactance arousal has recently been initiated by Carver and Scheier (1981). These investigators reasoned that since Carver (1977) had shown that an experimental manipulation of objective self awareness (Duval & Wicklund, 1972; Wicklund, 1975) could enhance reactance effects, chronic dispositions to be self-attentive should have a similar influence. The measure of attention to self used by Carver and Scheier was the Self-Consciousness Scale (Fenigstein, Scheier, & Buss, 1975). This scale has three factors, two of which were investigated by Carver and Scheier. Private Self-Consciousness includes items such as "I'm generally attentive to my inner feelings" and is supposed to reflect a person's awareness of his or her thoughts, feelings, and motives. Public Self-Consciousness includes items such as "I'm concerned about my style of doing things" and is supposed to measure a person's awareness of self as a social object. The literature cited by Carver and Scheier indicates that the Private Self-Consciousness subscale has been successful in obtaining effects similar to those obtained by at least some typical objective self-awareness experimental manipulations (e.g., exposure to a mirror). The relationship between the Public Self-Consciousness Subscale and objective self awareness is, apparently, less clear.

In their first study, Carver and Scheier selected male subjects who scored at the extremes on the Private Self-Consciousness scale and (using an experimental paradigm modeled after that of Snyder & Wicklund, 1976) exposed these subjects to a high or low threat attitude-consistent communication. Two significant interactions were obtained (threat × pre–post trials; subject type × trials), but the anticipated three-way interaction was not statistically reliable. Carver and Scheier, however, did examine pre–post attitude change scores among all the experimental groups (see Table 9.4). In this analysis, the only significant pre–post opinion change was found among high Private Self-Consciousness subjects who read the high threat communication. These subjects showed significantly less agreement with the position advocated by the communication after they read it.

Although subjects had been selected on the basis of their Private Self-

TABLE 9.4
Mean Opinion Change[a,b]

	High threat	Low threat
High private self-consciousness	− .74	.13
Low private self-consciousness	.13	.40
High public self-consciousness	− .04	.00
Low public self-consciousness	− .72	.45

[a] From Carver, C. and Scheier, M. Self-consciousness and reactance. *Journal of Research in Personality*, 1981, 15, 16–29, Tables 1 and 2, pp. 20 and 21.
[b] The same subjects were used for both analyses.

Consciousness scores, Carver and Scheier also investigated the effects of grouping subjects on the Public Self-Consciousness scale. Using a median split for subject type, a significant three-way interaction was obtained. Examination of the means of this interaction revealed that levels of threat to freedom had no effect on subjects high in Public Self-Consciousness. For those subjects low in Public Self-Consciousness, however, high threat led to significant negative attitude change, whereas low threat led to significant positive attitude change (see Table 9.4).

The second experiment reported by Carver and Scheier used the pre-decision convergence paradigm of Linder, Wortman, and Brehm (1971). As was noted earlier (see Chapter 8), Carver and Scheier replicated the Linder *et al.* finding that subjects who anticipated making a decision in 3 min rated the choice alternatives as more similar in attractiveness than subjects who anticipated making a decision in 10 min. A marginally significant interaction ($p = .065$) was also obtained by Carver and Scheier, such that the difference between the decision conditions was significant only for subjects high in Private Self-Consciousness (see Table 9.5). Additional analyses of the data using subjects grouped on the Public Self-Consciousness scale revealed no significant effects of this subject type.

Taken together, the data from these two studies have a number of possible implications for reactance theory. First, they serve to emphasize the importance of attention to one's own responses in generating opposition to influence attempts. While it is still not clear exactly what internal response is critical (e.g., focusing on one's attachment to the behavioral freedom versus focusing on one's responses to the threat to freedom), attention to the self does seem to increase opposition to freedom-threatening influence attempts. Attention to the self can be induced situationally as in the Carver (1977) study or can be examined as

TABLE 9.5
Absolute Difference in the Ratings of the Two Interviewers[a]

	Time to decision	
	10 min	3 min
High private self-consciousness	2.74	1.64
Low private self-consciousness	2.48	2.25

[a] See Table 9.4, Footnote a, Table 3, p. 25.

a relatively chronic individual difference variable. In the latter case, high Private Self-Consciousness appears to act in a similar fashion to high internality on the I–E scale, and not to resemble the threshold effect obtained by Carver (1980) for Type A males. Furthermore, as with I–E but not with the Type A CPBP, sex differences do not appear to mediate the effects of Private Self-Consciousness. Female subjects participated in the study by Carver (1977) and in the second study by Carver and Scheier; male subjects participated in Carver and Scheier's first study.

In their discussion of the distinction between the Private Self-Consciousness and Public Self-Consciousness subscales, Carver and Scheier suggest that Private Self-Consciousness produces effects analogous to those produced by some manipulations of objective self-awareness, while Public Self-Consciousness produces effects analogous to those produced by other manipulations of objective self-awareness. More important for the present consideration is the distinction between the two subscales in terms of their effects on responses to threats to freedom. High levels of Private Self-Consciousness appear to increase opposition to coercive influence attempts. High levels of Public Self-Consciousness appear to operate in a very different fashion. In the first experiment, where an external threat to attitudinal freedom was involved, high Public Self-Consciousness eliminated both reactance and compliance. In the second study, where an internal self-imposed threat to decisional freedom was involved, Public Self-Consciousness had no effect. The impact of Public Self-Consciousness thus seems restricted to external threats and, possibly, given the nature of the items on the scale, external threats from a social agent. Private Self-Consciousness has no such apparent limitation.

Moreover, the effects of high Public Self-Consciousness cannot be described as a simple reduction in reactance motivation for reestablishment of freedom. Rather, there seems to be a stiffening of one's initial opinion and relative invulnerability to either of the two motives aroused by a social influence attempt. The phrase "relative invulnerability" is vague, and purposely so. It is not clear whether the motives toward compliance and reactance are reduced in magnitude, or whether the behavioral tendencies usually produced by such motives are suppressed. Hopefully, further research in this area will attempt to articulate in more detail the effects of Public Self-Consciousness on responses to persuasive communications.

CONCLUSION

This has been a rather restricted examination of individual difference variables that may have a significant impact on reactance processes. We have chosen not to speculate about the possible relationships between reactance and a host of other individual difference variables that have been found to moderate people's responses to influence attempts. In the case of such variables (e.g., psychopathy: Johns & Quay, 1962, Quay & Hunt, 1965; authoritarianism, Rubin & Moore, 1971; need for approval, Smith & Flenning, 1971; cognitive complexity: Suedfeld & Vernon, 1966, Tetlock & Suedfeld, 1976), there may be a relationship, but the theoretical variables involved would be difficult to determine. Instead, we have focused on individual difference variables that have either a compelling relationship to the processes of theoretical interest (I–E) or have been explicitly investigated in terms of their impact on reactance (Type A CPBP and Public and Private Self-Consciousness).

Throughout our discussion of this selected research, we have tried to make explicit connections between the psychological processes denoted by the individual difference measure and those processes addressed by the theory. These interpretations were seldom without ambiguity and necessarily entailed a good deal of speculation. Many of the empirical findings we have reported are of considerable interest. The problem arises in trying to specify what exactly it is about the individual difference dimension that interacts with the experimental manipulations and the theoretical variables they operationalize. We hope that future research on reactance and individual differences makes this problem a central focus. It is interesting to obtain more powerful reactance effects with one group of subjects than with another. It is theoretically much more meaningful, however, if one also can specify the psychological processes that differ between these two groups of people.

SUMMARY

Three individual difference variables were considered in relation to reactance theory. For Rotter's (1966) locus of control variable, a review of the literature suggested that internals are more resistent to influence than externals (especially under conditions where the magnitude of threat is great and/or the importance of the freedom is high) but that internals will conform once the pressure to conform is removed. The latter finding seems similar to the "sleeper effects" discussed in Chapter 6. Moreover, it is possible that internals and externals differ in terms of the type of threat that will arouse reactance, with internals reacting to personal threats to freedom and externals reacting more to impersonal threats.

The relationship between the Type A coronary-prone behavior pattern and reactance arousal was also considered. It was suggested that Type A individuals may have a lower threshold for reactance arousal than Type B individuals, perceiving coercion at, and experiencing reactance arousal against, lower levels of threat. The two types, however, do not appear to differ at higher levels of threat. These comparisons seem to hold only for males; with females, the existing data are complex and to some extent contradictory.

Finally, the relationships between two factors of the Self-Consciousness Scale and reactance were examined. High Private Self-Consciousness appears to increase opposition to freedom-threatening influence attempts. The effects of high Public Self-Consciousness appear more complex, and it was suggested that this individual difference variable may act to strengthen initial position in the face of external threat to freedom, such that neither conformity nor reactance are manifest.

CHAPTER 10

Reactance Theory and Impression Management Formulations

Two studies by Heilman and her associates (Heilman & Garner, 1975; Heilman & Toffler, 1976) have raised several significant theoretical issues for reactance theory. In this chapter, we shall examine Heilman's work, seeking to explicate the issues that are in dispute and to respond to Heilman's position. At the end of the chapter, a more recent version of an impression management interpretation of reactance effects is considered.

Promises versus Threats

An initial issue raised by Heilman is whether there is a theoretical difference between using promises to reward compliance and inducing compliance by threatening to punish noncompliance. Heilman proposes that only the latter instance constitutes a threat to freedom. For Heilman, "needs derived from self-concept maintenance, fear of appearing weak and foolish before others, and concern about the relationship with the threatener [Heilman & Garner, 1975, p. 911]" stimulate resistance to threats, and are not evoked by promises. When promises are made, "feelings of autonomy are not similarly jeopardized [Heilman & Garner, p. 911]."

Reactance theory takes a different approach to possible differences between threats and promises. First, both threats and promises are seen as threats to freedom. Offers may be punishing or rewarding, but if they pressure one to behave in a certain way, they threaten one's freedom not to behave in that way. That, under conditions specified by the theory, a promised reward can arouse reactance has been demonstrated by Brehm and Mann (1975), who used a proffered bribe to induce subjects to change their opinions.

It may be, however, that threats and promises threaten different numbers of freedoms. Threats (e.g., "You must do X or I'll punish you by doing Y") typically involve taking away something (e.g., love, money, the state of physical and/or psychological well-being that was expected prior to imposition of a threat of punishment) that one already has. Promises of reward (e.g., "You must do X and I'll reward you by giving you Y") offer to provide a person with something desirable he or she does not have (e.g., love, money, time to do other things). Any threat would thus threaten the freedom not to do the behavior of interest *and* the freedom to keep that which you presently possess. Promises of reward, however, would typically threaten only the freedom not to engage in the behavior under consideration. Promises cannot be said to threaten your freedoms to have or not have the proposed *reward* because the reward is controlled by the influence agent and does not exist as a freedom for the target of the influence attempt. Since two threats to two different freedoms would be expected to create more reactance than one threat (see previous discussion of summation and possible carry-over effects in Chapter 4), reactance arousal may typically be greater in response to threats than to promises.

We have stated earlier that whether or not the person attempts to restore freedom will depend, in part, on the cost of noncompliance. Typically, the cost of noncompliance will be greater when a threat is involved than when a promise has been made. If you do not comply with a threat, you will lose that which you already have. You will be worse off than before the influence attempt. If you do not comply with the influence exerted by a promise, you will fail to gain something you do not currently have. You will stay the same as you were prior to the influence attempt. Assuming that the threat and the promise involve items equally important to the person, noncompliance with the threat will be more psychologically costly than noncompliance with the promise, and thus direct restoration of freedom in response to a threat will be less likely to occur than in response to a promise. It is important to realize, however, that suppression of restorative behavior in response to a threat will only take place if the cost of noncompliance with a threat is relatively high.

Another difference between threats and promises occurs in regard to the interpersonal relationship between the influence agent and the target of the influence attempt. Heilman's analysis stresses the importance of this relationship for determining the person's response to threats and promises. We agree that it is important but would discuss the relationship in terms more relevant to the theory. We also view the relationship variable as more complex than Heilman's analysis would indicate.

A person who threatens to punish noncompliance may be perceived differently from a person who promises to reward compliance. The former individual may be seen as more hostile and, therefore, less attractive. The relationship between attractiveness of the influence agent and the amount of influence obtained has been discussed previously (Chapter 6) and was investigated in the study by Brehm and Mann (1975) that was described in the earlier discussion. It will be remembered that Brehm and Mann found that the more attractive influence agents obtained more compliance when the freedom that was threatened was relatively unimportant. When, however, the threatened freedom was important, the unattractive influence agents obtained more compliance than the attractive ones, and, indeed, negative attitude change was exhibited in response to the influence attempt by the attractive agents.

The difference in perceptions of a threatener and a promiser are further accentuated if the target person believes that the influence agent had a choice of using either a threat or a promise. If the influence agent who has such a choice chooses to offer a promise, this indicates relative good will toward the target. If, on the other hand, the agent who has a choice decides to threaten punishment, this choice will have serious implications about that person's intent. First, it will probably indicate to the target that the influence agent has a strong intent to obtain compliance; this perceived intent will increase the magnitude of the threat to freedom perceived by the target. Second, if the target individual expects future interactions with the influence agent, the choice of a threat over a promise may imply the distinct possibility of coercive attempts by the influence agent in the future, and, by implication, threaten future freedoms. Both heightened perceptions of perceived intent and implied threats to future freedoms should increase the magnitude of reactance aroused.

Let us at this point summarize the relationship between threats and promises as we would see this relationship in terms of reactance theory.

1. Both threats and promises threaten the freedom *not* to engage in the behavior X that the influence agent seeks to obtain.
2. Threats threaten the freedom not to engage in X *and* the freedom to keep that which is threatened with removal. Promises only threaten the freedom not to engage in X. Threats, therefore, should arouse greater reactance.
3. If a threat and a promise involve punishments and rewards of equal importance, noncompliance with a threat will be more psychologically costly to the person than noncompliance with a promise. If the cost of noncompliance is relatively high, restorative behavior will be suppressed more often in response to a threat than to a promise.
4. A threatener will likely be seen as less attractive than a promiser. If the freedom being threatened is unimportant, the promiser should obtain more compliance. If the freedom being threatened is important, the promiser may obtain less compliance.
5. If the influence agent can choose between threats and promises, the choice of a threat may signify greater intent to persuade and, if future interaction is anticipated, greater likelihood of threats to future freedoms. In such a case, reactance arousal would be greater in response to threats than to promises.

Modes of Compliance

A second theoretical issue raised by Heilman should be considered before turning to her empirical research. Heilman proposes that giving an individual the opportunity to choose the mode of compliance should counteract the restrictiveness of threats and reduce reactance arousal. Again, our analysis of this proposition would take a somewhat different approach.

Let us imagine that an influence agent is strongly urging a target person to engage in a certain behavior that we will designate as "X." The freedoms to do X and not to do X represent a set of freedoms distinct from the freedom of how to do X. To provide the freedom of how to do X does not restore the freedom not to do X, nor, theoretically, should this provision of freedom reduce the magnitude of reactance that is aroused when the freedom not to do X is threatened.

Consider, however, the situation where the target individual knows that the freedom of how to do X does exist for a number of individuals in the present situation, and that the influence agent can determine whether or not the specific target person will be allowed to exercise this freedom. Assuming that the target person expects to have the freedom to decide how to do X, an influence agent who threatens the freedom not to do X *and* eliminates the freedom of how to do X has impinged upon a greater number of freedoms than an influence agent who threatens the freedom not to do X and allows the person to exercise the freedom of how to do X. Reactance arousal should thus be greater in the former case than in the latter.

Furthermore, the context in which the freedom to decide upon how one will comply with an influence attempt is granted or not will play a large part in determining the target person's response. What if you believe that the influence agent will obtain a direct benefit from your behavioral compliance, but that the way in which you comply will not affect the influence agent's gains? In such a situation, the influence agent's attempt to get you to do X is understandable and, to some extent, justified. Denying you the freedom to choose the mode of compliance is not, however, justified, and, if future interaction is expected, may well imply that the influence agent will try to threaten or eliminate future behavioral freedoms. When, on the other hand, the influence agent does allow you to exercise choice in regard to the mode of compliance, this act indicates a restriction on future threats. With this influence agent, threats to your behavioral freedoms are likely to occur only if your behavior directly affects the influence agent's well-being.

We would expect, therefore, the provision of choice of mode of compliance to affect one's compliance with an influence attempt under the following conditions.

1. The freedoms to engage in the advocated behavior or not, and the freedom to choose the mode of compliance must be perceived as psychologically connected. The most obvious way to connect these freedoms, and make them relevant to each other, would be for both freedoms to be vulnerable to threat or elimination by the same influence agent.
2. If these freedoms are perceived as a related set of freedoms, reactance arousal and opposition to influence will be greater if choice of mode of compliance is not provided than if it is. When choice is not provided, a greater number of freedoms are threatened, and implications for future threats may be increased.

Heilman's Research

With this theoretical background, let us examine the procedures used and the results obtained in the two relevant studies by Heilman and her colleagues (a third study by Heilman, 1976, was discussed previously in Chapter 7). The studies by Heilman and Garner (1975) and Heilman and Toffler (1976) used virtually identical procedures. In both, female subjects were recruited from a high school and told they would earn "from $2.00 to $3.00" (Heilman & Garner) or "an average of $2.50" (Heilman & Toffler) for their participation. Subjects participated in large groups (15–30). Subjects in these groups either were led to believe that another group was participating at the same time (Heilman & Garner), or two groups actually were run simultaneously in different rooms (Heilman & Toffler).

All subjects were told they would work in pairs with a peer who was in another room; they were also told they would not learn the identity of their partner nor she theirs. Subjects were led to believe that some subjects would be acting as "tasters" in the experimental task, while others would be acting as "tabulators." Actually, all subjects were told they would be tasters and their partners would be tabulators.

As tasters, subjects expected to taste either orange juice or vinegar. They were told they would be paid a basic rate of $2.50 for the session, but that their partner's earning depended on what they, the subjects, chose to taste. If subjects chose to taste orange juice, their partner's earnings would be less than if they chose to taste vinegar. Subjects were also informed that their partners could fine or reward the subject 50¢ if they chose. In addition, subjects learned that although there was only one type of orange juice to taste, there were four different types of vinegar available. In the Heilman and Garner study, subjects were told that their partners could determine whether or not subjects could choose which kind of vinegar to taste. In the Heilman and Toffler study, subjects were told that either their partners could determine whether or not subjects could choose which kind of vinegar to taste, or that a random process would determine whether they chose or not.

All subjects in both studies then received a message from their supposed partner. Half the subjects received a threat in which the partner threatened to fine them 50¢ if they did not taste vinegar; half received a promise in which the partner promised to give them a bonus of 50¢ if they would taste vinegar. (Heilman and Garner also examined the possible effects of different ways of wording threats and promises. Since this variable did not affect their results, it will not be discussed here.) For subjects in the Heilman and Garner study, a printed statement at the bottom of the message gave the partner a chance to indicate who would choose the type of vinegar tasted if the subject chose to taste vinegar. An additional statement, supposedly written by the partner, also was included. Half the subjects were informed by the partner that, "The decision would be up to you. You can choose whatever kind you want." The other half were told, "I will choose the type of vinegar."

Subjects in the Heilman and Toffler study expected either that their partner could determine whether the subject could choose the type of vinegar (interpersonal condition) or that a random process would determine this (noninterpersonal condition). For those subjects in the interpersonal condition, a printed question at the bottom of the message they received ("If your pairmate chooses vinegar, will she have a choice of which kind she tastes?") allowed partners to designate choice or no choice by checking "yes" or "no." Subjects who believed whether or not they would have choice would be determined by a random process were informed after reading their partner's threat or promise message that the random process ("on the basis of your ID number") had selected them either to have a choice or not to have a choice.

All subjects then chose whether to taste orange juice or vinegar, and this constituted the major dependent variable. Questionnaire items also obtained the subject's opinion of her partner and the message.

Obviously, this is a rather complicated procedure. A great many potentially important psychological factors are involved that might affect subjects' compliance. For purposes of the present discussion, let us go back over the summarized points that we noted earlier.

Threats versus Promises
1. Both the threat and the promise threaten the subject's freedom not to taste vinegar.
2. Although the two studies used slightly different monetary inducements for recruitment purposes, subjects in both studies were told they would earn a "basic payrate of $2.50." The threat, therefore, threatened the freedom not to taste vinegar as well as the freedom to keep the full $2.50 subjects believed they had earned. The promise threatened only the freedom not to taste vinegar.
3. Although the cost to subjects in the threat conditions should have been psychologically greater for noncompliance (they would lose 50¢ they thought they had) than for subjects in the promise conditions (they would keep their full $2.50 but fail to earn 50¢ more), the cost for noncompliance is not particularly high in either case.
4. The freedom not to taste vinegar is, presumably, of little importance, and, thus, the more attractive influence agent should obtain more compliance.
5. The influence agent could choose to use either a fine or a bonus.

Although subjects were told they would not learn the identity of their partner, the fact that all subjects were students at the same high school may have rendered this supposed anonymity suspect. Subjects may have thought there was a fairly good chance that they would find out who their partner was. In any case, subjects certainly expected future interaction with their fellow students.

Choice of Mode of Compliance

1. For subjects in the Heilman and Garner study and in Heilman and Toffler's interpersonal condition, the freedoms to taste or not taste vinegar and the freedom to choose which type of vinegar to taste were connected. In the noninterpersonal condition of the latter study, the choice of which type of vinegar to taste was not relevant to subjects' responses to the influence attempt by their partners.

2. In the Heilman and Garner study and the interpersonal condition of the Heilman and Toffler study, subjects believed that their partners would determine whether or not they could choose the type of vinegar they would taste (*if* they chose to taste vinegar). Subjects also were not told that the type of vinegar tasted would affect their partners' earnings (and we presume that they believed that type of vinegar tasted was irrelevant to partner earnings, although we cannot find any explicit instructions to this effect in the procedures for either study). If our presumption is correct, denying choice of vinegar may well have been seen by subjects as a gratuitous and unjustified abrogation of freedom.

The results obtained in these two studies are displayed in Tables 10.1 and 10.2. Table 10.1 shows the proportion of subjects in each experimental condition that chose to taste vinegar. As can be seen, these results are consistent with both Heilman's analysis and ours. Promises produce a uniformly high level of compliance. Threats coupled with a denial of the freedom to choose by the partner produce a low level of compliance. When, however, the freedom to choose was provided by the partner, considerable compliance was obtained. This pattern holds true only when the partner determines whether or not the subject can choose which type of vinegar to taste. When this choice was supposedly determined randomly in the Heilman and Toffler study, compliance to threats is uniformly lower than compliance to promises regardless of whether choice is provided or not. We shall discuss Heilman's analysis of this difference between the interpersonal and noninterpersonal conditions in the following section.

Before turning to this issue, however, let us also examine the attractiveness ratings of the partner (displayed in Table 10.2). In the Heilman

TABLE 10.1
**Percentages of Subjects Choosing to Comply
with Partners' Influence**

	Choice provided (%)	Choice not provided (%)
Heilman & Garner, 1975[a]		
Threats	79	38
Promises	83	79
Heilman & Toffler, 1976[b]		
Interpersonal		
Threats	91	55
Promises	91	100
Noninterpersonal		
Threats	64	64
Promises	100	100

[a] From Heilman, M. D. & Garner, K. A. Counteracting the boomerang: The effects of choice on compliance to threats and promises. *Journal of Personality and Social Psychology*, 1975, *31*, 911–917, Table 1, p. 914. Copyright 1975 by the American Psychological Association. Reprinted by permission.

[b] From Heilman, M. D. & Toffler, B. L. Reacting to reactance: An interpersonal interpretation of the need for freedom. *Journal of Experimental Social Psychology*, 1976, *12*, 519–529, Table 1, p. 525.

TABLE 10.2
Perceptions of the Partner: Mean Factor Scores for the Evaluative Factor

	Choice provided	Choice not provided
Heilman & Garner, 1975[b]		
Threats	7.196[a]	8.344
Promises	4.021	5.604
Heilman & Toffler, 1976[c]		
Interpersonal		
Threats	6.78	8.44
Promises	3.18	4.24
Noninterpersonal		
Threats	8.00	8.60
Promises	4.71	4.06

[a] Higher means indicate more negative evaluations on 9-point scales.
[b] See Table 10.1, Footnote *a*, Table 2, p. 915.
[c] See Table 10.1, Footnote *b*, Table 2, p. 526.

and Garner study, promisers were rated significantly more favorably than threateners, and partners who provided choice were rated significantly more favorably than partners who did not. In the Heilman and Toffler study, only a significant difference between ratings of threateners and promisers was reported. For both studies, however, favorability ratings of the partner parallel obtained compliance. The most negative rating of the partner in the Garner and Heilman study occurred in the threat–no choice condition where the least compliance was obtained. In the Heilman and Toffler study, partners were rated negatively in the interpersonal-threat–no choice, noninterpersonal-threat–choice, and noninterpersonal-threat–no choice conditions, all conditions in which low levels of compliance were obtained. These attractiveness ratings seem generally consistent with our analysis, in which we have stressed the gratuitous nature of the partner's denial of the subject's freedom to choose among the different types of vinegar, and the irrelevancy of the random process's provision of choice for responses to the partner's influence attempt.

Reactance as Impression Management

In the interests of an organized presentation, we have put off discussing the rationale behind Heilman and Toffler's interpersonal versus noninterpersonal conditions until this point. We wanted to discuss first the theoretical issues of threats versus promises and choice of mode of compliance. We differ from Heilman on the interpretation of these issues but it is important to note that her interpretations on these issues offer challenges only to specific aspects of the theory. They do not propose an alternative for the theory as a whole.

The third theoretical issue raised by Heilman, however, does propose a radical revision of the basic premises of the theory. Heilman and Toffler (1976) argue that "the motivation to regain personal freedom stems from the desire to project to the other an image of oneself as an autonomous being [p. 520]." More specifically, they propose "that the effects of threats can be mitigated by freedom-affirming interventions *only when the intervention has consequences for the relationship between the individual and the influencing agent* [p. 521]." These statements indicate that, for Heilman and Toffler, reactance is aroused *and* reduced as a function of concerns that one has about the impression one makes on the influence agent.

In regard to the arousal of reactance, the Heilman and Toffler proposition is as difficult to address as Mugny and Doise's (1979) notion of catching a "glimpse" of a social agent behind every threat to or elimination of freedom. As we stated earlier in Chapter 2, it is a matter of how much of a glimpse will suffice. We do assume, however, that Heilman and Toffler are making a somewhat different point than that made by Mugny and Doise. The latter argue that no matter what is the apparent agent that threatens freedom, a social agent will always be viewed as the ultimate source of the threat. Heilman and Toffler, on the other hand, do not address explicitly whether nonsocial agents can threaten or eliminate freedom, but, instead, argue that reactance in response to any type of threat or elimination will occur only when impression management concerns are present.

Unfortunately, it is not clear whether Heilman and Toffler mean to imply that reactance arousal will occur only when a social agent threatens freedom, or if, in their view, nonsocial agents could threaten freedom and reactance arousal would be produced as long as there was someone around to impress. The latter interpretation recalls the ubiquitous experimenter who figured prominently in our earlier discussion of social versus nonsocial threats and, just as then, suggests that such a possibility will be difficult to rule out.

Heilman and Toffler's hypothesis about freedom-affirming interventions is, however, considerably more specific and more amenable to empirical investigation. While the phrase "freedom-affirming intervention" is somewhat ambiguous, we presume they are talking about something analogous to restoration of freedom, and to help us define this phrase, we can examine their empirical operations. In the Heilman and Toffler study, choice of mode of compliance was used as the freedom-affirming intervention and, as predicted, it was found that this intervention resulted in high levels of compliance only when it came from the influence agent and not when it came from another source (i.e., the random process).

Let us address this hypothesis and its empirical support on two levels. First, it should be clear from our previous remarks that choice of mode of compliance does not restore the person's freedom not to engage in the behavior desired by the influence agent. The only way for the influence agent to restore the person's freedom not to do X is to tell the person he or she does not have to do X. Telling the person that the choice of how to do X is available is an important event (as discussed previously), but it does not restore the freedom not to do X. As we have indicated, we believe that the obtained difference between the interpersonal and noninterpersonal conditions can be explained in a way that is quite consistent with reactance theory.

Second, there are a number of studies in which an individual's freedom has been restored and increased compliance obtained. Heilman and Toffler would have us believe that in all of these studies, the restoration of freedom had consequences for the relationship between the individual and the influencing agent. We can examine these studies to see if this was this case.

Let us consider the studies by Worchel and Brehm (1971); Andreoli, Worchel, and Folger (1974); McGillis and Brehm (1975); and Brehm and Mann (1975). In none of these studies did the influencing agent restore the target individual's freedom, and yet reactance was reduced and increased compliance obtained. It seems clear, then, that in order to reduce reactance arousal, restoration of freedom (and, presumably, "freedom-affirming interventions") does not have to be presented by the influencing agent who threatened the freedom.

The way in which Heilman and Toffler's hypothesis is stated, however, raises the more general issue of whether the freedom restoration need only be somehow relevant to ("has consequences for") the relationship between the influencing agent and the target, even if the influencing agent does not actually restore freedom. This is more difficult to determine, but a reasonable rule of thumb would seem to be that restoration of freedom could be relevant to the relationship only if the influence agent knew it had occurred.

For three of the four studies we are considering, the influence agent did know this. In Worchel and Brehm (1971) and Andreoli et al. (1974), the restoration of freedom by the third party was stated in the presence of the influencing agent. In Brehm and Mann (1975), the influencing agents (i.e., other group members) knew that the possibility of their using a bribe to induce compliance was no longer available. It should be noted, however, that in none of these studies was there any reason for subjects to think that the influencing agent would know about their freedom-restoring behavior (i.e., their opinions as stated on the dependent measures). Thus, although in a broad sense, the freedom restoration was relevant to the relationship between the influence agent and the target, there was no clear opportunity for the target person to demonstrate the effects of the restoration of freedom to the influence agent. These circumstances make an impression management interpretation of these studies difficult to maintain.

Moreover, in the study by McGillis and Brehm (1975), there is no reason to believe that subjects thought the influencing agent would know about the restoration of freedom that occurred. As described earlier, (Chapter 5), shoppers' freedom not to buy a certain brand of bread was threatened by a promotional campaign. When shoppers observed another shopper restoring her freedom, buying the bread being promoted increased over both baseline and no restoration conditions. The restoration of freedom occurred in an aisle of the supermarket (near the designated bread) and out of sight of the person who had given the shopper the promotional information (and certainly out of sight of the bread company officials and the advertising executives who, presumably, were the actual influencing agents). There would seem to be no possible way in which the results of this study could be interpreted in terms of impression management.

Reactance as Impression Management Revisited: Prior Exercise of Freedom

A recent paper by Baer, Hinkle, Smith, and Fenton (1980) extends the impression-management interpretation of reactance effects into the domain of prior exercise of freedom as explicated by Wicklund (1974) and investigated by Snyder and Wicklund (1976). We have considered the principle of prior exercise of freedom at some length in Chapter 6 and, here, will only summarize the Snyder and Wicklund view. According to Snyder and Wicklund, reactance arousal is reduced in response to a freedom-threatening communication if, prior to the communication, the person has had the opportunity to advocate the position opposite to that urged by the communication.

Baer et al. (1980) propose that the prior exercise of freedom proposition can be interpreted in terms of impression management efforts by the individual. Specifically, they argue that only public prior exercise of freedom (i.e., known to the communicator) should be effective in reducing reactance arousal. Moreover, they also take the Heilman view that only public expressions of attitude should serve to reduce reactance, since only public expressions will project the threatened individual's autonomy from the threatener. Baer et al. (1980) acknowledge that in the Snyder and Wicklund studies, subjects' prior exercise of freedom was not brought to the attention of the communicator. They suggest, however, that "concerns for self-presentation may have been directed toward another person whom the subjects perceived was evaluating their psychological worth, the experimenter [Baer et al., 1980, p. 417]."

To test their hypotheses, Baer et al. (1980) had undergraduate subjects either write or not write an essay arguing against the position that they supported (and that was to be advocated in the forthcoming persuasive communication). Of those subjects who wrote this essay, half believed it would be seen by their partner (supposedly another, same sex subject in a separate room); half were instructed to seal their essays in envelopes and place them with a pile of other sealed envelopes, thus ensuring confidentiality from both the partner and the experimenter. Control subjects who did not write an essay spent this period of the experiment composing a list of important issues. All subjects then completed a 12-item attitude questionnaire, one item of which assessed their attitude on the experimental issue.

Subjects next received a persuasive communication, supposedly written by their partner, that advocated an attitude-consistent position. Subjects in the high threat condition received a communication liberally sprinkled with "you must" and "you have no choice" statements, while subjects in the low threat condition received the same communication without the threatening statements. Subjects' postcommunication attitudes were then assessed. Half of the subjects were told their attitudinal expressions would be shown to their partners "with whom they would meet for a brief discussion"; the other half were instructed to put their opinion statements in sealed envelopes.

The overall design of this experiment was, thus, a 3 (prior exercise: public, private, none) × 2 (threat: high vs. low) × 2 (postcommunication attitude expression: public vs. private) factorial. On the analysis of attitude change scores, the predicted three-way interaction was obtained, although it slightly exceeded the conventional .05 level ($p < .059$). Within private postcommunication expression conditions, there was no interaction between threat and prior exercise. Within the public expression conditions, however, threat and prior exercise did interact, with only the private exercise and the no exercise conditions evidencing significant negative attitude change. Since these were the two cells in which Baer et al. (1980) had predicted that concerns for personal autonomy should be most salient and should not have been appeased by prior (public) exercise, Baer et al. concluded that their results were "consistent with a self-presentation interpretation of psychological reactance [p. 421]."

From our point of view, these results are also quite consistent with a more traditional reactance theory formulation. In order to explain this interpretation, it is necessary, as it was with Heilman's work, to consider carefully the procedural details of the study. First, while Baer et al. (1980) propose that the attitudinal issue used in this study (i.e., "that student government should have a role in university administrative affairs") was "highly important," their evidence for this is rather weak. In pretesting various issues, they found that this issue received a mean importance rating of 7.15 on a 10-point scale and that it was given the highest importance ratings relative to 11 other issues that were pretested. A mean of 7.15 seems more appropriately characterized as moderately important instead of highly important, and that it was the highest in importance among the 12 issues that were pretested may simply tell us something about 1970s-style student apathy and/or the other issues that were pretested.

Second, the methodology of this study was such that the attitudinal postmeasure appears to have been taken only minutes after the attitudinal premeasure. The only intervening experimental procedure was for subjects to read the persuasive communication, and there is nothing in the report of the procedure that would lead one to believe that this communication was especially lengthy. Taking repeated measures of attitudes over such a short period of time typically reduces the amount of attitude change that one will obtain—regardless of what goes on during the intervening few minutes. Indeed, mean attitude change for 10 of the 12 cells in the present experiment ranged from $-.10$ to $+.67$.

The two points made in the preceding paragraph suggest an alternative explanation of Baer et al.'s (1980) results. We would propose that subjects were confronted with a not very important attitudinal issue and that, because of this relative lack of importance, not very much reactance arousal could be created by any threat to the individual's freedom to hold his or her own opinion on it. Moreover, the short time period between attitudinal measurements restricted all attitude change (both positive and negative). Thus, for private postcommunication subjects, there was little reactance, little persuasion, and little motivation to change the attitude they had expressed minutes previously.

For public postcommunication subjects, however, an entirely new situation had been created. They expected to meet with and discuss the attitude issue at hand with the author of the communication they had read. Low threat condition subjects, having read an innocuous presentation of an opinion with which they agreed, were not particularly affected by this—again, it is dramatic how little *positive* attitude change was obtained in these conditions. High threat condition subjects were affected, but only if they had *not* previously written an essay opposing the communicator's position that had been seen by the communicator.

We would suggest that high threat condition subjects who had "sent a message" to their partner were *not* affected by the persuasive communication because the heavy-handed influence attempt they received was justified by the fact that their partner had received their (counterattitudinal) essay *before* sending subjects the one they read. High threat condition subjects in the private prior exercise and no exercise conditions, however, had no such way to legitimize the communication they received. For these subjects, the communication was not reciprocal, it was heavy-handed, and, most important, it was made by someone with whom they expected to interact. Subjects in the two conditions where Baer *et al.* (1980) found negative attitude change (with means of − 1.6 and − 1.7) may then have experienced reactance arousal not in response to a specific threat to a specific attitudinal freedom, but in response to a threat to their expected freedom to hold their own vis-a⁻ vis a supposed equal both in regard to the attitude issue at hand and to any other issues that would come up in their subsequent discussion. Only in these two cells, then, was an important freedom threatened in such a way that there were implications for other freedoms as well.

Now, at this point, the reader may wonder if we ourselves have not skirted awfully close to an impression management interpretation of reactance. Actually, we have not. Reactance theory has never claimed that reactance could not be aroused by social threats to social freedoms. It does claim that the processes underlying this type of reactance are not different from the processes underlying responses to nonsocial threats to nonsocial freedoms. In Baer *et al.*'s (1980) study, we believe that the only important freedom that was significantly threatened was the social freedom of interpersonal autonomy. If, however, an attitudinal issue had been used that clearly was of high importance to subjects (or procedures were used that would be more conducive to attitude change), then we would have expected reactance to have been aroused and expressed under private as well as public conditions when no prior exercise had been provided. It might well be the case, however, that even if such an issue had been used, reactance would have been greater in the public postcommunication–private exercise and public postcommunication–no exercise conditions due to the addition in those cells of a significant threat to interpersonal freedom as well (see Chapter 4 on multiple threats to freedoms).

Two final caveats concerning the Baer *et al.* (1980) study are worth noting. The first concerns the effect of the prior exercise of freedom manipulation on "initial" attitudes. The Snyder and Wicklund studies found that prior exercise of freedom (making a counter-attitudinal statement) produced significant amounts of attitude change. One would plausibly expect similar effects to have occurred in the Baer *et al.* experiment, particularly where the prior exercise of freedom was public (to the supposed partner and the experimenter). Because this effect might have made subjects in the public exercise condition less "pro" to begin with, obtained differences in attitude change between this condition and the private exercise and no exercise conditions become confounded with initial position on the issue. Unfortunately, Baer *et al.* do not report whether prior exercise affected subjects' attitudes.

Finally, we might address the reasonableness of suggesting that subjects in the Snyder and Wicklund studies were concerned about presenting themselves to the experimenter. For such self-presentation concerns to be viable, we would assume that it would be necessary for an individual subject to believe that his or her opinions could be individually identified by the experimenter. Given the procedures of the Snyder and Wicklund studies, it is highly unlikely that subjects could have believed this. In their first experiment, subjects participated in groups that averaged around 30 subjects each; in Experiment II, subjects participated in groups that averaged around 80 individuals each. These seem sufficiently large crowds that subjects should have felt considerable anonymity. Anonymity was further enhanced by having the two booklets that subjects filled out (one containing the premeasure; the other containing the postmeasure) identified only by the subject's seat number in the large auditorium where the experiment was conducted (Snyder & Wicklund, 1980). This kind of anonymity seems as likely to assure subjects of the privacy of their opinions as the Baer *et al.* private conditions in which subjects sealed their opinion questionnaires in envelopes. Indeed, given that Baer *et al.* had only two subjects participate in each experimental session, it could be argued that the Snyder and Wicklund studies were *less* likely to induce concerns about self-presentation to the experimenter.

Conclusion

We have covered Heilman's work and the Baer *et al.* study in considerable detail. There are several reasons for this. At an operational level, the experimental procedures in these studies turn out to be very complex in terms of the theoretical variables involved. More important, however, we believe that a good deal of detail was necessary to adequately discuss the positions advocated by these investigators. Their writings provide the most articulated set of alternative theoretical proposals currently available. They deserve to be taken seriously, and we wished to do so.

Although we do not agree with the specific propositions of either Heilman or Baer *et al.*, we readily acknowledge that their emphasis on the interpersonal setting in which reactance effects often take place is an important and valuable contribution. Like European theorists such as Mugny and Doise, these researchers urge us to examine more closely the *social* psychology of psychological reactance. We have tried to do so in a variety of ways throughout this volume.

SUMMARY

A major qualification of reactance theory has been proposed by Heilman and others. This qualification is that reactance is aroused and reduced only in social relationships. Heilman's main argument is that the motivation to regain freedom comes from the desire to impress the threatener of freedom with an image of oneself as an autonomous person. That is, the threat to freedom must occur in a social context, and the response to that threat is designed to demonstrate one's autonomy in regard to that social agent. Reactance theory, on the other hand, assumes that threats can come from impersonal sources and that restoration of freedom can occur without the source of the threat being aware of restoration.

Heilman also proposes that only threats of punishment for noncompliance constitute threats to freedom; promises of reward for compliance do not. In contrast, reactance theory holds that regardless of their source or character, pressures to give up freedoms will arouse reactance. However, it was pointed out that negative pressures (threats of punishment) can arouse more reactance than positive pressures because the former pressure one to give up something already in one's possession, while the latter only threaten to withhold something that is presently not in one's possession. In addition, threats of punishment, compared to promises of reward, may convey a picture of more hostility and intent to influence on the part of the threatener.

Heilman further proposes that giving an individual the opportunity to choose the mode of compliance should counteract the restrictiveness of threats and reduce reactance. In contrast, our analysis in terms of reactance theory suggests that restrictions on modes of compliance will have no effect on reactance unless modes previously have been established as freedoms. Furthermore, reactance aroused by pressure to comply will not be affected by threats to mode of compliance unless the freedoms not to comply and to select different modes have been established as a set.

Two experiments by Heilman and her colleagues were described and discussed in some detail. It was concluded that the evidence lends support to Heilman's theoretical position as well as to the traditional form of reactance theory. More recent research relevant to an impression management form of reactance theory was also discussed. It was noted in discussing impression management formulations of reactance that some previous demonstrations of reactance are quite difficult to explain in terms of an impression management formulation. However, it may be impossible to rule out the possible role of a loosely conceived form of impression management processes.

CHAPTER 11

Developmental Aspects of Psychological Reactance[1]

Reactance theory addresses itself to basic motivational processes that are assumed to be ubiquitous and universal. As we have noted (Chapter 2), the content of these processes (i.e., the perceived freedom and the perceived threat) would be expected to vary widely among different individuals and different cultural milieus, but the processes themselves should remain constant. Constancy of motivational process is also assumed in regard to age and developmental status of the organism. While the vast majority of reactance research has been conducted with adults, the theory presumably would be applicable to children as well.

This chapter will review three categories of literature. First, we will review the existing reactance research that has been conducted with children. These investigations, while not designed with this purpose in mind, do seem to indicate that the theory "works" with children as well as with adults. The second category of literature to be discussed is more

---

[1] Portions of this chapter appear also in S. Brehm, "Oppositional behavior in children: A reactance theory approach." In S. S. Brehm, S. M. Kassin, and F. X. Gibbons (Eds.), *Developmental Social Psychology: Theory and Research* (New York: Oxford University Press, 1981).

diverse. Three topic areas involving different aspects of oppositional behavior in children have been selected for more extensive examination. Some of the research on these topics has been conducted within the rubric of reactance theory; most, however, stems from other theoretical perspectives. In the present consideration of these topics, reactance theory will be used in an attempt to provide an integrative approach to these various research findings. Finally, we shall conclude this chapter with a brief discussion of helplessness effects in children.

REACTANCE RESEARCH WITH CHILDREN

Importance of Freedom

A study by Worchel (1972) demonstrated that reactance arousal could be increased for children when the importance of the freedom that was threatened was increased. Subjects in this study were boys and girls between the ages of 6 and 12 who were attending summer camp. Subjects were either shown a movie or not. Of those who were shown a movie, half saw an aggressive movie about boxing, and the other half a nonaggressive movie about boats and ships. All subjects were led to believe that they would choose to engage in one of two activities: having a pie fight or riding one-person rubber rafts. When a second experimenter entered to get their choices, this experimenter (same sex as subjects) verbally pressured subjects to choose the pie fight, to choose the raft, or did not pressure them to choose either of the two alternate activities. The major dependent measure was subjects' choice of their subsequent activity.

Worchel had reasoned that viewing a movie would make the freedom to engage in activities similar to those depicted in the movie more salient and more important. Reactance arousal was, therefore, expected to be greatest for subjects who saw a movie and were then pressured to choose the activity that was *different* from that depicted in the film. These subjects should restore freedom by choosing the activity that was similar to that shown in the movie.

The results from this study are displayed in Table 11.1. First, let us examine subjects' choices when they either saw a movie *or* were pressured to choose a subsequent activity. Although these differences were not statistically reliable, it can be seen that subjects who saw a movie but did not receive any verbal pressure tended to choose a subsequent activity that was similar to the one in the movie, whereas subjects who had not seen a movie tended to choose in line with the verbal

TABLE 11.1
Percentages of Subjects Who Chose the Film-Related Activity[a]

	Verbal pressure		
Movie seen	To choose the pie fight (%)	To choose the raft (%)	None (%)
Aggressive movie	56[b]	88	67
Boat movie	100	67	78
No movie			
% choosing pie fight	67	25	33
% choosing raft	33	75	67

[a] Adapted from Worchel, S. The effects of films on the importance of behavioral freedom. *Journal of Personality*, 1972, 40, 417–435, Table 1, p. 424. Copyright 1972 by Duke University Press.

[b] There were nine subjects in every condition except the no movie–verbal pressure to choose raft, in which there were eight subjects.

pressure they received. Second, when we consider only those subjects who both saw a movie *and* were verbally pressured, significantly more subjects chose the film-related activity when the verbal pressure was to choose the dissimilar activity (94%) than when the verbal pressure was to choose the similar movie (61%). Pressuring children *not* to choose a film-related activity thus led to more choices of this type of activity than when they were pressured to choose a film-related activity.

Proportion of Freedoms

A study by Brehm, McQuown, and Shaban (reported in Brehm, 1966) demonstrated that reactance arousal in adolescents was a function of the proportion of freedoms that was eliminated. This study has been discussed previously (see Chapter 3), but we shall briefly review the experimental procedures here. Eighth-grade students read a brief description of each of six movies, and rated and ranked these movies according to how much they would like to see each one. In a later session, groups of subjects were told either that they could choose one of the movies to see from a list provided by the experimenter, or that they would be assigned one of the movies. Subjects were then provided with lists of either all six movies or of each individual's top-ranked three movies. Following inspection of the list, subjects in the no elimination condition were asked to rerate all six movies. For all other subjects, before they could begin to fill out the rating questionnaire again, an assistant entered the room and whispered something to the experimenter. After this, the experimenter announced that one of the movies did not arrive with the others and, therefore, could not be seen.

The experimenter and assistant then went to each subject individually and marked off his or her second-ranked movie. Subjects were instructed, however, to go ahead and rerate all of the six original movies. The data from this study confirmed the theoretical predictions that had been made (see Table 3.1). Subjects who expected to choose a movie and who had a high proportion of their freedoms eliminated (1 movie from the list of 3) became more favorable to the eliminated movie than did subjects in the choice–low proportion condition (1 movie eliminated from the list of 6), the no choice–high proportion condition, or the no elimination control group (although this last difference was only marginal, $p = .10$). Reactance arousal was thus maximized when the freedom to have any one of the choice alternatives had been established and when the elimination of one of these freedoms eliminated a large proportion of the subjects' available freedoms.

Threat to Freedom

A study by Weiner (reported by Brehm, 1966) examined children's responses to a peer's threat to their decisional freedom. Subjects in this study were first-grade students who were seen individually and told that they would get to choose a gift toy for themselves as a reward for helping out the experimenter. All subjects rank-ordered seven toys. About a week later, these children were asked to rank the toys again, and this second ranking was described as constituting the child's final choice of a gift. Half of the subjects reranked the toys without further comment from the experimenter. To the other half, the experimenter remarked, "Oh, by the way you remember the day when all the boys [girls] came to look at the toys for the first time? Well, one of them said something to me about you. Let's see, he [she] said, '[Name of subject] has to choose the [name of subject's preferred toy]. He [she] can't choose anything else.' So I asked him/her why he [she] said that, and he [she] said he [she] didn't know, just that '[Name of subject] has to choose it, that's all.'" These subjects then reranked the toys. As had been predicted, children who had been told that a peer was pressuring them to choose their initially most preferred toy reduced the ranking of that toy ($M = -1.38$) significantly more than children who were not informed of any peer pressure ($M = -.43$).

Elimination of Freedom

Two studies by Hammock and Brehm (1966) investigated children's responses to an elimination of freedom. While procedures and results of the first of their studies were described briefly earlier (see Chapter 5), we shall provide a more detailed examination of their research for the purposes of the present discussion. Subjects in Hammock and Brehm's first study were black male and female children ranging in age from 7 to 11. Each child was seen individually in the experiment. When subjects arrived at the first experimental room, they were randomly assigned to either a choice or no choice condition. Subjects in the choice condition were told that, as a reward for telling the experimenter how much they liked each of nine candy bars, they would be allowed to choose one of the two candy bars that were in another room. No choice subjects were given the same information, except that they were told they would be *given* one of the two candy bars in the other room.

All subjects then ranked the nine candy bars (by a process of eliminating the one the subject liked best from each set of diminishing number). On the pretext of obtaining a form, the experimenter left the room and informed the second experimenter in the other room of the subject's third- and fourth-ranked candy bars. The experimenter then returned to the subject and escorted him or her to the other room. For choice subjects, the experimenter told the second experimenter that they could choose whichever candy bar they wanted. For no choice subjects, the experimenter stated that the subject should be given a candy bar. After the first experimenter left the room, the second experimenter displayed the child's third- and fourth-ranked candy bars and gave the child his or her third-ranked candy; no child was given an opportunity to express a preference. The child was then returned to the first room and the first experimenter, claiming that he had made a mistake in recording the subject's preferences, asked all subjects to rerank all the candy bars.

Hammock and Brehm had predicted that, relative to the rankings by subjects in the no choice conditions, children in the choice condition should increase their rankings of the candy they had been denied (initially fourth-ranked) and decrease their rankings of the candy they had been given (initially third-ranked). Their results provided partial support of these hypotheses. Although a total reactance score (combining changes from both items) was significantly different between the two groups, the separate components of this total score were not particularly robust. For the candy they had not received, choice subjects tended to rate ($p = .08$) this candy bar as more attractive than subjects

TABLE 11.2
Mean Ranking Changes

Initial rank:	No choice conditions		Choice conditions	
	Eliminated Fourth	Given Third	Eliminated Fourth	Given Third
Hammock and Brehm, 1966, Study I[a]	− .43	.00	.23	− 1.23
Brehm, in press[b]				
Males	− .97	− .66	− .08	− 1.50
Females	.13	− .97	− .82	− 1.00

Initial rank:	Eliminated Third	Given Fourth	Eliminated Third	Given Fourth
Hammock and Brehm, 1966, Study II[c]	− .94	.00	− .11	− .86

[a] See Table 5.1, Footnote a.
[b] See Table 5.1, Footnote b.
[c] See Table 5.1, Footnote a, Table 2, p. 552.

in the no choice condition (see Table 11.2). For the candy they were given, no choice subjects did not differ significantly from choice subjects. Thus, while the general pattern of results supported the experimental hypotheses, the effects were somewhat weak.

In their second study, Hammock and Brehm used a similar procedure with some modifications. Subjects were white, all male, and ranged in age from 8 to 12. Instead of nine candy bars, ten toys each costing $1.00 were used as stimulus materials. It was made explicit to all subjects that the two toys (that, as in the first study, either they could choose between, or one of which would be given to them) would be two of the ten they ranked, although possibly not the two they liked best. One further modification in this study was especially important: All subjects were given their fourth-ranked toy and denied their third-ranked one.

This latter change in procedure creates some interpretive ambiguity. The procedure used in the first study (giving subjects the more preferred of the two toys) clearly rules out frustration as an alternative explanation for the obtained results. In the second study (where the subjects were given their less preferred toy), the elimination of frustration is not so clear. Neither of the toys was the subjects' favorite, or even their next most favored toy, and yet it could be argued that subjects would be frustrated by being denied that toy (of the two available) that they found most attractive. Moreover, frustration might be increased for subjects who had expected to choose and who had, presumably, intended to choose the toy they liked best. In any case, the results continued to be somewhat weak statistically. Again, the total reactance score was significantly different between the two experimental conditions, but the component comparisons were only marginal. For the toy they were denied, choice subjects tended ($p = .09$) to rank this toy as more attractive than no choice subjects, while for the toy they were given, choice subjects tended ($p < .08$) to rank this toy as less attractive (see Table 11.2).

The Hammock and Brehm studies have recently been replicated by Brehm (in press). Following essentially the same procedures used in their second experiment, Brehm was particularly interested in possible differences between the sexes and different ages. Although Hammock and Brehm had included both boys and girls in their first study, the number of members of each sex was quite small and precluded obtaining any sex differences unless these differences were quite strong. A similar problem existed in regard to age. It is important to note that Brehm attempted to eliminate frustration by following Hammock and Brehm's initial procedure of giving the child his or her more attractive (third-ranked) alternative and denying the child the less attractive (fourth-ranked) one.

Subjects for this experiment were 140 first- and sixth-grade children from two public elementary schools. An overall analysis of the ranking changes of the eliminated toy revealed a significant interaction between experimental condition and sex of subjects, and separate analyses by sex were performed. Such an interaction was not obtained for the ranking changes of the given toy, but separate analyses by sex were also conducted on these data in order to parallel the analyses done on the eliminated object. For males, a clear confirmation of the reactance theory prediction was obtained (see Table 11.2). Relative to males in the no choice condition, males in the choice condition were significantly more favorable to the eliminated alternative and significantly less favorble to the given alternative. For females, theoretical predictions were not confirmed. Females in the no choice condition were more favorable to the eliminated object than those in the choice condition, and females in the two conditions did not differ in regard to the given alternative. Grade did not interact with either experimental condition or sex on the rankings of either toy.

The behavior of female subjects in this study was not predicted and is not easy to explain. One possibility is that female subjects anticipated being able to influence what toy they were given and that, for them, the interpersonal situation of being given a toy constituted a more important freedom than the situation of making one's own choice between two, not very attractive toys. The preemptory behavior of the second experimenter may have constituted a threat to the freedom of being given what they wanted, thereby enhancing the attractiveness of the eliminated toy in that condition. While this interpretation is entirely speculative, it is interesting to note that the only evidence of an absolute increase in attractiveness (initial rank = 4; final mean rank = 3.87) for either toy occurred when female subjects in the no choice condition reranked the eliminated object.

The studies described thus far offer fairly good support for the general applicability of reactance theory to children's motivation and behavior. Children, ranging in age from the early elementary school years to middle-level junior high school students, have displayed reactance in response to threats to and eliminations of freedom. Reactance arousal has been increased by increasing the proportion of freedoms eliminated and the importance of the freedom threatened. Children in these studies have opposed a choice forced on them by an adult as well as one supposedly advocated by a peer. Items eliminated by circumstance as well as by a social agent have become more attractive. Except for the study by Brehm (in press), however, these studies were not designed with any specifically developmental issues in mind. But there are a number of topics that have received considerable attention by developmental psychologists and that are clearly relevant to reactance theory. In the following sections, three such topics will be discussed. The relationship between reactance theory and research conducted on these topics will be described, and an effort will be made to sketch out the implications of reactance theory for a variety of developmental processes.

SELECTED DEVELOPMENTAL TOPICS

Barriers

Oppositional behavior can occur in response to physical obstructions as well as in response to directives or prohibitions by social agents. Since physical barriers do not involve the myriad interactive factors that often complicate interpersonal relationships, responses to barriers offer a particularly suitable paradigm for studying children's oppositional behavior.

Barriers and Object Attractiveness

A number of studies have investigated the relationship between physical barriers and children's perceptions of object attractiveness. For example, in their classic study of frustration and regression in young children, Barker, Dembo, and Lewin (1941) presented children aged 28–61 months old with a variety of attractive toys behind a transparent but insurmountable barrier. Although the toys differed in attractiveness, the procedures of this study (in which many toys of many different attractiveness levels were used) make it difficult to determine what effects the barrier had on toy attractiveness.

A series of studies by Wright (1934, 1943) provided a more detailed examination of barriers and object attractiveness. Working with children 4 to 8 years of age, Wright obtained evidence of a general preference for barricaded objects when these objects were *not* identical to the nonbarricaded choice alternatives. Subsequent studies by Child and Adelsheim (1944) and Child (1946) failed to replicate Wright's work and did not obtain evidence that children preferred barricaded over nonbarricaded objects. Unfortunately, it is highly questionable whether these latter two studies constituted an acceptable test of Wright's hypothesis; both studies utilized choice alternatives that were either identical or only minimally different.

Furthermore, there are a number of methodological problems with the studies conducted by both Wright and Child. Both investigators allowed an experimenter to remain in the room while the child approached the choice alternatives; in Wright's work it is clear that this experimenter was aware of the experimental hypothesis. Wright's studies and Child's (1946) investigation may also have been affected by communication among subjects. Moreover, the ages of the children participating in these various experiments covered a wide range, and only Child (1946), who conducted the only study that did *not* include preschool children, provided an analysis of differences between age groups. Neither Wright nor Child mention possible sex differences in children's responses to barriers.

The hypothesis that object attractiveness should be increased by barriers is consistent with reactance theory as well as with the Lewinian notions that stimulated much of the previous work. Brehm (1966) discussed this relationship and reported a study with Hammock that examined this hypothesis. Subjects for this study were boys and girls from the first, fourth, and fifth grades of a public elementary school. The experimenter took each individual child to an experimental room where there was a table. Subjects in the choice condition were told they could choose between two different pieces of candy and have whichever one they thought was best. Subjects in the no choice condition were told they could have a piece of candy and were asked to tell the experimenter which of the two *other* pieces was the best. For all subjects, the experimenter then placed 1 piece of candy 3 inches from the near edge of the table and another piece 33 inches from the same edge. Candies were pink and yellow after-dinner mints, and the colors were rotated between the two different placements. No choice subjects were told they would receive a green mint, which the experimenter held up to them while giving them their instructions.

Brehm and Hammock expected that giving subjects choice would establish the two freedoms of having the yellow mint and having the pink mint. Since the candy that was furthest removed from the subject should be more difficult to obtain, distance was expected to act as a barrier and, therefore, as a threat to the child's freedom to have the further candy. Subjects in the no choice condition had not had the freedoms to have either candy on the table established. It was predicted that the reactance aroused by the distance-barrier should lead more children in the choice condition than in the no choice condition to designate the further candy as "the best one." There was a trend for this expected difference, but it did not reach acceptable levels of statistical reliability. Of the subjects in the no choice condition, 47% said that the far candy was best, while 65% of the subjects in the choice condition said the far one was best. This difference is significant only at the 12% level.

There are a number of methodological problems with this study. Again, the experimenter was present during the child's choice, and, indeed, Brehm refers to the seemingly large effect that experimenter behavior had on children's choices. Very similar items were used as choice alternatives, and possible inter-subject communication cannot be ruled out. Moreover, Brehm and Hammock did not analyze for sex or age differences.

Sex Differences in Barrier Response

As it happens, there is a fair amount of evidence that would suggest that sex and age differences may be important in determining children's responses to barricaded items. Goldberg and Lewis (1969) reported that 13-month-old children behaved differently in reaction to barriers as a function of sex. Males in their study spent more time at the ends of an insurmountable barrier than females, while females spent more time at the center of the barrier and cried more. These behaviors can be interpreted as indicating more effort on the part of males to get around the barrier and obtain the barricaded object. In their extensive longitudinal study of newborns and preschoolers, Bell, Weller, and Waldrop (1971) also obtained sex differences in young children's (27–33 months of age) responses to contrived barriers.

Males showed a cluster of behaviors involving variations in goal directedness and vigorous, sustained response to two different levels of contrived barriers. In females, a cluster of barrier behavior featuring variations in speed and persistence was organized around only one contrived barrier in which cognitive aspects appeared important, and in which an assertive response to the barrier was modeled by teachers [Bell *et al.*, 1971, p. 80].

On the other hand, Jacklin, Maccoby, and Dick (1973) obtained findings that do not support those reported by Goldberg and Lewis. For 13- and 14-month-old children, these investigators found no evidence of males' making more purposive efforts to surmount the barrier and found that girls cried more than boys only in a moderate stress condition (and not in a high stress condition also included in their study).

Data obtained by Van Lieshout (1975) suggest that age as well as sex differences may play a role in determining young children's responses to barriers. Van Lieshout had Dutch children at 17–19 months and then again at 23–25 months of age interact with their mothers through a series of experimental procedures. At one point, the mother placed a toy inside a plexiglass box that the child could not open. Although the sex of the child did not affect behavior directed at the box, negative emotional responses (e.g., crying, anger) to the mother who placed the toy in the box differed as a function of the child's sex and age. Males and females did not differ in negative emotional response at the younger age period (17–19 months), but males displayed more negative emotional response than females at the older age period (23–24 months). Examining this interaction from a different perspective, negative reactions for females significantly decreased between 18 and 24 months, whereas negative reactions for males tended ($p < .10$) to increase across this age span.

These studies suggest, then, that sex differences in responses to barriers are more likely to occur around the age of two than before. Of the three studies in which children before the age of two participated, only Goldberg and Lewis obtained sex differences. For the most part, Jacklin *et al.* did not, nor did Van Lieshout find sex differences when the children in his study were under two years of age. On the other hand, both Bell *et al.* and Van Lieshout obtained sex differences with children around the age of two, although it should be noted that Bell *et al.* found differences in manipulative behavior while Van Lieshout obtained sex differences only in emotional response.

Physical Barriers and Psychological Reactance

Consideration of the literature described above suggested a number of elements that would need to be taken into account in order to generate an adequate examination of children's responses to barriers. First, the age of two is suggested by empirical evidence as well as anecdotal report ("the terrible two's") as being of distinctive interest. Second, males and females need to be included in a study of barrier behavior to see if sex differences might appear. Third, a variety of methodological cautions are necessary: the experimenter should not be in the room when the child interacts with the barrier; inter-subject communication should be minimized; and while objects (both barricaded and not) should be equally attractive, they should be clearly different.

The need for this latter design characteristic is theoretical as well as methodological. As discussed in Chapter 3, if a person is choosing between two items and one is threatened with elimination, reactance arousal should result only if the two are not identical. Identical items do not provide unique instrumental value for satisfying needs, and an object or behavior must be of unique instrumental value in order for it to constitute a sufficiently important free behavior. Finally, it would also be important to show that preference for a barricaded object would increase as the barrier becomes more difficult to overcome. The barrier, according to reactance theory, acts as a threat to freedom, and with increasing threat, motivation to reestablish the freedom should increase.

With these theoretical and methodological points in mind, the following study was conducted to examine the relationship between physical barriers and reactance arousal. Brehm and Weinraub (1977) recruited volunteer parents and children from the local community. Two-year-old children (range: 21–27 months) were brought individually by their mothers to a university laboratory, the age of the subjects and the experimental setting thus eliminating inter-subject communication about the experimental procedures. After the experimental procedures were explained to the mother, she and her child were brought to the door of the experimental playroom where the experimenter was standing in the middle of the room in clear sight of the mother and child. The experimenter proceeded to hold up and name each of two toys, placed each toy at an equal distance from the child, and informed the child that he or she could play with whatever toy he or she wanted. The mother then was seated unobtrusively in a corner of the room, and the experimenter left the room.

The toys used in the experiment were a Fisher Price Ring Stack and a Fisher Price Color Stack, shown in a pilot study with other children this age to be equally attractive. These toys are similar in color and size, but clearly different in shape. For each child, a toy was placed either behind the barrier or beside it. The barrier was always located to the right of the child, and consisted of a blue-tinted, transparent Plexiglass sheet inserted into a wooden base.

Three experimental conditions were run in this study. In two conditions, both toys were used (and counterbalanced between being behind the barrier or being beside it), and the barrier was either small (.33 m high) or large (.66 m high). In the third condition, only the large barrier was used, but the toys were identical (and counterbalanced between the Ring Stack and the Color Stack). Children's behavior toward the toys and the barrier was videotaped from behind a one-way mirror. The major dependent measure was the child's latency before touching each toy.

Brehm and Weinraub predicted that maximum reactance arousal, and thus maximum initial preference for the barricaded toy, should occur when the barrier was large and the toys were different. For males, this prediction was confirmed (see Table 11.3). When the two toys were identical, boys touched the free-standing toy somewhat more quickly than the barricaded toy, although this difference is not statistically significant. When the toys were different and the barrier was small, latency to touch was essentially equivalent for both toys. When, however, the toys were different and the barrier was large, 2-year-old males touched the barricaded toy significantly sooner than they touched the free-standing toy. The behavior of female subjects did not conform to the reactance theory prediction. Female two-year-olds touched the free-standing toy more quickly (M = 30.19 sec) than the barricaded one (M = 57.65 sec) regardless of the size of the barrier or the difference between the toys.

These findings are essentially consistent with those of previous investigations of 2-year-olds' responses to barriers. Two-year-old males do seem to oppose the barrier (or the social agent who has implemented it), and the conditions under which this opposition occurs can be predicted from reactance theory. Two-year-old females, however, appear not to oppose physical barriers. This latter finding is perhaps best

TABLE 11.3
Latency to Touch (in seconds) for 2-Year-Old Males[a]

	Large barrier, identical toys	Large barrier, different toys	Small barrier, different toys
Barricaded toy	56.00	22.30	45.22
Free-standing toy	37.33	70.10	47.33

[a] From Brehm, S. S. & Weinraub, M. Physical barriers and psychological reactance: 2-year-olds' responses to threats to freedom. *Journal of Personality and Social Psychology*, 1977, *35*, 830–836. Table 1, p. 833. Copyright 1977 by the American Psychological Association. Reprinted by permission.

regarded in light of Van Lieshout's research. His data suggest that at an early age, males and females behave similarly in response to a barricaded object, but that as development proceeds the sexes begin to differ. With age, male children appear to become more negative in their responses toward barriers, while female children appear to become less negative. Taken together, the Van Lieshout and Brehm and Weinraub studies raise the possibility that for male children, the freedom to oppose physical obstructions is affirmed, while for females either the freedom itself becomes irrevocably eliminated or the cost of engaging in direct restorative action becomes prohibitive. As has been noted previously, there are important psychological differences between irrevocably eliminating a freedom versus suppressing freedom-restorative behavior, and it would seem important that future research on young children's responses to barriers try to determine which of these processes might be affected during the socialization of young girls.

Compliance with Adult Social Influence

When an adult tries to influence the behavior of a child, the pressures on the child to conform will be considerable. Many adults control resources that are essential for the child's survival or, at least, for his or her psychological well-being. Most adults are capable of physically enforcing their demands on the child by brute force; even if, in actuality, this force is not likely to be used, the very fact that it could occur may be sufficient to enforce compliance by the child. Furthermore, even if a specific adult does not control resources valuable to the child and does not have direct physical power over the child, most children are quite aware that relatively nonpowerful adults can frequently enforce compliance by communicating with the more powerful adults in their lives. Adults, then, are extremely powerful social influence agents in relation to children.

This power can have a variety of effects on the possiblilities for reactance arousal. Because of their power, adults have extensive control over defining the child's behavioral freedoms. This would be especially true for young children, who typically spend more time with adults than do older children and on whom other sources of information, such as peers and TV, have less impact. For example, the young child who has never been allowed to snack after dinner time probably does not see himself or herself as free to do this. Continued enforcement of such a regulation by adults, then, would not be expected to arouse reactance.

Children do, however, come to perceive themselves as having certain freedoms. Sometimes these freedoms are established by the parents, sometimes by other sources of information. Whatever the source, once the child perceives engaging (or not engaging) in a certain behavior as a specific behavioral freedom, then the possibility for reactance arousal is created, and if this freedom is threatened or eliminated by an adult, reactance arousal should occur. These conditions are not, however, sufficient to generate freedom-restorative behavior. For children, the cost of noncompliance may often be too high and, if so, opposition to the adult's influence will be suppressed. This analysis suggests that, at least for preadolescent children, compliance with adult requests will be more likely to occur than opposition. In order to obtain actual behavioral opposition, it will be necessary to ensure that (a) a freedom of sufficient importance is established for the child, (b) a threat of sufficient magnitude occurs, and (c) the cost of noncompliance is not so high that opposition is suppressed.

When we examine the research on children's compliance with adult requests that has been generated from theoretical perspectives other than reactance, we find, as might be expected, a mixed picture. Clearly, children often do comply, and factors such as contingent reinforcement (e.g., Goetz, Holmberg, & LeBlanc, 1975) and verbal reprimands for noncompliance (e.g., Forehand, Roberts, Doleys, Hobbs, & Resick, 1976) can increase compliance.

Children do not, however, *always* comply, and some of the variables that have been found to reduce compliance are consistent with a reactance theory analysis. For example, Forehand and Scarboro (1975) found that as mothers increased the number of commands to their children (in an observed interaction in the laboratory), compliance decreased. The procedure in this study involved mothers' instructing their children to play with each of six toys, one at a time, and giving each instruction twice. Each single freedom was, therefore, threatened twice, and, over time, the number of freedoms threatened increased.

A study by Patterson, Littman, and Brown (1968) found that *implied* influence by an adult model can also increase oppositional behavior. In this study, male first-graders were first asked to designate their preferred picture in each of 68 pairs of pictures of objects. The pictures were presented in drawings contained in a booklet. Approximately two weeks later, subjects were exposed to these picture pairs projected on a screen and again asked to indicate the one in each pair that they preferred. The first 28 slides presented were used to measure variability in picture preferences by comparing children's preferences when the slides were shown with those expressed earlier in response to the drawings in the booklet. During the next 40 slides, a female adult who was seated beside the child indicated her preferences prior to the child's response. On 31 of the 40 slides, the adult's preference disagreed with the child's initial preference; on 9 of the slides, the adult's preference agreed. The number of times the preferences expressed by the child disagreed with those of the model constituted the major dependent measure.

The data obtained in this study indicated a considerable amount of oppositional behavior. The mean variability for picture preference (established during the baseline) was 37%. When the model disagreed with the child's initial preferences, variability was significantly lowered to 18%; children opposed the model by staying with their previous initial preferences. When, however, the model's preferences agreed with the child's initial preferences, variability was significantly increased to 71%; children opposed the model by reversing their own initial preferences. In a second study reported by Patterson et al. only "negative set" variability (i.e., children's opposition to an agreeing model) was examined. Male children between the ages of 6 and 10 participated, and it was found that the younger children (6–7) had significantly higher negative set scores than the older children (8–10).

The influence in Patterson et al.'s study was implicit rather than direct. The adult model did not tell the child which picture to prefer; she simply stated the one that she preferred. While this may have constituted a threat of low magnitude, this kind of influence may also have implied to the child that the costs of noncompliance were not potentially high, and allowed the reactance that was created to be expressed in direct restorative behavior.

Theoretically, this kind of trade-off is problematic; it is difficult to predict whether the sort of implicit influence that will reduce the perceived costs of noncompliance might also reduce the magnitude of threat to such a degree that little reactance would be aroused. It is possible, however, to reduce the perceived costs of noncompliance without simultaneously reducing the magnitude of the initial threat. One way to do this would be to have the adult not to be present when the child has the opportunity to restore freedom by opposing the adult's influence. Although the evidence is somewhat mixed (see, for example, Redd, 1974, and Winston and Redd, 1976), there are some studies that have found that having the adult who has given instructions to a child leave the room decreases the child's compliance with these instructions (Peterson & Whitehurst, 1971; Redd & Wheeler, 1973).

Conflict between Adult Influence Agents

Another way in which an adult's social influence power over a child can be reduced was suggested in a study by Brehm (1977). Subjects in this study were male and female first- and fifth-graders who participated in a modified version of the paradigm used earlier by Worchel and Brehm (1971). Each individual child was taken by Experimenter 1 to the experimental room and, there, introduced to Experimenter 2. The children were told that both experimenters were trying to find out what children like and dislike about toys. All subjects were informed that they would look at some toys, tell another person (Experimenter 3) how much they liked the toys, and then get to choose a toy and play with it.

In the no influence condition, children simply looked at two toys displayed on a table; two different sets of toys were used for the two grades to ensure sufficient toy attractiveness. In the influence condition, subjects' inspection of the two toys was interrupted by E1's saying, "Of course, I think you should choose this one. There's no question about it." As she made this statement, E1 touched one of the displayed toys. Subjects in the restoration condition received the same influence attempt by E1, but immediately after this statement, E2 (who had been quietly working at a desk) looked up and said, "Wait a minute, I think you should choose whichever one you want." For all subjects, E1 and E2 left the room, and E3 then entered the room to assess subjects' ratings of each of the two toys. Children were asked whether they liked or disliked a given toy, and, if they said they liked it, were asked to point to one of a set of 5 blocks of increasing size (displayed on a poster board) that were verbally labeled for the child as indicating increasing amounts of liking. Which toy the child was urged to choose and rate first, or (in the no influence condition) only rate first, was counterbalanced. After ratings were obtained, all subjects chose the toy they wished to play with.

Brehm had predicted that children's responses to these experimental procedures would be similar to those obtained by Worchel and Brehm with college-age adults. That is, liking for the advocated toy was expected to decrease in the influence condition and to increase once freedom was restored in the restoration condition. The rating data obtained did not confirm these predictions (see Table 11.4). Instead, children complied with the adult influence in the influence condition,

TABLE 11.4
Mean Compliance Ratings[a]

	No influence	Influence	Restoration
First-graders	.42[b]	1.6	− .75
Fifth-graders	− .17	1.9	1.00

[a] From Brehm, S. S. The effect of adult influence on children's preferences: Compliance versus opposition. *Journal of Abnormal Child Psychology*, 1977, 5, 31–41. Table 1, p. 37. Copyright 1977 by Plenum Publishing Corp.

[b] Ratings of the toy-not-urged (and/or the toy rated second) subtracted from the ratings of the toy-urged (and/or the toy rated first). In the influence and restoration conditions, therefore, negative scores indicate opposition to the advocated choice alternative.

although the difference between the influence and no influence conditions was significant only for fifth-graders. Moreover, first-graders displayed significantly less compliance with the advocated choice in the restoration condition than in the influence condition. For fifth-graders, there was only a nonsignificant trend for compliance to be reduced in the restoration condition relative to the influence situation. In general, children's choices were consistent with their rating preferences, only 13% of them choosing their less favorably rated toy.

Although these findings failed to confirm Brehm's initial predictions, they are congruent with the analysis offered in this chapter. While the children in this study had their freedoms to choose and evaluate the toys according to their own preferences clearly established, there is no reason to believe that these freedoms were of any great importance. Moreover, the adults who interacted with the child were strangers and had no direct power over the child's behavior, but they appeared in the child's classroom with permission from the child's teacher. Thus, in the influence condition, a reasonably powerful adult threatened a relatively unimportant freedom. Furthermore, E1's advocacy of a particular toy was received in silence by E2; this lack of response on E2's part may have suggested to the child that she agreed with E1's advocacy. Although the child's ratings of and choice between the toys was obtained by a third individual and neither E1 nor E2 remained in the room, children may have presumed that the other experimenters would learn of their behavior. Given this context, one can (admittedly, after the fact) understand the high levels of compliance that were obtained in the influence condition.

This type of analysis can also suggest an explanation of why there was some tendency for first-grade children in the restoration condition to oppose the experimenter's influence attempt. It does not appear that this opposition to E1 was generated by compliance with E2. E2 never directly expressed a preference, and, indeed, one-third of the first-grade subjects did *not* see E2's preferences as differing from those of E1. Furthermore, the same proportion of children in both grades (one-third) perceived their choice as agreeing with E2's preference and disagreeing with E1's preference. Thus, the majority of children in both grades did not see themselves as agreeing with E2 and opposing E1, and the level of this perception was constant across grade and did not parallel the greater oppositional tendencies on the part of first-graders.

Instead of complying with E2, then, it seems possible that the younger children in this study perceived E2's statement as undercutting the power of the influencing agent, E1. By supporting the child's freedom to choose, E2 may have implicitly opposed the first adult's control over the child's behavior. This reduction in power may have signaled to children that E1 would have reduced ability to punish noncompliance and, thus, may have made it permissible to oppose her influence. To push these speculations one step further, it would also seem possible that fifth graders have a more long-range view of the power of adults and that E2's statement supporting the child's freedom to choose was less effective in reducing E1's power for them than for the more socially naive first-graders.

Given our previous references to possible sex differences in children's responses to adult influence, it should be noted that the above effects obtained by Brehm were not modified by the sex of the child. However, very few subjects of each sex were available in each of the relevant experimental conditions and only very strong sex differences could have shown up on the statistical analyses that were conducted. (For further discussion of sex differences in reactance, see Chapter 12).

Compliance in Naturalistic Settings

All of the above studies examined children's responses to adult influence in experimental settings. It would seem of interest to provide a brief review of some of the findings on such behaviors that have been obtained in naturalistic settings (i.e., in the family's home). None of the studies described below was conducted with reactance theory in mind, and the reader is cautioned that all of the following interpretative statements are sheer, if rather intriguing, speculation.

In a study of the interactions between mothers and year-old infants, Stayton, Hogan, and Ainsworth (1971) reported that compliance to mothers' commands was not a function of either frequency of verbal commands or of frequency of physical interventions. Instead, maternal sensitivity, acceptance, and cooperation were found to be "the primary correlates of an infant's compliance to commands [Stayton *et al.*, 1971, p. 1065]." Stayton *et al.* concluded that a "disposition toward obedience" will emerge in a supportive social environment and that calculated attempts to shape the emergence of compliant behavior are not necessary.

A similar picture of the predominance of compliance with maternal directives was reported by Minton, Kagan, and Levine (1971). Even with the supposedly "terrible" two-year-olds who served along with their mothers as subjects, these investigators observed little disobedience. It was noted, however, that "disobedience among boys . . . was positively associated with frequent physical punishment and maternal failure to explain prohibition [Minton *et al.*, 1971, p. 1889]."

Lytton and his associates have published a number of studies describing the interaction between parents and their 25- to 35-month-old male children (both twins and single children being included in the sample). Lytton and Zwirner (1975) concluded that maternal consistency, play with the child, use of psychological rewards, and reasoning facilitated compliance. Maternal use of psychological punishment and material reward as well as paternal use of physical punishment was, however, negatively associated with compliance. Similar findings were reported in Lytton's 1977 paper, with the additional observation that maternal use of physical punishment was a negative predictor of compliance. In a more recent presentation of the findings from this research project, Lytton (1979) found that physical control when combined with verbal commands detracted from compliance, while the combination of positive action (e.g., smiling, expression of love or approval, hugging) and commands increased compliance.

These findings would appear to be quite consistent with the general analysis offered earlier in this chapter. Among these very young children, compliance appears to be overwhelmingly more frequent than disobedience. Considering both the physical power (i.e., physical control and control of resources) and the informational power (i.e., defining the child's behavioral freedoms) that parents have over young children, this is presumably what any of us would expect. With children beyond the infancy stage, however, compliance is not all-pervasive. Disobedience appears linked to the use of strong control techniques (such as physical punishment and control, and—at least, for mothers—use of psychological punishment and material rewards). An additional factor promoting noncompliance appears to consist of the way in which information is presented to the child. Maternal failure to explain prohibition was cited by Minton *et al.* as related to disobedience among male 2-year-olds, while Lytton has pointed to consistent enforcement of rules by the mother and reasoning as facilitating compliance.

All of these factors are easily encompassed within a reactance theory framework. The use of strong control techniques can be seen as increasing reactance arousal by increasing the magnitude of threat to the child's freedom. Failure to explain prohibition or to use reasoning may also increase reactance arousal by increasing implications for future threats to future freedoms. When a prohibition is clearly explained, the child knows the limits of the threat to or elimination of freedom. In the absence of a clear explanation, other free behaviors may be threatened by implication.

Lytton's emphasis on the importance of consistency in rule enforcement also would appear related to a central tenet of reactance theory. The inconsistent parent may, in effect, "mislead" the child into thinking that he or she has a freedom that the parent does not regard as a freedom. Consequently, when the parent does attempt to enforce the rule, the child perceives this as a threat to or elimination of a freedom, and psychological reactance should be aroused. If, however, rule enforcement is consistent, then parental control is more likely to be exercised over those behavioral acts that the child has never regarded as free. In this case, reactance should not be aroused and neither the motivation to oppose the parent nor actual behavioral opposition would be produced.

As a final point, we might note that enforcement of rules is often a two-person endeavor. Based on both Lytton's findings and the experiment by Brehm (1977), we would expect that disobedience from a child should be increased by conflict between the parents about rules as well as by inconsistent rule enforcement by a single parent. When parents disagree, and the child knows about this disagreement, the child may perceive a specific behavioral freedom to be established that will not be seen as a free behavior for the child by at least one parent, and the social power of both parents may well be reduced by the conflict between them.

Modifying Noncompliant Behavior

So far in this chapter, we have considered what might be termed "normal" oppositional behavior. In the case of children, this normal oppositional behavior may be unpleasant for the adult recipients of it (usually parents or teachers), but such opposition, in general, would be seen as a positive developmental event indicating the child's increasing autonomy.

Beyond these normal levels of failure to comply, many clinicians have encountered what might be called "deviant" oppositional behavior. This type of oppositional behavior is considered deviant presumably because it occurs more frequently, more intensely, and/or over a longer period of time than the "normal" type. Some children are brought to mental health professionals specifically because of problems with oppositional behavior. Indeed, the recent DSM–III (*Diagnostic and Statistical Manual of Mental Disorders*, 3rd ed.: American Psychiatric Association, 1980) includes the category "oppositional disorder" for diagnostic use with children and adolescents.

Other children are brought to mental health professionals or to governmental agencies, such as the police or the court system, because they have violated more formalized societal norms. Cohen (1955) has emphasized that delinquent behavior frequently consists of direct opposition to more general norms: "The delinquent's conduct is right, by the standards of his subculture, precisely because it is wrong by the norms of the larger culture [p. 28]."

Furthermore, children whose problems are severe and of psychotic proportion may also display deviant oppositional behavior (see, for example, Cowan, Hoddinott, & Wright, 1965). DesLauriers and Carlson (1969) have noted this feature of some autistic children and have described a procedure that uses this problem behavior to benefit the child's treatment.

> The most general strategy used here is neither uncommon, nor is it unknown to most mothers confronted with the *No, No* phase of their young child. It consists, essentially, either of demanding of the child the exact opposite of what one might actually want him to do, or of pretending convincingly that one doesn't really care one way or the other whether the child does what he is asked [DesLauriers & Carlson, 1969, p. 156].

There have been three major theoretical approaches to the treatment of deviant oppositional behavior. In this section, we shall describe each briefly and then outline some possible treatment strategies that could be derived from reactance theory.

Psychoanalytic Approaches

Psychoanalytic approaches (based on Freud's writings and the work of later neo-Freudians such as Erikson) have been remarkably nonspecific in their treatment of deviant oppositional behavior. For example, in Anthony and Gilpin's (1976) consideration of oppositional behavior, psychotherapy with oppositional children is described as focusing on the therapist–child relationship, with the therapist calling attention to the oppositional behavior and attempting to elevate the child's self-esteem. Very little of this would seem specific to oppositional behavior, and, yet, it should be noted that such an approach would presumably minimize direct therapist control over the child's behavior, and, thereby, oppositional behavior by the child might be reduced at least within the confines of the therapeutic relationship. Whether or not any such reductions will generalize to other aspects of the child's life is debatable. Gilpin and Worland (in Anthony & Gilpin, 1976) report successful interventions in 4 out of 15 completed cases of deviant/excessive oppositional behavior. In the absence of any kind of placebo or waiting-list controls, however, it is impossible to evaluate this rate of success.

Behavioral Approaches

A more clearly effective therapeutic intervention has been generated by behavior therapists. The general approach is to combine modified parental attention (i.e., attention and praise for desirable/compliant behavior) with the use of time-out (i.e., placing the child briefly in a nonreinforcing environment) in response to undesirable/oppositional behavior. Describing this approach, Wahler (1969) noted that in his study, (a) parental reinforcement value was initially low and increased as a function of the treatment program and (b) oppositional behavior was reduced. The theoretical questions raised by these findings are summarized by Wahler. "First, if parental reinforcement value was initially quite low, why should the timeout procedure be effective? . . . Secondly, if parental reinforcement value was initially quite low, what was maintaining the children's oppositional behavior during baseline? [p. 170]." Wahler proposed that a "plausible answer" to the second question would be that the oppositional child suffers not from an excess of oppositional behavior, but rather from a deficit of cooperative behavior. Low parental reinforcement would, then, be consistent with such a deficit condition.

This explanation would appear to run into difficulty on two fronts. First, as we have seen, compliant behavior seems to develop quite easily and spontaneously among most children, without specific parental strategies to induce it. Contrary to this view, Wahler seems to be suggesting that some more active intervention (i.e., higher parental reinforcement) is needed either for all children or, at least, for the specific children in his study. However, he does not explicitly address the latter possibility. Second, Wahler's explanation would still seem to leave unanswered the question of why time-out was effective and why parental reinforcement value increased during treatment. While numerous other investigators (e.g., Baer, Rowbury, & Baer, 1973; Forehand, Cheney, & Yoder, 1974; Forehand & King, 1974; Scarboro & Forehand, 1975; Walter & Gilmore, 1973) have confirmed the effectiveness of combined modified attention and time-out in reducing oppositional behavior, these theoretical issues raised by Wahler still appear to be largely unresolved.

A reactance theory approach to Wahler's findings would be substantially different. First, reactance theory would not find it peculiar that certain kinds of parent–child interactions could lead to both low positive effects on behavior (i.e., low reinforcement value) and high negative effects (i.e., high levels of opposition). Instead, this theoretical perspective would hypothesize that the parents are not serving as effective control agents over the child: Freedoms have been established for the child that the parents do not regard as free behaviors; social influence attempts are of sufficient magnitude to arouse reactance and of insufficient magnitude to irrevocably eliminate freedom; and the costs of noncompliance are not sufficiently high to suppress direct opposition.

Second, the effectiveness of time-out may, from a reactance theory point of view, reflect parental reassertion of control in a dramatic and unmistakable way. Time-out may redefine free behaviors for the child such that what was perceived as a freedom no longer is, or it may increase the costs of noncompliance such that direct restorative behavior is suppressed. If time-out operates through either (or both) of these theoretical pathways, there may be undesirable psychological costs associated with its use. If too many freedoms are eliminated (or eliminated in such a way that elimination of a large number of freedoms is implied), the child may become not only nonoppositional, but helpless and unmotivated to engage in desirable as well as undesirable behaviors. (Typical treatment programs try to counter such a possibility by including positive reinforcement for desirable behaviors.) On the other hand, if restorative behavior is merely suppressed, rather than reactance arousal being eliminated, the reduction in oppositional behavior may not generalize to other settings with other social agents.

Furthermore, it might be noted that using time-out as a treatment procedure has become highly controversial (Anderson & King, 1974; White, Nielson, & Johnson, 1972) and has been banned with some populations (*Wyatt v. Stickney*, 1973). As Forehand *et al.* (1976) have noted, such concerns over severe restrictions of children's behaviors highlight the need to develop alternative methods of reducing oppositional behavior.

Patterson's Approach

The third major approach to the treatment of excessively oppositional children is a combination of systems analysis and behavior therapy. This approach is largely associated with the work of Patterson (e.g., Patterson, 1974; 1976a). Although there has been some dispute about generalization and persistence of the reduction in oppositional behavior attained by this treatment method (see Kent, 1976; Reid & Patterson, 1976), Patterson's treatment approach appears to be reasonably successful in reducing oppositional behavior in the immediate environments of concern (i.e., home and school).

Patterson (1976a) describes the theoretical context that has formed the basis for his treatment of conduct disorder boys. First, he hypothesizes that the parents of conduct disordered children will often use both punishment and reinforcement inconsistently. Undesirable behaviors will be rewarded (at least by parental attention), while desirable behaviors will often go unnoticed. Thus, a major element of Patterson's treatment program is to generate more consistent use of reinforcement and punishment. Parents and teachers are taught to reward desirable behaviors consistently and to respond to undesirable behaviors by withdrawing reinforcers (including the use of time-out, as described in Patterson, 1975, 1976b). This treatment approach is, then, essentially equivalent to that employed by Wahler and the other investigators cited previously. The theoretical rationale, however, is quite different. Patterson does not maintain Wahler's position that the problem lies in a deficiency of compliant behaviors brought about because parents are not sufficiently reinforcing to induce compliance. Instead, he proposes that the inconsistent use of punishment and reinforcement by parents decreases parental control over the child's behavior and allows oppositional behavior to flourish.

Patterson's second major concern is with the coercive system that he sees as developing within the family of a conduct disordered child. He contends that when one person uses "pain control techniques" over another, the second person will learn to use these same techniques: "Presumably, as one member of a system applies pain control techniques, the victims will eventually learn, via modeling . . . and/or reinforcing contingencies . . . , to *initiate* coercive interactions [Patterson, 1976a, p. 269]."

This interactive learning can, according to Patterson, lead to "extended interchanges in which *both* members of the dyad apply aversive stimuli [p. 269]." Moreover, increases in the intensity of the aversive stimuli will tend to be reinforced whenever an increment in intensity results in the most coercive person's "winning" the immediate battle and the other person's ceasing his or her attack.

Both of Patterson's hypotheses about the kind of family environment that is most likely to produce an excessively oppositional child are congruent with a reactance theory analysis. As described earlier, inconsistency can (unwittingly) establish freedoms. Moreover, being aggressed against by another can also establish a freedom—the freedom to counter-aggress (Nezlek & Brehm, 1975)—and watching other people interact aggressively can serve to increase the importance of acting aggressively oneself (Worchel, 1972).

Unfortunately, the data reported by Patterson (1976a) are somewhat at odds with these hypotheses about the etiology of excessive oppositionalism. First, it is not clear that consistency of parental reinforcement schedules is as important as either Patterson initially believed or, indeed, as one would expect in terms of reactance theory.

> Several reviewers, including the present writer . . . , have suggested that training parents to reduce positive consequences for coercive behaviors would be followed by reductions in rates for these behaviors. Analysis by Taplin (1974) showed that the hypothesis may not be tenable. The analysis showed a nonsignificant correlation between children's baseline Total Deviant behavior scores and the parents' schedules of positive consequences for these behaviors. A cross-lag correlational analysis also showed no support for the hypothesis. Finally, his data showed significant *reductions* for mean rates of the child's Total Deviant behavior during the initial phases of treatment at which point parental mean rates of positive consequences for these behaviors were *increasing!* [Patterson, 1976a, p. 304].

These findings led Patterson to believe that the modeling provided by coercive disciplinary acts may be more important than parental schedules of punishment and reinforcement. This hypothesis received only partial support.

> It was hypothesized that as the behavior of the problem child was brought under control, the coercive behaviors of all other family members would display commensurate reductions. . . . In keeping with the hypothesis, the data at termination showed reductions in Total Deviant scores for all family members. However, only the changes for siblings were significant [Patterson, 1976a, pp. 304-305].

Although Patterson's specific hypotheses regarding the role of reinforcement consistency and modeling of coercive behaviors in the generation and maintenance of excessive oppositional behavior have not been fully supported, there is evidence that, at a general level, disciplinary inconsistency and punitiveness are both associated with undesirable behavior in children. For example, Rosenthal, Finkelstein, Ni, and Robertson (1959) found that maternal inconsistency and punitiveness were related to the problem behavior of children seen at the Illinois Institute of Juvenile Research; paternal punitiveness and authoritarian control were also associated with problem behavior in these children (Rosenthal, Ni, Finkelstein, & Berkwits, 1962). Inconsistency *between* parents has been found to be related to undesirable behavior in young children (Baruch & Wilcox, 1944; Read, 1945), delinquency (Glueck & Glueck, 1950; McCord, McCord, & Zola, 1959), and excessive aggressiveness (Bandura & Walters, 1959).

These findings are strikingly similar to the data on noncompliance in normal children that have been described previously in this chapter and suggest that rather than focusing on inconsistent (or inappropriate) reinforcement schedules per se, an alternative approach would be to investigate parental formulation of rules that define desirable and undesirable behaviors. Such an approach would be highly consistent with reactance theory's emphasis on the need for a freedom to exist in order for a threat to that behavior to evoke opposition.

Reactance Theory Approaches

In the preceding sections, various treatments of and conceptual approaches to excessive oppositional behavior in children have been interpreted in terms of reactance theory. All of this has been, of course, strictly *post hoc,* and it would be valuable to have a more direct application of the theory to the problem behavior of interest. One such application is described by Ayllon, Allison, and Kandel (1980). These investigators made use of a treatment for oppositional behavior based on Varela's (1971) "persuasion by successive approximation using reactance." The initial component of this technique is the formulation of a hierarchy of statements relevant to the desired behavior, which range from the most likely to be accepted by the client to the least likely. The therapist then tries to persuade the client of the opposite of each statement, attempting, thereby, to create reactance and motivate the client to publicly commit himself or herself to the desired statement. The therapist progresses up through the hierarchy until the client has committed himself or herself to all the desired statements. Typically, the last statement(s) concerns a behavioral intention on the part of the client that, if carried through, would ameliorate the problem behavior.

Ayllon *et al.* report two interventions with normal children who were classified by their teacher as the most disruptive in the class. All were male, from 11 to 13, and all were performing poorly in their academic subjects as well as being disruptive. The teacher considered all four boys as capable of at least average work and repeated efforts by the teacher to discourage the disruptive behavior as well as conferences with the parents had failed to improve the children's classroom behavior.

After a baseline of the children's disruptive behavior and academic performance had been established, each of the four children was counseled successively by one of two therapists. The therapist (presumably in consultation with the teacher and the parents) drew up the hierarchy of statements that the therapist wished each child to agree with. A condensed version of that hierarchy is displayed in Table 11.5 along with a few excerpts from the dialogue between one of the students and his therapist.

For three of the children in this study, the successive persuasion technique was quite successful. Disruptive behavior was reduced from a mean of 47% to a mean of 19%; academic performance in math increased from 22% correct to 83% correct. Ayllon *et al.* report that these children's desirable behavior increased dramatically on the first day after "behavioral persuasion," and that the desired changes were maintained for the rest of the study (an average of 12 days for each child).

For the fourth child, success was only temporarily achieved. While there was impressive improvement in both disruption and math performance on the first day after the intervention, these improvements vanished the following day. Ayllon *et al.* decided to repeat the behavioral persuasion session with this child, but this time with the school principal, the teacher, and the child's father in attendance. After this session, this child's disruptive behavior decreased from a mean of 50% to a mean of 30%, and his math performance increased from 11% correct to 73% correct; the improvement figures are averages of the six days after the second treatment session during which this student's behavior was monitored.

It would be inappropriate to generalize too much from these findings. A very small sample of subjects was used, and, although all of the subjects in this study exhibited problem behavior in school, the level of their problem behavior was far less than that exhibited by, for example, the children in Patterson's project (who are typically referred by community agencies including the Juvenile Court, schools, and community mental health clinics). Nevertheless, Ayllon *et al.*'s findings are

TABLE 11.5
Persuasion by Successive Approximation Using Reactance[a]

Condensed hierarchy
1. What I will say will be the truth.
2. I am not working too hard in school right now.
3. I care about school.
4. When I'm disruptive, it is on my own volition.
5. I can change on my own volition.
6. I can do academic work on my own volition.
7. I will commit myself to doing my school work.

Transcript excerpts

Therapist: Before we even start talking, I must admit I'm not sure whether we should even bother. I have found that a lot of students don't even tell the truth and can't keep their word. You probably won't tell the truth, either.

Student: I'll tell the truth to you.

T: Well, that's good to hear; we won't be wasting our time talking, then. I guess you must really be working hard in school these days.

S: Myself, I'm not. I'm really just kind of loafin' around. The other kids are workin' hard. You know, the ones who get good grades.

. . .

T: I guess it's hopeless, then. You wouldn't even consider trying it the other way around—work first, play later.

S: No. Well, I could try. I know what you're trying to do—you're trying to get me to do my work in school, aren't you?

T: I'm not trying to get you to do anything—I can't make you do anything you don't want to do.

S: But you and Mrs. Q would like me to do my work, right?

T: I would like it if you would like it. But I know you aren't willing to even give it a try.

S: I would give it a try.

. . .

T: Would you write something for me?

S: Like what?

T: Like what you have told me you are going to do.

S: You write it. I don't like to write. You write it and I'll sign it.

T: You dictate it to me, OK? I, [*student's name*] . . .

S: I, [*student's name*], give my word that I will get my seat work done and handed in by Mrs. Q's deadline. I will do this until the end of school. [Student then signs the statement immediately].

T: [*Student's name*], are you sure you want to do this until the end of school? We could make it for just a couple of days instead.

S: No, I'll work until the end of school.

[a] Adapted from Ayllon, Allison, and Kandel, 1980. Reprinted by permission.

extremely interesting. They suggest the possibility that the reactance techniques developed by Varela and used by him with adults (see Chapter 13) can be effectively applied to children. They also point out that one cannot assume that the immediate improvement that may be obtained through such a technique will be maintained. For the fourth student, a booster session that involved a stronger public commitment (and, thus, presumably came closer to actually eliminating his freedom *not* to carry out the behaviors to which he had committed himself) was necessary. Moreover, Ayllon *et al.* point out the need to integrate the new behaviors into the child's social environment by taking "steps to assure that new behavior patterns come under reinforcing environmental contingencies."

Another possibly effective intervention technique to enhance student compliance has been described by Miller, Brickman, and Bolen (1975). In their first study, fifth-grade students were exposed to eight days of either attribution or persuasion treatments addressing the topic of littering. The attribution treatment consisted of a variety of ways of telling students in one class that they were neat and tidy. The principal, the teacher and the janitor were all involved in telling the class how neat and tidy it was. In the persuasion treatment, the same school personnel delivered a variety of messages informing another class that it should be neat and that students should not litter. A third class served as a no treatment control and no messages about neatness were delivered to it. On both an immediate (2 days after the treatment) and a delayed (2 weeks after the treatment) posttest, the classroom that had received the attribution treatment was more conscientious about discarding litter than either of the other two classrooms.

In their second study, Miller *et al.* (1975) focused on second-graders' math-related self-esteem and math skills. All experimental conditions were presented individually to children in each of four classrooms. Children in the attribution ability condition were told they were doing very well in arithmetic; children in the attribution motivation condition were told they were working hard in arithmetic; children in the persuasion ability condition were told they should do well in arithmetic; children in the persuasion motivation condition were told they should be working harder at arithmetic; children in the reinforcement condition were praised for their progress in arithmetic; and children in the control condition received no treatment whatsoever. The various treatment conditions lasted eight days and involved a number of variations on each treatment theme. On math self-esteem, only the two attribution groups were significantly different from the control group in their increase in self-esteem from pre- to posttest (which took place the day after treatment ended). A similar pattern of results was obtained on both immediate and delayed posttests of math skills.

Miller *et al.* (1975) suggest two advantages for their approach to inducing behavioral compliance and attitudinal acceptance. First, attribution techniques appear to be more effective than either persuasion or reinforcement (at least, the social reinforcement used in their study). Relative to persuasion, Miller et al. (1975) suggest that attribution may be more effective "because it is less easily recognized as persuasion, and hence less likely to arouse resistance, counterarguing, or reactance [p. 438]." Second, Miller et al. note that attributional techniques may have longer lasting effects than behavior change induced by reinforcement. Attributional techniques such as those used by Miller et al. do have clear reinforcing properties; however, they also presumably serve to induce intrinsic motivation to perform the desired behavior that will not be dependent on receiving extrinsic reinforcement. As they put it, "Thus to some extent a reinforcement procedure that produces enduring change may require elements of attribution, while successful attribution treatment may involve elements of reinforcement [Miller et al., 1975, p. 439]."

It is important to remember that although the Miller et al. studies involved an intervention technique designed to increase compliance, the targets of this intervention were normal children who, on the whole at least, had not displayed excessive oppositional behavior. It remains to be seen whether such a technique would be successful with chronically disobedient children, but the Miller et al. findings coupled with other investigators' observations (e.g., Ayllon & Roberts, 1974) that "indirect" methods may be more effective than direct ones certainly support the need for future research on such reactance-minimizing techniques.

WHEN REACTANCE FAILS: HELPLESSNESS IN CHILDREN

Repeated failure to control behavioral outcomes can occur to children in real life as a function of the characteristics of their environment. Rodin (1976) has suggested that children's living situations may influence their attempts to master and control the environment around them. In her first study, Rodin found that 6- to 9-year-old black males were more likely to prefer self-selected over experimenter-administered rewards if they lived in a low density (fewer people per number of rooms in home) than if they lived in a high density home environment. A second experiment reported by Rodin presented seventh-grade children (mostly black) with either soluble or insoluble problems in either a crowded or uncrowded experimental room (i.e., room size was varied as was space between chairs; number of subjects was constant across conditions). All subjects then received a second set of similar problems that were soluble. Although laboratory-created density had no effects on children's success in solving the second set of problems, home environment interacted with treatment experience to affect children's subsequent success. When the first problem was not solvable, high density children did more poorly on the second (solvable) task than other children from high density homes who had experienced an initial solvable problem. Low density children, however, "showed this difference less strongly [Rodin, 1976, p. 575]."

Rodin suggests that "chronic high density living may reduce one's feeling of choice and control . . . by fostering conditions in which both negative and positive events may be unpredictable and/or uncontrollable [p. 576]." These conditions might then, according to this interpretation, lead children to value choice less and to be more vulnerable to becoming helpless after a failure experience. There is, however, a question that should be raised about Rodin's experiment and her interpretation of these data.

Rodin did not separate the training task (solvable versus unsolvable) from the test task (solvable problems). The same room, the same experiment, and the same type of problem were used in both. As has been discussed previously (Chapter 4), failure to separate training and test tasks creates considerable theoretical ambiguity. In this specific case, one wonders if the children from high density homes were simply more cynical than those from low density homes. High density children who received unsolvable problems initially might simply have assumed that the second set would be unsolvable as well and not tried as hard to succeed. While this is helplessness of a sort, it is very specific to the given situation and may, indeed, be the most realistic way of coping in that situation.

The most elaborate theoretical and empirical consideration of children's helplessness has been articulated by Dweck and her associates (Diener & Dweck, 1978; Dweck, 1975; Dweck & Bush, 1976; Dweck, Davidson, Nelson, & Enna, 1978; Dweck & Gilliard, 1975; Dweck & Goetz, 1978; and Dweck & Reppucci, 1973). According to this model, interactions with social agents create expectations and attributions about success and failure, and these expectations and attributions, in turn, influence whether or not children become helpless in response to failure. The model is generally consistent with the present theoretical view. Attributing a failure to lack of effort allows an individual to maintain the perception of control or freedom, whereas attributing failure to lack of ability signifies that the individual never thought he or she had the freedom, or that he or she has given it up. Despite these consistencies in theoretical approaches, the evidence gathered by

Dweck and her associates is extremely difficult to discuss within a reactance theory framework and, therefore, will not be reviewed here.

SUMMARY

The possibility of using reactance theory as a framework for understanding oppositional behavior in children was explored. First, a number of studies from the reactance literature in which children participated as subjects were considered. Children, ranging from first-graders to eighth-graders, have displayed reactance in response to threats to and eliminations of freedom. Reactance arousal has been increased by increasing the importance of the freedom threatened and the proportion of freedoms eliminated. Children in these studies have opposed a choice forced on them by an adult as well as one supposedly advocated by a peer. Items eliminated by circumstances as well as by a social agent have become more attractive. The results from these studies offer support for the general applicability of the theory to children's motivation and behavior.

Second, a number of topics that have received considerable attention in the developmental literature were examined in terms of reactance theory. *Physical barriers* were viewed as threats to freedom, and a study was reported in which 2-year-old males found a barricaded item more attractive than a nonbarricaded one when the barrier was large (i.e., the threat to freedom was great) and when the items were not identical (i.e., each item had unique instrumental value for satisfying a specific motive). Consistent with previous research, female 2-year-olds did not show this preference and, indeed, preferred the nonbarricaded item regardless of experimental condition.

Children's *compliance* in both the laboratory and naturalistic settings was discussed. It was hypothesized that oppositional behavior would be displayed by children only when (a) a freedom of sufficient importance was established, (b) a threat of sufficient magnitude was brought to bear against that freedom, (c) the cost of opposition to the influence attempt was not so great as to suppress behavioral opposition. Parental consistency was seen as affecting both the establishment of freedom and the cost of noncompliance. An inconsistent parent may unwittingly establish a freedom for a child; once the freedom has been established, future attempts at controlling the child's behavior in regard to this freedom may arouse reactance. Moreover, parents may differ in what behaviors they establish as freedoms for the child. Interparental inconsistency also may affect the cost of noncompliance, with conflict between adults over each one's control of the child reducing the social power of both.

Various approaches to *modifying children's noncompliant behavior* were then examined: psychoanalytic, behavioral, and family systems. The reactance theory analysis was seen as especially similar to the family systems approach, with both emphasizing the role of excessive punitiveness and parental inconsistency as variables promoting noncompliant behavior. The possibility of reactance-based treatments to decrease noncompliance and increase compliance was discussed.

Finally, helplessness effects in children were briefly considered. Both life experiences that decrease the importance of choice and attributional processes that lead to the perception that one does not have control over one's outcomes were seen as potentially facilitating helplessness.

CHAPTER 12

Sex Differences in Psychological Reactance

In a number of places throughout this volume, we have described reactance findings that differed as a function of the gender of the subjects. These findings trace an intriguing and somewhat puzzling thread through the literature relevant to the theory. It is important to emphasize that sex difference findings represent only a small portion of this body of literature. Reactance studies have been conducted with male and female subjects, and predictions from the theory have been confirmed with both. There is no reason to believe that the theory "works" better for one sex than the other. A number of studies suggest, however, that gender may interact with theoretical variables such that arousal of reactance in specific situations is affected by the sex of the individual involved. In this section, we shall summarize the sex differences that have been obtained and examine the theoretical implications of these findings.

Sex Differences in Pre-School Age Children

One convenient way to organize these findings is to categorize them by the age of the subjects. This organization allows us to look for possible developmental trends as well. Beginning with children below the age of two, we find that there is little evidence of sex differences in behaviors relevant to reactance. As was stated in Chapter 11, of the three studies that examined young children's responses to barriers, only one (Goldberg & Lewis, 1969) found a sex difference. The longitudinal study by Van Lieshout (1975) is particularly interesting in this regard. Van Lieshout found no sex differences in children's negative emotional responses to the mother (who had barricaded an attractive toy) at 17–19 months, but did find a sex difference later (at 23–25 months). Sex differences in 2-year-olds' barrier responses were also obtained by Bell et al. (1971) and Brehm and Weinraub (1977). Taken together, these findings suggest that the potential for reactance arousal in response to barriers exists early in development for both males and females. Somewhere around the age of two, however, sex differences begin to appear, with males trying harder to overcome the barrier (Bell et al.), showing more negative responses toward the agent that imposed the barrier (Van Lieshout), and, under conditions specified by the theory, being more attracted to the barricaded object (Brehm & Weinraub).

Although the determinants of these differences between the sexes are not known, the developmental pattern is suggestive of the effects of socialization. Perhaps the freedom to have a barricaded object has been affirmed for males and undermined for females. Perhaps the cost of expressing the motivation to have that which is physically difficult to obtain has remained low for males and has become high for females. Whatever the causal path, it may be important that barrier situations would typically involve negative emotions on the part of the child as well as physical obstruction. It is possible that in these types of situations, boys and girls receive different socialization experiences. Whether or not other types of reactance-producing situations (that, for example, are not so associated with anger toward the agent and/or that do not involve physical obstruction) would also produce sex differences at this age would seem an important question for future research.

Staub's 1971 study suggests that sex difference findings for kindergarten children may be highly dependent upon the type of measure that is used. It will be recalled (see Chapter 4) that Staub found that each of two different methods of inducing prosocial behavior was more effective alone than when the two were combined. We have suggested that the latter situation may have involved posing two threats to the same freedom, and thus that the magnitude of threat created by combining the two persuasive methods may have been greater than the magnitude of threat created by either method alone. Both boys and girls displayed this one-is-better-than-two effect, but on different measures of prosocial behavior: helping another child in distress for females, and sharing for males.

If, as Staub's study suggests, sex differences in reactance to persuasive inductions of prosocial behavior depend on what behavior we observe, it would be important to attempt to determine what parameters define these different behaviors. For instance, one could speculate that girls are socialized more to respond to overt displays of physical and/or emotional distress than are boys. If so, then a victim in emotional distress should create more pressure on girls to be helpful than on boys. Pressure to help that stems from characteristics of the victim would combine with pressures to help created by persuasive appeals, and should, therefore, produce more reactance in girls than in boys. These comments point to the need to anchor future research on sex differences in reactance to the two major components of the theory. What is the freedom that is being threatened and might it be more firmly established or more important for one sex than the other? What is the threat that is being posed and might it be greater for one sex than the other?

Sex Differences in Preadolescence

A number of studies have investigated children's conformity to influence attempts by both adults and peers. Sex difference findings in this literature have been erratic, with some investigators having found levels of conformity to differ according to sex (e.g., Allen & Newtson, 1972; Hamm & Hoving, 1969; Pasternack, 1973) and others not having obtained such a difference (e.g., Strassberg & Wiggin, 1973; Utrech & Hoving, 1969). The potential demographic complexity involved in conformity is illustrated in a study by Cantor (1975), in which sex differences in conformity were obtained with a lower-class sample but not with a middle-class sample. One sex difference in conformity that does appear to have some stability is reported by Bronfenbrenner (1970) and Bixenstine, DeCorte, and Bixenstine (1976). Using hypothetical situations, these investigators found that females said they would be more resistant to misbehavior sponsored by their peers than did males.

The results of these various studies suggest that rather than focusing on whether or not there are sex differences in conformity, a more profitable research tactic would be to specify those conditions that will produce such differences and those that will not. From our perspective, we are again back to the determination of the freedom involved and of the nature of the threat to that freedom. Working with adult subjects,

Sistrunk and McDavid (1971) have suggested that the topic of social influence will play a large part in determining whether females conform more than males or vice versa. The same reasoning would seem appropriate throughout the developmental spectrum. Moreover, a reactance theory analysis would also focus on characteristics of the social influence attempt itself—such as the agent who makes the attempt, the force of the attempt, the implications posed by the attempt for other freedoms—and the costs of noncompliance. While this approach is obviously more complex than the search for "pure" sex differences in conformity, we believe that it is also more likely to yield coherent and reliable findings.

Two studies suggest that the importance of the freedom that is threatened may play a role in mediating sex differences in reactance among preadolescent children. Leventhal and Mace (1970) report an examination of the effects of laughter on evaluation of a slapstick film. In their first study, elementary school age children were instructed to laugh or instructed not to laugh at a W. C. Fields' movie, and then answered a series of evaluative questions about the film. Although subjects in all conditions complied with instructions to laugh or not laugh, evaluations of the movie were a function of an interaction between instructions and sex of subject (see Table 12.1). Male subjects tended to evaluate the film more positively when instructed not to laugh than when instructed to laugh; females tended to evaluate the film more positively when instructed to laugh. Looking across the two sexes, boys and girls did not differ in their evaluations of the film when told to laugh, but when told not to laugh, boys were more favorable to the film than girls.

We can presume that all the children entered this study feeling free both to laugh and not laugh at a movie. Some children then had their freedom to laugh threatened by the instruction not to laugh, while

TABLE 12.1
Mean Evaluations of the W. C. Fields' Movie[a]

	Instructions	
	Laugh	Don't laugh
Males	4.05	4.45
Females	4.15	3.60

[a] From Leventhal, H. & Mace, W. The effects of laughter on the evaluation of a slapstick movie. *Journal of Personality*, 1970, *38*, 16–30, Table 1, p. 20. Copyright 1970 by Duke University Press. Reprinted by permission.

others had their freedom not to laugh threatened by the instruction to laugh. Because there is no condition without instructions about laughing, we cannot tell whether for males there is a decrement in evaluation in the laugh condition, an enhancement of evaluation in the don't laugh condition, or both (although the pattern of sex differences that was obtained is more consistent with the second type of effect). All we can conclude is that among males, the instructions about laughter appear to have created a reactance effect on movie evaluation. Furthermore, it is interesting to note that no expression of reactance arousal was obtained on actual laughter. It would appear that the costs of failing to comply with the adult experimenter's instructions were prohibitive. Since, however, no direct instructions about evaluations of the film had been given, the behavior offered an opportunity for any reactance that was aroused to be expressed.

A study by Brehm (in press) suggests the possibility that female children may be more concerned about being given objects than about choosing them, especially if neither object is particularly attractive. This study (described earlier in Chapter 11) replicated Hammock and Brehm's (1966) experimental procedures with a large enough sample to adequately investigate the possibility of age (first- and sixth-graders) and sex differences. Subjects were led to believe that they would be allowed to choose between two different objects or that they would be given one of two different objects. All subjects were then shown the items they had ranked third and fourth on an initial evaluation of a set of ten objects, and all subjects were given their third-ranked alternative, without any of them being allowed to state a preference. Subjects then reranked all ten objects.

Changes in ranking (displayed in Table 11.2) indicated that males behaved as had been predicted. Although males devalued both the object they had received as well as the one they had not received, males who had expected to choose devalued the eliminated object *less* than males who had not expected to choose. Males in the choice condition also devalued the given object more than males who had not expected to choose. Changes in ranking by females, however, did not conform to prediction. For the object they were given, females in both the choice and no choice condition devalued it and equally so. For the object they did not receive, females in the choice condition devalued it *more* than those in the no choice condition. Indeed, the only evidence of an absolute increase in attractiveness was found for no choice females when they reranked the eliminated object; their rankings of this object increased slightly from their initial ranking ($M = 4.00$) to their final ranking ($M = 3.87$).

It is important to emphasize that the no choice instructions in this experiment did not stress subjects' lack of choice. Instead, it was stated that subjects would be given one of two objects. The assumption was made that telling someone he or she would be given an object was equivalent to saying that he or she had no choice in the matter. For male subjects, this equivalence appeared to hold. For females, however, it is possible that to be given something constituted a freedom in itself. Females may have assumed that their wishes would have some impact on what they were given, and the freedom to be given what they wanted may have been more important to them than the freedom to choose between two, not terribly desirable objects. The preemptory behavior of the second experimenter who handed subjects one item without any consultation with them about their wishes may, then, have aroused more reactance for female subjects in the condition in which they expected to be given something than in the condition in which they expected to choose. This interpretation is quite speculative and completely *post hoc*. It does, however, point again to the need to assess what particular freedom is being threatened and to the possibility that freedoms may be differentially important to males and females.

High School Age

In the article by Leventhal and Mace (1970) already cited, a study with high school age subjects is also reported. For this study, subjects were classified as either high or low laughers depending on their response to a pretest slapstick movie. Subjects then watched a second movie for which canned laughter was either present or not, and evaluated the film. Again, subjects complied with the experimental manipulation, although the difference in laughter between the experimental condition (with canned laughter) and the control condition was only marginal ($p < .07$). Evaluations of the film (on two of the three evaluation questions asked; in the first experiment, the mean of eight evaluation questions was used in the analysis) were a function of a significant interaction between level of pretest laughter and experimental condition. Subjects who laughed a lot in the initial pretest tended to evaluate the film less positively when canned laughter was present than when it was not. Subjects who laughed at a low level on the pretest tended to evaluate the film more positively when canned laughter was present than when it was not. Although the interaction of sex with these variables was not significant, inspection of the data reveals that this pattern of results was much stronger for boys than for girls. Indeed, the means for high laughter girls are essentially equivalent regardless of whether canned laughter was present or not.

These data provide only a partial fit with the results of Leventhal and Mace's first study. In the first study, males differed from females only when instructed *not to* laugh; when instructed *to* laugh, there were no sex differences. These results, then, suggest that the freedom to laugh was especially important to males. In the second study, there were no instructions not to laugh. Instead, there was only the implicit instruction (via the canned laughter) to laugh. The data from this study appear to indicate that the freedom not to laugh was especially important to males who had displayed high levels of initial laughter. Thus, males in both studies displayed more (indirect) opposition to the experimental instructions/procedures than did females, but the threatened freedom that elicited this opposition differed between the two studies. Since the age of the subjects also differed across the two studies, it is conceivable that these results reflect a developmental shift in males' valuing of the freedoms to laugh and not to laugh.

The *post hoc* interpretation that was offered for the behavior of female subjects in Brehm's (in press) study suggests that females may be especially likely to experience reactance arousal in interpersonal situations. A study by Brehm and Sensenig (1966) obtained results that were consistent with this suggestion. As described previously (Chapter 3), male and female high school students received a note from their supposed partner that either stated a preference (control) for choosing one rather than another of a pair of pictures or contained a strongly worded, directive statement that both subjects should choose one rather than the other (implications). Some subjects believed they would receive a note only for the first of five pairs of pictures (low implications); others believed they would receive a note for each of five pairs of pictures (high implications). The results of this study provided only partial support for the experimental hypotheses. As expected, more subjects in the control condition complied with the choice advocated by the note (73%) than in the implications conditions (43%). Contrary to prediction, however, more opposition was not created in the high implications condition than in the low implications conditions, there being only a trend in this direction (respectively, 40% complied vs. 47%). Moreover, Brehm and Sensenig note that the difference between these two conditions was accounted for entirely by the behavior of female subjects, male subjects actually tending in the opposite direction.[1]

In interpreting these data, it is important to examine the experimental task that subjects expected to perform. Subjects were told that they

---

[1] As noted earlier, Sensenig and Brehm (1968) revised the procedures of this study and, with *female* undergraduates as subjects, were able to obtain a significant difference between high and low implications conditions. See also, however, Footnote 3 in Chapter 3 for evidence that the Sensenig and Brehm effects can be obtained with both sexes.

would look at whatever picture was chosen and make judgments about what the people in the pictures were thinking, feeling, and doing. Females may have felt more competent to perform this kind of interpersonal judgment task than males, and/or they may have valued their freedom to choose a picture for the task more. Since, in addition, the threat in this study was supposedly delivered by a peer, the Brehm and Sensenig experiment was highly interpersonal and suggests that females may be especially reactive to social threats to their interpersonal freedoms.

Sex Differences in Adults

Interpersonal Freedoms

Some of the complexities of the relationship between gender and responses to threats to interpersonal freedoms are illustrated in a study by Archer and Berg (1978) on disclosure reciprocity. Subjects in this experiment were mainly adults (age range: 15 to 64 with a mean of 24.79) contacted in public places in Austin, Texas. Subjects were approached by either a male or female experimenter who explained that he or she was conducting a class project on self-descriptions. For subjects who agreed to participate, the experimenter said that the project was comparing self-descriptions among different people, and that first the experimenter would write a self-description and then the subject was to read it and write one about himself or herself. All self-descriptions began with the statement, "Hi, I'm a junior [senior] at U.T. I'm pretty depressed today because everyone is so into getting drunk." Low intimacy was created by following this with, "I just saw some friends and that's all they could talk about." Medium intimacy used the ending, "I just read in a letter from home that my brother went drinking with his friends instead of going to school," while high intimacy was created by ending the self-description with, "I got a call from my father this morning and he says he's going to leave my mother. I always knew she was an alcoholic, but I didn't know what to do."

Cross-cutting the manipulation of intimacy, subjects either had or did not have their freedom restored. For no restoration subjects, the subject was asked to write his or her own description after reading the experimenter's self-description. For restoration subjects, the experimenter told the subject, before the subject could write anything, "Oh, I'm supposed to tell you at this point that anything you want to write about yourself is okay. It's completely up to you." Subjects then wrote their self-descriptions and answered some questions about the experiment.

The major dependent measure used by Archer and Berg was the number of words contained in the subjects' responses. The mean number of words for each experimental condition is displayed in Table 12.2.

In their analysis of the disclosure situation, Archer and Berg reasoned that people feel obligated to reciprocate disclosures at the level of intimacy of the initial disclosure. Thus, a very intimate disclosure will pressure individuals to reveal intimate material about themselves, while a disclosure low in intimacy will pressure a person to reveal less intimate material. Since people will generally be more reluctant to reveal intimate information about themselves, the highly intimate disclosure will threaten a more important freedom than the nonintimate disclosure. Moreover, since highly intimate disclosures, from strangers at least, would usually be viewed as unlikely and inappropriate, intimate disclosures may threaten other freedoms by implication (e.g., "What's he [she] going to do next?") and, through this process as well, arouse greater reactance.

As had been predicted, a significant interaction between level of intimacy and restoration was obtained. In the no restoration condition, the mean number of words written by subjects tended to increase from low

TABLE 12.2
Mean Number of Words Written by Subjects[a]

	Level of intimacy of initial disclosure		
	Low	Medium	High
No restoration			
Male experimenter			
Male subjects	63.4[b]	62.2	39.8
Female subjects	30.2	65.8	30.8
Female experimenter			
Male subjects	52.0	40.6	47.0
Female subjects	40.8	30.8	34.4
Restoration			
Male experimenter			
Male subjects	49.4	48.2	53.2
Female subjects	39.2	60.0	51.8
Female experimenter			
Male subjects	42.6	48.8	71.6
Female subjects	42.0	64.8	92.0

[a] From Archer, R. L. & Berg, J. H. Disclosure reciprocity and its limits: A reactance analysis. *Journal of Experimental Social Psychology,* 1978, 14, 527–540, Table 2, p. 533.

[b] Actual mean number of words per condition. In their data analysis, Archer and Berg used logarithmically transformed data.

to medium intimacy and then to decrease under high intimacy; none of these differences, however, was significant. In the restoration condition, increasing intimacy led to increasing word production. The critical comparison between restoration and no restoration under high intimacy was significant, with restoration subjects writing more words than no restoration subjects. These effects, however, need to be placed in the context of the numerous effects of sex that were obtained.

First, there was a marginal ($p < .07$) interaction between sex of experimenter and intimacy. For male experimenters, number of words tended to increase from low intimacy to medium and then to decrease when a high level of intimacy was used. For female experimenters, however, number of words increased as intimacy level increased. Thus, highly intimate self-disclosures from females appeared to pose less of a threat to freedom than the same disclosures from males. Second, there was a marginal ($p < .10$) interaction between sex of subject and restoration, with females showing a larger increase in the number of words written after freedom was restored. This finding suggests that females were more sensitive to the restoration of their interpersonal freedom than were males.

Third, Archer and Berg report subjects' ratings on the likeability and openness of the experimenter. On both measures, there was a marginal ($p < .08$) interaction between sex of experimenter and restoration. Female experimenters who restored freedom were perceived as more likeable and open than male experimenters who restored freedom. Also, female experimenters who restored freedom tended to be seen as more likeable and open than female experimenters who did not restore freedom. These data suggest that, at least in terms of general interpersonal impact, females who restored freedom were particularly successful.

Within this context of sex differences, it might be helpful to examine the effects of sex on the critical comparison between restoration and no restoration under high levels of intimacy. Regardless of sex of experimenter or sex of subject, more words were written by subjects who had had their freedom restored after a high intimacy disclosure than subjects for whom freedom was not restored. The smallest difference, however, was obtained for male subjects interacting with male experimenters, while the greatest difference was obtained for female subjects interacting with female experimenters. These comparisons suggest that the general reactance theory formulation of disclosure reciprocity can be applied across gender; the magnitude, however, of the predicted effects seems to depend on the sex of the discloser as well as on the sex of the person to whom the disclosure is made.

One additional study is consistent with the notion that females are especially sensitive to reactance arousal in regard to interpersonal free-doms. As was noted earlier (see Chapter 3), Davis and Martin (1978) found that there was a trend for female subjects to reduce the pleasur-able vibrations they administered to their partners when this partner was a stranger and when he had been verbally responsive to the vibra-tions. Davis and Martin suggested that the freedom not to become inti-mate was more important to females, especially when they were inter-acting with unfamiliar males.

Competency at Exercising a Freedom

The possible role of competency in mediating sex differences in reac-tance arousal has been discussed earlier (see Chapter 2) in our descrip-tion of the supermarket studies by Regan and Brehm (1972; also reported in Brehm, 1966) and McGillis and Brehm (1975). It will be recalled that only female shoppers in these studies were less compliant under high threat conditions than low. Regan and Brehm suggested that females might perceive themselves as more competent in food shopping than males and, since a freedom cannot exist without some minimal level of perceived competence to exercise the freedom, the high pres-sure advertisement campaign may have threatened a freedom for fe-male shoppers but not for males. The generality of this finding is some-what impaired by the failure of Gilbert and Peterson (1971) to find any sex differences in their replication of this experimental paradigm.

Motivational Tendencies

Another possible area of differences between the sexes that may mediate reactance arousal involves motivational tendencies. Aletky and Carlin (1975) alluded to such a difference in their study of the rela-tionship between sex differences and placebo effects. As we described earlier (see Chapter 4), Aletky and Carlin postulated that males would be motivated to display strength of grip, whereas females would not be so motivated. Both sexes were assumed to be motivated to display good health, and both sexes were thought to be susceptible to demand char-acteristics of a placebo. Thus, for males, three important pressures to perform well on the experimental task (squeezing a dynamometer) were possible (motive to appear strong, appear healthy, and confirm the effectiveness of the placebo); for females, only the latter two were important. The greater number of pressures on males can be construed as increasing the magnitude of threat beyond the level experienced by females. In support of this analysis, males in the condition where all three pressures were applied declined in performance, but females in the same experimental condition improved.

The possibility of more complex relationships among gender, motivation, and reactance arousal is raised by Carver's (1980) study of the Type A coronary prone behavior pattern. We have described this study previously in Chapter 9, and it will be recalled that although Type A males did seem more reactance prone (at lower levels of threat) than Type B males, the Type A versus Type B distinction did not reliably predict the behavior of female subjects.

This pattern of results raises the possibility that the Type A–B distinction may involve different parameters for males as compared to females. In particular, it is possible that both sexes can be classified according to whether or not they exhibit Type A behavior, but that the motivational bases for this behavior differ. Some evidence consistent with this hypothesis has been obtained by Smith and Brehm (in press). Table 12.3 displays the results of their correlational study in which scores for the student version of the Jenkins Activity Survey (Glass, 1977) were correlated with the Jones (1969) Irrational Beliefs Test. The former is an often used measure of the Type A coronary prone be-

TABLE 12.3

Correlations Between the JAS (Student Version) and the Irrational Beliefs Test[a]

	Jenkins activity survey		
Irrational beliefs test	Full sample	Males	Females
Demand for approval	−.16**	−.16	−.16
High achievement	.11	.24**	.01
Blame proneness	.17**	.15	.19*
Frustration reactivity	.12	−.02	.24**
Emotional irresponsibility	−.14*	−.07	−.20*
Anxious overconcern	.18**	.05	.31***
Problem avoidance	−.41****	−.51****	−.32***
Dependency	−.15*	−.15	−.14
Fatalism	.12	.06	.16
Perfectionism	.03	.13	−.04
IBT total	.01	−.05	.01
	N = 149	N = 72	N = 77

[a] From Smith, T. W. & Brehm, S. S. Cognitive correlates of the Type A coronary-prone behavior pattern. *Motivation and Emotion,* in press. Copyright pending by Plenum Publishing Corp.

*p ≤ .10
**p ≤ .05
***p ≤ .01
****p ≤ .001

havior pattern. The latter generates 10 scale scores (10 items each) corresponding to Ellis' (1962) specific irrational beliefs as well as an overall score for general irrational thinking.

The strongest and most consistent relationship between these two measures was found for problem avoidance. Type A's, male and female, tended to disagree with the idea that one should avoid problems and, instead, appeared to be endorsing a belief in an active-mastery style of coping rather than a passive-avoidant style. This type of belief is highly consistent with the behaviors associated with the Type A pattern (i.e., time urgency, impatience, achievement striving, etc.), and an association between Type A's and disbelief in problem avoidance was also found by Lohr and Bonge (1979) in their sample of college age males.

Lohr and Bonge, however, did not include females in their study, and the data obtained from college age individuals of both sexes by Smith and Brehm suggest that important sex differences may exist. In the Smith and Brehm study, male Type A's tended to endorse a belief in high achievement standards. It is obvious how Type A behaviors such as competitiveness, job involvement and achievement striving could reflect this belief. Female Type A's, however, did not evidence a belief in the need for high achievement. For females, the cognitive correlates were somewhat more diffuse, with particular association between the Type A pattern and frustration reactivity and anxious overconcern. This set of beliefs is consistent with Glass's (1977) notion that the Type A pattern reflects an attempt to maintain control over environmental demands and requirements.

In light of Carver's results, these correlational findings are intriguing. The pattern of results obtained by Smith and Brehm does not suggest that Type A males are more concerned with general control issues than Type A females. In fact, just the opposite may be suggested. Moreover, the correlational data obtained by Smith and Brehm generate a number of hypotheses about the types of situations in which gender and Type A may combine to maximize reactance arousal. One could speculate that Type A males should react to any threats to their freedoms to behave competently and achieve, whereas Type A females should react to threats to their freedoms to order the world in the way they think best. On the other hand, one would hypothesize that *both* male and female Type A's should show considerable reactance to any attempts to get them to avoid their responsibilities.

The data gathered by Smith and Brehm do not allow us to explain Carver's findings, nor do they serve to enable us to make simple statements about the relationship among gender, Type A, and reactance.

They do, however, illustrate possible sex differences within the Type A–B distinction and, most important, they assist us in formulating testable hypotheses about how these differences might affect reactance arousal in specific situations.

SUMMARY

Although there is no reason to believe that reactance theory is sex-specific, predictions from the theory having been confirmed repeatedly with both male and female subjects, it is quite possible that gender may interact with theoretical variables such that arousal of reactance in specific situations is affected by the sex of the individuals involved. A survey of sex-difference findings relevant to reactance theory indicated that such differences have been obtained across a wide age span, with subjects ranging from young children to adults, and suggested that the following theoretical tenets are crucial for an understanding of how those differences may arise.

First, it is necessary to ask whether the freedom has been firmly established for both males and females. It is possible that any specific freedom might exist in a given culture only for one sex; if so, only that sex possessing the freedom would be expected to experience arousal in response to threats to that freedom. Second, is the freedom equally important for both sexes? It may be, for instance, that personal interactions are more important for females than for males. If so, threats to interpersonal freedoms might create more reactance among females than among males.

Another theoretical variable that may well produce differential reactance among the sexes is the perceived competence of exercising a freedom. Threats to freedom should produce reactance only when one believes oneself competent to exercise the freedom. If members of one sex perceive themselves as more competent than members of the other sex to exercise a specific freedom, then the former will experience more reactance if this freedom is threatened.

Characteristics of the threat may also interact with gender. Especially interesting in this regard are differences between males and females in preexisting motivational tendencies. When an individual is already motivated to act in a particular way, this internal pressure may combine with any external pressure that is then applied such that the magnitude of threat to the freedom *not* to act is increased relative to a person who is not internally motivated. Thus, it has been suggested, some sex differences in opposition to influence may arise because of preexisting sex differences in the motivation to perform the action advocated by the influence attempt.

Finally, it should be noted that developmental level may affect any of the above variables. Gender specific establishment of freedom, importance of freedom and competence in exercising a freedom may vary as a function of age. Similarly, different motivational tendencies may exist for the two sexes at some ages but not at others.

PART III

Applications of the Theory

CHAPTER 13

Clinical Applications

In this chapter and the following ones in this part of the book, we will explore the utility of reactance theory for generating practical approaches to and understanding of a wide variety of real world events. One applied area in which reactance effects would seem particularly important is that of the psychological treatment of psychological problems. Clinicians have approached reactance theory (and related conceptions) from two different perspectives. On the one hand, the arousal of the motivation to oppose the therapist has been seen as undesirable and something to be minimized in therapy. On the other, induced opposition to the therapist's direction has been suggested as a feasible treatment technique for at least some specific problems. Our discussion in this chapter will be organized in terms of these two perspectives.

Before addressing these issues, however, a few remarks about the more general relationship between reactance and therapy are in order.[1]

---

[1] In this chapter, we shall use the term *therapy* to refer to the general class of procedures in which psychological interventions are used to try to ameliorate psychological problems. Within this general class, three more specific categories will be distinguished. Those approaches to therapy termed *psychodynamic* include both orthodox Freudian analysis as well as more recent neo-Freudian modifications. The term *behavior therapy* will be used to refer to therapeutic interventions based on operant conditioning, classical conditioning, and/or social learning theory. Third, the term *client-centered* will refer to

Along with many other writers (e.g., Carson, 1969; Frank, 1961/1973; Goldstein, Heller, & Sechrest, 1966; Sheras & Worchel, 1979; Winett, 1970), we view therapy as, at least in part, a process of persuasion and attitude change. This is not to say that we see therapy as consisting solely of the therapist's giving direct advice to the client (although, of course, this does happen at times), but, rather, this view indicates our belief that through a variety of techniques—some quite subtle, others more overt—the therapist endeavors to provide the client with experiences that will facilitate both attitudinal and behavioral change. Moreover, the therapeutic interaction usually involves explicit differences in the social power of the participants. Although clients do have power over their therapists (and probably more than they recognize), the social power of the therapist can usually be considered to be greater than that of the client.

This general context suggests that much of the material covered earlier in this volume would be relevant to therapeutic endeavors. We have discussed persuasion and attitude change, social power and interpersonal relationships, and, as part of this latter topic, being asked to help and receiving it. There is no reason to repeat what we stated previously in regard to these topics, but we do want to bring the connection between these previous chapters and the present one to the reader's attention.[2]

Reactance Arousal as an Undesirable Aspect of Therapy

That clients can oppose the efforts of their therapists is a therapeutic truism as old as the concept of systematic psychological intervention itself. In psychodynamic theory, resistance is a cornerstone of both the theory and the therapy. Resistance to dealing with unconscious conflictual material is viewed as inevitable and as an obstacle that must be

---

approaches such as Rogerian and Gestalt therapy. We fully recognize that these are relatively crude distinctions that eschew many important specific differences and that fail to classify a number of specific therapeutic approaches adequately. These distinctions, however, would seem sufficient for the general points that we are trying to make in this chapter.

[2] The previous discussion in Chapter 11 on modifying noncompliant behavior in children is also relevant to any general consideration of clinical applications to reactance theory. It is, however, important to note that, among other things, the difference in the balance of social power between adults and children is of such magnitude that it may be difficult, and misleading, to generalize very much from interventions with children to interventions with adults.

overcome if therapy is to be successful. Behavior therapists also have been sensitive to the issue of client opposition. Davison (1973) points out that "nearly everything we do in behavior modification requires the active cooperation of the client [p. 154]." Presumably, without that cooperation, effective therapeutic intervention would be exceedingly difficult (see also, Goldfried & Davison, 1976). Finally, client-centered therapies conceptualize spontaneous and autonomous self-directed behavior to be the primary therapeutic goal, and coercive direction by the therapist is seen as the antithesis of effective therapeutic behavior, regardless of whether the client complies with or opposes this direction.

If client resistance to therapeutic interventions can reduce the effectiveness of these interventions, how might this resistance be avoided or, at least, minimized? There seems to be virtual consensus on the answer to this question. Psychodynamic therapists are cautioned to avoid giving interpretations before the client is "ready" for them. Client-centered therapists are enjoined to avoid directing the client in any way. In regard to more specific techniques, Kidder (1972) suggests that the "permissive approach" to hypnosis might produce more attitude change than the "authoritarian approach." Beutler (1978) has pointed to the reduction in effectiveness that can occur when clients are pressured into engaging in role-playing exercises.

At a more general level, a variety of social psychological theories (i.e., reactance, dissonance, self-perception) have suggested that the likelihood of sustained therapeutic improvement will be enhanced by maximizing clients' perceptions of free choice in therapy and minimizing clients' perceptions of therapist pressure. The convergence of these theoretical perspectives has been discussed elsewhere (e.g., Beutler, 1978; Brehm, 1976; Brehm & McAllister, 1980) and will not be detailed here.

While the prediction that choice would be more effective than coercion in eliciting lasting behavior and attitude change is well supported theoretically, anecdotally (virtually every clinician is pessimistic about therapy outcomes for clients who are involuntarily consigned to treatment), and empirically in the laboratory, there is little evidence of the specific effect of choice on therapeutic endeavors. Part of the reason for this lack of evidence is endemic to clinical research. Methodologically adequate studies of the effects of actual therapy with actual clients are exceedingly expensive and difficult; they are, therefore, rare. Moreover, when such studies are done, they are usually restricted to relatively global comparisons of treatment strategies (e.g., psychodynamic versus behavior therapy, as in Sloane, Staples, Cristol, Yorkston, & Whipple, 1975).

More detailed consideration of the relative effectiveness of components of therapy are frequently conducted with nonclinical populations (such as test-anxious or snake-phobic college students). Although generalization of the results obtained with such populations to "true" clinical populations is difficult and a continuing source of debate for clinical researchers (e.g., Cochrane & Sobol, 1976; Kazdin, 1978), analogue studies such as these can provide hypotheses about the possible therapeutic effectiveness of more specific treatment components. Unfortunately, however, even if we restrict our consideration to analogue studies, specific examinations of the effects of choice are sparse and, as will be seen below, difficult to interpret.

Choice and Reactance: Analogue Studies

An early study on the effects of choice of treatment was conducted by Devine and Fernald (1973). College undergraduates were selected who both reported extreme fear of snakes and who, in a behavioral pretest, refused to even lift the lid of a cage containing the snake to be used in the study. Since experimental procedures involved more than the one hour required for course credit, all subjects were told that they did not have to participate; all, however, did choose to continue. This particular aspect of the study indicates that all subjects initially were given the freedom to decide whether or not to participate in the treatment study, and all can be considered to be "volunteers."

Two-thirds of the subjects in the study were then shown a 40-minute video-tape of four different therapists each conducting one of four different types of therapy (systematic desensitization, encounter, rational-emotive, and behavioral rehearsal with modeling). These subjects were asked to rate their preferences about having each of the therapies and were interviewed about their preferences. Half of these subjects were then assigned to the therapy that they had strongly preferred; the other half were assigned to the therapy that they had strongly preferred *not* to receive. The remaining one-third of the subjects were told that the videotape machine was broken and, thus, they could not see the film; they were randomly assigned to type of therapy. All subjects received two 1-hr sessions of the designated type of therapy.

Devine and Fernald then ranked the performance of all subjects on the behavioral approach posttest and performed one-way Kruskal-Wallis analyses of ranks. There was no significant effect for type of therapy, but therapy preference did have a significant effect on post-therapy performance. While the vast majority of subjects in all conditions showed improvement over their initial approach behavior, subjects receiving their preferred therapy improved more than subjects receiving either the randomly assigned therapy or their nonpreferred therapy.

The nonpreferred therapy condition in this study appears to be a rather strong reactance manipulation. After being given choice about participation in the study, these subjects watched a videotape of different therapies and expressed their therapy preferences in both written and oral form. It appears a reasonable assumption that they expected to receive their preferred therapy and that assignment to the therapy they strongly preferred not to receive eliminated this expected freedom. Moreover, this type of manipulation can be assumed to have created frustration as well as reactance (see Chapter 5 for discussion of frustration and reactance).

The random assignment condition, though intended as a baseline control, may also have created reactance. Subjects in this condition may have reacted similarly to subjects in studies concerned with the effects of censorship (see Chapter 6). Upon being informed that the tape existed, they may have perceived that they had the freedom to see the tape (after all, why could not another machine be obtained?) and, more inferentially, that they had the freedom to use the videotape material as a grounds for deciding upon the type of therapy they wished to receive. A more appropriate baseline control would have been to make it quite clear to subjects that they would not have the freedom to choose the type of therapy they received, and then to mention (or, even, show) the videotapes. In this way, knowledge of the tapes' existence (or content) would be kept constant across conditions, but in the condition where no decisional freedom was established, no reactance arousal should take place.

The lack of an adequate baseline control condition creates difficulties in interpreting the results of this study. We cannot know whether obtaining one's preferred therapy *enhanced* therapeutic effectiveness or whether both the random assignment condition and the nonpreferred therapy conditions *reduced* therapeutic effectiveness. Furthermore, since this study was not conducted in order to test a reactance theory hypothesis and since, therefore, establishment of subjects' freedoms was not strictly controlled, the possibility that reactance was aroused in the two conditions in which therapy was less effective is certainly plausible but necessarily speculative.

In a study by Gordon (1976), the effects of volunteering and choice of treatment were examined with college undergraduates. Gordon defined volunteers as those subjects who immediately signed up for an offered experience with relaxation training; nonvolunteers were undergraduates who did not at first volunteer, but who later agreed to participate when their professor told them they would receive extra credit for participating in psychology experiments. Subjects either choose between two hypothetical treatments or were assigned to a treatment chosen by another subject. All subjects actually received the same standard relaxation training.

Significant interactions between volunteer status and choice of treatment were obtained on measures of perceived value of the treatment and on self-reports of degree of relaxation achieved. On both of these measures, choice did not affect the nonvolunteers. Choice did, however, have an impact on those subjects who had signed up immediately. For these subjects, choice led to significantly more perceived value of the treatment than reported by no choice subjects. Choice also produced a significant increase from pre to post reports of relaxation, while the no choice condition failed to produce a significant difference across the two measures of relaxation. On both dependent measures, the same general pattern of results was obtained. Volunteer–choice subjects tended to report the greatest perceived value and effectiveness of treatment, while volunteer–no choice subjects tended to report the lowest levels. The nonvolunteer subjects reported intermediate levels of value and effectiveness.

This study has been extensively critiqued by Harris and Harvey (1978), who contend that both experimental manipulations in Gordon's study were quite problematic. Harris and Harvey point out, for instance, that the "nonvolunteers" did actually volunteer, but at a later time. Moreover, "volunteers" reported being somewhat less relaxed than "nonvolunteers" prior to treatment. Thus, "volunteers" were both more interested in becoming relaxed and more tense. These differences may have led to increased sensitivity by "volunteer" subjects to the variation in choice of treatment.

Harris and Harvey also take issue with Gordon's suggestion that no choice–volunteers may have experienced reactance arousal. They note that the right to choose was never clearly established for any of the subjects, and, therefore, that the no choice condition did not eliminate an established behavioral freedom. The way in which the no choice condition was operationalized, however, may be considered to have frustrated subjects. No choice subjects, especially those volunteers who felt tense and desired relaxation, might have been frustrated and angered by seeing another subject receive his or her preferred treatment—simultaneously in the same room—but not being allowed to choose a treatment for themselves. Any such anger and frustration could have reduced subjects' perception of the value of the treatment and, indeed, made it difficult for them to become relaxed.

All of Harris and Harvey's points are well taken. It should be noted, however, that Gordon's data can be construed to fit a reactance theory interpretation. For the sake of argument, let us suppose that all subjects perceived that they had the freedom to choose their treatment: choice subjects because they were allowed to choose and no choice subjects because they saw a similar other make a choice. If this freedom was perceived by no choice subjects, the elimination of it *might* create reactance. Two ambiguities here should be noted. First, as in Devine and Fernald's study and as pointed out by Harris and Harvey, there is the possible confounding of frustration and reactance. Second, as we have described previously (see Chapter 4), if the elimination of freedom was perceived to be irrevocable, reactance should not be of very long duration. If, however, sufficient reactance of sufficient duration was aroused, the desirability of the treatment received should be decreased and the desirability of the treatment *not* received should be enhanced. These effects on treatment desirability could then influence perceived value and effectiveness of the two treatments.

That this effect occurred only for Gordon's volunteer subjects can also be seen as consistent with reactance theory. The volunteer subjects may have perceived themselves as more in need of relaxation than the nonvolunteer ones. If so, the importance of the freedom to choose and obtain an effective treatment would be greater for volunteer than for nonvolunteer subjects, reactance arousal should be greater if this freedom was eliminated, and subsequent attitudinal and behavioral effects also should be greater.

This interpretation is offered quite speculatively. Gordon's results would have been much easier to interpret if the methodological and theoretical problems noted by Harris and Harvey had been avoided. In addition, even if all our "supposed's" were granted, Gordon's results, like those of Devine and Fernald (1973), can be as easily interpreted as supportive of dissonance theory as of reactance theory. Subjects who made a voluntary commitment on an important decision should experience dissonance between the choice they made and any negative aspects of the chosen alternative. Dissonance could then be reduced by perceiving the choice alternative more favorably and, perhaps, by being more positively affected by this alternative.[3]

[3] See, however, Harris and Harvey's (1978) discussion of why specific procedures used by Gordon create difficulties for interpreting his data in terms of dissonance theory. See also Cooper (1980; Axsom & Cooper, 1981) on dissonance processes in therapy.

Thus, although as Harris and Harvey point out, Gordon's study cannot provide fully adequate support for the hypothesis that not allowing clients choice in the treatment situation creates reactance and decreases the perceived value and effectiveness of the treatment received, we regard Gordon's data as suggestive that such an effect could occur for clients for whom treatment is especially important. Another suggestive study on the topics of subject status and treatment effectiveness as a function of choice of treatment was conducted by Kanfer and Grimm (1978).

Nonvolunteer subjects in this study were undergraduates who had been assigned to the experiment as one of the five they were required to participate in for course credit. These subjects had no choice in the experiment to which they were assigned, but they could refuse to participate in any specific experiment. Volunteers were those who were solicited through campus newspaper ads inviting participation in "a study concerning increased reading speed and comprehension." Subjects were seen individually and were given descriptions of three different supposed types of techniques for improving reading skills. Free choice subjects chose the technique they wished to have administered to them. Lost choice subjects "stated a preference," but then were told the experimenter could not give them that one, and had to give them another type instead. No choice subjects were told that while the three types were generally used in research of this sort, in this experiment only one type was being used. All subjects actually received the same type of training, descriptions of the three types having been sufficiently vague that subjects would believe they were receiving the specific one they had chosen or been assigned to.

Reading comprehension and reading rate were measured both before and after the training. No effects were obtained on comprehension, but two main effects were found for reading rate. Volunteers showed marginally ($p = .06$) more improvement than nonvolunteers. In addition, individual comparisons on the significant effect of experimental conditions revealed that free choice subjects improved significantly more than lost choice subjects and that no choice subjects did not differ significantly from either of the other two groups.

This study shares some of the problems we have noted in the studies by Devine and Fernald (1973) and Gordon (1976). The manipulation of volunteer versus nonvolunteer status is highly questionable. Kanfer and Grimm's "nonvolunteer" subjects could choose not to participate in any specific experiment and thus, in this sense, all subjects could be considered to have volunteered. On the other hand, "nonvolunteers" may have differed from "volunteers" on variables other than choosing to participate in the experiment. "Volunteers" may have been older than the "nonvolunteers," may have perceived themselves as more in need of improvement in reading skills, and may have made a greater effort to participate in the study. All of these differences make it impossible to tell which among them might have been crucial in affecting subjects' responses to the training they received. It should be noted, however, that "volunteers" and "nonvolunteers" did not differ in pretraining reading rate.

Kanfer and Grimm's manipulation of choice also creates some ambiguity. Although their no choice baseline condition is well conceived, there remains no way to distinguish between frustration and reactance effects in their lost choice condition. Moreover, the failure to obtain a significant difference between the no choice condition and either of the other two conditions makes it impossible to determine the direction of the obtained effect. Reactance (and/or frustration) may have led to decreased treatment effectiveness; dissonance reduction may have led to increased treatment effectiveness; or both may have occurred.

Thus these three studies on the effects of choice on treatment effectiveness obtained rather similar effects and suffer from similar methodological problems. All three found a positive effect of choice for at least some subjects on some measures. All three, however, also failed to provide an adequate no-freedom baseline condition (the no choice condition used by Kanfer and Grimm being the exception), confounded frustration and reactance, and did not provide data that can distinguish between a positive effect for choice and a negative effect for no choice or lost choice.

Reactance as a Characteristic of the Client

Another perspective on the issue of client choice has been suggested in a recent paper by Beutler (1979). Beutler suggests that rather than enunciating overall dicta that would apply to all clients, a more effective way to proceed might be to designate those specific therapeutic interventions that would be effective for specific psychological conditions. Beutler (1979) then describes "three assumedly independent patient-symptom dimensions [that] could account for a large portion of the variability which has been obtained in many comparative studies [p. 882]" of therapeutic outcome effectiveness.

Among these three dimensions, Beutler describes a dimension of patient reactivity. For "high reactance" patients, he proposes, "Insight treatments will be superior to most forms of behavioral treatments since they involve less direction by the therapist. Affective insight therapy will be superior to cognitive insight therapy for the same reason [Beutler, 1979, p. 884]." For "low reactance" patients, he hypothesizes that "non-insight treatments will be superior to insight treatments because such patients are assumed to seek external direction [Beutler, 1979, p. 884]." As measures of patient reactivity, Beutler used I–E scores or patient populations in which he assumed generalized reactance tendencies would be high (e.g., adolescent delinquents).

Before describing the results of Beutler's use of patient reactivity to account for differential outcome effectiveness, we should note a few theoretical points. Although reactance theory has concerned itself more with the situational determinants of reactance than with individual difference characteristics that might affect the arousal and expression of reactance, the studies reviewed in Chapter 9 do appear to demonstrate a relationship between Rotter's I–E scale of locus of control and psychological reactance. Beutler's notion that patients might differ in their potential for (or in readiness of) reactance arousal and that the I–E scale might be a measure of such a difference is consistent with the conclusions of this review. It should be noted, however, that there is no tenet in reactance theory that would generate the prediction that patients low in reactance potential would "seek external direction." This hypothesis could be valid, but it must be made outside the context of reactance theory.

In order to test his hypotheses, Beutler identified 52 "methodologically adequate" comparative outcome studies. Each study was rated by two independent raters on the three patient-symptom dimensions (i.e., reactance plus two others) examined in Beutler's review. On these three dimensions, interrater agreement was lowest on the patient reactivity dimension (66% versus 95% and 80%).

There were six studies on which the two independent raters agreed that patient reactivity was an important variable in the study and on which the raters agreed in their classification of the level of this reactivity. In two of these studies, the patients participating were judged as high in reactivity (Novaco, 1976: volunteers with "anger control problems"; Jesness, 1975: adolescent inpatient delinquents). Both studies compared a cognitive modification technique (self-instructional treatment or transactional analysis) with a behavior modification treatment (relaxation or contingency contracting). While Beutler would have expected the cognitive modification techniques to be superior with these patient samples, the two treatments did not differ in effectiveness in either study.

The results of the four other studies cited by Beutler are summarized in Table 13.1. All four exposed patients varying in locus of control to

TABLE 13.1
Differential Treatment Effectiveness as a Function of Patient Locus of Control[a]

Subjects	Treatments	Results[b]
Abramowitz, Abramowitz, Roback, & Jackson, 1974		
Mildly distressed college students	Directive (D) versus nondirective (ND) group therapy	E: D more effective than ND I: ND more effective than D
Friedman & Dies, 1974		
Test-anxious college students	Systematic desensitization (SD) versus automated desensitization (AD) versus counseling (C)	E: C & SD, too much control by self I: C, optimal control by self SD & AD: I more resistant than E
Kilman & Howell, 1974		
Institutionalized female drug addicts	Directive versus nondirective group therapy	D = ND
Kilman, Albert, & Sotile, 1975		
Students recruited for a "growth group"	Structured (S) versus unstructured (US) group therapy	E: S more effective than US I: US more effective than S

[a] Adapted from Beutler, 1979.
[b] E = externals; I = internals.

treatments that differed in amount of direction provided by the therapist. After reviewing these studies (as well as those relevant to the other two patient-symptom dimensions he considered), Beutler (1979) concluded that "The most consistent support provided by this review has been for hypotheses regarding the level of patients' reactance. However, these were also the hypotheses least often evaluated [p. 894]." Our conclusion would be somewhat more cautious. Of the six studies used to test the patient reactivity hypothesis, only three provided support for the hypothesis, and one of these (Friedman and Dies, 1974) did not report any differences on the target behavior (i.e., test anxiety).

Other studies not reviewed in Beutler's article have examined the relationship between I–E and treatment effectiveness. These too appear to have provided suggestive yet sketchy evidence in support of using the I–E dimension as a factor in determining the treatment modality most likely to be effective. For example, Best and Steffy (1975) and Best (1975) report two studies examining the effect of I–E classification on responses to smoking withdrawal programs. In the Best and Steffy study, subjects (volunteers from the local community) were exposed to either satiation (i.e., smoking double their original rate) or nonsatiation. Reduction of rate of smoking outside the clinic sessions was requested as well, and this reduction rate was planned either by the client or by the therapist. Immediate reductions in smoking were obtained for all groups. Over the follow-up period, therapist-planning versus client-planning had no effect. Locus of control did, however, interact with satiation. Internal subjects who received satiation smoked less over time than internals who did not receive satiation; externals did not differ as a function of satiation. Further examination of Best and Steffy's data indicates that the two groups showing a trend toward most reduced smoking at the last (4-month) follow-up were the internal–satiation and the external–no satiation groups. The groups showing the most backsliding from their immediate posttreatment reductions were internal–no satiation and external–satiation.

In Best's study, subjects were exposed to either an internal focus of treatment (i.e., satiation) or an external focus (i.e., situational analysis of those environmental events associated with smoking). Relative to a control group that received the "core treatment" of concentrated cigarette smoke and rapid smoking, internal locus of control subjects who had received the internal focus treatment were equivalent at a 6-month follow-up, external locus of control subjects who had received the external focus reported somewhat greater smoking, and the other two experimental conditions reported the greatest amounts of smoking.

Thus, while this study replicated the general pattern of Best and Steffy's results—finding that satiation for internals and nonsatiation for externals were more effective than the other two combinations of personality and treatment types—no experimental group was better off at follow-up than the core treatment control group. In reviewing this pattern of results, Best (1975) suggests that "Tailoring [of the therapy to individual difference characteristics of the client] does not so much serve to augment treatment efficacy as to prevent the added components from doing harm and reducing the clinic's value [p. 7]." The simpler procedure in such circumstances, it would seem to us, would be not to add any additional components.

Wallston, Wallston, Kaplan, and Maides (1976) offer an interesting perspective on the use of the I–E scale to predict differential treatment effectiveness. These investigators contend that the I–E scale is too general to serve as an effective predictor. Rather, they suggest, what is needed is a more specific locus of control scale designed to measure people's attitudes and beliefs about personal control that are specifically relevant to a particular situation. Wallston et al. report the development of one such scale: the Health Locus of Control (HLC)

Scale. In their study, overweight female subjects were exposed to either a self-directed program or a group project for losing weight. The former program was seen as more consistent with HLC internals and the latter program with HLC external personality types. At the end of treatment, subjects with a personality-consistent program reported more satisfaction than subjects with a personality-inconsistent program. Weight loss data also followed this pattern, although no significant differences were obtained. The authors note that when these same subjects were classified on Rotter's I–E scale, no interactions between subject type and program were found.

Finally, we should point out that there are other populations besides the anger-control patients and the adolescent delinquents mentioned in Beutler's review article that might classify as high in reactance potential. Rice and Schoenfeld (1975), for example, suggest that alcoholics may be relatively internal in their locus of control and might, therefore, resist aversive conditioning procedures in which the client is a passive participant. Love, Kaswan, and Bugental (1972) report a study in which upper socioeconomic class parents responded more favorably to a less directive treatment for their children's difficulties than to a more directive treatment. Lower socioeconomic class parents (primarily mothers) responded in the opposite fashion. Love et al. suggest that the greater financial and personal autonomy of upper class individuals may lead them to resist directive treatment procedures, whereas the lower autonomy of lower class individuals may lead them to respond favorably to such interventions.

Overall, then, one would have to conclude that the evidence for either general therapeutic disadvantage for lack of (or deprivation of) choice, or for more specific interactions of type of therapy with personality characteristics of clients is mildly supportive. From a reactance theory viewpoint, the weakness of the available support may stem from the use of overly inclusive categories. An I–E scale designed for the specific area of concern (as advocated by Wallston et al.) would seem a clear improvement over a general measure of locus of control. Even this, however, is a long way from assessment of a specific freedom of specific importance possessed by a specific individual. Over-inclusiveness can be observed in terms of the treatments as well. Treatments tend to be complex and, although one may be more or less directive than another, both directive and nondirective components are likely to be included in both.

Since it is not possible to make the kind of fine distinctions in the real world that one grows accustomed to in the laboratory, overinclusiveness to some degree is probably inevitable. Nevertheless, it would seem helpful if future research efforts in this area, so much as is realistically possible, would focus on more specific variables. In such a pursuit, we would like to suggest that reactance theory can provide a number of specific variables that may influence therapeutic effectiveness.

The Interaction of Client Freedoms
and Therapist Communications

One set of theoretically relevant variables that might be involved in treatment effectiveness was investigated in a study by Stivers and Brehm (1980). Stivers and Brehm reasoned that some problem situations would promote the importance of the freedom to try to exert personal control over the problem, while other situations would increase the importance of the freedom *not* to try to exert personal control. While any number of factors might serve to enhance the importance of either freedom, Stivers and Brehm suggested that such factors as direct impact of the problem on the person's life and expectations of being able to resolve the problem through exerting personal control would increase the importance of the freedom to try to exert personal control. On the other hand, less direct impact, lower expectations of being able to resolve the problem by exerting personal control, and contemplation of unpleasant events while trying to solve the problem should increase the importance of the freedom not to try to resolve a problem through exerting personal control. Stivers and Brehm hypothesized that where the freedom to try to exert personal control is most important, greatest reactance should be aroused by communications emphasizing the individual's lack of control over the situation; where the freedom not to try to exert personal control is most important, reactance arousal would be expected to be greatest in response to communications stressing the person's possession of personal control.

In this study, female undergraduates participated in a role-play analogue of a therapeutic interaction. Each subject was met at the door of an experimental room that was arranged to resemble an office, and she was seated facing a desk with a tape recorder on it. The experimenter explained that she was interested in studying counselor–client interactions, and that due to the difficulties of studying actual therapeutic sessions, a role-play simulation had been created to examine those aspects of counselor–client interactions that were of interest.

Each subject was asked to role-play a client going to see a counselor at a university counseling center for the first time. She was given a written description of one of two client situations and asked to take her time reading it over, and to imagine herself in this person's place. One of the situations, a conflict about whether to stay in a troubled romantic relationship and try to work out the problems in the relationship, was designed to increase the importance of trying to exert personal control over the outcome of the situation. The other, a conflict about whether to stay in a friendship with a close friend who was severely depressed and try to help that friend work out the depression, was designed to increase the importance of the freedom not to try to exert personal control.

When the subject reported herself ready to identify with the role of the client, she was asked to imagine that she had just presented the problem to the counselor. She then heard a tape that presented stereotypical views from either a behavioristic, psychodynamic, or client-centered perspective. The behavioristic tape emphasized rewards and punishments in the environment as determinants of problem outcomes, and the psychodynamic tape stressed deeply rooted personality traits as determinants. The client-centered tape emphasized the client's own decisions and deliberate actions as key determinants. Thus, the first two tapes emphasized determination of the outcome of the situation by something outside the client's personal control, whereas the third emphasized client responsibility for the outcome. After the subject had listened to the tape, the experimenter (who had left the room during the tape and was blind to all experimental conditions) interviewed the subject about her reaction to the supposed couselor. Subjects responded to all interview questions by giving ratings on a scale from 1 to 10.

Two measures are of major interest for our present discussion. Heightened reactance arousal was expected to lead to both motivational and attitudinal effects. As a measure of motivation, subjects were asked how much they intended to exert control over the outcome of their presenting problem. A significant interaction between freedom made important and counselor communication was obtained. Planned individual comparisons within each level of freedom made important were then performed to see if the means for the behavioristic and psychodynamic conditions were, as they were expected to be, equivalent. For the freedom not to try condition, this was the case (see Table 13.2). The combined mean of these two conditions was then compared to the mean for the client-centered condition. As had been predicted, motivation to exert personal control was significantly lower for those subjects who heard the counselor communication that emphasized that problem outcomes were determined by one's own actions. Thus, for subjects who valued the freedom not to try to exert personal control,

TABLE 13.2

Mean Ratings for Subjects' Reported Intention to Exert Personal Control and for Their Evaluations of the Counselor[a]

	Type of counselor communication			
	Behavioristic	Psychodynamic	Behavioristic and psychodynamic[b]	Client-centered
High importance of the freedom *not* to try to exert personal control				
Intention (Pretest = 5.13)	5.20[c]	5.10	5.15	4.40
Evaluation	6.55[d]	5.45		3.88
High importance of the freedom to try to exert personal control				
Intention (Pretest = 8.13)	8.20	9.40		8.20
Evaluation	3.43	2.90	3.17	8.05

[a] From Stivers and Brehm, 1980.

[b] Conditions combined only when statistically equivalent.

[c] The greater the number, the greater the intention to exert personal control.

[d] The greater the number, the more positive the evaluation.

the communication emphasizing one's possession of control reduced the motivation to try.

Within the freedom to try condition, the means for the behavioristic versus psychodynamic communications were significantly different. In light of this unexpected difference, each mean was then compared individually with the client-centered condition. For subjects who had heard the psychodynamic tape, motivation to try was significantly greater than for subjects who had heard the client-centered tape, but subjects in the behavioristic and client-centered conditions did not differ in reported intention to try to exert personal control. The former result was in accordance with theoretical predictions; the latter was not. Thus, for subjects who valued the freedom to try to exert personal control, one communication (i.e., psychodynamic) emphasizing determinants other than personal control increased the motivation to try, whereas the other freedom-inconsistent communication (i.e., behavioristic) appeared to have no effect.

Subjects were also asked to evaluate the counselor on a number of measures (i.e., agreement with the counselor, perceptions of counselor helpfulness, desire to see the same counselor again, and desire to see a different counselor). These measures were combined in an overall evaluative index, and a significant interaction between freedom made important and counselor communication was obtained. Using the same set of planned comparisons described above for the motivation measure, it was found that, although the means for the behavioristic and psychodynamic communications were significantly different for subjects who had read the problem designed to enhance the importance of the freedom not to try to exert personal control, each differed significantly from the mean for the client-centered subjects. As had been predicted, client-centered subjects were *less* favorable toward the counselor than subjects in the other two conditions. For subjects who had read the problem designed to increase the importance of the freedom to try to exert personal control, the behavioristic and psychodynamic conditions (combined) differed significantly from the client-centered condition. Among these conditions, client-centered subjects were, as had been predicted, *more* favorable toward the counselor.

Some other data are helpful in interpreting these findings. First, it should be noted that freedom-consistent communications (i.e., those communications that emphasized the degree of personal control that was consistent with the important freedom created by the presenting problem) did not appear to affect reported motivation. The means for pretest subjects who simply read one of the two problem descriptions and responded to the question, "How much do you feel that your decisions and actions control the outcome of this situation?" are given in Table 13.2. It can be seen from these data that the mean levels of intention reported by subjects to freedom-consistent communications were highly similar to pretest means. On the other hand, opposition to the counselor's communication was produced in two of the three conditions in which subjects heard freedom *in*consistent communications. In this study, then, freedom-consistent communications did not appear to affect motivation; *in*consistent communications, however, did appear to induce motivational change.

Second, subjects' anticipated outcome for the problem they had assumed in the role-play did not differ as a function of experimental condition, and, indeed, was relatively positive (overall mean = 6.58, where 10 indicated the most positive outcome). Differential expectations about the outcomes of the two problems cannot, therefore, explain the obtained interactions between freedom made important and counselor communication.

The results of this study suggest that in situations where counselor communications about personal control are inconsistent with the client's perceived freedom regarding his or her efforts to exert personal control, opposition to the counselor and derogation of the counselor's efforts may occur. A few caveats, however, are in order. This was a role-play study, and these results can provide only hypotheses about what might happen in an actual clinical setting. Moreover, even within the controlled laboratory setting, one important unpredicted effect was obtained. Subjects in the freedom to try condition who heard the behavioristic tape reported intentions to exert personal control that did not differ from the intentions reported by subjects in the client-centered condition, nor, it appears, from the baseline level of motivation expressed by pretest subjects responding to the same presenting difficulty. It should be noted, however, that subjects in this condition did evaluate the counselor in accordance with a priori predictions.

These findings suggest the possibility that at least some therapeutic messages about environmental control may lead to conflicting interpretations in relationship to one's desired personal control. Perhaps such messages may be interpreted as *either* implying an individual's lack of control—by emphasizing a source of control outside the individual—or as implying the individual's possession of personal control by suggesting an ability to influence the environment. Such a possibility suggests that counselors who emphasize the power of environmental contingencies might be well advised to assess the way in which their clients are interpreting the personal control implications of such an emphasis.

In spite of the role-play nature of this study, then, the theoretical analysis employed by Stivers and Brehm (1980) may have applicability both for clinical practice and research. Different clients have different problems; some of these problems may be perceived as under their own control, but most problems that bring clients to therapists are probably not viewed as subject to their own control. Virtually all clients, however, presumably have the freedoms *to try* and *not to try* to exert personal control. Further, while therapists would not be expected to convey the kind of stereotyped messages about personal control used by Stivers and Brehm, all therapists probably do convey their notions about whether or not the client should be trying to exert control. Both client perception of the importance of the freedom to try (or, not to try) to exert personal control and the therapist's beliefs about the client's personal control can be assessed—by asking the appropriate questions and/or by observation or transcripts of the therapy session.

It would seem, therefore, that variables of the type examined by Stivers and Brehm are important therapeutic elements that are rather easily measured. Moreover, these variables are specific instances of the critical theoretical components of freedoms and threats. From a reactance theory point of view, understanding the way in which reactance arousal might be created and expressed in therapeutic settings would be approached through such an assessment of the specific important freedoms held by the client and the specific threats to these freedoms posed by the therapist.

Reactance as a Treatment Strategy

In this section, we shall discuss ways in which reactance arousal might be generated in therapy as a desired part of treatment. A recent paper by Tennen, Rohrbaugh, Press, and White (1981) provides an extremely helpful conceptual framework in which to consider the therapeutic uses of reactance arousal. "Paradoxical" therapeutic interventions—where the therapist urges the client to engage in symptomatic behavior rather than to avoid it or overcome it—have been described by a number of clinicians. Tennen *et al.* suggest that such paradoxical interventions can be viewed as representing either compliance-based or defiance-based therapeutic strategies. In compliance-based paradoxical interventions, the therapist actually does want the client to engage in the symptom. Tennen *et al.* (1981) hypothesize that this sort of therapeutic approach may be most helpful "with symptoms such as obsessions, panic attacks, and various somatic complaints which seem to be maintained by attempts to stave them off [p. 18]." Conversely, defiance-based paradoxical prescriptions would be used by therapists who want the client to disobey. Since the therapist has told the client to perform the symptom, disobedience would result in a decrement of symptomatic behavior.

Tennen *et al.* propose that whether compliance-based or defiance-based strategies would be more useful can be ascertained by consideration of two client-symptom characteristics. The first variable is the reactance potential of the client; the second is the client's perception that the symptomatic behavior in question is either free (under his or her control) or unfree (not under his or her control). Compliance-based paradoxical interventions are viewed as most appropriate when reactance potential is low and the symptom is an unfree behavior. Defiance-based strategies are seen as most likely to work when reactance potential is high and the symptom is a free behavior. Use of paradoxical strategies in the other two cells of the fully crossed two-by-two model is seen as more problematic.

Tennen et al. suggest that reactance potential can be assessed in a number of ways. They hypothesize that some clients may possess a general trait of high reactivity due to such factors as regarding all behavioral freedoms as important and/or having relatively few behavioral freedoms such that a threat to any one poses a threat to a large portion of their total available freedoms. This notion of a general trait of reactivity is also consistent with the relationship between Rotter's I–E scale and reactance, discussed earlier in this chapter as well as in Chapter 9. Another source of high reactivity noted by Tennen et al. involves developmental variables. These investigators suggest that adolescents and older people may be especially prone to resist control over their behavior. Third, Tennen et al. point out that high reactivity can be produced situationally through characteristics of the behavioral freedom (i.e., its importance, number of freedoms threatened) and/or of the specific threat (i.e., magnitude of threat).

The distinction between free and unfree behaviors seems a more complicated matter. Tennen et al. acknowledge that there is not likely to be any objective way of assessing this distinction, and they suggest that the client's perceptions of "freeness" are the important issue. They also acknowledge that, as we have remarked earlier, clients may come into therapy presenting relatively few symptoms that they themselves regard as free. In this case, Tennen et al. (1981) believe that one can prescribe engagement not in the symptom itself, but in what they term "collateral behaviors": "Thus a client whose problem is fear of crowds would almost certainly view his panicky feelings around people as 'unfree,' yet might acknowledge that riding in a car to Times Square is something he could do, but would rather not [p. 20]."

Although Tennen et al.'s idea about using collateral behaviors rather than the symptom per se in paradoxical injunctions is an intriguing and potentially useful notion, the admission that much of client behavior is probably regarded as unfree would seem to vitiate the utility of the free versus unfree distinction. Moreover, as we have indicated earlier, the "freeness" of the symptom may not be as relevant to therapy as the "freeness" of trying to cope with the symptom.

If one eliminates, then, the free versus unfree distinction from their model, the two operative characteristics in Tennen et al.'s framework appear to consist of the characteristics of the symptoms and the reactance potential of the specific client in regard to specific behavioral

freedoms. For symptoms that are presumed to be maintained by attempted avoidance of the symptom and where reactance potential is
low, a compliance-based therapeutic intervention would seem appropriate. In this general class, one could include the obsessions, panic
attacks, and somatic complaints mentioned by Tennen *et al.* as well as
phobias and symptoms such as insomnia and stuttering that are believed to be exacerbated by the anxiety produced in attempting to
avoid them (see Storms & McCaul, 1976, for an interesting discussion of
exacerbation effects). When a compliance-based strategy is used, the
therapist will want to take every precaution to ensure that reactance
potential is and remains low, since disobedience in this case would
mean trying harder to avoid the symptom and would, therefore, worsen
the client's condition (see Brehm, 1976, for an extensive consideration
of ways in which therapists can avoid creating reactance).

Defiance-based paradoxical interventions would seem most appropriate in conditions where reactance potential is high and the symptom is presumed not to be maintained by efforts to avoid it. Hostile
interpersonal behaviors, various antinormative behaviors (such as ad-
dictions), and symptoms that function, as least in part, to control the
behavior of others would seem good candidates for this type of intervention. For defiance-based strategies, the therapist would want to
use the theory as a guide for generating as much reactance arousal as
possible.

Use of the compliance versus defiance distinction proposed by Tennen *et al.* is especially helpful in sorting through the wide variety of
techniques that have been viewed as "paradoxical" (see reviews by
Newton, 1968a, 1968b, and Raskin & Klein, 1976). In our following
discussion, we shall briefly describe a number of different paradoxical
interventions.

Varieties of Paradoxical
Intervention: Compliance-Based

Probably the earliest reference to encouraging clients to engage in
symptomatic behavior is found in the writings of Dunlap. In his initial
consideration of this technique, Dunlap (1932) based his therapeutic
approach on a rather idiosyncratic version of learning theory in which
the response that was practiced was distinguished from the response
that was to be performed. Dunlap appears subsequently to have deleted this particular theoretical rationale, and in a later paper (1942)
makes the argument that by voluntarily performing something that was
previously regarded as involuntary, new "affective and ideational"

elements become associated with the behavior. Presumably, these new elements allow the person to stop engaging in the behavior. Dunlap called his technique "negative practice" and treated individuals by instructing them to perform the undesirable behavior over and over again. In his 1942 paper, Dunlap stated that he had used negative practice successfully with motor patterns such as stammering and with "affective and ideational habits."

Massed practice is very similar to Dunlap's negative practice. Again, the client is instructed to repeat the behavior over and over. The rationale behind this treatment, however, is based on Hullian theory and particularly on the theoretical postulate that reactive inhibition will build up as a behavior is frequently repeated. Problem behaviors that have been reported to have been successfully treated with massed practice include tics (Yates, 1958), examination anxiety (Malleson, 1959), and the Gilles de la Tourette syndrome (tics and compulsive swearing; Clark, 1966).

Another type of paradoxical technique is *paradoxical intention* described by Frankl (1960, 1966). Frankl (1966) views paradoxical intention as a therapeutic strategy most useful for those symptoms that are maintained by the client's anticipatory anxiety: "Anticipatory anxiety triggers off what the patient so fearfully expects to happen. . . . A symptom evokes a phobia and the phobia provokes the symptom [p. 254]." Frankl's theoretical framework is complex, but one critical component he cites for the effectiveness of paradoxical intention is that the technique creates a sense of detachment from the symptom. Presumably, this new perspective by the client (which involves the client's recognition of the absurdity of the symptom and, perhaps, of even its humorous elements) facilitates elimination of the undesirable behavior. Gerz (1966) reported that 88.2% of a group of 51 phobic and obsessive-compulsive clients recovered or made significant improvement in response to treatment based on paradoxical intention. Solyom, Garza-Perez, Ledwidge, and Solyom (1972) reported a 40% specific recovery rate for 10 clients troubled with obsessive thoughts. Neither of these two studies provided any kind of no-treatment control group and, thus, the meaning of their reported recovery rates is difficult to assess. Successful treatment of a case of erythrophobia (excessive blushing) by paradoxical intention was reported by Lamontagne (1978).

All the techniques we have discussed would seem clearly compliance-based. They also seem to be used primarily with symptoms in which anxiety plays a large role: either anxiety about the occurrence of an undesired symptomatic behavior, or anxiety about a desired but fearfully avoided object or behavior. Presuming that reactance potential is low in clients treated with these approaches, negative practice, massed practice and paradoxical intention all seem to fit the criteria that we derived from Tennen et al.'s description of compliance-based strategies.

There is some question, however, about whether compliance-based paradoxical interventions would be the best treatment approach for the kinds of problems to which they have been applied. One major difficulty with compliance-based strategies is that if the client were to try to oppose the therapist's instructions to engage in the symptom, the client's anxiety about engaging in the behavior (as he or she tried not to engage in the behavior) might well increase and symptomatic behavior could become worse.

Opposition to the therapist's instruction seems a great deal less likely when anxiety-generated symptoms are treated with systematic desensitization (Wolpe, 1959). In systematic desensitization (SD), clients are asked to imagine (in some cases, actual presentation of the feared stimulus takes place) fearful stimuli. The imaginative process proceeds along a hierarchy, in which initial images of objects or situations that evoke little anxiety are gradually replaced by stimuli that usually would elicit greater and greater anxiety. Prior to engaging in SD, the client is trained to relax, and the original theoretical rationale for SD was that relaxation reciprocally inhibits the anxiety response.[4] By gradually proceeding up a hierarchy, the client is supposed to be able to face what would have been anxiety-producing images without anxiety. Given the strong evidence for the effectiveness of SD (e.g., Kazdin & Wilcoxon, 1976; Rumm & Masters, 1979), SD is currently the psychological treatment of choice for the reduction of anxiety.

Another type of treatment approach to anxiety-generated symptoms is implosive therapy (Stampfl & Levis, 1967, 1973). In this technique, fearful stimuli are imagined by the client, but no hierarchy is used. Instead, extremely fearful images are presented from the outset in an effort to "flood" the client with anxiety and, thereby, allow this anxiety to extinguish. There would seem to be a fine line between compliance-based paradoxical interventions and implosive therapy—though implosive therapy makes more use of images rather than actual behavior and exaggerates the anxiety-producing stimulus. Raskin and Klein (1976) regard implosive therapy, but not systematic desensitization, as a type of paradoxical intervention. In his review of the relative treatment effectiveness of implosive therapy compared to systematic desen-

---

[4] More recent theoretical explanations of the effects of systematic desensitization have stressed the importance of cognitive mediation.

sitization, Morganstern (1973) suggested that, in general, systematic desensitization appears the more effective technique. Our consideration of compliance-based paradoxical interventions raises the possibility that client opposition to implosive therapy may be a factor in limiting its effectiveness.

Varieties of Paradoxical
Intervention: Defiance-Based

In terms of defiance-based paradoxical strategies, several writers have reported the use of such techniques with schizophrenic clients. Like Frankl, Lindner (1954) stressed the creation of a detached attitude on the part of his client that allowed this client to reject his delusional system. A somewhat more aggressive use of a defiance-based technique was described by Rosen (1953): "Whenever your hunch tells you the patients are in danger of repeating some characteristic irrational behavior, you beat them to the draw by demanding that they reenact just exactly the piece of psychotic behavior that you fear they may fall into again [p. 27]." Davis (1965–66) reported the successful use of paradoxical statements with hospitalized schizophrenics in short-term psychoanalytic therapy.

Other clinicians who have advocated the use of paradoxical instructions as one part of the therapeutic repertoire are those who originally worked with the Bateson project on family therapy in schizophrenia. Jackson (1963) described what may still be the ultimate use of paradoxical instructions. He suggested that therapists might try teaching their paranoid clients to be more suspicious. While Jackson's stated goal for this therapeutic behavior was to increase the paranoid's attention to the real world, such an intervention would also create an extreme double-bind for the client. If the paranoid person obeys the therapist, then the paranoid, who trusts no one, is trusting the therapist with direction of his or her major symptom (and major view of the world). If, on the other hand, the paranoid disobeys the therapist, then the paranoid must become less paranoid.

The inherent relationship between double-binds and paradoxical interventions is pointed out by Watzlawick, Beavin, & Jackson (1967), who state that what they call "prescribing the symptom" is a specific technique included in the larger class of behaviors that create a double-bind for the individual. Watzlawick *et al.* appear to view prescribing the symptom as an appropriate treatment for numerous types of symptoms. "Paradoxical injunction" as described by Haley (1963, 1973) has obvious similarities to the Watzlawick approach.

Haley emphasizes the power relationship that exists between therapist and client, and between the client and his or her social environment. If a client's symptom serves, at least in part, to control the behavior of others, instructing the client to engage in the symptom effectively "turns the table." It is now impossible for the client to use the symptom to control the therapist; to engage in the symptom is to be controlled by the therapist. Moreover, Haley sees paradoxical injunctions as essentially "no lose" therapeutic strategies. If the client complies, control over the symptom is given over to the therapist. If the client defies the therapeutic prescription, symptom occurrence is decreased or eliminated.

Defiance-based paradoxical strategies can be interpreted from a reactance theory framework. For example, Fish (1972) reports a case of fused identity that he was able to treat effectively in one therapeutic session. In this case, three women in their first year of college came to him complaining that their identities had merged, and that they were spending virtually all their time together. Rather than opposing these behaviors, Fish got them to give him a list of when they would be together the next day. He instructed them that he wanted them to follow this list absolutely to the letter and that it was very important that they spend the designated times together. Follow-up indicated that two of the women became considerably less interested in being together and began to spend much less time with each other. One woman did become upset over the dissolution of the supposedly fused identity.

A reactance theory analysis would suggest that, initially, the freedom to be together was very important for all three women. One can understand this in terms of the anxiety created by one's freshman year at college and the need for social support during this time. If Fish had opposed their being together, he would have threatened this important freedom and may well have increased their "identity fusion." For at least two of these women, however, the freedom not to be together was apparently also an established freedom. While this freedom was presumably less important than the freedom to be together, the strong directive statements by Fish seem to have been a sufficient threat to freedom to create reactance arousal; freedom was restored directly by reducing contact with each other. This case study is a good example of the way that defiance-based paradoxical techniques make use of the client's existing motivational structure, rather than trying to change this structure such that more straight-forward efforts to motivate engagement in the desired behavior could be effective.

Another type of defiance-based strategy is Varela's (1971, 1977, 1978) "persuasion by successive approximation using reactance." This technique (which was described previously, Chapter 11, in regard to Ayllon et al.'s, 1980, treatment of disruptive male children) consists of constructing a hierarchy of statements concerning the client's attitudes and behavioral intentions. The therapeutic goal is to get the client to adopt these attitudes and intentions. Starting with the most acceptable statement for the client and working up to the least acceptable statement, the therapist urges the *opposite* of the statement and attempts, thereby, to provoke the client to resist the therapist and agree with the statement that is actually desired by the therapist.

This technique is explicitly defiance-based, but differs from the techniques described previously in its use of a hierarchy. Use of the hierarchy allows the therapist to progress from eliciting reactance where reactance potential is high (i.e., on statements where the importance of the freedom to disagree with the therapist would be high) to eliciting reactance where reactance potential is initially low. For example, consider the transcript provided by Ayllon et al. (1980), a section of which is reprinted in Table 11.5 of this book. Suppose the therapist had *started* the session by saying to the disruptive child, "I know you aren't willing to even give [doing your work] a try." Starting the session this way might well have elicited the child's agreement with the therapist's statement instead of the desired ("I would give it a try") disagreement that was obtained through use of a hierarchy.

Although the way in which this kind of hierarchy functions to increase the level of reactance arousal generated by later statements is not entirely clear, Varela's description of the process provides one feasible explanation. Varela reasons that having committed oneself publicly to, for example, the first statement in a hierarchy, both the salience and the importance of the freedom to take the position represented in the second statement are increased. Whatever the theoretical process underlying this technique, "persuasion by successive approximation" would seem an ingenious way to change low reactance potential into high, and, thus, to increase the probable success of a defiance-based therapeutic intervention.

Unfortunately, however, none of the defiance-based strategies discussed above has received adequate empirical support. Most of the evidence for the effectiveness of the technique comes from case study material provided in the writings already cited. The study by Ayllon et al. in which a multiple baseline design was used to assess causal relationships provides reasonably good support for the effectiveness of Varela's persuasion technique, but, as noted earlier, this study involved a very small sample of essentially normal children exhibiting a mild behavior problem. Defiance-based therapeutic interventions have, then, shown considerable promise (both theoretically and in terms of case study material) for providing therapists with a uniquely different approach to the therapeutic endeavor. This promise needs now to be pursued vigorously with more adequate evaluation research. We would hope that the theoretical framework offered by reactance theory would assist in the operationalization of defiance-based strategies in both practice and research.

In addition to obtaining more compelling evidence on the treatment effectiveness of defiance-based interventions, it will be important to ascertain the effects of such strategies on the relationship between the client and the therapist. The results from the role-play study by Stivers and Brehm (1980) suggest that oppositional motivation created by therapist communications may be accompanied by derogation of the therapist and his or her therapeutic efforts. Presumably, whether any given therapist is willing to pay such an interpersonal cost will depend on numerous factors, such as the perceived resiliency of the specific therapeutic relationship and the likelihood of success with defiance-based in contrast to more traditional therapeutic techniques. Thus, the possibility that defiance-based strategies may damage the therapeutic relationship does not indicate that such strategies are, therefore, too risky for use, but does point out the need for taking such possible damage into account prior to using these techniques.[5]

SUMMARY

Reactance arousal during therapy can be viewed from either of two perspectives. On the one hand, the arousal of the motivation to oppose the therapist traditionally has been seen as undesirable and something

---

[5] In some instances, it would be possible to combine compliance- and defiance-based interventions in a single treatment package. For example, an increasingly common approach taken in the treatment of sexual dysfunction is to prescribe extended sessions of foreplay *and* to prohibit intercourse. Use of this technique assumes that anxiety plays a large part in the creation of sexual difficulties and that initial compliance by the client will allow the client "safe" sexual experiences that do not generate high levels of anxiety. At some point, however, it is expected that the client will "rebel" and actually go ahead and engage in intercourse, without anxiety about his or her sexual performance. In this treatment approach, the timing of the client's switch from compliance to defiance would seem critical, and one might expect that if reactance were aroused too early in the treatment program (either due to the client's characteristics, characteristics of the partner, or features of the therapist's communications), clients might rebel before their sexual anxieties had been sufficiently reduced to allow successful and satisfying intercourse.

to be minimized in therapy. On the other, induced opposition to the therapist's direction has been suggested as a feasible treatment technique for at least some problems. Both points of view were examined in this chapter.

In terms of reactance arousal as an undesirable effect in therapy, a series of analogue studies were reviewed that appear to suggest that deprivation of client choice can hinder effective treatment. Unfortunately, none of these studies was able to distinguish the possible negative effects of deprivation of choice as opposed to the possible positive effects of provision of choice. A more client-specific approach to reactance arousal in therapy has been offered by Beutler. He suggests that reactance is more likely to occur with certain clients than with others, and that for reactance-prone clients less directive therapeutic techniques should be more effective than highly directive ones. A review of the relevant literature indicated some support for this contention. Another approach to predicting differential levels of reactance arousal in therapy involves specification of the freedom that the client views as important and the characteristics of the therapist's communications relevant to this freedom. It was suggested that when an important freedom is threatened by the therapist's communication, both opposition to and derogation of the therapist can occur.

Reactance arousal as the basis for facilitating therapeutic goals was considered in terms of paradoxical therapy. Two types of paradoxical interventions were described. In compliance-based paradoxical interventions, the therapist desires the client to comply with therapeutic directives and engage in the symptomatic behavior. Typically, problems treated with these techniques involve anxiety that is generated by attempts to avoid engaging in the symptom. Thus, compliance-based paradoxical therapy that creates reactance arousal and opposition to the therapist's directives could lead the client to attempt even harder to avoid symptom engagement, experience even more anxiety, and have his or her difficulties increased rather than reduced. Defiance-based paradoxical interventions do not run this risk. These interventions are designed to motivate the client to oppose the therapist's directives (should, instead, the client comply, then the therapist is viewed as having obtained control over the symptom). It was pointed out, however, that defiance-based paradoxical interventions do run the risk of damaging the therapeutic relationship, and that this risk needs to be considered when use of this technique is contemplated.

CHAPTER 14

Social Influence:
Social Problems
and Consumer Behavior

Social influence in modern society is ubiquitous and seemingly inescapable. Although the goals of the influence can vary from altruistic (e.g., providing medical care for the aged) to commercial (e.g., making a larger profit on a certain brand of designer jeans) and the source can vary widely (e.g., governmental agencies, business enterprises), the formal process of one group of people trying to influence another (usually larger) group remains constant. In this chapter we shall consider a variety of ways in which social influence tactics in the real world may arouse reactance, and, thereby, reduce compliance or foster opposition.

SOLVING SOCIAL PROBLEMS

In order to solve many of society's problems, a cooperative effort on the part of many people is required. Because this cooperative effort does not necessarily spring "full blown" into the minds and behavior of the populace, government agencies and various special interest groups often find themselves attempting to elicit certain behaviors in order to obtain what they see as a solution to a given social problem. These attempts to elicit or change a particular behavior (e.g., obey the 55 mile an hour speed limit, stop smoking) sometimes involve persuasion and sometimes involve more or less coercive tactics. While both approaches can arouse reactance, coercive ones are more likely to be perceived as threats to freedoms and are therefore more likely to result in noncompliance or overt opposition.

The potential importance of reactance motives in solving social problems is highlighted in a study by Summers, Ashworth, and Feldman-Summers (1977). These investigators contacted a random telephone sample in Seattle, Washington and obtained agreement from 55% of the people they contacted to participate in a survey of attitudes about proposed solutions to overpopulation. Respondents rated the similarity of pairs of solutions and judged the acceptability of each solution. Multidimensional scaling of the similarity judgments revealed two dimensions that accounted for 64% of the variance: voluntary versus nonvoluntary and economic versus noneconomic. The first dimension contrasted solutions in which coercion was high versus those in which participation in the solution was voluntary. The second dimension contrasted solutions in which an economic incentive or penalty was used to elicit compliance with solutions in which no economic feature was involved. Each participant's judgments of solution acceptability were then regressed on the dimensional coordinates associated with each solution. The median multiple correlation R that was obtained for the original sample was .81. Summers et al. also applied this model to the acceptability judgments of small cross-validation samples of students and nonstudents. For students, the median R was .79, while for nonstudents ("similar in composition to the primary sample"), the median R was .81. All three samples tended to judge as unacceptable the more coercive solutions as well as those solutions that involved economic incentives or penalties.

Although these two dimensions were orthogonal in Summers et al.'s analysis, both can be viewed as related to potential reactance arousal. Coercive solutions pose a threat to freedom, while noncoercive solutions pose either no threat at all or a mild one. Economic incentives and penalties act to increase the magnitude of threat to behavioral freedom; by making it harder to refuse to comply, they can increase the motive to refuse to comply. Summers et al. (1977) make a similar analysis of these two dimensions and comment,

> What is surprising . . . is the finding that such a high proportion of the response variance can be accounted for in terms of perceived threat to freedom—to the exclusion of other characteristics of the solutions. Such an outcome suggests that persons who wish to persuade others about the merits of one solution or another would

be well advised to focus upon the restrictive or nonrestrictive aspects of the solutions in question. Persuasion attempts which focus on other dimensions—e.g., cost, technical feasibility, time required for impact, etc.—might well be seen as irrelevant [p. 172].

A number of other writers have pointed out the potential relationship between attempted solutions to social problems and reactance arousal. Like Summers et al., Cooper (1974) discusses the possibility of reactance arousal to coercive solutions to overpopulation. Samuel (1972) and Berkowitz (1974) have pointed out how reactance may be aroused in obtaining support (i.e., signatures on a petition) for political positions. Parental resistance to innovations in public schools is seen by Bridge (1976) as an instance of reactance arousal. Wandersman (1976) has suggested that efforts to involve more people in the planning of built environments could reduce reactance responses to the restrictions imposed by such environmental structures. Citing the possibility of reactance arousal to more coercive attempts (e.g., starter-interlocks and mandatory seatbelt laws) to get people to wear seatbelts, Elman and Killebrew (1978) propose the use of small incentives to minimize reactance.

Although the relationships between societal problem solutions and reactance arousal suggested by the above authors are intriguing, the empirical evidence for these relationships is scant. There are, however, some other areas of societal problem solutions in which the possible role of reactance has received more compelling empirical documentation. In the remainder of our discussion of this topic, we shall consider each of these areas.

Antipollution Measures

A study by Mazis and his associates (Mazis, Settle, & Leslie, 1973; Mazis, 1975) suggests that banning certain substances from the market may create wide-spread attitudinal opposition and some behavioral opposition as well. Subjects in this study were housewives from either Miami or Tampa who lived in randomly selected middle-income neighborhoods and who fit demographic and detergent-use characteristics imposed by the investigators. Miami consumers had been legally prohibited from purchasing phosphate laundry detergents, whereas Tampa consumers had not. Since all the subjects had had the freedom to purchase phosphates prior to the ban and were included in the sample only if they had, in fact, used a phosphate brand "most often during the preceding six months," the initial freedom to use phosphates was firmly established for all subjects, and reactance should have been aroused for Miami housewives who were now forbidden the use of their regular detergent.

Two types of analyses were conducted with the interview data that were obtained. First, Miami and Tampa housewives were compared on their views of the effectiveness of phosphate detergents and on their attitudes toward governmentally imposed solutions to pollution problems. On three of the seven attributes investigated (e.g., whiteness, stain removal, cleans in cold water), Miami housewives rated phosphate detergents more favorably than Tampa housewives. Miami housewives were also more negative toward legal restrictions on the sale of detergents and on the need for the government to play an important role in reducing water pollution. In the second analysis, the Miami housewives interviewed were classified as either nonswitchers (who could continue to purchase their favorite brand since a nonphosphate detergent of this brand was available), switchers (who were forced to change their brand, since the producers of these brands did not distribute nonphosphate detergents for several months after the ban), and violators (those who either hoarded phosphates before the ban or who smuggled phosphates in from neighboring localities that did not have a ban). Comparing switchers and nonswitchers on their perceptions of phosphate versus nonphosphate detergents, switchers viewed phosphates as much more effective than nonphosphates; nonswitchers saw only a slight edge for phosphates. For five out of the seven attributes surveyed, the favorability difference perceived was significantly greater for switchers than for nonswitchers. Finally, it is interesting to note that 12% of the Miami sample admitted to violating the law by using phosphate detergents.

While these data are consistent with a reactance theory analysis and certainly indicate widespread opposition to the banning law in question, they do not rule out the role of frustration. Miami housewives could no longer purchase their favorite type of detergent, and switchers could no longer purchase even their usual brand. Since it will be difficult in most applied studies to rule out a frustration explanation, it might be noted again (see Chapter 5) that in the one laboratory study in which frustration and reactance were directly compared (Worchel, 1974), the potency of reactance in creating hostility toward the agent who had eliminated a behavioral freedom was greater than either sheer frustration (not getting one's most favored item) or frustrated expectancies (not getting what one had expected to have). While Worchel's study cannot be used to rule out the role of frustration in other settings where both frustration and reactance are theoretically possible explanations, it does suggest that where the two are confounded, reactance arousal is likely to be at least as psychologically significant as frustration.

Fair Employment Practices

Rosen and Mericle (1979) investigated the effects of fair employment regulations on hiring and salary decisions. Subjects in this study were predominantly male municipal administrators who participated in a management simulation. Subjects were given either a strong or weak fair employment practices regulation to follow and read descriptions of either a male or female applicant for a job. Although type of policy and sex of applicant did not affect hiring decisions, there was a significant interaction between policy and sex on salary recommendations (made only by those subjects who recommended hiring the applicant). The means in this interaction were not significantly different, but there was a trend for males to be paid more when the fair practices policy was strong and for females to be paid more when the fair practices policy was weak.

These data are quite interesting. Taken at face value, they suggest that a weak affirmative action position (our city is "an equal employment opportunity employer") is as effective as a strong affirmative action position (our city is "under considerable pressure to carry out its affirmative action goals and to hire more women and minorities"), and that both produce equivalent hiring of men and women (there was no condition without a fair employment practices statement to see if any sex discrimination would have occurred there). On the other hand, sex discrimination does appear to occur, when it comes to salary decisions, and this discrimination appears to go both ways: Women get the edge in salary when hired under a weak fair employment policy and men when hired under a strong fair employment policy.

One can, however, look at these data in another way. The subjects in this experiment were real administrators, but they were making only simulated decisions. It would be expected that they would try to present themselves in a favorable light to the experimenters who were obviously interested in the effects of affirmative action policies. All the demand characteristics run, then, toward being fair and even-handed. This analysis suggests that we should not take the results indicating equal effectiveness on hiring too seriously, and that the evidence for sex discrimination on salary decisions may be only a minimal expression of a much stronger effect in real life. It would be enlightening to obtain data on these questions under conditions where demand characteristics were less obtrusive. This is purely a speculative comment on our part, but we would not be surprised if, under these conditions, the strong fair employment policy was more effective than the weak one in obtaining nondiscriminatory hiring, but salary decisions continued to reveal discrimination against women who were hired under the strong fair employment policy. If obtained, such data would suggest that the coercive policy is sufficiently strong to effect behavioral compliance (presumably through making noncompliance too costly), but that the reactance aroused by such coercion would lead to freedom restoration on related decisions. Such a dilemma—between obtaining direct behavioral compliance, but risking indirect opposition—may not be at all unusual in the field of social policy.

Sex and Violence on TV

It has become fairly commonplace to use advisories to indicate to TV viewers which programs will contain especially violent or sexual material. A study by Herman and Leyens (1977) examined the effects of these advisories. Data were collected from a permanent panel for French-speaking Belgian Television. This panel is composed of 400 individuals, selected to be representative of French-speaking Belgium. The panel works for one week every sixth week, and 20% of the sample is changed after a week's work. Panel members note which program they are watching (at quarter-hour intervals) and evaluate each program they watch. Advisories are given for violence, sex, and "climate" of movie (e.g., depressing, tense), and there are three different levels of advisories: announcer warning, announcer warning plus the word "qualification" (*réserves*), and "white square" in which a small white square is displayed in a corner of the screen for the entire broadcast.

Herman and Leyens restricted their examination to sex and violence advisories on Thursday-evening movies for a 4-year span (1972–1975). For the first three years (although not for 1975), it was found that movies with advisories had a larger audience than movies without advisories, and these differences were obtained for both sex and violence. Level of advisory had no effect. Analysis of evaluative ratings indicated that there was no tendency for movies with advisories to be rated more favorably than movies without.

There are obvious problems with these data: one would like a comparison between the advisory movies and the nonadvisory movies when the advisory system was not in effect; the lack of effect of advisory level (especially the obtrusive little white square) is puzzling; evaluative ratings are confounded by coming from those who chose to watch that program rather than another; and, of course, people may simply be more interested in viewing programs containing sex and violence. These are, however, just the sorts of problems that one encounters in applied research. Stacked against these methodological problems is a large and representative sample of people performing a real behavior in the real world. It does seem clear that advisory programs are more watched than nonadvisory programs, and it is possible that reactance arousal is a viable explanation for this effect.

Littering

Several studies have suggested that littering behavior may be affected by reactance arousal. Jorgenson (1978) found that his experimental group (told to "please throw this away") littered more than his control group (who were not told anything about what to do with the political literature they had received). Reich and Robertson (1979) report three studies in which littering was complexly affected by message content and, apparently, socioeconomic class of the subjects. In general, however, Reich and Robertson found that stronger demands (such as "don't litter" and "don't you dare litter") produced more littering than polite requests ("help keep your pool clean"; "keeping the pool clean depends on you") or irrelevant messages on driving and pool safety.

Geller and his associates have been especially interested in possible reactance effects produced by antilittering messages. Geller (1973) found that a specific antilittering prompt that specified the trashcan to be used was less effective than a general prompt requesting people not to litter. Geller, Witner, and Orebaugh (1976) found that a message demanding ("you must not . . .") that people not litter was equally effective as a polite request not to litter. Brasted, Mann, and Geller (1979) have suggested that this failure of the demanding message to secure more compliance than the polite request reflects the reactance aroused by the demand. Stronger evidence for the role of reactance arousal would, of course, have been obtained if the demand had produced less compliance than the polite request.

Brasted et al. (1979) also cite an unpublished study by Mann, Brasted, and Geller (1979) in which compliance was complexly affected by type of message, obtrusiveness of trash cans, and difficulty in complying with the antilitter message.

For those individuals who received the handbill at the two entrances located a considerable distance from the can specified for disposal ($n = 1440$), significantly fewer individuals ($p < .01$) disposed of the handbill in the specified can with the demand prompt ("You must . . . ") than with the specific prompt ("Please dispose . . . ") *if* the obtrusive trash receptacle was available as an alternative [Brasted *et al.*, 1979, p. 80].

This finding suggests that a stronger worded antilitering message will produce reactance arousal and direct restoration of freedom when (*a*) compliance is difficult and (*b*) a direct way to restore freedom is easily available.

When the attractive trash can was at the specified disposal point, those individuals who received the demand-prompt handbill directly in the vicinity of this can ($n = 1200$) obeyed the behavioral request significantly *less* often than did those who received the handbill conveying the specific prompt ($p < .01$) [Brasted *et al.*, 1979, p. 80].

This finding suggests that a stronger worded antilitttering message will produce reactance arousal and direct restoration of freedom when there are two sources of threat to freedom: (*a*) the demanding message and (*b*) an obtrusive, attractive receptacle which, in effect, demands to be used. When there was only the threat to freedom from the message (and the designated can was ordinary and unobtrusive), the demand message did not produce less compliance than the specific (and undemanding) prompt.

There is, thus, a fair amount of evidence that antilittering messages may produce reactance arousal and oppositional behavior. There is also the suggestion from the Reich and Robertson study as well as the Mann *et al.* experiment that these reactance effects may be affected by a variety of characteristics of either the target individuals or the environmental situation. Although complexities such as these obscure a parsimonious theoretical interpretation, they probably are also inevitable in the real world and in applied research.

CONSUMER BEHAVIOR

Clee and Wicklund (1980) provide an extensive and detailed review of the possible effects of reactance on consumer behavior. There is no need for us to duplicate that review here. Instead, we shall examine some selected studies (some cited by Clee and Wicklund, some not) that investigate a variety of ways in which the arousal of psychological reactance might affect consumer behavior.

Reactance-Producing Properties of the "Hard Sell"

All other things being equal, it would be expected that a strong threat to an established freedom would create more reactance than a mild threat to freedom. Since "hard sell" messages to consumers can be viewed as threats of greater magnitude than "soft sell" messages, reactance arousal should be greater in the former case than in the latter. Several studies suggest that hard sell messages are at a disadvantage in producing compliance.

One set of relevant studies has already been described. It will be remembered that the supermarket study by Regan and Brehm (1972; also reported in Brehm, 1966) found that the most effective market promotional technique was to provide the price of the item being advertised with a low pressure verbal message to buy the product. Increasing the amount of money provided and/or increasing the coerciveness of the verbal message reduced purchases of the desired item. This pattern of results, however, was obtained only for female shoppers.

Two replications of the supermarket study have been conducted. Gilbert and Peterson (1971) found that the combination of high verbal pressure and the provision of more money than was needed to buy the bread produced the lowest number of purchases, and there was no effect of sex of shopper. Sex of shopper did, however, affect the results of a second replication by McGillis and Brehm (1975). In their study, purchase price of the bread was provided in all experimental conditions, and only the coerciveness of the verbal promotional message was varied. Although (as in the Regan and Brehm study) all experimental conditions produced increased buying of the designated item relative to baseline, high pressure verbal messages produced fewer purchases among female shoppers than low pressure verbal messages. The McGillis and Brehm experiment also included a restoration condition in which shoppers saw a supposed other shopper (actually an experimental confederate) restore her own freedom not to purchase the brand being promoted. Restoration produced very high levels of purchases of the designated item for both male and female shoppers, regardless of the type of verbal promotional message they had received.

These studies provide rather good evidence of the drawbacks of hard sell messages. There is no evidence that such messages reduce purchases below baseline levels, but there are now three studies indicating that, for female shoppers at least, the hard sell at the supermarket is less effective than the soft sell. (See Chapters 2 and 5 for further discussion of these studies).

In a role-play study where undergraduates pretended to be choosing among different patterns of lead crystal, Reizenstine (1971) exposed subjects to persuasive messages designed to get them to change their preferences between their first- and second-ranked alternatives. When a hard sell message was used, only 13% reversed their preferences, but 73% reversed their preferences in response to a soft sell message. These findings can be compared to the 33% level of reversals obtained for a control group that was not exposed to any persuasive message, and to the virtual absence of change that was obtained for subjects urged to change their preference between their first- and *sixth*-ranked alternatives. These data suggest that a mildly worded persuasive statement can elicit considerable compliance when two alternatives similar in attractiveness are being considered; a hard sell, however, produces little compliance, as does any type of message aimed at changing preferences for items disparate in attractiveness. The finding that the hard sell message (in the conditions where the target preferences were those items ranked first and second) tended to produce less compliance than no message at all is suggestive of a relatively strong reactance effect.

One aspect of hard sell messages is that they disclose the persuasive intent of the person delivering the message. Robertson and Rossiter (1974) found that perceptions of persuasive intent correlated with less favorability toward consumer items. Subjects in this study were 289 male elementary school children who were interviewed about their attitudes toward TV commercials. It was found that perceptions of the commercials' intent to persuade increased with age and that children who perceived persuasive intent were likely to believe the commercial messages less, to like commercials less, and to report less desire for the advertised products.

A study by Seipel (1971) with Swedish housewives suggests that offering gifts to consumers can, under some conditions, be considered a hard sell. Subjects in the study were sent a gift offer (an item worth about $2.50) from a Swedish food producer. Subjects in the low reciprocation condition were merely asked to mail a request in order to receive the item; subjects in the medium reciprocation condition were asked to include $.50; and subjects in the high reciprocation condition were asked to include $1.00 and to answer a questionnaire. In order to receive the gift, subjects had to respond within a fourteen day period; after this period, subjects were contacted by phone and interviewed about a variety of attitudes and behaviors relevant to the gift offer.

Seipel reports a number of measures taken as part of this study. Three of these are most relevant to our present discussion. First, attractiveness of the gift offer (as measured by actual requests for the gift and by reported attractiveness) did not increase as a function of reciprocation required. Gifts requiring low or medium reciprocation were clearly *more* attractive than gifts requiring high reciprocation, but within the low and medium conditions, there was a consistent trend for the gift in the low reciprocation condition to be perceived as *less* attractive than the one in the medium condition. Second, reported purchases of the company's products were greater in the low reciprocation than in either of the other two reciprocation conditions or in the no gift control group. Third, attitudes toward the company's brand tended to be only slightly more positive in the low reciprocation condition than in the other two experimental conditions. This study suggests that offering free gifts may have the effect most desired by the company offering the gift (i.e., increasing purchases of their products), but that general attitudes are not as positively affected as one might expect and that specific attitudes toward the gift are considerably less positive than would be expected. These latter effects possibly reflect reactance aroused by the hard sell offer of a free gift.

Purchaser Visibility

One usually thinks of anonymity as facilitating the expression of reactance arousal (e.g., Heilman, 1976). Anonymous behavior avoids any potential costs for noncompliance, and thus any reactance aroused should be freely expressed. It is possible, however, that anonymity also can act to reduce threat to freedom. If one knows that one will make a decision or perform a behavior privately, the inability of any observer to punish noncompliance may reduce the perceived threat to freedom. Conversely, public behavior makes potential punishment for noncompliance possible; this potential may constitute an additional pressure on the person to conform and, thereby, increase the magnitude of reactance that is aroused (see Chapter 7 for discussion of the effects of social power and surveillance).

Such an analysis may account for the findings reported by Burnkrant and Cousineau (1975). These investigators presented college undergraduates with supposed information about other people's opinions about a supposed new brand of instant coffee. Some subjects were instructed to indicate their evaluation of the coffee by placing a tag with their name on it on a favorability display (visible condition); other subjects were instructed to indicate their evaluation by placing a blank tag on this display (anonymous condition). Control subjects evaluated the coffee with a blank tag and without being exposed to information about other people's ratings.

Burnkrant and Cousineau found a significant effect for visibility.

Although subjects in both experimental conditions rated the coffee more favorably than subjects in the control group, subjects in the visible condition rated the coffee less positively than those in the anonymous group. In their discussion Burnkrant and Cousineau (1975) interpret these findings in a manner similar to our previous comments:

> If the subjects in the visible condition perceived the requirement that their product evaluations be visible and identifiable by others who follow them as constraining their freedom to act in the situation, psychological reactance may have been aroused. This psychological reactance could have moderated the positive effect of the influence [p. 213].

Contracts: Freedom-Reduction and Reactance

In a study of the relationship between government agencies (i.e., the Defense Department and NASA) and their principle contractors, Hunt and Hunt (1971) propose an intriguing possibility of relationship-generated reactance arousal. We think their account speaks best for itself and will provide it without further comment.

> Paradox arises because as the parties seek to stabilize the reliability of a valued exchange relation, their attachment and commitment to it and its preservation tends to deepen and, with that, dependency and an attenuation of "usable" power. . . . In its turn, this will tend to instigate search for and attraction to alternatives, probably, all things equal, in direct proportion to the achieved reliability of the initial relation. . . . Thus, assuming commitment and attenuation of power, the more stabilized, reliable, or crystallized an exchange relation . . . , the stronger will be the motivation to seek alternatives to it [Hunt & Hunt, 1971, p. 430].

A Potpourri of Other Consumer Effects

Using a very broad definition of consumerism—when an individual seeks to obtain a certain item or behavioral interaction for himself or herself—we would like to briefly indicate some other consumer behaviors that might be affected by reactance. It is important to note that all of the applied studies below that obtained possible reactance effects are amenable to alternative explanations involving psychological processes other than reactance. We mention these studies as instances of hypotheses about reactance effects in the real world, not as conclusive evidence for reactance arousal in the situations of interest.

Studies by Spitz, Gold, and Adams (1975) and by Bracken and Kasl (1975) mention the possibility of reactance responses in the general area of human sexuality. Spitz et al. found that their sample of 24 sexually active female undergraduates (approximately half using birth-control pills and the other half not) reported the lowest frequency of intercourse during menstruation and the highest in the postmenstrual period. This effect of greater sexual activity after a period of restricted sexual activity was found for both mutually-initiated and male-initiated sexual intercourse. (An interesting sidelight to these data is found in the authors' comment that, "The number of female-initiated intercourse experiences was too small to detect any meaningful changes in levels throughout the cycle [Spitz et al., 1975, p. 256]".)

In their paper discussing reasons why women may delay seeking abortions, Bracken and Kasl (1975) point to the possibility of prechoice convergence (see Chapter 8) as a woman considers whether to have a baby or to seek abortion. Such convergence would make any decision harder to make and thus increase the time needed to make a decision. Bracken and Kasl also note that such a process may mean that as the possibility to obtain an abortion decreases (due to increased gestational size or increased opposition from important people in the woman's life), the motivation to obtain an abortion may increase.

Ventimiglia (1977) raises the possibility that reactance arousal may affect one's career commitment. He reports that the "drop-out" priests among his sample of seminary students reported more vocational encouragement from their mothers than did their classmates who remained in seminary.

Another possible area for reactance to affect career commitment would seem to be the mid-life crisis so beloved by the popular press these days. As one grows older, one may perceive the impending loss of some behavioral freedoms. In terms of one's career, what once seemed a free choice may increasingly be perceived as the only choice, and, thus, as no choice at all. Alternative careers that once seemed possible choices may be seen as quickly dropping out of the realm of possibility. Under these circumstances, those other career possibilities may increase in attractiveness, while the career one is pursuing may decrease in attractiveness. Countering this process, one would expect dissonance reduction to operate such that one makes the best of the career alternative one chose. At the moment, the empirical evidence appears on the side of dissonance. Kopelman (1977) reported a 4-year longitudinal study of 182 engineers, with 74% of his sample ranging from 30 to 49 years of age. He found that career expectations and career values tended to correlate positively over time, with subjects in his study tending to value less those career outcomes they perceived themselves as unlikely to obtain. This rather sanguine picture of responses to one's career certainly conflicts with that painted for us by the popular press, and it will be interesting to see if Kopelman's findings are replicated by other investigations.

Scarcity

Supply and demand are basic facts of economic life, and, as such, can be expected to impact on consumer behavior. In his commodity theory, Brock (1968) hypothesizes that "any commodity will be valued to the extent that it is unavailable [p. 246]." A study by Worchel, Lee, and Adewole (1975) examined the possible effects of commodity scarcity on perceived value. Three consumer items were displayed to female undergraduate subjects, and subjects were told that the first item to be rated would be some cookies contained in a glass jar on the table. For half of the subjects, there were 2 cookies in the jar; for the other half, there were 10. At this point a second experimenter entered the room and either left the cookies in the jar as they were or substituted a new jar. For some subjects, the jar that was substituted increased the number of cookies (from 2 to 10); for others, the new jar decreased the number of cookies (from 10 to 2). Subjects in the latter condition were told either that the second experimenter needed more cookies because his subjects had eaten more of them than he expected or that the first experimenter had accidentally taken the second experimenter's cookies. Subjects who received a substitute jar containing more cookies than they had at first also received either a social demand (subjects had eaten less than expected) or accidental explanation for the exchange. In addition to these manipulations, half of the subjects were told that only a small number of subjects would be run in the study, while the other half were told that a large number of subjects still remained to be run. Subjects were then asked to taste a cookie and complete various ratings.

This study is quite complex and it may be helpful to summarize the design. When subjects rated the cookies, cookies were either scarce or abundant. Some cookies had always been this way, others became scarce or abundant due to social demand, some became scarce or abundant due to an accident. Subjects either expected low participation by other subjects or high participation. Worchel, Lee, and Adewole (1975) asked subjects to rate how much they would like to eat more of the cookies (liking), how attractive they thought the cookies, and how much they thought the cookies should cost. The data from these measures are displayed in Table 14.1.

The general pattern of results can be summarized as follows. Scarce cookies were liked more than abundant ones. Within scarcity, relative deprivation (i.e., change from an abundant state) led to greater liking and valuing of the cookies than constant scarcity. Within scarcity, a social demand cause for the scarcity led to greater liking and valuing of the cookies than an accidentally caused scarcity. Within abundance,

TABLE 14.1
Means for Liking, Attraction and Estimated Cost (per Pound)[a]

	Reason for change in supply		
	Demand	Accident	No change
Scarcity			
High participation			
Liking	2.25[b]	3.27	4.08
Attraction	2.33[b]	3.00	4.00
Cost	71.5	60.9	45.8
Low participation			
Liking	3.00	3.75	4.40
Attraction	3.18	3.75	4.40
Cost	60.3	52.4	56.2
Abundance			
High participation			
Liking	7.17	6.30	5.64
Attraction	6.58	6.40	5.64
Cost	37.5	45.9	46.2
Low participation			
Liking	6.82	6.64	5.46
Attraction	6.64	6.27	5.73
Cost	37.5	46.4	45.8

[a] From Worchel, S., Lee, J., & Adewole, A. Effects of supply and demand on ratings of object value. *Journal of Personality and Social Psychology*, 1975, *32*, 906–914, Table 1, p. 909. Copyright 1975 by the American Psychological Association. Reprinted by permission.

[b] The lower the number, the more favorable the evaluation.

cookies made abundant were liked less than cookies that were always abundant. The effect of participation was expected to occur in the no-change scarcity condition. Contrary to prediction, there was no difference as a function of participation on the liking and attraction measures, and low participation subjects valued the cookie more in terms of cost than high participation subjects.

By and large, these results provide strong support for Brock's commodity theory. Scarcity increased value, and, in particular, scarcity due to social demand increased value. The notions that relative scarcity would increase demand and relative abundance would decrease demand, though not derived from commodity theory, were also supported. Although Worchel, Lee, and Adewole (1975) intended their manipulation of participation to vary subjects' perceptions of the level of social demand, this manipulation was quite weak. It was apparently never stated whether other subjects would be asked to taste cookies rather than the other two products and, besides, whatever other subjects did, it would happen after the subject finished. Given the ambiguity and weakness of this manipulation, its lack of predictable effects is not surprising.

Worchel, Lee, and Adewole state that commodity theory "does not speculate about exactly how scarcity enhances value [p. 911]" and suggest that reactance theory may serve as a theoretical explanation of the processes involved. If we review their results in terms of reactance theory, some findings seem consistent with the theory, whereas others would seem to be outside the purview of the theory. Reactance theory could not make the general prediction that scarce objects would be valued more than abundant ones. This effect would only be expected by the theory if the person's freedom to have an object was firmly established. Thus the comparison of major interest for reactance theory would be between scarcity that existed continuously and scarcity that was introduced after a period of abundance. This difference was significant. It should be noted, however, that reactance theory could not easily predict the difference between the scarcity-no change condition and the abundant-no change condition. In order to predict this, one would have to assume that subjects entered the laboratory with the established freedom to have more than two cookies, and that this freedom applied to the laboratory situation as well as to their previous experience.

The difference between the effects of scarcity due to social demand and scarcity due to accidental event is also difficult for reactance theory to predict. One would have to suppose that the social demand explanation carried more threats for future freedoms than the accidental explanation. Given that subjects apparently expected only to taste cookies, it is not clear what future freedoms would have been threatened by the second experimenter's action taken to provide for his subjects—unless, subjects thought he might come back and take the two remaining cookies away from them! Finally, it should be noted that reactance theory would not attempt to make predictions about abundance per se. The nearest thing to abundance that has ever been studied within a reactance theory framework is the Brehm and Rozen (1971) study where newly created abundance threatened old freedoms. Since all the cookies were the same in the study by Worchel, Lee, and Adewole (1975), one cannot talk about the newly added eight cookies as constituting different freedoms from the original two.

These comments indicate, then, that although there is some overlap between commodity theory and reactance theory, this overlap is not complete. Both can address scarcity, but they do so with different prerequisites in mind and formulate a somewhat different set of predictions. The data obtained by Worchel, Lee, and Adewole (1975) basically support both theoretical perspectives and suggest, then, that both may be of value in understanding consumer reactions to situations of scarcity.

SUMMARY

The application of reactance theory to the solving of social problems yields some understanding of why attempted solutions frequently fall short of their mark. Proposed solutions frequently threaten freedoms and thereby create resistance to their acceptance. A survey of people's feelings about proposed solutions to overpopulation, a study of housewives' reactions to the banning of phosphate detergents, a simulation study of how administrators respond to affirmative action programs, a survey of audience reactions to warnings about the sexual or aggressive nature of TV programming, and several field experiments on methods to cope with littering all illustrate the possible role of reactance and consequent resistance to problem solutions.

Research on consumer behavior reveals another arena in which reactance may play a large role. For example, in a number of studies, the hard sell has been found to reduce the effectiveness of sales compaigns relative to a soft sell. Other possible reactance effects have been noted in regard to long-term purchasing contracts, women's decisions concerning having an abortion, and career commitment, although evidence in each of these specific areas is minimal. Finally, scarcity of a product has been found to increase its attractiveness, and both reactance theory and commodity theory appear useful in understanding people's responses to conditions of scarcity.

CHAPTER 15

Applications to Formal and Informal Power Relations

Social power relationships provide a setting to which reactance theory is readily applied. The establishment of power relationships through formal agreement or by custom and experience defines what freedoms individuals have in that relationship. Accidental or intentional overstepping of established power can easily constitute a threat to the freedom of other individuals involved in the power relationship, with consequent reactance arousal.

Although this application of reactance theory appears reasonable and straightforward, actual real world settings are frequently difficult to analyze. Exactly what freedoms people believe themselves to have and exactly what power-relevant behaviors will be seen as threats to those freedoms are not always so clear. In part, then, the task of applied research is to come to a clearer understanding of the freedoms that people hold in different circumstances and of what they perceive to be threats to those freedoms. This aspect of the application of reactance theory to real life problems is evident in the following report of research on superior–subordinate relationships, judge–jury relationships, and interpersonal space and crowding.

Superior-Subordinate Relationships

The possibility that reactance might occur in superior–subordinate relationships has been noted by a number of authors. Rosen and Jerdee (1975) suggest that "overzealousness" on the part of employees might create managerial reactance. Tjosvold (1978) hypothesizes that "control-minded" school administrators may provoke reactance in teachers. Taylor (1979) points out that "bad patients" may be reacting to the loss of many behavioral freedoms that is entailed by traditional hospital procedures. These authors suggest, then, that reactance can be created "up the line" of command or down.

Unfortunately, there are few applied studies that have obtained empirical evidence in support of this proposition. For example, Rosen and Jerdee posit the possibility of reactance arousal, but their simulation study (with bank employees serving as subjects) found that aggressive appeals from hypothetical employees were well received. The study by Organ (1974) that was described previously (Chapter 7) did find evidence of reactance arousal when subordinate-subjects expected to have their agreement with the "supervisor's" recommendations inspected by the supervisor and when this supervisor made flattering remarks about the subject. This study was also a simulation, however, involving undergraduate business majors role-playing a managerial situation. The study by Piliavin and Gross (1977), also described previously (Chapter 7), on AFDC recipients' responses to different types of social services did involve "real people" in real life situations. No evidence of reactance was found in that study, but, then, as we pointed out, there was little reason to think that significant levels of reactance would be aroused.

A correlational study by Mowday (1978) provides suggestive evidence about the role that reactance may play in superior–subordinate relationships. In this study, 65 elementary school principals rated, among a variety of measures, the method they would be most likely to use to influence others and were rated on effectiveness by their immediate supervisor. It was found that those principals who endorsed the use of "manipulation" were most likely to be rated as effective by their supervisors. Manipulation was defined to the principals as a way of "providing information to the individual in such a way that they [sic] are *not* aware you are trying to influence them [Mowday, 1978, p. 146]." Other possible forms of influence that could be endorsed were threats (e.g., going to the school board), appeals to authority (e.g., to school board policies), persuasive arguments, and using rewards or exchanging favors. In his discussion, Mowday suggests that those principals who used manipulation had opted for a covert use of power rather than an overt use, and that this method of influence was more successful because it ran less risk of arousing reactance. Although these results are quite interesting and do involve real-world relationships, the fact that the influence ratings were self-reported and not verified by other sources suggests caution in interpreting these data.

Judge and Jury

Another source of empirical evidence on reactance and power relationships is found in a series of studies examining the effects on juries of judicial rulings that certain evidence is inadmissible. In his review of jury research, Wrightsman (1978) poses the question of whether a judge's instruction to disregard specific evidence may serve to produce reactance or whether it may simply increase the jury's attention to the information ruled inadmissible. The way in which this interpretive ambiguity arose can be seen when the three major studies relevant to this issue are examined.

The earliest empirical evidence on jurors' responses to rulings of inadmissibility was reported by Broeder (1959). Working with experimental juries composed of persons on jury duty, Broeder presented the critical piece of information in two ways. In one condition, it was disclosed that the defendant in the case possessed insurance; in another, this disclosure was followed by the judge's instruction that it be disregarded. A third condition was included in which no information about insurance was presented. The average award in the no information condition was $33,000. In the information condition, this increased slightly to $37,000; in the information-inadmissibility condition, the average award was $46,000. Broeder attributed the rather dramatic effect obtained by ruling the insurance information inadmissible to sensitization of the jurors to the information presented.

Using Broeder's basic experimental paradigm, Sue, Smith, and Caldwell (1973) changed the content of the trial and varied the evidence presented against the defendant. In this study, college undergraduates were asked to imagine themselves members of an actual jury, and read a summary of a supposed murder trial. For half the subjects, the summary provided strong evidence of the defendant's guilt; for the other half, weak evidence of guilt was provided. Cross-cutting this manipulation, subjects either received no further information, were given additional information consistent with the defendant's guilt that was admitted by the judge, or were given additional information and then told the judge had ruled it inadmissible. Two significant main effects were obtained. Subjects who received weak evidence were less likely than subjects who received strong evidence to find the defendant guilty (see Table 15.1). Receiving additional information (whether admissible or not) also led to more guilty verdicts than not receiving additional information. There was a slight, but nonsignificant trend, for more subjects in the weak evidence condition who received inadmissible information to find the defendant guilty than subjects in the admissible evidence condition. In the strong evidence condition, this trend was reversed. Thus, while Sue *et al.* replicated Broeder's findings that inadmissible evidence is not disregarded, they found only a slight and restricted trend for this type of evidence to have more impact than the same evidence ruled admissible.

Wolf and Montgomery (1977) point out that there is a difference between a straightforward ruling of inadmissibility (e.g., "this evidence is inadmissible") and a combination of inadmissibility with admonishment from the judge ("this evidence is inadmissible and you, the jury, must disregard it"). The latter type of wording was used by Sue *et al.,* but it is not clear from Broeder's article what type of wording was used. To investigate this issue, Wolf and Montgomery presented undergraduate students, serving as mock jurors, with a summary of a supposed criminal case (i.e., a stabbing during a barroom brawl). Subjects in the six experimental conditions received additional information that was in favor of either the prosecution or the defense. For some subjects, this information was ruled admissible; for others, it was ruled inadmissible; and for a third experimental condition, it was ruled inadmissible and the judge admonished the jury, "You have no choice but

TABLE 15.1
Percentage of Guilty Verdicts[a]

Initial evidence	Additional evidence			
	Inadmissible (%)	Admissible (%)	Control (%)	Total (%)
Strong	53	68	47	57
Weak	35	26	0	21
Total	44	47	24	

[a] From Sue, S., Smith, R., & Caldwell, C. Effects of inadmissible evidence on the decisions of simulated jurors: A moral dilemma. *Journal of Applied Social Psychology,* 1973, *3,* 345–353, Table 1, p. 350. Copyright 1973 by V. H. Winston & Sons. Reprinted by permission.

to disregard it." A control group read the summary without the additional information. Subjects were asked to rate the defendant's guilt or innocence on a 31-point scale.

Subjects' mean ratings of guilt are provided in Table 15.2. As can be seen, the core case material was essentially neutral, with control subjects showing only a slight tendency to rate the defendant as guilty. An overall ANOVA of the experimental conditions revealed a significant interaction between direction of critical evidence and judge's ruling. The individual comparisons reported by Wolf and Montgomery indicated that prosecution-consistent evidence created higher judgments of guilt than defense-consistent evidence in both the admissible and inadmissible with admonishments conditions; direction of the evidence did not create a significant difference in the inadmissible condition. Wolf and Montgomery argue that their findings effectively rule out the sensitization hypothesis. The inadmissibility statement per se should have drawn subjects' attention to the evidence, but this statement did not lead to differential ratings of guilt. They suggest, instead, that the kind of inadmissibility ruling that is coupled with an admonishment creates a significant threat to the jurors' freedom to consider that evidence. This threat should arouse reactance, and freedom can be restored by considering that evidence in some detail, indeed by acting counter to the judge's instruction to let it have no effect on the outcome of the case. Rulings of inadmissibility with admonishment could be viewed, then, as a kind of belated attempt to censor information, and the reactance created by such judicial procedures would be analogous to the reactance created by censorship (see previous discussion, Chapter 6).

Examination of these studies suggests that the present evidence on

TABLE 15.2
Mean Ratings of Guilt[a]

Direction of critical evidence	Judge's ruling		
	Admissible	Inadmissible	Inadmissible with admonishment
Prosecution consistent	6.25	1.25	4.00
Defense consistent	−8.46	−2.04	−3.17
Control = 1.38			

[a] From Wolf, S. & Montgomery, D. A. Effects of inadmissible evidence and level of judicial admonishment to disregard on the judgments of mock jurors. *Journal of Applied Social Psychology*, 1977, 7, 205–219, Table 1, p. 213. Copyright 1977 by V. H. Winston & Sons. Reprinted by permission.

[b] The higher the number, the greater the guilt.

the effects of inadmissibility rulings is rather much of a hodgepodge, with definite inconsistencies among the results of these studies. Broeder found, relative to a no information control, little effect of admissible evidence and a large effect of inadmissible evidence. Sue *et al.* found that both admissible and inadmissible evidence were persuasive, but only slight evidence (under only one level of strength of initial evidence) that inadmissible evidence could have a greater impact than admissible evidence. Wolf and Montgomery do not report individual comparisons among their admissibility conditions. Inspection of their data indicates, however, that compared to their no additional information control, admissible evidence had a large impact, inadmissible with admonishment had some impact, and inadmissible had virtually no impact. Broeder's study is thus the only one that provides clear evidence of a boomerang effect—in which the impact of inadmissible evidence is more than that same evidence when admitted—and, as Wolf and Montgomery note, we cannot be sure what kind of inadmissibility statement he used.

It is important to realize, however, that Broeder's study was the only one of these three that made much of an attempt to simulate actual courtroom procedures. The studies by Sue *et al.* and Wolf and Montgomery used responses from individual subjects who role-played being jurors. These subjects read case summaries in which the admissibility statements were made, not to them, but to the original jury in the supposed trial. While studies by Worchel and his colleagues suggest that reactance can be aroused by observing another person's freedom being threatened (Andreoli, Worchel, & Folger, 1974) and can be accurately attributed to an observed other (Worchel, Insko, Andreoli, & Drachman, 1974), having reactance aroused firsthand would surely constitute a better test of the hypothesis. This does not mean that an actual jury must be studied. (Besides being almost impossible to get permission to do so, there are many inherent methodological problems to such an approach.) It does suggest that future experimental tests of the effects of inadmissibility rulings might be well advised to create conditions more similar to those of an actual trial, and to ensure that the judge's ruling of inadmissibility is directed at the actual subjects in the experiment.

Crowding and Personal Space

A number of writers have suggested a relationship between behavioral freedom and perceived crowding.[1]

[1] The effects of high density have also been studied in relationship to helpless behavior (see, for example, Sherrod, 1974; Rodin, 1976; and Baum *et al.*, 1978). The

Crowding occurs when the number of people an individual is in contact with is sufficient to prevent him from carrying out some specific behavior and thereby restricts his freedom of choice [Proshansky, Ittelson, & Rivlin, 1970, p. 182; see also revised edition, Proshansky et al., 1976.]

A person's realization that he is unable to supplement his supply of space evokes an awareness that his range of behavioral freedom is restricted [Stokols, 1972, p. 86].

The less [space] one has, the more one wants—a spatial analogue, in fact, to reactance theory [Edney, 1975, p. 1114].

Although all of these writers make reference to reactance as a possible explanatory framework for the effects of crowding, they all fail to emphasize an essential component of the theory. As has been stated repeatedly throughout this book, reactance does not assume that behavior restriction per se will arouse reactance and lead to attempts to restore freedom. Only when the person has established a behavioral freedom and that specific behavioral freedom is threatened or eliminated should reactance be aroused and direct attempts at freedom restoration occur. Manderscheid (1975) makes what appears to be an implicit reference to this theoretical assumption when he discusses the discrepancy between actual density and normatively specified density that must occur in order for an environment to be perceived as crowded. We would put the point more broadly.

We would propose that the motivation to restore one's personal space and/or reduce the number of people in a specified environmental unit will be aroused when an established behavioral freedom is perceived to be threatened by intrusions into one's personal space and/or a change in the number of people present in the environmental unit. It is also possible that a certain area of personal space becomes established as a behavioral freedom in and of itself. If so, intrusions into one's personal space should in and of themselves threaten a freedom (regardless of effects on other free behaviors), and the motive to restore that space should be aroused. Under conditions of strong reactance arousal, this motive could result in a desire for an area of personal space that is larger than the preintrusion area. One could also suppose that the number of people expected to be present in an environmental unit could itself become a behavioral freedom, although this expectation would surely have to vary widely, depending on the unit and the occasion. If so, the same analysis that was applied to an established

---

literature on this topic will not be reviewed here, but the latter two studies were, respectively, discussed in Chapter 11 and mentioned briefly in Chapter 4.

freedom of personal space could be applied to an established freedom of density.

Given the lack of attention that most writers on crowding have paid to the need for a freedom to be established in order for reactance to be aroused, it is not surprising that there is very little empirical evidence documenting a relationship between responses to crowding (or personal space violations) and reactance. We will, however, examine two studies that purport to provide evidence on this point.

Edney, Walker, and Jordan (1976) report both a field and a laboratory study where the relationship between personal space and feelings of control was examined. In the field study, people on a beach were observed and interviewed. Dividing subjects into those whose average distance to neighbors was more or less than 7 feet, Edney et al. found that for those with neighbors 7 feet away or closer, individuals who reported feeling little "control over the situation" they were in designated a larger area surrounding them "to be their own" than individuals who reported feeling greater control (see Table 15.3). This relationship did not hold for people with neighbors more than 7 feet away.

In the laboratory study, pairs of subjects were told to stand facing each other at distances of 3, 7, 15 and 30 feet. A relationship similar to the one found in the field study was obtained. When subjects were standing 7 feet and 3 feet away, those who reported feeling that the other person had higher than average control *over them* indicated a personal space boundary that was greater in area than that indicated

TABLE 15.3
Mean Personal Space Radii (in Inches)[a]

	Interpersonal distance	
	Under 7 feet	Over 7 feet
Study I: Beach		
Felt control (median split)		
Low	93.00	108.33
High	67.89	101.04
Study II: Laboratory		
Control by other subject		
High	48.17	39.34
Low	27.40	48.17

[a] From Edney, J. J., Walker, C. A., & Jordan, N. L. Is there reactance in personal space? *Journal of Social Psychology*, 1976, *100*, 207–217, Table 1, p. 212. Copyright 1976 by The Journal Press. Reprinted by permission.

by those who felt the other subject had lower than average control over them. Again, for interpersonal distances above 7 feet, no differences in personal space as a function of perceived control were obtained.

Both of these studies suffer from a number of methodological problems. In the field study, all data are, of course, correlational, and causal relationships can only be hypothesized. In the lab study, one variable (interpersonal distance) was manipulated, but both the measures of control and personal space were elicited from the subjects. Furthermore, subjects were asked how much control they had over the other subject as well as how much control the other subject had over them, and Edney et al. report that these two measures were highly positively correlated (.68). Thus, it would be assumed that many of the individuals who were reporting that the other subject had higher than average control over them were also reporting that they themselves had higher than average control over the other subject. This type of correlation raises some difficult questions about what kind of "control" was involved here and whether or not this kind of control was the same as the control reported by subjects in the field study (who were only asked how much control *they* had).

Even if we ignore, for the moment, these methodological problems, the pattern of data obtained by Edney et al. is not what would be expected by reactance theory. If personal space violations *and* feelings of not being in control of environmental events are seen as arousing reactance and creating the motive to extend one's personal space, we might expect that those individuals who did react would designate personal space territories larger than individuals who still felt in control and/or for whom the interpersonal distance was so great that there was little chance that a personal space violation had occurred. We would expect, then, a three-by-one contrast, with subjects who had an interpersonal distance of 7 feet or under and who felt low control (or, in the second study, felt high control of the other over them) having the largest area of personal space.

While a three-by-one contrast does appear to describe the data from both experiments, the deviant cell is not the one that would be expected by reactance theory. Instead, the data indicate that the interaction is caused by subjects with 7 feet or under interpersonal distances who *felt* high in control over environmental events (or who felt the other subject had less than average control over them). These subjects reported *smaller* personal space areas than subjects in the other three cells.

In a study of perceived crowding and control, Schmidt, Goldman, and Feimer (1979) report the results of a questionnaire study of residents of San Bernadino and Riverside, California. Subjects were administered a number of scales and interviewed about their perceptions of crowding at the residence, neighborhood and city levels. Schmidt *et al.* report that perception of crowding was significantly predicted by scales measuring attainment of privacy, freedom to get away, attitudes toward limitation of development in the city, and importance of spatial factors in selecting a residence. The need to attain privacy also significantly predicted perceptions of crowding at the neighborhood and city levels. Schmidt *et al.* (1979) summarize their data by stating, "The proposition that crowding may be related to the restriction of behavioral freedom is a common theoretical position that runs through many of the predictors at the neighborhood and city levels of analysis as well [as at the residence level] [p. 125]."

Again, although reactance theory is referenced in relationship to the restriction of behavioral freedom, these authors do not distinguish between the restriction of a free behavior and the restriction of one that has never been established as free. Their results do suggest that there is a connection between perceived crowding and needs for privacy and freedom of movement, but it is not possible to determine whether this connection has anything to do with reactance theory. It would be hoped that future research on possible reactance effects from crowding or personal space violations would be more sensitive to the need to show that a freedom has been established and would move toward examining whether variables relevant to the theory (e.g., importance of freedoms, proportion of freedoms threatened, magnitude of threat) influence people's perceptions of and responses to high density situations and violations of personal space.

SUMMARY

Formal and informal power relationships offer a fertile setting for the occurrence of reactance. Few studies, however, have examined this possibility in formal organizations, though there is some simulation and correlational evidence consistent with the general proposition.

Simulation studies of the formal relationship between judges and juries have produced some evidence that jurors may experience reactance when instructed to disregard evidence deemed inadmissible by the judge. The data from the relevant studies are somewhat inconsistent, however, and the majority of studies have not attempted to simulate actual courtroom procedures.

Several investigators working in the area of crowding and personal space have suggested that invasions of personal space can arouse reactance. In most cases, however, these investigators have failed to emphasize that there must be a prior establishment of freedom in regard to space before crowding or invasions of space can be said to arouse reactance. The small amount of relevant research evidence on this problem, while suggestive of reactance effects, does not permit a clear interpretation in terms of reactance theory.

PART IV

Control

CHAPTER 16

Reactance Theory and Control

Control has become a popular term in psychological theory and research. It has been used to help explain why people organize their perceptions (Kelly, 1955), why they make causal attributions (Kelly, 1971), why people are biased to see the world as just (Lerner, Miller, & Holmes, 1976), why people want to be *origins* rather than *pawns* (de Charms, 1968), why stressful conditions are not always debilitating (e.g., Glass & Singer, 1972), why helplessness is produced by noxious events (Seligman, 1975) and why choice can enhance learning (Savage, Perlmuter, & Monty, 1979). Apparently, there is almost no end to the (usually beneficial) effects of control. As we indicated earlier in Chapters 1 and 4, there is an intimate relationship between the notion of control and reactance theory. In the present chapter, we will delineate this relationship and explore how the notion of control and reactance theory illuminate one another.

Two questions are useful in organizing this discussion: (a) What is the relationship between a freedom as defined by reactance theory and the notion of control? and (b) What is the relationship between reactance as a motivational state and "control motivation?" After addressing these two questions, we will discuss the effects of control and how control relates to helplessness.

357

FREEDOM AND CONTROL

The concept of freedom as used in reactance theory has been defined conceptually and empirically throughout this volume, and we need only summarize the conceptual definition. Freedom refers to an individual's belief that he or she can engage in a particular behavior. The freedom can pertain to what one does, how one does it, or when one does it, and it may concern the accomplishment of attaining a potentially pleasant outcome or avoiding an unpleasant one. As a belief, a freedom can be conceived of as an expectancy with a particular degree of strength. In addition, by virtue of its unique instrumental value for the satisfaction of a motive, a freedom gains importance to the individual. A freedom that has the unique ability to satisfy a potentially strong or important motive will have more importance than one that can satisfy only a trivial motive. In summary, a freedom is an expectancy that one could engage in a particular behavior, and that expectancy can vary in strength and importance.

Reactance and Locus of Control

The concept of control has also been defined as an expectancy or belief. Perhaps the most influential such definition is that given by Rotter (1966) in his discussion of locus of control. According to this view, individuals acquire generalized expectancies that their reinforcements are controlled by themselves (internal control) or by factors in the environment (external control). As a generalized predisposition, the belief in internal versus external control refers equally to all situations and response dimensions, and varies only in the degree to which the individual is characterized as "internal" or "external" in his or her belief. Lefcourt (1979), however, has suggested that the belief in internal versus external control may be more fruitfully conceptualized in terms of specific situations or behavioral dimensions. Such a suggestion has implicit within it the idea that the belief in internal versus external control of reinforcers may vary in its strength according to the specific goals involved.

The conceptual relationship between Rotter's approach and reactance theory's view of freedom is somewhat unclear. While an intuitive conclusion might be that those individuals who are high on internality would generally have more freedoms, hold them more firmly, and perhaps value them more (i.e., perceive their freedoms as more important), there is no clear correspondence between reactance theory's conception of specific freedoms and the idea of generalized beliefs about internal versus external control of reinforcers. In addition, the experiment by Cherulnik and Citrin (1974), described earlier in Chapter 9, suggests that individuals who believe their reinforcements are controlled externally also have freedoms. It will be recalled that Cherulnik and Citrin found reactance effects (increased attractiveness of an eliminated choice alternative) for a personal elimination of freedom for internals, and for an impersonal elimination of freedom for externals. Although some questions can be raised concerning the methodology of their experiment, the results suggest that individuals who are high in externality may best be considered as having freedoms to receive reinforcements even though those reinforcements are controlled externally. This conception of freedom, it should be noted, is not unlike that in our earlier discussion of how the disconfirmation of expectancies concerning uncontrollable events (e.g., the weather) can arouse reactance (see Chapter 2).

Despite the lack of clarity in the relationship between reactance theory's view of freedom and the conception of internal versus external locus of control, it should be remembered that a number of studies have obtained results suggestive of a relationship. In general, what those studies indicate (see Chapter 9) is that people who are high on internality, compared to those high on externality, show resistance to external influence.

Control, Stress, and Reactance

Another approach to the understanding of control has been offered by Averill (1973). Although not stated in terms of beliefs or expectancies, this approach may easily be translated into cognitive terms. Averill is concerned with the effect that different kinds of control have on an individual's response to stress, an impending noxious event. It must be assumed that in order for these different kinds of control to affect an individual's responses, the individual must be cognizant of having control.

Three kinds of control were distinguished by Averill: behavioral, cognitive, and decisional. Behavioral control is the ability of the individual to modify the impending noxious event or the situation in which it is to occur. Cognitive control is the acquisition and appraisal of information about the impending noxious stimulus. Decisional control is having alternative courses of action.

It will be apparent that each of these types of control fits the definition of freedom within reactance theory. An individual can have the freedom to avoid or modify a potentially noxious outcome, to obtain and/or form a judgment about a potentially noxious outcome, and to have or avoid one outcome rather than another. Averill, like others who have discussed control, does not make explicit statements about the strength of the impression of control or of the importance of control, though it is perhaps implicit that the effects of having control are a function of the noxiousness of the threatening stimulus.

The primary difference between Averill's view and that of reactance theory lies in the stipulated consequences of control. Like many others who have investigated one or another aspect of control over aversive stimuli (e.g., Bowers, 1965; Geer, Davison, & Gatchel, 1970; Glass & Singer, 1972; Hokanson, DeGood, Forrest, & Brittain, 1971; Houston, 1972; Langer & Rodin, 1976; Mandler, 1972; Rodin, 1976; Schulz, 1976; Seligman, 1975; Sherrod, 1974), Averill is primarily interested in the ameliorative effects of control on stress. The question addressed by these various investigators is whether and under what conditions having control of one kind or another over an impending negative event reduces stress and/or debilitating aftereffects of the experience of stress. The comparison of interest is always between a condition in which stress is unavoidable and one in which some sort of control is available, in order to see whether or not that particular type of control alleviates the physiological and behavioral consequences of unavoidable stress. In contrast, reactance theory, as we have seen, is directed at an understanding of the psychological consequences of *loss* of control.

There is a fascinating issue raised by this difference in perspective. Research on reactance theory has necessarily been concerned with the individual's expectancies of control because a proper test of the theory requires a comparison of a condition where control of a particular kind is first expected and then threatened or lost with a condition in which there is no threat or loss, or with a condition in which no control is expected. The latter two would be interesting conditions to compare in order to examine the psychological effects of control. Unfortunately, reactance research has been confined almost entirely to potential positive rather than negative outcomes, so that the ameliorative effects of control over potentially aversive stimulation in these settings has not been examined.

But if we turn the question around and ask about potential reactance effects in stress research on control, an interesting implication appears. Although the examination of the effects of control on responses to noxious stimulation has seldom involved the explicit reduction of expected control, a condition that theoretically should arouse reactance, the prior expectancies of subjects (animal or human) about control have not been of particular concern to investigators. It is clear, however, in terms of reactance theory that if subjects have prior expectancies of being able to avoid the kind of noxious stimulation presented to them in the experiment, then being placed in a low or no control condition should arouse reactance. The consequence of such reactance arousal would be to make the experience more aversive to the subject unless and until the subject gives up the freedom to avoid the noxious stimulation. In other words, what is taken in stress research to be a baseline comparison condition for the effects of control (or predictability of stimulus, etc.) may in fact be a condition in which responses to stress are exacerbated by the arousal of reactance.

The importance of this criticism of stress research can be seen in the work on human helplessness. As noted earlier in Chapter 4, college students are likely to believe that they can solve the kinds of problems given to them in helplessness experiments, and when they find themselves failing to do so, they frequently show intensified efforts at problem solution (e.g., Pittman & Pittman, 1979; Roth & Kubal, 1975; Wortman, Panciera, Shusterman, & Hibscher, 1976). This effect is predictable from reactance theory, and there is no particular reason to believe that it would be limited to the helplessness paradigm in stress research. To the extent that subjects expect that they should not be exposed to noxious conditions when participating in research, their being placed in a condition of no control will increase their feelings of overall stress. It is for this reason that experimenters should examine the general perceptions and feelings that subjects have about the experimental situation. Subjects in whom reactance has been aroused are likely to indicate anger and the feeling that they have been treated unfairly. Such responses would be indicators that the condition of no control (or, perhaps, of particular types of control) had aroused reactance and instigated negative or stressful responses that were greater than would have occurred to the noxious stimulus per se.

To summarize this discussion of control in regard to stress, we have seen that the types of control stipulated by Averill (1973) can be subsumed under the concept of freedom as defined by reactance theory, but that investigations of the effects of control on stress have concentrated on different aspects of control than has reactance theory. For researchers on stress, control is a condition under which the detrimental effects of stress are usually reduced, though sometimes increased, whereas for reactance research, control is a condition under which reactance can be produced if there is a threat to, or elimination of, that control. Because stress researchers have not explicitly studied the effects of expectancies about control, and because reactance researchers have confined their research efforts to positive as opposed to negative potential outcomes, there is only a hypothetical overlap between these two lines of work. This hypothetical overlap, however, suggests a promising line for further research.

Another potential area of overlap involves aspects of control that affect the stressfulness of exposure to a noxious stimulus. These characteristics, in some instances, may be viewed as important freedoms in terms of reactance theory. For example, Sherrod, Hage, Halpern, and Moore (1977) reported that control over the onset *and* offset of an aversive stimulus produces a multiplicative improvement in persistance and accuracy on poststress tasks over having either type of control alone. These effects suggest that the importance of having one freedom can be increased by having a second, related freedom. Theoretically, the loss of the two kinds of control together (onset and offset of the noxious stimulus) would produce a multiplicative amount of reactance compared to the loss of either type of control by itself (see discussion of summation effects in Chapter 4).

This discussion of the relationship between control and behavioral freedoms would not be complete without mention of an issue raised by Lacey (1979) and previously discussed in the context of the application of reactance theory to clinical practice (Chapter 13). In our earlier discussion it was noted that some clinical investigators such as Haley (1963, 1973) have suggested that a therapist can order a client with a symptom to engage in that symptom. By making this an order, the therapist forces the client to give up his or her use of the symptom as a means of having power over the therapist. Either the client complies with the therapist's order and thereby gives control over the symptom to the therapist, or he or she defies the therapist and gives up the symptom. As may be seen, this is a case in which the strategy of the therapist is to arrange the situation so that he or she has control over the client's behavior, no matter what the client does. It is, in short, an example of what Lacey referred to as the slave driver and the slave. The issue presented here for the understanding of control is that while an individual slave has control over some of his activities, such as whether he starts building the pyramid on the north side or the south, he has no control over superordinate goals and policies such as whether or not to build a pyramid at all. A slave cannot determine the agenda; she can control only what she is allowed to control. There are, in other words, different levels of activities and goals over which a person can have control or not.

Translated into reactance theory, levels of control are conceptualized as different freedoms. This adds nothing to reactance theory, of course, because freedoms are specific to the time and situation in any case. The freedom to decide on which side of the pyramid to start building is not qualitatively different from the freedom to decide whether to build a pyramid or an obelisk. Although objectively it might be thought that one freedom is more important than the other, the importance of a freedom is subjective; the determination of the location of the starting point for building may be just as important to the slave as is the choice between a pyramid and an obelisk for the slave driver.

The idea of levels of control is important in understanding the organization of social groupings. It harks back to sociological analyses in terms of position (status) and function (role) and how these notions help in the understanding of job performance and job satisfaction. For reactance theory, such analyses are important because they indicate what freedoms are held by a person in a given position in an organization and thereby allow the prediction of the arousal of reactance when there is interference with a function (freedom). For the task of understanding how control ameliorates stress, however, there may be few or no implications from conceiving of control as having different levels.

The foregoing discussion has made clear, we hope, that there is an intimate relationship between at least some ideas of perceived control and reactance theory's definition of freedom. It may be helpful, therefore, to close this analysis of the perception of control with an explicit definition of control that is compatible with reactance theory's conception of freedom. This definition, as will be seen, is general and is compatible with that used by many investigators working on stress and helplessness. Perceived control, according to our view, consists of the belief or perception that one can affect the probability of occurrence of a potential outcome. This definition is equivalent to saying that a person has (some degree of) freedom in regard to the outcome. Like a freedom, control is conceived as specific to a particular event rather than being a generalized characteristic (applicable to all or many kinds of events). Thus, if one can also specify the firmness of the perception of control and the importance to the individual of the potential outcome, one could just as well use the term *freedom* as it is used in reactance theory. Moreover, to the extent that perceived control is equivalent to the concept of freedom, loss of control or threats to control should arouse reactance and the theoretically expected consequences of reactance.

CONTROL MOTIVATION

Reactance theory conceives of the perception of control as specific to a particular outcome; however, the perception of control could be understood more broadly in terms of whether or not a person views himself or herself as having control *in general*. Control motivation is also subject to these two perspectives: as specific to a given outcome or as general across outcomes. A logically independent issue is whether control motivation is conceived as directed only toward the restoration of threatened or lost control, or toward having and gaining control. In the discussion to follow, we shall consider each of these issues separately: specificity of motivation and goal of the motive. However, it should be noted that these two conceptually distinct dimensions can be combined to form four different possibilities for the conceptualization of control motivation.

1. Control motivation is general across all possible outcomes, and is directed toward having and gaining control.
2. Control motivation is specific to a particular outcome, and is directed toward having and gaining control in regard to that outcome.
3. Control motivation is general across all possible outcomes, and is directed toward regaining generalized control when there has been some threat to or loss of control.
4. Control motivation is specific to a particular outcome, and is directed toward regaining threatened or lost control over that outcome.

These four ways to conceptualize control motivation have not been equally popular with investigators, as will be seen in the following discussion. Indeed, we know of no instance in which a specific motive to gain control has been postulated (No. 2 in the foregoing list). Furthermore, the major issue that evolves from extant theoretical approaches is whether the first or the fourth of the listed possibilities is the better way to conceptualize control motivation: Is control motivation best conceived as a general motivation to gain control, or as a specific motivation to regain threatened or lost control over a specific potential outcome? In the following discussion, it should be kept in mind that though control is uniformly thought to have functional value for the individual (control allows the maximization of benefits and the minimization of harm), control motivation means a motive to have control for its own sake rather than to have control simply because it allows one to satisfy another motive. Our critique of various approaches depends heavily on this distinction. In addition, it should be noted that for the purposes of comparing reactance theory with other conceptions of control, we are not interested in the distinctions that can be made between general control motivation, mastery motive, and effectance; the latter notions are all motives to have or gain generalized control.

The Specificity of Control Motivation

Many theorists and researchers have posited a mastery, or general control, motivation (e.g., de Charms, 1968; Deci, 1975; Kelley, 1971; White, 1959). The function of such a motive is to increase the amount of control that the individual has over his or her outcomes and thereby increase the quality of his or her life. Such a motive is necessarily conceived as being very general in nature because it pervades all activities and has implications for the satisfaction of all other motives. Other theoreticians or investigators (e.g., Lerner, Miller, & Holmes, 1976; Walster, 1966) have taken the more modest position that control has functional value for the individual, and that people will have a tendency to perceive themselves as having control. Both of these schools of thought suggest a generalized conception of control motivation.

In contrast, reactance theory, as well as some theoretical statements about response to stress (e.g., Lazarus, 1966; Mandler, 1972), takes the more limited view that control motivation is specific to the situation. Rather than conceiving of the individual as having a general need for control, these latter views suppose that the motivation to control is elicited by a particular event (a potential noxious outcome or the loss of control over important outcomes).

The utility of the specific view of control motivation is seen in the considerable evidence in support of reactance theory, described in the previous chapters of this volume. On the other hand, it is difficult to document the utility of a more general conception of control motivation. Indeed, it is not clear just what implications there are of such a view. One possibility, however, is that reduction in control over one aspect of an individual's life would lead to seeking more control over other aspects. That is, if general in nature, control motivation that is aroused by loss of control would be evidenced in any other way that would satisfy the motive to control. Thus, where reactance theory stipulates that reactance is directed toward restoration of the threatened freedom (or toward restoration of that freedom by implication), a generalized notion of control motivation would predict that the loss of freedom could just as easily result in attempts to increase unrelated kinds of control.

Two recent experiments provide some support for this position. Pittman and Pittman (1980) had subjects who had been exposed to no, low, or high helplessness training make causal attributions from a case history that contained "mand" (behavior under the control of external reinforcement contigency) or "tact" (behavior reflecting a characteristic of the individual) information. Subjects who had received helplessness training, compared to those who had not, made greater use of the mand-tact information. Also, Swann, Stephenson, and Pittman (1981) found that subjects who had been exposed to helplessness training, compared to those who had not, selected questions of higher 'diagnosticity" when given the task of interviewing another person. The findings from both experiments were interpreted as evidence for a motive to control after an experience with control deprivation. These results, then, can be viewed as support for the third type of theoretical formulation described earlier; they do not, however, lend support to the more general formulation of control motivation (number 1 in our list of different types of formulations) that will be discussed in the following section.

Reactive versus Generalized Control Motives

As noted above, some theoreticians have explicitly postulated a general type of control motivation. White (1959), in his discussion of competence, postulated an *effectance motivation*, a motive to deal effectively with the environment. Because of this motivation, an individual will supposedly experience feelings of pleasure (and efficacy) when he or she produces changes in the environment. A statement of mastery motivation is found in de Charms' (1968) concept of the individual as an *origin*. De Charms postulated that a person strives to be a causal agent rather than to be controlled by his or her environment (i.e., to be a *pawn*). More recently, de Charms (1979) has eliminated his emphasis on individuals' perception of themselves as causal agents in the world, and has replaced this perceptual view with the notion of *experience*. According to this revised conception, the individual does not perceive control, rather he or she experiences or feels control. Whether or not this revised view has additional implications for our understanding of the mastery motive remains unclear.[1] Yet a third general motive position appears in Deci's (e.g., Deci & Porac, 1978) theory of intrinsic motivation. This theory, like that of White, assumes that people have a need to be competent and effective in dealing with their environment.

[1] A more elaborate theory about the phenomenal state of control is found in Chanowitz and Langer (1980). However, the application of their distinction between mindful and mindless behavior appears to apply primarily to learning versus performance of tasks, and has limited implications for the general understanding of control.

In contrast to the view that there is a motive to control or master the environment, reactance theory assumes that control motivation (reactance) is aroused when there is a threat to preexisting control (see discussion of freedoms, Chapter 2). According to reactance theory, the acquisition of freedoms occurs through experience, formal agreements, the establishment of laws, and, possibly, through social comparison as well. No motive is postulated to account for any of these ways of establishing freedoms.

Although many investigators posit a need to have or gain control, which would imply an ongoing motive to aquire more and more control, the evidence that can be adduced to support such a notion is sorely deficient. That conditions can be produced that increase self-direction (de Charms, 1979) or intrinsic motivation (Deci, 1975) does not make a cogent case for the postulation of a mastery motive. And persuasive as it is, White's (1959) argument for effectance motivation is not quite convincing. The question that must be raised is the following. If there is a motive to be effective in dealing with the environment, or a motive to master the environment, or a motive to control the environment and one's own behavior and its outcomes, why, by this late date, is there not abundant experimental evidence to demonstrate such motives? It is difficult to believe that there has been insufficient interest in these ideas to have produced many experimental attempts. What one is led to suspect is that many attempts have been made and they have failed. Let us, therefore, review the evidence in which a need for control has been posited, and see what we might conclude about the existence of such a motive. Our review will be quite selective because of the large number of studies on control, but we believe that it is reasonably representative.

Experimental Evidence on a
General Motive to Control

An experiment by Russ, Gold, and Stone (1979) was explicitly designed to examine the effect of effectance arousal on interpersonal attraction. Patterned after a study by Byrne and Clore (1967), effectance motivation was aroused by showing subjects a movie that was very difficult to make sense of. In two additional conditions, subjects were shown either the same film but were first given a way to make sense of the movie, or subjects were shown a film that was easy to understand. Subjects were run in small groups. Each subject was first asked to fill out a survey of attitudes, was shown one of the movies, was then shown attitude responses supposedly from another subject who was present in the group, and finally, for the dependent measure, was asked to indicate on another questionnaire how attractive that other subject was. The similarity of the fictitious other to the subject on the attitude dimensions was manipulated to be high or low.

Russ et al. expected that in low effectance arousal conditions, the usual relationship would be found between attitude similarity and attraction: the greater the similarity, the greater the attraction. This effect was obtained for the subjects who saw the easy-to-understand movie and the subjects who saw the difficult-to-understand movie but were first given an explanation. The investigators reasoned, however, that where effectance motivation was high, subjects would find dissimilar others attractive because they would expect to find dissimilar people more useful for helping them to understand a movie that they themselves could not understand. This effect, too, was obtained, thus confirming their analysis in terms of effectance motivation.

Using a very different setting, Walster (1966) examined the idea that people have a need to see themselves in control of their own fates, and that when they observe an accident that has a negative consequence, they will be motivated to assign blame for the accident so as to reassure themselves that the accident could not happen to them. In her study, subjects read a description of an accident in which the severity of the consequences was systematically varied. As predicted, she found that more blame was put on the perpetrator of the accident when the severity of consequences was high. It should be noted, however, that this effect has frequently failed to replicate (e.g., Shaver, 1970) and is amenable to a nonmotivational explanation (e.g., Wortman & Linder, 1973).

Along a similar vein, Lerner, Miller, and Holmes (1976) report a series of studies designed to demonstrate that people believe in a just world. According to this line of thought, a just world, in which people receive outcomes that they deserve, preserves predictability and controllability for the perceiver. If others' outcomes are in accord with what they deserve, then the perceiver can expect his or her own outcomes to be in accord with what he or she deserves. Typical of the research in support of this line of reasoning is a study by Lerner and Simmons (1966), which found that when a participant in an experiment was assigned to receive electric shock, that person was derogated.

More directly relevant to the effect of control motivation on interpersonal attributions is a study by Miller, Norman, and Wright (1978). According to these investigators, the need for effective control will lead individuals to bias their judgments about others toward a dispositional, as opposed to a situational, attribution. Being stable over time and situations, dispositional attributions enable one to predict future behavior.

To test their analysis, Miller *et al.* (1978) had four different kinds of observers for a prisoner's dilemma game. All observers were told that two games would be played. One observer thought he or she was Player B, playing two games against another subject, Player A, actually simulated by the experimenter. A second observer expected to passively observe the game played (supposedly) by A and B. A third observer passively observed the first game and expected to play against Player A in the second game. Finally, the fourth subject expected to passively observe both games but, after the first game, was informed that he or she would play the second game against Player A. The play of Player A was manipulated to appear relatively cooperative for half the observers and relatively competitive for the other half. The investigators expected to replicate earlier results by Miller and Norman (1975) that showed that a player who expected to play against Player A tended to make more dispositional inferences about that player than did a passive observer. This effect was indeed replicated. In addition, these investigators predicted that the observer (post-expectant condition) who did not initially expect to play against Player A at all, but who was then informed after the first game that he or she would play against Player A in the second game, would also show an enhanced tendency to make dispositional attributions. Relative to passive observers, this effect was obtained. Miller *et al.* (1978) concluded that because subjects in their post-expectant condition were treated exactly the same way as subjects in the passive observer condition until the observation period was over, increased dispositional attributions by post-expectant subjects could not be due to selective information processing and must therefore be due to a motivational process. That process, according to the authors, reflects the need for effective control.

Before proceeding with our examination of other evidence on control motivation, let us summarize and evaluate what we have reported to this point. In the study by Miller *et al.* (1978), even though the authors invoke a "need for effective control," there is no evidence for control motivation independent of other reasons that make control desirable (such as being successful in an upcoming task). If controlling behaviors —in this case making dispositional attributions—occur only in the service of other motives, then there seems no reason to posit a need for control. Unless control motivation occurs in the absence of other motives, as White (1959) assumes to be the case for effectance, then it has no separable identity and its functions can be stated without appeal to a separate motive.

The more interesting cases for the present discussion are the experiments and theoretical propositions of Russ *et al.* (1979), Walster (1966), and Lerner *et al.* (1976). As Wortman (1976) has noted, the latter two implicitly assume a desire for control in their reasoning, and the study by Russ et al., of course, was explicitly designed to test for effectance motivation. None of these studies, however, demonstrates the existence of a mastery motive, effectance, or a motive to control. Rather, what happens in each experiment is that people are presented with a "problem" or "challenge" to their preexisting conceptions or abilities. That is, in each case, the motivation that occurs is aroused by the situation that confronts the subject. While this arrangement of experimental affairs is not inconsistent with White's (1959) description of effectance in infants and children, it is inconsistent with the conclusion that White draws from his examples.

That conclusion is that effectance is an inherent part of human nature; it is always there and will operate when conditions permit. One of the conditions necessary is that there be something in regard to which to become effective. Unfamiliar stimuli (strange situations) would be a prime example. But one must distinguish between strange situations that are simply available for the operation of effectance and those that elicit a response for other reasons. The concept of effectance or of a mastery motive locates the motivating force within the individual and implies a seeking out of situations in which the motivation can operate. The motive to be effective with, or master, the environment is intrinsic rather than being generated in the service of satisfying other motives such as hunger or affiliation.

Experiments like those we have reviewed fail to make a convincing case for an intrinsic control motive because they present individuals with problems or challenges in their immediate environment. If one expects to make interpersonal judgments that are supposed to be affected by a confusing movie, one must necessarily strive to come to some understanding of what the movie was about. In the experiments by Walster and by Lerner and Simmons, the subjects were confronted with a violation of their preconceptions of how the world should be ordered. Given that problems or challenges are presented to subjects in all of the control motivation research we have reviewed here, it is impossible to conclude that the operation of effectance or a mastery motive has been demonstrated.

More Direct Attempts to Demonstrate
a General Motive to Control

Let us turn at this point to an explicit attempt to demonstrate a motive to *increase* control. Ferebee (1975) carried out an elaborate experiment to see if various conditions of partial control over and predictability of a stressor would produce evidence of a desire to increase control. Basing her analysis on prior research on the effects on stress of predictability and control over stressors, and on Lazarus' (1966) notion of counterharm resources, Ferebee predicted that attempts to increase control over the stressors would be a direct, joint function of the magnitude of the stressor, amount of prior control over the stressor, and predictability of the stressor. Ferebee postulated that if there is no prior control over the stressor, the individual will adopt a passive stance and be unmotivated to increase control.

The following six conditions were included in the experiment. Under high magnitude of the stressor, prior control was either high or low, and predictability of the stressor was either high or low. Under low magnitude of the stressor, subjects were given high prior control and exposed to either high or low predictability of the stressor. The stressor was described to subjects as either a very mild electric shock, or a moderately severe shock. The predictability of shocks was varied by indicating that they would occur either regularly in time (e.g., once each minute) or that the period between shocks would vary between 5 sec and 3 min. Prior control was varied by giving high control subjects a button that they could press and informing them that if they pressed it during the 10 sec preceding a shock, the shock would not occur. In order to hold constant the number of shocks that each subject expected to receive, the number of shocks programmed and button presses allowed were varied according to the condition. Low control subjects, who had no button to press, were informed that there would be 20 shocks. High control subjects were told that there would be 40 shocks, and those who expected predictable shocks were allowed 20 button presses, thus allowing them to avoid 20 of the 40 shocks. High control subjects in the unpredictable condition were told they would have 60 button presses, which would allow them to avoid all but about 20 of the 40 shocks.

After receiving the information about shock intensity, predictability, and prior control, subjects were informed of a way in which they could reduce the aversiveness of the shocks. They were informed that by first working on a reaction time task, they could mobilize "aminopyrines" in their bodies, which were said to be pain reducers. Persistence and effort at the reaction time task were intended as measures of the motivation to increase control. In addition, prior to working on the reaction time task, subjects filled out a questionnaire to check on the effectiveness of the manipulations, and a second questionnaire, ostensibly from the departmental ethics committee, concerning how well they were treated in stress research. This latter questionnaire was designed to measure further aspects of subjects' motivation to control their exposure to stressors.

In order to dramatize the effectiveness of the reaction time task on pain perception, subjects were exposed to blasts of white noise that actually decreased in intensity over a 1.5-min period from 87 dbs to 77 dbs. At the same time, they were shown a meter that supposedly indicated that the intensity of the electrical noise signal had remained constant while the noise level decreased. Thus, subjects should have perceived that work on the reaction time task decreased the perceived intensity of the noise. Subjects were then allowed to work on the reaction time task until they signaled that they wished to stop or until they had completed 25 trials.

The questionnaire checks on the manipulations indicated that they were all reasonably successful. Subjects in the high control conditions, however, expected to receive somewhat more shocks than did those in the low control condition, perhaps indicating they did not believe that their button pressing would be sufficiently accurate to avoid the maximum number of shocks. As intended, subjects felt they had between "slight" and "moderate" control over the painfulness of the shocks, and they thought the effect of aminopyrines was between slight and moderate in effectiveness in reducing pain. The appropriate conditions were therefore established for examining the extent to which being confronted with a stressor under various conditions of prior control and predictability would produce a motive to increase control over the stressor.

Neither the behavioral measure of performance on the reaction time task nor the questions pertaining to control over participation in stress research revealed any reliable differences due to the experimental manipulations. In short, this elaborate and carefully designed study failed to produce evidence for any sort of motivation to increase control over an aversive stimulus.

Ferebee's experiment, like most experiments that produce null effects, would not be very informative about control motivation except for a number of post hoc analyses she carried out. Included in the second questionnaire (ostensibly from the ethics committee) were questions that asked subjects how much choice they should have about participating in stress research, and how much choice they did have about participating in the present project. It will be recognized that to the extent subjects reported they should have had more choice than they had, reactance (reactive control motivation) should have been aroused. What Ferebee found was that there was a fairly strong tendency for subjects to say that they should have had more choice than they were given. Furthermore, when subjects were divided into two groups according to the size of the discrepancy between the amount of choice they thought they should have and what they felt they actually had, a number of findings emerged on the measures of motivation. For example, average reaction time was found to vary as a joint function of discrepancy score on choice and intensity of the shocks, and as a joint function of discrepancy score and control over the shocks. It appears, for example, that subjects who had high discrepancy scores on choice and who were in the high intensity of shock, high control, condition did indeed work harder at the reaction time task, as was originally expected.

Further details of Ferebee's results, however, are not germane to the present point. Rather there are two important lessons to take from this research. First, stress research does indeed have the potential for arousing reactance, as noted earlier, and as a consequence of this potential, conditions of no control, normally taken as baselines against which to examine the effects of different kinds of control or predictability, are suspect. They may easily involve reactance responses to a greater degree than do conditions that allow the subject some degree of control over the stressor.

Second, under conditions in which a motive to increase control had a good opportunity to reveal itself (as demonstrated by the sensitivity of the motivational measures in the post hoc analyses), no evidence for such motivation was found. What was found, however, was evidence of control motivation as a function of the discrepancy between how much choice subjects thought they should have about participating in stress research and how much they thought they actually had. This discrepancy, which should arouse reactance, then interacted with the experimental manipulations to affect the various motivational measures. It seems there is a strong clue here about the direction in which our theoretical thinking should proceed.

Two important attempts to make a direct test for effectance motivation have recently been reported by Solomon (1976) and Rodin, Rennert, and Solomon (1980). These investigators reasoned that if there is a general effectance motive, it should be reflected in a desire to have choice even when that choice has little or no instrumental value for outcomes. They also reasoned that the act of choice should enhance self-esteem in so far as the act reflects active control over the environment (being competent).

In order to demonstrate the existence of effectance motivation, Solomon (1976) gave college students the impression that they were to work on a perception task and then they would repeatedly taste one of four flavors provided for each subject in an individual taste packet. The flavors had ostensibly been previously rated for pleasantness, and all were described as pleasant.[2] To test the proposition that people are motivated to attain control per se, some subjects were told that there was no contingency between their performance on the perception task and which flavor they would taste; others were told that if they performed well on the perception task, they would be allowed to choose which flavor they would taste. In another condition, subjects were informed that if they performed well they would be given a pleasant flavor to taste but that if they did not perform well, they would receive a less pleasant flavor. For this latter group of subjects, then, there was clear instrumental value in performing well on the perception task.

The amount of work performed on the perception task indicated that subjects who had a pleasant outcome to gain worked harder than those for whom there was no contingency between performance on the perception task and what they would taste. This difference indicated that the performance on the perception task measured motivation as intended. Nevertheless, those who could obtain a choice between four pleasant flavors by performing well on the perception task worked no harder than did subjects who could not influence which flavor they received. Thus, there was no evidence that subjects were motivated to attain control for its own sake.

Solomon's results are quite clear in showing that her subjects did not put out any extra effort to attain a choice between taste alternatives that were rated equally pleasant. The inference may therefore be drawn that these subjects exhibited no control motivation. It is possible, of course, that experiments of this kind are not well suited to demonstrating effectance motivation because subjects' concerns are focused on understanding the experimental procedure and, perhaps, on not looking foolish. Such conditions would presumably be less than conducive to the operation of effectance motivation.

The potential delicacy of demonstrating the operation of effectance was largely circumvented by the research reported by Rodin *et al.* These investigators attempted to validate White's assertion that if people are motivated to be effective, then an act of choice should raise self-esteem. In a series of three different experiments, it was demonstrated that the act of choice *lowers* rather than raises self-esteem. In the first experiment, compared to subjects who had no choice, those who had some choice about which personality tests to take and in which order

---

[2] Conditions were also run in which tastes were unpleasant, but these conditions produced ambiguous results and will not be reported here.

to take them subsequently had lower self-esteem. In the second experiment, a replication and extension of the first, it was found that making the tests appear important (e.g., highly valid) further lowered the self-esteem that choice subjects showed relative to no choice subjects. The third experiment gave subjects the impression that they did or did not have choice about what kinds of questions to ask an interviewee in the second part of an interview. As in the first two studies, those who had choice, compared to those who did not, showed a greater decrement in self-esteem.

In contrast to what White indicated should be the relationship between exercising control (having choice) and effects on self-perception, these studies uniformly indicated that, at least under some conditions, exercise of control *lowers* self-esteem. In discussing these results, Rodin *et al.* point out that decrements in self-esteem from having made a choice probably are due, at least in part, to feelings of responsibility for possibly bad decisions, and to lack of adequate information about the alternatives when the choice had to be made. In summarizing all of their evidence, these investigators state that "there does not appear to be an innate need or drive to manipulate the environment and . . . exercising control does not necessarily have positive effects on self-perception, which is clearly the implication one would derive from White (1959) [Rodin *et al.*, 1980, pp. 143–144]."

To summarize our review to this point, we have seen that purported demonstrations of control motivation have in reality presented people with problems or challenges with which they had to cope. Furthermore, direct attempts to demonstrate control motivation, as seen in the work of Ferebee and of Rodin *et al.*, have failed to obtain confirming evidence.

On the other hand, what has been demonstrated in the experimental literature is a *reactive* effectance or control motivation. The evidence for this kind of motivational process is overwhelming. A problem threatens control, whether it is a matter of understanding, attitudinal disagreement, or explicit loss of control. It is the threat to control (which one already had) that motivates an attempt to deal with the environment. And the attempts to deal with the environment can be characterized as attempts to regain control. Thus it is that Walster's subjects assigned blame; Lerner's subjects derogated an unfortunate individual; Russ *et al.*'s subjects sought help for understanding; and in the research described throughout this volume, subjects have evidenced motivation to regain their threatened freedoms. Indeed, it is the latter body of evidence that best makes the case for a motivational process that is peculiar to the act of control. For in many of the experiments designed to test reactance theory, there has been an explicit attempt to rule out alternative interpretations based on frustration of other motives. These experiments have demonstrated rather clearly that loss of control, per se, is motivating.

It would be unwise, of course, to foreclose on the idea that there is a mastery motive, a motive to control. Perhaps the best evidence for such a motive comes from research on aspiration level (e.g., Lewin, Dembo, Festinger, & Sears, 1944) and on achievement motivation (e.g., Atkinson & Feather, 1966). This body of research has shown that people tend to raise their aspiration levels to a point slightly above their past performance, and it is not difficult to read a mastery motive into this effect. Unfortunately, this effect may be highly culture bound, and in our own culture, this effect may be due to impression management. To the best of our knowledge, no aspiration level studies have eliminated this possible source of bias. Similarly, the fact that in achievement research people tend to select a task with a probability of success that is on the low side (.3 to .4) could be interpreted as reflecting a mastery motive. However, this body of research, too, seems subject to the possible bias of impression management.

In summary, there is abundant evidence that people attempt to regain control either in the service of other motives or for the sake of control itself when they are confronted with challenges, problems, or in other words, threats to their control. On the other hand, while it is possible that we have missed some crucial evidence, we have found nothing that makes a convincing case for a general motive to control, to master, or simply to be effective.

THE FACILITATIVE AND BENEFICIAL EFFECTS OF CONTROL

Much of the concern with the concept of control comes from the notion that to have control is good, not to have it is bad. In light of our discussion to this point, it is easy to distinguish two quite different reasons why having control could be beneficial in a wide variety of situations. First, because control means being able to affect the probability of occurrence of a potential outcome, having control over an outcome means that one can increase or decrease the likelihood of attaining or avoiding the outcome. Thus, having control means that one can maximize desirable outcomes and minimize undesirable ones.

The second possible benefit of control stems from its possible motivational component. Quite obviously, if there is a generalized motive to control, a person in a situation that allows no control is in a state of frustration. To put the extreme case, even if all of the individual's other physiological and psychological needs (hunger, sex, defecation, affiliation, etc.) were met, frustration would ensue if there were no way to exercise control over anything. Thus, if there is a generalized control motivation, lack of control, whether in the context of pleasant or unpleasant activities, would presumably have detrimental psychological effects—e.g., feelings of frustration.

While lack of control would presumably produce frustration of the motive to control, having control would take advantage of that motive. Thus, whenever any motive was served by instrumental behavior, there would be additional motivation from the control motive. This seems to be the conclusion that Savage, Perlmuter, and Monty (1979) draw from their research on paired associate learning under various conditions of choice. These investigators have found that allowing people to make a choice of which response word is to be paired with a stimulus word prior to learning the pairs by the anticipation method enhances the rate of learning. In a series of studies built on this paradigm, they and their associates have been able to show that the beneficial effect on rate of learning is not due to an improvement in associative bonds made possible by response selection, nor even to the act of having chosen, but rather is due to the anticipation of having choice. Furthermore, they have shown that where the choice is made from words having different values of meaning, the choice must be a significant one (e.g., between two words of high meaning rather than between one of high meaning and one of low).

A conceptually similar effect has been found in a series of schoolroom experiments carried out by Brigham (1979). Brigham and his associates have found that children learning mathematics work faster when allowed to choose their own reinforcers, and when allowed to control such aspects of their work as pacing, scheduling of work periods, and goal setting.[3]

Although these motivating effects of having choice or control are interesting, they do not necessarily point to a motive to control. An alternative interpretation, for example, is that the condition of choice allows the individual to focus on intrinsic motives that otherwise would not operate. Second, choice may focus attention on the difficulty of the task, and a number of theorists (e.g., Atkinson, 1957; Brehm, 1979; Kukla, 1972) have suggested that motivation can be enhanced by

---

[3] See also the studies of the effects of choice on therapeutic effectiveness reviewed in Chapter 13.

the perception of difficulty. Third, having to make a choice in and of itself can be energizing, either because of the difficulty of making the choice (Brehm, 1979), because of the frustration entailed in making a choice (Brown & Farber, 1951), or because of dissonance from having chosen (Festinger, 1957). Thus, it is important to recognize not only the value and interest of these recent findings on the effects of choice, but also the remaining theoretical ambiguities surrounding the process by which these effects are brought about.

CONTROL AND HELPLESSNESS

We have previously described in Chapter 4 the Wortman and Brehm integration of reactance theory and the learned helplessness model (Seligman, 1975), as well as the evidence relevant to that integration. The main argument, it will be recalled, is that when a person who expects to be able to control outcomes is exposed to uncontrollable outcomes, such as repeated failure, the effect of that experience is first to arouse reactance (control motivation) and consequent increased striving, and after repeated failure, to cause a feeling of helplessness and a decrement in motivation and consequent performance.

The other half of the Wortman and Brehm model concerns the effect of uncontrollable outcomes on people who have no prior expectation of having control. Because without prior expectation of control there is no possibility of reactance arousal, the model predicts decreased motivation to exert control as the amount of experience with lack of control increases. Furthermore, the decrease is said to be proportional to the importance of the outcome that is uncontrolled. The usefulness of this part of the model can be seen in the work of Glass and Singer (1972) and their associates.

These investigators demonstrated the effects of predictability and control of stressors such as noise, electric shock, and social situations on various kinds of performance measures *after the stress was over.* Like the human helplessness research paradigm, in which a helplessness (failure) treatment is followed by a test of performance on a different task, the effects of interest were that unpredictability of the stressor, and lack of control over it, seemingly produced decrements in performance on proofreading, in persistence at working on an insoluble puzzle, and slowness in performance on the Stroop (response conflict) task. What is interesting about these findings for the present discussion is that the experiments were carried out in such a way that in most of them, there was no reason for subjects to expect to be able to have a predictable stressor or control over the stressor. Where reactance theory calls for prior expectations of control in order for lack of control to arouse reactance, subjects in much of the Glass and Singer research were never led to expect control, and they demonstrated clear deficits on the performance tests.

It is conceivable, of course, that subjects in the Glass and Singer research believed that they had the freedom to avoid exposure to the stressor. As Glass and Singer report in the last chapter of their book, a number of subjects did in fact choose not to participate after having heard a few seconds of noise blasts. It is therefore possible that some of the effects observed by Glass and Singer in their conditions of no control were due to reactance, just as was found in the Ferebee experiment, described earlier. However, it would be difficult to account for all of their experimental results in this way.

Glass and Singer invoked the concept of helplessness to explain their obtained effects. Acccording to their view, individuals who find themselves confronted with a stressor over which they have no control become helpless, and that state of helplessness then presumably lasts long enough to interfere with functioning on the performance tests. As we have said, from the Wortman and Brehm model, one would predict helplessness effects without reactance unless there had been some prior expectation of control.

Although the Wortman and Brehm model describes helplessness effects as they were known at the time it was formulated, it does not really increase our understanding of helplessness as a process. To explain how helplessness effects can occur in the absence of prior expectancies of control, a more general model is required. Abramson, Seligman, and Teasdale (1978) have formulated an attributional model that attempts to stipulate conditions under which expectancies of no control (helplessness) will transfer from one situation to another. This model is a clear improvement over the earlier learned helplessness model (Seligman, 1975), but it has already drawn criticism (e.g., Wortman and Dintzer, 1978), in part because of the failure of attributional processes to operate as supposed in the determination of helplessness effects (e.g., Hanusa & Schulz, 1977; Wortman, Panciera, Shusterman, & Hibscher, 1976).

Another approach to the problem of understanding control and helplessness is seen in a recent motivational theory (Brehm, 1979). It is important to note that although this recent theory of motivational energization addresses some of the same issues with which reactance theory is concerned (e.g., expectations of control, experiences with uncontrollable outcomes), the energization model approaches these issues from a distinctly different perspective. The energization model, then, in no way offers a substitute for or replacement of reactance theory as it currently stands and as it has been described throughout this volume. It does offer what we believe to be an interesting and provocative framework in which to examine various fundamental motivational issues as well as the specific effects of experiencing uncontrollable outcomes.

The energization model addresses the energizing function of motivation. It hypothesizes that the magnitude of energization is a function of what the individual perceives can and must be done in order to satisfy a motive. When a motive exists—for example, when a person has been deprived of food or is confronted with the possibility of receiving electric shock—the amount of energization that actually occurs is controlled by the perceived difficulty of satisfying the motive (e.g., eating or avoiding shock). If the instrumental behavior required for motive satisfaction is seen as easy, very little energization will occur; if it is seen as difficult, relatively greater energization will occur; and if it is seen as impossible, no energization should occur because no instrumental behavior is to be carried out.

How much energy the individual is willing to mobilize in order to carry out instrumental behavior is limited by the strength of the motive, that is, for example, by the degree of food deprivation or by the perceived strength of the shock that one might receive. Strong motives obviously are capable of producing more energization than are weak or trivial motives. Furthermore, if the motive is too weak to produce the amount of energization required for motive satisfaction, then, again, there will be little or no arousal of energy because the individual has judged that he or she will do nothing to try to satisfy the motive. Thus, what is seen as "too difficult" to do will vary with the strength of the motive: The weaker a motive, the more likely it is that a given degree of perceived difficulty of instrumental behavior will be seen as "too difficult" to do. In some instances, of course, the individual will perceive that motive satisfaction is literally impossible, and when this occurs, there will be no energization no matter how strong the motive, for there is simply nothing that can be done.

What this theoretical view says about "helplessness" is, first, that there are conditions under which it is normal for individuals to be unmotivated in regard to potential outcomes, even very important potential outcomes. Whenever the individual perceives that motive satisfaction is clearly too difficult or is literally impossible, he or she will experience no motivational arousal (energization) in regard to that motive. A person, for example, who loves the ocean beach and finds him or herself living in Kansas without time or money to make a trip to a beach will simply be unmotivated to go to a beach. The perceived attractiveness of an ocean beach will be relatively low for that person as long as he or she sees no way of getting there. In this case, a prior expectation of attaining the outcome is not necessary, the state of low motivation is produced simply by the perceived impossibility of attaining the outcome.

A second way in which a person can become "helpless," according to this motivational model, is to start out with the perception that outcome attainment (or avoidance) is difficult though clearly within one's control, and then to discover that attainment (or avoidance) is impossible. In this case, the individual is moved from a firm expectation of control to a condition of no control. The prior expectation, however, that one could attain or avoid the potential outcome is not sufficient to produce "frustration" when it is perceived subsequently that the outcome cannot be controlled. For the prior expectation that one can control an outcome, even if difficult, is not in and of itself energizing. Only when the individual anticipates immediate instrumental activity, or has actually begun to engage in that activity, does energization occur. Once energy has been mobilized, however, the discovery that there is nothing that can be done to attain or avoid the outcome should result in a feeling of frustration and probably depression. This latter way of becoming helpless, in which energy is first aroused, is similar to Mandler's (1972) analysis of helplessness except that it does not require that the individual be engaged in ongoing behavior that is interrupted. All that is required is anticipatory energization prior to the discovery of impossibility. This view also has close parallels to Klinger's (1975) description in terms of "current concerns" and a cycle of energization, trying, failing, and depression.

It seems likely, though not certain, that the generation of feelings of depression depends on the prior arousal of energy. In those instances, mentioned earlier, in which the individual perceives that he or she has no control over a potential outcome and never becomes energized in anticipation of performing instrumental behavior, the individual would presumably describe himself or herself as helpless but not as depressed.

These theoretical expectations have been supported by recent research (Brehm, Solomon, Silka, & Toi, 1980). In two experiments, subjects were confronted with easy, difficult, or impossible tasks to perform in order to attain an attractive incentive. Then, just prior to trying to perform the task, they were asked to indicate how attractive they perceived the incentive to be and to describe their current feelings on an adjective checklist. As would be expected from the energization model, subjects who anticipated a difficult task rated the incentive as more attractive than did those who anticipated either an easy or impossible task. In addition, those subjects who were in the impossible condition rated themselves as more helpless but not more depressed than those in the easy and difficult conditions. Parallel to the above studies on positive outcomes, Wright and Brehm (1980) found that a potential electric shock was rated as more unpleasant by subjects who anticipated a difficult task of avoidance of the shock than by subjects who anticipated either an easy or impossible avoidance task. Again, subjects in the impossible condition in one of the two experiments reported rated themselves as helpless but not as depressed.[4] Furthermore, these effects of task difficulty on the perception of shock and on mood were produced only when subjects anticipated immediate work on the task; they did not occur for subjects who expected to wait half an hour before doing the task.

The mere perception of impossibility, then, is sufficient to produce a state of helplessness, or low motivation, without affective consequences. Unfortunately, at the time they did their research, Glass and Singer were not particularly interested in the mood states of their subjects and so they did not obtain the information that would be relevant to the present argument. We would guess, however, that had they measured moods, they would have found helplessness without depression in those subjects who were exposed to uncontrollable stressors. Indeed, as Cohen (1980) has noted, most of the studies that have examined after-stress mood states have failed to find differences as a function of control or perceived control (e.g., Cohen & Spacapan, 1978; Frankenhaeuser & Lundberg, 1974).

A more important question that concerns the applicability of the energization model to the understanding of the Glass and Singer aftereffects, and to the helplessness paradigm in general, is why the experience of helplessness at Time 1 should affect behavior at Time 2. Even if it is granted that the perception of impossibility produces less energization than the perception of (difficult) control, why should this difference persist long enough to affect the postnoise tests used in the Glass and Singer research or the test tasks used in the helplessness paradigm (e.g., Roth & Kubal, 1975)? At present, there is no clear theoretical answer to that question, nor is there any experimental evidence that demonstrates that the low energization produced by the perception of

---

[4] Subjects in the impossible condition of the other experiment rated themselves as less happy but not as more helpless or depressed than those in the easy and difficult conditions.

impossibility persists after one is no longer confronted with the impossible task. In a word, the suggestion that the energization model may account for the helplessness effects demonstrated by Glass and Singer remains highly speculative.

Although our motivational explanation of the Glass and Singer research is far from elegant, it is perhaps as good or better than other explanations that have been offered. The aftereffects of uncontrollable stressors are particularly hard to understand when the uncontrollability is due not to failure at an instrumental task, but simply to the fact that one has no control over the stressor in the experimental situation. Under these conditions, where there is no instrumental response to try or make in the presence of the stressor, there is neither learning about noncontingency of responses (there are no responses), nor is there failure. Furthermore, the experimental treatment of being exposed to an uncontrollable stressor is so unlike the posttest tasks of proofreading, tracing geometric patterns, and responding to the Stroop test, that application of an attributional model, such as that by Abramson *et al.* (1978), appears to be impractical. It is for these reasons that a simple motivational explanation seems most appealing.

Cohen (1980), in his review of research on the aftereffects of stress, agrees that a simple motivational approach (a frustration-mood hypothesis) has a great deal of appeal, but points out the viability of several alternative interpretations (adaptive-cost hypothesis, information overload, persistent coping strategies, etc.). He concludes that the aftereffects of stress may represent a complex process and may therefore require more than one theoretical approach. In all of the experimental literature on control over stressors, aftereffects remain the single most challenging set of phenomena in need of explanation. Whether these findings are best understood as due to the ameliorative effects of perceived control or to the detrimental effects of perceived lack of control, or both, remains to be seen.

SUMMARY

The concept of control, which has been enjoying increasing usage in the understanding of psychological phenomena, is related to reactance theory in two ways. To have control can be seen as equivalent to having one or more specific freedoms. To be motivated to regain control can be seen as equivalent to reactance. Conceived in this way, control refers to the ability to effect a specific outcome, and control motivation refers to a motivational state directed toward regaining control over a specific outcome.

Some investigators, however, have posited a generalized motivation to control—a mastery or effectance motivation. This view suggests that people are motivated to increase control rather than simply to reestablish threatened control. A review of the experimental evidence failed to find support for this more general form of control motivation. Indeed, explicit experimental attempts to demonstrate a motivation to increase control and an effectance motivation failed to produce any support at all.

The research literature indicates that having control over outcomes can have beneficial effects on, for example, learning. Other studies demonstrate that lack of control can have detrimental effects on responses to stress and on poststress performance. Having, losing, and not having control can also be used to explain many of the phenomena of learned helplessness. Various theories have attempted to account for the effects of control, and a motivational model that depends on the perceived difficulty of controlling an outcome was outlined, along with some supporting experimental evidence.

PART V

Conclusion

CHAPTER 17

Conclusion:
Reprise and Future Themes

The previous chapters describe abundant evidence that people are motivated to restore freedoms when those freedoms are threatened. Frequently the motivation to restore a freedom is so great that individuals act contrary to the pressure put on them to give up the freedom. The determinants of the magnitude of the motivation to restore freedom and, consequently, the determinants of whether people will or will not conform to pressure have been spelled out in some detail. These determinants, in general, are the importance of the freedom, the strength of the threat to that freedom, and the extent to which other freedoms are threatened simultaneously, either directly or by implication. Although this general outline of reactance theory is supported by considerable experimental evidence, there are a number of less fully investigated issues that have emerged from our examination of the theory. It is these issues that we will highlight and discuss in this concluding chapter.

The Concept of Freedom

We have stated that because a freedom is a belief, it can vary in the strength with which it is held. What this assertion implies is that some freedoms will be maintained almost no matter how much pressure there is to give them up, whereas other freedoms will be relinquished for little reason. In theory, this dimension of strength is independent of how important the freedom is to the individual though, in practice, strongly held freedoms probably tend to be relatively important. In any case, what is interesting about strength of freedom is that it sets an upper limit on the amount of reactance that can be aroused by any given threat. Regardless of its importance, a freedom may be given up quickly if it is not firmly held. On the other hand, a threat to a firmly held freedom, as we have seen throughout this volume, arouses reactance only to the extent that the freedom is important. Thus, it is apparent that there is a complex interplay between the strength and importance of a freedom and the magnitude of threat to it in determining the magnitude of reactance and whether positive or negative responses will be made to pressure to give up the freedom. However, little attention—either theoretically or empirically—has been given to this relationship. Aside from a handful of experiments that have attempted to manipulate freedom in an all or none fashion, there has been no attempt to examine responses as a joint function of strength of freedom and strength of threat. This, then, is a fundamental aspect of the theory that requires experimental examination.

Related to the present emphasis on freedom as a belief is the issue of how freedoms are acquired in the first place. Although reactance theory does not make the acquisition of freedom a formal part of its structure, there is an obvious relationship between how a freedom is established and the strength of the freedom. For example, the observation by a professor new to a department that all professors do not attend departmental faculty meetings may suggest that there is a freedom not to attend such meetings. But is such an observation sufficient to establish a firm freedom? What additional factors would strengthen or weaken this freedom? To answer these questions, one should turn to what is known about the acquisition of beliefs in general and then, perhaps, make a special analysis concerning beliefs about behavioral freedoms. An approach of this kind would presumably lead to hypotheses about the strength with which a freedom would be held, and would go hand in hand with investigation of the interactive effects of strength of freedom and strength of threat. A particularly interesting aspect of how freedoms are acquired would involve a developmental perspective. Special attention might also be paid to differences in gender and in psychological dimensions such as the belief in external versus internal locus of control of reinforcers.

Yet a third aspect of freedoms that remains poorly understood is how they may be perceived as sets. Because the magnitude of reactance is a direct function of the proportion of freedoms threatened, understanding of magnitude depends on understanding what freedoms are available and on how many of these are threatened. We have seen that this problem is easily solved in laboratory experimental research by giving subjects multiple alternatives from which to make a selection—the set of freedoms being determined by the set of alternatives. However, if the proposition about proportion threatened is to have some general utility in the understanding of behavior, principles are needed by which to map what freedoms belong together in the eyes of the actor. A secretary, for example, typically has a variety of freedoms connected with work—how and in what order to deal with typing letters and other materials, whether or not to drink coffee or chew gum while working, when and how much to order in the way of secretarial supplies, etc. Are all such freedoms seen as a set? Probably not. It seems more likely that a set would include only those freedoms that one contemplates exercising at a given point in time. Thus, a secretary might contemplate different orders in which to carry out typing jobs A, B, C, and D, and the freedoms involved in this ordering would not be affected by, for example, a threat to the freedom to drink coffee while typing. This sort of detailed analysis of what freedoms constitute a set may seem rather tedious, yet it is undoubtedly required if the proportion proposition of reactance theory is to be useful, especially when the theory is applied to natural as opposed to laboratory situations.

In addition to questions about how freedoms are acquired, how their strengths are determined and how they are grouped, there remains an interesting question about whether or not freedoms can be negatively valued. An affirmative answer has clear intuitive appeal as well as conceptual support. Freedoms imply responsibility for outcomes, and where those outcomes are of great consequence for the individual, the responsibility can weigh heavily. For just as the possession of freedoms has functional value for maximizing benefits and minimizing harm, so the exercise of freedoms carries the potential of making mistakes. Moreover, positions of power, which by definition include freedoms over a wide range of events that can affect not only the self but outcomes for other people as well, require the exercise of those freedoms that come with the position. As people move through their personal and working lives, they tend to acquire more and more freedoms that they must exercise, and at some point, they may find that they have more responsibilities than they want or feel able to handle. At this point the freedoms become onerous, and the individual may well prefer to give them up rather than have to exercise them.

Having to exercise a freedom that one does not want to exercise is an interesting case for reactance theory. A person typically has the freedom to stick a finger into an electrical outlet and receive a shock or to put a hand in boiling hot water and be scalded, but one does not normally wish to exercise either of those freedoms. Indeed, the freedoms that are important in this case are those to avoid the electric shock and the scalding water. But if, through peculiar circumstances, a person were forced to have to experience one or the other of these noxious events, the importance of the freedom to avoid each would determine which would be selected, and a threat to or elimination of either avoidance freedom would theoretically arouse reactance and its usual consequences. The alternative forced on one would tend to become even more unattractive and the threatened or eliminated alternative would tend to become less unattractive. In other words, this analog hypothetical situation implies that even where one wishes to avoid the exercise of freedom, reactance theory still applies. What is different is that the freedoms to avoid outcomes become more important than the freedoms to attain outcomes. What should also be clear is that where avoidance motives predominate, the individual, in the absence of forces to exercise a freedom, would do nothing. In effect, the individual would escape from the freedoms that were available. Unfortunately, there is almost no experimental evidence on reactance processes where avoidance motives predominate, and the validity of our analysis remains in question until additional relevant research is done.

Finally, an intriguing question must be raised about the role of personal responsibility in the conceptualization of freedoms. Because the supposed functional value of a freedom is that it allows one to maximize benefits and minimize harm to the self, there is the apparent implication that to have a freedom means to have personal control over an outcome. Indeed, this was the view emphasized in the original formulation of reactance theory, in which *behavioral* freedoms were stressed. Given the present emphasis on freedom as an expectancy, however, it is possible to conceive of freedoms more broadly. Rather than limit freedoms to behaviors, one can define freedoms as expectancies about outcomes over which the individual may or may not have control. Thus, a person might expect to receive a particular positive outcome or not receive a particular negative outcome, and for that person, this expectation constitutes a freedom. For example, a single mother with a dependent infant may believe that she has the freedom to receive welfare payments to support herself and her child. At most, the mother has limited, if any, control over reception of these payments because they are determined by federal and state regulations. If a change in regulations resulted in a reduction or loss of payments, there would be little that she could do. Yet, such a loss may be seen as a threat to or elimination of a freedom, and reactance aroused.

If there is no perceived control over an outcome freedom, there will probably be no perceived way to restore it. Therefore, following the reactance–learned helplessness model, we would expect that the arousal of reactance would be followed quickly by a state of helplessness and feelings of depression and apathy. These consequences would ensue, of course, whether the outcome in question was reception of a positive event or avoidance of a negative event. Thus, the sheer violation of an expectancy may be sufficient to arouse reactance and consequent helplessness effects.

We do not wish to review here the evidence for this modified view of freedoms. Suffice it to say that there is suggestive evidence from the research on the internality–externality dimension and reactance, the internality–externality dimension and learned helplessness, and the fact that personal causation does not enhance freedom-restoration effects. All of this evidence suggests that personal control is not a necessary condition for either the arousal or the reduction of reactance. The apparent role of control or behavioral freedom, then, is to establish one general condition under which there will be expectancies about outcomes. It is possible that expectancies about uncontrolled outcomes also can serve as freedoms.

The Necessary and Sufficient Conditions for Reactance Arousal: Alternative Views of Reactance Phenomena

How freedoms are best conceptualized has critical implications for our understanding of the necessary and sufficient conditions for the arousal of reactance. It is quintessential that there be a freedom, that it have some importance, and that there be a threat to it in order for reactance to occur. Whether or not these conditions are sufficient, however, has been questioned by several investigators, all of whom have proposed that reactance is basically a social phenomenon. In its most extreme form, their view would be that freedoms are social in nature, that threats must be social, and that restoration of freedom can occur only through social events.

The pro and con arguments in light of the evidence have been discussed at length, and need not be repeated here. What we wish to reiterate is that (a) there is no argument about social variables being important in reactance theory, and (b) there is already some reactance evidence in the literature that is difficult to interpret as social in nature. One possibility, raised by the impression management formulation in particular, is that the creation in the laboratory of a sufficiently important freedom and a sufficiently important threat may frequently, even typically, involve social interaction of some sort. Moreover, it is virtually impossible in the laboratory to remove the possibility that subjects may have thought that the experimenter could examine their responses. Field studies, then, may be a more appropriate format for the demonstration of reactance effects that cannot be explained in terms of impression management processes.

Reactance as a Motivational State

Subjectively, reactance may be an intense experience. It presumably includes a strong urge to do something (toward restoring a freedom), and it may be accompanied by feelings of hostility. Given the presumed intensity of the experience, and the relatively strong behavioral effects observed in some research, it would seem plausible to expect that there is concomitant physiological arousal. To the best of our knowledge, however, there has been no attempt to measure physiological effects of reactance. While we would not expect such attempts to produce any theoretical insights, the successful measurement of physiological effects could open avenues to the study of some of the more subtle theoretical questions. For example, what happens to reactance when a freedom is eliminated? Does it take a long time to disappear or does it decay quickly? Does hope for restoration of an eliminated freedom maintain arousal or not? Does the restoration of freedom by implication reduce reactance as much as direct restoration? These and many other questions could be examined in terms of physiological measures, if such measures proved to be sensitive.

It should also be possible to demonstrate the effect of reactance on processes that are known to be affected by drive. For example, performance on strongly versus weakly learned habits should interact with amount of reactance arousal, as has been demonstrated with other motivations, including cognitive dissonance.

Threats to Freedoms

Any event that makes it more difficult for a person to exercise a freedom constitutes a threat to that freedom. By and large, strong threats produce stronger reactance effects than do weak threats. Theoretically, one might expect that when two or more threats are applied to the same freedom, stronger reactance effects would occur than when these same threats are applied singly. This expectation has been supported by considerable research, but it has failed to receive support in certain instances. The variation in patterns of reactance effects to multiple threats to the same freedom raises a number of theoretical issues about how threats work.

One issue concerns the possibility that as the perceived difficulty of exercising a freedom increases, there is a threshold at which the perception of threat occurs. This means that the perceived difficulty of exercising a freedom can increase from zero up to a certain point without creating the perception of a threat to freedom. What is interesting about this possibility is that two or more independent events that increase the perceived difficulty of exercising a freedom, each of which is subthreshold, can combine to form a threat to freedom. This possibility has not yet been systematically investigated, though there is a small amount of research that is interpretable in this way.

A second issue concerning two or more threats to the same freedom has to do with whether the effects on reactance are additive or multiplicative. If each of two threats increases the difficulty of exercising a freedom by the same amount, the combination of the two threats should be additive and produce twice the amount of reactance. To examine this possibility in research, however, is tricky because, as we have seen in earlier discussions, increasing force on a person to give up a freedom can first result in increasing amounts of negative influence followed by decreasing amounts and eventual positive influence. Thus, to inspect the effects of two or more independent threats to freedom, one must be sure that the combination of threats does not reach beyond the maximum amount of reactance that can be aroused, given the importance of the freedom. If the combination does go beyond the maximum amount of reactance that can be aroused, then it will appear that the combination produces less reactance than would be expected from an additive effect. It is even possible that a combination of threats could produce compliance or positive influence, whereas each threat by itself would produce negative influence. Knowing exactly how strong the threats are relative to the importance of the freedom could be a difficult methodological problem to solve.

Another interesting, and perhaps methodologically more straightforward, problem concerning two or more threats to freedoms is the possibility that the reception of one threat sensitizes a person to any other threats. If sensitization occurs, it might plausibly be thought to magnify the amount of reactance that would occur in response to a particular threat in the absence of sensitization. In other words, if threat A causes

X amount of reactance, it might cause 2X amount of reactance if it occurs after the individual has been sensitized by a prior threat to the *same* freedom. The possibility that this sort of sensitization can occur with different threats to *different* freedoms also was discussed earlier in this volume. It was pointed out that a threat to one freedom might plausibly be expected to sensitize a person to threats to other freedoms, and that this sensitization would presumably depend on reactance from the first threat continuing to exist at the time that the second threat occurs. That is, the sensitization is assumed to be due to the existence of reactance, not to the fact that a prior threat has occurred.

The notion that when reactance exists, people may be hypersensitive to threats to their freedoms has important implications for the understanding of numerous kinds of relationships. For example, if one's spouse or roommate inadvertantly threatens a freedom and the resulting reactance is not reduced, one will then be in a state of hypersensitivity such that the least imposition by the other will be seen as a threat to freedom and a great deal of reactance will result. Small interpersonal problems can thus quickly become blown into major conflicts over control. A similar analysis could be applied to union–management relationships, racial relations, international conflict, etc. The potential importance of a sensitization effect is great and clearly justifies further research to establish if and how it works.

Just as sensitization to threats could account for unusually large reactance effects, so can implied threats. These effects have been found in research already done. What remains to be understood more clearly about implied threats, however, is the rules by which implication operates. This problem is not unlike that of determining what freedoms go together in sets, discussed earlier. What appears to be needed is some sort of mapping of the relationship between freedoms and threats. Without such mapping, the application of reactance theory to real life settings will be constrained.

Loss of Freedom

While the loss of a freedom should arouse some reactance, the present view of reactance theory emphasizes that a person will give up a freedom when it is clear that there is no way to recover it. Presumably, then, the reactance that occurs from the loss dissipates once the freedom has been given up. For example, if a ten-year-old boy is told by his father that he can no longer ride his bicycle on a certain busy street where the boy had been riding for the last year, the well-established freedom would be eliminated. To the extent that this freedom was important to the boy, reactance would be aroused and would impel him to try to restore his freedom. Indeed, we can easily imagine that he would argue vociferously that there was no danger or other reason that he should not go on the busy street as witnessed by his success in the past. If his father were adamant, however, the boy would have to obey or risk parental disapproval, withholding of spending money, etc. If these expected punishments clearly outweighed the importance of the freedom (the potential benefits of riding on the busy street), the boy could be expected to comply with his father's request. As we have already mentioned, there will be some initial reactance from the elimination of freedom, causing initial compliance to be reluctant and partial.

The interesting question, however, is whether the elimination of the freedom will result in the freedom being given up. It is entirely possible for the boy to entertain the idea that through social influence or other events (his father has a spontaneous change of mind) he will soon have his freedom back. How best to conceptualize this state of affairs is not clear. On the one hand, if it is appropriate to say that the freedom has not been given up, then there should be a continued state of reactance with the consequences that (a) compliance will be less than complete, and (b) the desirability of riding on the forbidden street will be relatively great. We might expect, then, that the boy would actively engage in trying to restore his freedom (e.g., persuading his mother to intervene on his behalf), and that so long as the impasse lasted, he would feel intensely frustrated.

But perhaps people respond to eliminations of freedom in a different way. It is at least conceivable that after the initial arousal of reactance due to the elimination, a person can temporarily relinquish a freedom. That is, the boy might concede that for the moment he does not have the freedom but still believe that he will soon regain it. In this case, reactance would dissipate, there would be total compliance, and there would be little frustration. In terms of subjective feelings, the boy would presumably be less unhappy by giving up the freedom than by maintaining it. At the same time, he might hold some hope for future restoration of the freedom, but any motivation to restore freedom would have to come from some source other than reactance (e.g., a belief in an equitable or just world).

In summary, we have little understanding as yet of how people respond to eliminations of freedom. Although there is evidence from research on human helplessness that people whose freedoms are eliminated may feel anxious, angry, and possibly depressed, we do not know how long these effects last nor how they may be affected by hope for or expectations of future restoration of freedom.

The Cognitive Effects of Reactance

The literature on reactance theory attests to the fact that threatened choice alternatives tend to become more attractive, and threats to attitudes can produce boomerang attitude change. Are these reactance effects a direct reflection of the motivational state directed toward restoration of freedom, or are there mediating cognitive processes? If there are mediating cognitive processes, do they take place before, during, or after the change in attractiveness or attitude has occurred?

Reactance aroused in regard to a threatened choice alternative adds to the total amount of motivation to have that alternative. Thus it is reasonable to assume that the resultant increase in the subjective attractiveness of the goal simply reflects this higher motivation. This is equivalent to the notion that a steak looks more attractive to a hungry person than to a satiated person. If this direct linkage holds between motivation and subjective attractiveness, there would seem to be no reason to posit any kind of cognitive mediating process prior to the change in attractiveness. However, there could be cognitive processes that would occur in support of the change in attractiveness and these could occur either during or after the change. That is, attention might be focused on positive characteristics of the outcome in question, or there might be an active search for positive aspects that would justify the increased attraction.

We could further speculate that the stability of the change in attractiveness would then depend on the success there was in finding or focusing on positive characteristics of the threatened alternative. If there were no success, we could expect the attractiveness of the alternative to revert to its original level once freedom was restored. On the other hand, if the search and focusing procedure were successful, the increased attractiveness of the threatened alternative should be stable and should remain even after the threat has been removed. Because the experimental restoration of freedom has typically been immediately after the threat, it has not permitted examination of the possibility that permanent change in attractiveness could occur. However, recent research that has studied the effects of delay in restoring freedom suggests that evaluative changes have some permanency (they are not completely eliminated by a delayed restoration of freedom), and that there are some cognitive (informational) differences associated with reactance effects. It is not yet clear, however, just what role these cognitive processes play concerning reactance-induced change in attractiveness of an alternative.

The role of cognitive processes in association with reactance in attitude change phenomena is potentially important and complex. For example, boomerang attitude change created by the threat in a persuasive communication (e.g., "you must agree") occurs in a context of implicit or explicit pro and con reasons for holding a particular attitudinal position. Hence, we might well expect differential processing of the relevant information as a function of the state of reactance. It would be interesting, for example, to compare attention to or recall of pro and con arguments in a persuasive communication when the freedom threatening statement was at the beginning rather than at the end of the communication. Similarly, it would be interesting to see if either encoding or retrieval of arguments is affected by reactance. It is possible, of course, that encoding and retrieval of arguments would be unaffected, but evaluation of those arguments would be affected.

In short, there are numerous questions about cognitive processes that may mediate or be associated with reactance effects, especially in regard to attitude-change phenomena. These questions, like the others we have raised in this chapter, are fully amenable to empirical investigation. It is our hope that this volume will serve as much to stimulate the endeavors of the future as to mark what has accumulated from the past.

References

Abramowitz, C. V., Abramowitz, S. I., Roback, H. B., & Jackson, C. Differential effectiveness of directive and non-directive group therapies as a function of client internal-external control. *Journal of Consulting and Clinical Psychology*, 1974, *42*, 849–853.

Abramson, L. Y., Seligman, M. E. P., & Teasdale, J. D. Learned helplessness in humans: Critique and reformulation. *Journal of Abnormal Psychology*, 1978, *87*, 49–74.

Albert, S., & Dabbs, J. M. Physical distance and persuasion. *Journal of Personality and Social Psychology*, 1970, *15*, 265–270.

Aletky, P. J., & Carlin, A. S. Sex differences and placebo effects I: Motivation as an intervening variable. *Journal of Consulting and Clinical Psychology*, 1975, *43*, 278.

Allen, V., & Newtson, D. Development of conformity and independence. *Journal of Personality and Social Psychology*, 1972, *22*, 18–30.

Allport, G. W., Vernon, P. E., & Lindzey, G. A. *A study of values.* Boston: Houghton Mifflin, 1960.

American Psychiatric Association Task Force on Nomenclature and Statistics. *Diagnostic and statistical manual of mental disorders* (3rd ed.). Washington, D. C.: American Psychiatric Association, 1980.

Anderson, K. A., & King, H. E. Timeout reconsidered. *Instructional Psychology*, 1974, *1*, 11–17.

Andreoli, V. A., Worchel, S., & Folger, R. Implied threat to behavioral freedom. *Journal of Personality and Social Psychology*, 1974, *30*, 765–771.

Anthony, E. J., & Gilpin, D. C. (Eds.) *Three clinical faces of childhood.* New York: Spectrum Publications, 1976.

Archer, R. L., & Berg, J. H. Disclosure reciprocity and its limits: A reactance analysis. *Journal of Experimental Social Psychology*, 1978, *14*, 527–540.

Ashmore, R. C., Ramchandra, V., & Jones, R. A. *Censorship as an attitude change induction*. Unpublished manuscript, Livingston College, Rutgers University, 1971.

Atkinson, J. W. Motivational determinants of risk-taking behavior. *Psychological Review*, 1957, *64*, 359–372.

Atkinson, J. W., & Feather, N. T. *A theory of achievement motivation*. New York: John Wiley & Sons, 1966.

Averill, J. R. Personal control over aversive stimuli and its relationship to stress. *Psychological Bulletin*, 1973, *80*, 286–303.

Axsom, D., & Cooper, J. Reducing weight by reducing dissonance: The role of effort justification in inducing weight loss. In E. Aronson (Ed.), *Readings about the social animal* (3rd ed.). San Francisco: W. H. Freeman, 1981.

Ayllon, T., Allison, M. G., & Kandel, H. J. *Changing behavior through systematic verbal persuasion*. Unpublished manuscript, Georgia State University, 1980.

Ayllon, T., & Roberts, M. D. Eliminating discipline problems by strengthening academic performance. *Journal of Applied Behavior Analysis*, 1974, *7*, 71–76.

Baer, A., Rowbury, T., & Baer, D. The development of instrumental control over classroom activities of deviant preschool children. *Journal of Applied Behavior Analysis*, 1973, *6*, 289–298.

Baer, R., Hinkle, S., Smith, K., & Fenton, M. Reactance as a function of actual versus projected autonomy. *Journal of Personality and Social Psychology*, 1980, *38*, 416–422.

Bandura, A., & Walters, H. *Adolescent aggression*. New York: Ronald Press, 1959.

Barclay, A. M. Information as a defensive control of sexual arousal. *Journal of Personality and Social Psychology*, 1971, *17*, 244–249.

Barker, R., Dembo, T., & Lewin, K. Frustration and repression: An experiment with young children. University of Iowa Studies, *Studies in Child Welfare*, 1941, XVIII, No. 1.

Baron, R. M., & Ganz, R. L. Effects of locus of control and type of feedback on task performance. *Journal of Personality and Social Psychology*, 1972, *21*, 124–130.

Baruch, D. W., & Wilcox, J. A. A study of sex differences in pre-school children's adjustment coexistent with interparental tensions. *Journal of Genetic Psychology*, 1944, *64*, 281–303.

Baum, A., Aiello, J. R., & Calesnick, L. E. Crowding and personal control: Social density and the development of learned helplessness. *Journal of Personality and Social Psychology*, 1978, *36*, 1000–1011.

Bell, R. Q., Weller, G. M., & Waldrop, M. F. Newborn and preschooler: Organization of behavioral relations between periods. *Monographs of the Society for Research in Child Development*, 1971, *36*, Nos. 1–2.

Benson, P. L., & Catt, V. L. Soliciting charity contribution: The parlance of asking for money. *Journal of Applied Social Psychology*, 1978, *8*, 84–95.

Berkowitz, L. Resistance to improper dependency relationships. *Journal of Experimental Social Psychology*, 1969, *5*, 283–294.

Berkowitz, L. Reactance and the unwillingness to help others. *Psychological Bulletin*, 1973, *79*, 310–317.

Berkowitz, W. R. The impact of protest: Willingness of passersby to make anti-war commitments at anti-Vietnam demonstrations. *Journal of Social Psychology*, 1974, *93*, 31–42.

Best, J. A. Tailoring smoking withdrawal procedures to personality and motivational differences. *Journal of Consulting and Clinical Psychology*, 1975, *43*, 1–8.

Best, J. A., & Steffy, R. A. Smoking modification procedures for internal and external locus of control clients. *Canadian Journal of Behavioral Science*, 1975, *7*, 155–165.

Beutler, L. E. Psychotherapy and persuasion. In L. E. Beutler and R. Greene (Eds.), *Special problems in child and adolescent behavior*. Westport, Conn.: Technomic Press, 1978.

Beutler, L. E. Toward specific psychological therapies for specific conditions. *Journal of Consulting and Clinical Psychology*, 1979, *47*, 882–897.

Bickman, L., & Rosenbaum, D. P. Crime reporting as a function of bystander encouragement, surveillance, and credibility. *Journal of Personality and Social Psychology*, 1977, *35*, 577–586.

Biondo, J., & MacDonald, A. P. Internal-external locus of control and response to influence attempts. *Journal of Personality*, 1971, *39*, 407–419.

Birmingham, S. *Jacqueline Bouvier Kennedy Onassis*. New York: Grosset and Dunlap, 1978.

Bixenstine, V. E., Decorte, M. S., & Bixenstine, B. A. Conformity to peer-sponsored misconduct at four grade levels. *Developmental Psychology*, 1976, *12*, 226–236.

Bowers, K. S. Pain, anxiety, and perceived control. *Journal of Consulting and Clinical Psychology*, 1965, *32*, 596–602.

Bracken, M. B., & Kasl, S. V. Delay in seeking induced abortion: A review and theoretical analysis. *Journal of Obstetrics and Gynecology*, 1975, *121*, 1008–1019.

Brasted, W., Mann, M., & Geller, E. S. Behavioral interventions for litter control: A critical review. *Cornell Journal of Social Relations*, 1979, *14*, 75–90.

Brehm, J. W. *A theory of psychological reactance*. New York: Academic Press, 1966.

Brehm, J. W. Attitude change from threat to attitudinal freedom. In A. G. Greenwald, T. C. Brock, and T. M. Ostrom (Eds.), *Psychological foundations of attitudes*. New York: Academic Press, 1968.

Brehm, J. W. *Perceived difficulty and energization*. Unpublished manuscript, University of Kansas, 1979.

Brehm, J. W., & Cole, A. Effect of a favor which reduces freedom. *Journal of Personality and Social Psychology*, 1966, *3*, 420–426.

Brehm, J. W., Jones, R. A., & Smith, D. *A motivational factor in the prediction of choice*. Unpublished manuscript, Duke University, 1975.

Brehm, J. W., & Mann, M. Effect of importance of freedom and attraction to group members on influence produced by group pressure. *Journal of Personality and Social Psychology*, 1975, *31*, 816–824.

Brehm, J. W., & Rozen, E. Attractiveness of old alternatives when a new, attractive alternative is introduced. *Journal of Personality and Social Psychology*, 1971, *20*, 261–266.

Brehm, J. W., & Sensenig, J. Social influence as a function of attempted and implied usurpation of choice. *Journal of Personality and Social Psychology*, 1966, *4*, 703–707.

Brehm, J. W., Solomon, S., Silka, L., & Toi, M. *Energization and consequent goal attractiveness as a function of the perceived difficulty of a cognitive task*. Unpublished manuscript, University of Kansas, 1980.

Brehm, J. W., Stires, L. K., Sensenig, J., & Shaban, J. The attractiveness of an eliminated choice alternative. *Journal of Experimental Social Psychology*, 1966, *2*, 301–313.

Brehm, J. W., & Wicklund, R. A. Regret and dissonance reduction as a function of postdecision salience of dissonant information. *Journal of Personality and Social Psychology*, 1970, *14*, 1–7.

Brehm, S. S. *The application of social psychology to clinical practice*. Washington, D.C.: Hemisphere, 1976.

Brehm, S. S. The effect of adult influence on children's preference: Compliance vs. opposition. *Journal of Abnormal Child Psychology*, 1977, *5*, 31–41.

Brehm, S. S. Psychological reactance and the attractiveness of unobtainable objects: Sex differences in children's responses to an elimination of freedom. *Sex Roles*, in press.

Brehm, S. S., & Bryant, F. Effects of feedback on self-expressive decision making. *Journal of Personality.* 1976, *44,* 133–148.

Brehm, S. S., & McAllister, D. A. A social psychological perspective on the maintenance of therapeutic change. In P. Karoly and J. J. Steffen (Eds.), *Improving the long-term effects of psychotherapy.* New York: Gardner Press, 1980.

Brehm, S. S., & Weinraub, M. Physical barriers and psychological reactance: 2-year-olds' responses to threats to freedom. *Journal of Personality and Social Psychology,* 1977, *35,* 830–836.

Bridge, G. Parent participation in school innovations. *Teachers College Record,* 1976, *77,* 366–384.

Brigham, T. A. Some effects of choice on academic performance. In L. C. Perlmuter and R. A. Monty (Eds.), *Choice and perceived control.* Hillsdale, N. J.: Lawrence Erlbaum Associates, 1979.

Brock, T. Implication of commodity theory for value exchange. In A. G. Greenwald, T. C. Brock, and T. M. Ostrom (Eds.), *Psychological foundations of attitudes.* New York: Academic Press, 1968.

Broeder, D. The University of Chicago jury project. *Nebraska Law Review,* 1959, *38,* 744–760.

Broll, L., Gross, A. E., & Piliavin, I. Effects of offered and requested help on help seeking and reaction to being helped. *Journal of Applied Social Psychology,* 1974, *4,* 244–258.

Bronfenbrenner, U. Reaction to social pressure from adults versus peers among Soviet day school and boarding school pupils in the perspective of an American sample. *Journal of Personality and Social Psychology,* 1970, *15,* 179–189.

Brounstein, P., Ostrove, N., & Mills, J. Divergence of private evaluations of alternatives prior to a choice. *Journal of Personality and Social Psychology,* 1979, *37,* 1957–1965.

Brounstein, P., & Sigall, H. Effects of dependence and timing of a favor on liking for a favor doer. *Representative Research in Social Psychology,* 1977, *8,* 118–127.

Brown, J. S., & Farber, J. E. Emotions conceptualized as intervening variables—with suggestions toward a theory of frustration. *Psychological Bulletin,* 1951, *48,* 465–495.

Burnkrant, R. E., & Cousineau, A. Informational and normative social influence in buyer behavior. *Journal of Consumer Research,* 1975, *2,* 206–215.

Bushcamp, M. *The mediation of reactance effects through the saliency of another freedom dimension.* Unpublished masters thesis, California State University at Long Beach, 1976.

Byrne, D., & Clore, G. L. Effectance arousal and attraction. *Journal of Personality and Social Psychology Monograph,* 1967, *6* (Whole No. 638).

Cantor, G. N. Sex and race effects in the conformity behavior of upper-elementary school aged children. *Developmental Psychology,* 1975, *11,* 661–662.

Carlsmith, J. M., Ebbesen, E. B., Lepper, M. R., Zanna, M. P., Joncas, A. J., & Abelson, R. P. Dissonance reduction following forced attention to the dissonance. *Proceedings of the 77th Annual Convention of the American Psychological Association,* 1969, *4,* 321–322. (Summary)

Carson, R. C. *Interaction concepts of personality.* Chicago: Aldine, 1969.

Carver, C. S. Self-awareness, perception of threat, and the expression of reactance through attitude change. *Journal of Personality,* 1977, *45,* 501–512.

Carver, C. S. *Self-awareness, self-consciousness, and reactance.* Paper presented at the 1978 American Psychological Association Convention.

Carver, C. S. Perceived coercion, resistance to persuasion, and the Type A behavior pattern. *Journal of Research in Personality,* 1980, *14,* 467–481.

Carver, C. S., & Scheier, M. F. Self-consciousness and reactance. *Journal of Research in Personality*, 1981, *15*, 16–29.

Catania, A. C. Freedom and knowledge: An experimental analysis of preference in pigeons. *Journal of the Experimental Analysis of Behavior*, 1975, *24*, 89–106.

Chanowitz, B., & Langer, E. Knowing more (or less) than you can show: Understanding control through the mindlessness-mindfulness distinction. In J. Garber and M. E. P. Seligman (Eds.), *Human helplessness: Theory and applications*. New York: Academic Press, 1980.

Cherulnik, P. D., & Citrin, M. M. Individual difference in psychological reactance: The interaction between locus of control and mode of elimination of freedom. *Journal of Personality and Social Psychology*, 1974, *29*, 398–404.

Child, I. L. Children's preferences for goals easy or difficult to obtain. *Psychological Monographs*, 1946, *60* (4, Whole No. 280).

Child, I. L., & Adelsheim, E. The motivational value of barriers for young children. *Journal of Genetic Psychology*, 1944, *65*, 97–111.

Christensen, L. The negative subject: Myth, reality, or a prior experimental experience effect? *Journal of Personality and Social Psychology*, 1977, *35*, 392–400.

Clark, D. Behavior therapy of Gilles de la Tourette's syndrome. *British Journal of Psychiatry*, 1966, *112*, 771–778.

Clee, M. A., & Wicklund, R. A. Consumer behavior and psychological reactance. *Journal of Consumer Research*, 1980, *6*, 389–405.

Cochrane, R., & Sobol, M. P. Myth and methodology in behavioral therapy research. In M. P. Feldman and A. Broadhurst (Eds.), *Theoretical and experimental bases of the behavior therapies*. New York: John Wiley & Sons, 1976.

Cohen, A. *Delinquent boys*. Glencoe, Ill.: The Free Press, 1955.

Cohen, S. Aftereffects of stress on human performance and social behavior: A review of research and theory. *Psychological Bulletin*, 1980, *88*, 82–108.

Cohen, S., & Spacapan, S. The aftereffects of stress: An attentional interpretation. *Environmental Psychology and Nonverbal Behavior*, 1978, *3*, 43–57.

Cole, C. S., & Coyne, J. C. Situational specificity of laboratory-induced learned helplessness. *Journal of Abnormal Psychology*, 1977, *86*, 615–623.

Cooper, J. Population control and the psychology of forced compliance. *Journal of Social Issues*, 1974, *30*, 265–277.

Cooper, J. Reducing fears and increasing assertiveness: The role of dissonance reduction. *Journal of Experimental Social Psychology*, 1980, *16*, 199–212.

Cowan, P. A., Hoddinott, B. A., & Wright, B. A. Compliance and resistance in the conditioning of autistic children. *Child Development*, 1965, *36*, 913–923.

Crowne, D., & Liverant, S. Conformity under varying conditions of personal commitment. *Journal of Abnormal and Social Psychology*, 1963, *66*, 547–555.

Davis, D., & Martin, H. J. When pleasure begets pleasure: Recipient responsiveness as a determinant of physical pleasuring between heterosexual dating couples and strangers. *Journal of Personality and Social Psychology*, 1978, *36*, 767–777.

Davis, H. Short-term psychoanalytic therapy with hospitalized schizophrenics. *Psychoanalytic Review*, 1965–66, *52*, 421–448.

Davison, G. C. Countercontrol in behavior modification. In L. A. Hamerlynck, L. C. Handy, and E. J. Mash (Eds.), *Behavior change: Methodology, concepts, and practice*. Champaign, Ill.: Research Press, 1973.

de Charms, R. *Personal causation: The internal affective determinants of behavior*. New York: Academic Press, 1968.

de Charms, R. Personal causation and perceived control. In L. C. Perlmuter and R. A. Monty (Eds.), *Choice and perceived control*. Hillsdale, N. J.: Lawrence Erlbaum Associates, 1979.

Deci, E. L. *Intrinsic motivation.* New York: Plenum Publishing Corp., 1975.

Deci, E. L., & Porac, J. Cognitive evaluation theory and the study of human motivation. In M. R. Lepper and D. Greene (Eds.), *The hidden costs of reward: New perspectives on the psychology of human motivation.* Hillsdale, N. J.: Lawrence Erlbaum Associates, 1978.

DesLauriers, A. M., & Carlson, C. F. *Your child is asleep.* Homewood, Ill.: The Dorsey Press, 1969.

Devine, D. A., & Fernald, P. S. Outcome effects of receiving a preferred, randomly assigned, or nonpreferred therapy. *Journal of Consulting and Clinical Psychology,* 1973, *41,* 104–107.

Dickenberger, D. *Ein neues Konzept der Wichtigkeit von Feiheit: Konsequenzen für die Theorie der Psychologischen Reaktanz.* Doctoral dissertation, Universität Mannheim, 1978. (Weinheim: Beltz, 1979).

Dickenberger, D., & Grabitz-Gniech, G. Restrictive conditions for the occurrence of psychological reactance: Interpersonal attraction, need for social approval, and a delay factor. *European Journal of Social Psychology,* 1972, *2,* 177–198.

Diener, C. I., & Dweck, C. S. An analysis of learned helplessness: Continuous changes in performance, strategy, and achievement cognitions following failure. *Journal of Personality and Social Psychology,* 1978, *36,* 451–462.

Doob, A. N., & Zabrack, M. The effect of freedom-threatening instructions and monetary inducement on compliance. *Canadian Journal of Behavioral Science,* 1971, *3,* 408–412.

Dowd, J. J. Distributive justice and psychological reactance. *Pacific Sociological Review,* 1975, *18,* 421–441.

Driscoll, R., Davis, K. E., & Lipetz, M. E. Parental interference and romantic love: The Romeo and Juliet effect. *Journal of Personality and Social Psychology,* 1972, *24,* 1–10.

Dunlap, K. *Habits: Their making and unmaking.* New York: Liveright Publishing Company, 1932.

Dunlap, K. The teaching of negative practice. *American Journal of Psychology,* 1942, *55,* 270–273.

Durham (N. C.) *Morning Herald,* 16 July 1963.

Duval, S., & Wicklund, R. A. *A theory of objective self awareness.* New York: Academic Press, 1972.

Dweck, C. S. The role of expectations and attributions in the alleviation of learned helplessness. *Journal of Personality and Social Psychology,* 1975, *31,* 674–685.

Dweck, C. S., & Bush, E. S. Sex differences in learned helplessness: I. Differential debilitation with peer and adult evaluators. *Developmental Psychology,* 1976, *12,* 147–156.

Dweck, C. S., Davidson, W., Nelson, S., & Enna, B. Sex differences in learned helplessness: II. The contingencies of evaluative feedback in the classroom and III. An experimental analysis. *Developmental Psychology,* 1978, *14,* 268–276.

Dweck, C. S., & Gilliard, D. Expectancy statements as determinants of reaction to failure: Sex differences in persistence and expectancy change. *Journal of Personality and Social Psychology,* 1975, *32,* 1077–1084.

Dweck, C. S., & Goetz, T. Attribution and learned helplessness. In J. H. Harvey, W. Ickes, and R. F. Kidd (Eds.), *New directions in attribution research,* Vol. 2. Hillsdale, N.J.: Lawrence Erlbaum Associates, 1978.

Dweck, C. S., & Reppucci, N. D. Learned helplessness and reinforcement responsibility in children. *Journal of Personality and Social Psychology,* 1973, *25,* 109–116.

Edney, J. J. Territoriality and control: A field experiment. *Journal of Personality and Social Psychology*, 1975, *31*, 1108–1115.

Edney, J. J., Walker, C. A., & Jordan, N. L. Is there reactance in personal space? *Journal of Social Psychology*, 1976, *100*, 207–218.

Eisenberg, G. M. *The relationship of locus of control to social influence: A test of reactance theory.* Unpublished masters thesis, University of South Florida, 1978.

Ellis, A. *Reason and emotion in psychotherapy.* New York: Lyle Stuart Press, 1962.

Elman, D., & Killebrew, T. J. Incentives and seat belts: Changing a resistant behavior through extrinsic motivation. *Journal of Applied Social Psychology*, 1978, *8*, 72–83.

Feldman-Summers, S. Implications of the buck-passing phenomenon for reactance theory. *Journal of Personality*, 1977, *45*, 543–553.

Fenigstein, A., Scheier, M. F., & Buss, A. H. Public and private self-consciousness: Assessment and theory. *Journal of Consulting and Clinical Psychology*, 1975, *43*, 522–527.

Ferebee, N. S. *Motivation to increase control over an outcome.* Unpublished doctoral dissertation, Duke University, 1975.

Festinger, L. *A theory of cognitive dissonance.* Stanford, Calif.: Stanford Press, 1957.

Festinger, L. *Conflict, decision and dissonance.* Stanford, Calif.: Stanford University Press, 1964.

Fish, J. M. Dissolution of a fused identity in 1 therapeutic session: Case study. *Journal of Consulting and Clinical Psychology*, 1972, *41*, 462–465.

Fisher, J. D., Depaulo, B. M., & Nadler, A. Extending altruism beyond the altruistic act: The mixed effects of aid on the help recipient. In P. Rushton and D. Sorrentino (Eds.), *Altruism and helping behavior.* Hillsdale, N.J.: Lawrence Erlbaum Associates, 1981.

Forehand, R., Cheney, T., & Yoder, P. Parent behavior training: Effects on the noncompliance of a deaf child. *Journal of Behavior Therapy and Experimental Psychiatry*, 1974, *5*, 281–283.

Forehand, R., & King, H. E. Pre-school children's non-compliance: Effects of short-term behavior therapy. *Journal of Community Psychology*, 1974, *2*, 42–44.

Forehand, R., Roberts, H. W., Doleys, D. M., Hobbs, S. A., & Resick, P. A. An examination of disciplinary procedures with children. *Journal of Experimental Child Psychology*, 1976, *21*, 109–120.

Forehand, R., & Scarboro, M. E. An analysis of children's oppositional behavior. *Journal of Abnormal Child Psychology*, 1975, *3*, 27–31.

Frank. J. D. *Persuasion and healing* (Rev. ed.). Baltimore: The Johns Hopkins University Press, 1973.

Frankel, A., & Morris, W. N. Testifying in one's own defense: The ingratiator's dilemma. *Journal of Personality and Social Psychology*, 1976, *34*, 475–480.

Frankenhaeuser, M., & Lundberg, U. Immediate and delayed effects of noise on performance and arousal. *Biological Psychology*, 1974, *2*, 127–133.

Frankl, V. E. Paradoxical intention: A logotherapeutic technique. *American Journal of Psychotherapy*, 1960, *14*, 520–535.

Frankl, V. E. Logotherapy and existential analysis—a review. *American Journal of Psychotherapy*, 1966, *20*, 252–260.

Fraser, S. C., & Fujitomi, I. Perceived prior compliance, psychological reactance, and altruistic contributions. *Proceedings, 80th Annual Convention, American Psychological Association*, 1972.

French, J. R. P., Jr., & Raven, B. The bases of social power. In D. Cartwright (Ed.), *Studies in social power.* Ann Arbor: University of Michigan Press, 1959.

Frey, D., Kumpf, M., Ochsmann, R., Rost-Schaude, E., & Sauer, C. *Eine Theorie der*

Kognitiven Kontrolle. Vortrag gehalten beim 30. Kongress der DGFPs in Regensburg, September, 1976.

Friedland, N. Social influence via threats. *Journal of Experimental Social Psychology,* 1976, *12,* 552–563.

Friedman, M. *Pathogenesis of coronary artery disease.* New York: McGraw-Hill, 1969.

Friedman, M. L., & Dies, R. R. Reaction of internal and external test anxiety students to counseling and behavior therapies. *Journal of Consulting and Clinical Psychology,* 1974, *42,* 921.

Fromm, E. *Escape from freedom.* New York: Rinehart, 1941.

Geer, J. H., Davison, G. C., & Gatchel, R. I. Reduction of stress in humans through non-veridical perceived control of aversive stimulation. *Journal of Personality and Social Psychology,* 1970, *16,* 731–738.

Geller, E. S. Prompting antilitter behaviors. *Proceedings, 81st Annual Convention, American Psychological Association,* 1973.

Geller, E. S., Witner, J. F., & Orebaugh, A. L. Instructions as a determinant of paper-disposal behaviors. *Environment and Behavior,* 1976, *8,* 417–439.

Gergen, K. J. Toward a psychology of receiving help. *Journal of Applied Social Psychology,* 1974, *4,* 187–193.

Gergen, K. J. Experimentation in social psychology: A reappraisal. *European Journal of Social Psychology,* 1978, *8,* 507–528.

Gergen, K. J., Ellsworth, P., Maslach, C., & Seipel, M. Obligation, donor resources, and reactions to aid in three cultures. *Journal of Personality and Social Psychology,* 1975, *31,* 390–400.

Gerz, H. O. Experience with the logotherapeutic technique of paradoxical intention in the treatment of phobic and obsessive-compulsive patients. *American Journal of Psychiatry,* 1966, *123,* 548–553.

Getter, H. A personality determinant of verbal conditioning. *Journal of Personality,* 1966, *34,* 397–405.

Gilbert, L., & Peterson, P. D. *Replication of the Regan and Brehm supermarket study.* Unpublished manuscript, Whitman College, 1971.

Girard, G. The influence of environmental requests on decision: A conflict reduction approach. *Italian Journal of Psychology,* 1977, *IV,* 299–311.

Glass, D. C. *Behavior patterns, stress, and coronary disease.* Hillsdale, N.J.: Lawrence Erlbaum Associates, 1977.

Glass, D. C., & Singer, J. *Urban stress.* New York: Academic Press, 1972.

Glass, D. C., Snyder, M. L., & Hollis, J. F. Time urgency and the Type A coronary-prone behavior pattern. *Journal of Applied Social Psychology,* 1974, *4,* 125–140.

Glueck, S., & Glueck, E. T. *Unraveling juvenile delinquency.* New York: Commonwealth Fund, 1966.

Goetz, E. M., Holmberg, M. C., & LeBlanc, J. M. Differential reinforcement of other behavior and noncontingent reinforcement as control procedures during the modification of a preschooler's compliance. *Journal of Applied Behavior Analysis,* 1975, *8,* 77–82.

Goldberg, S., & Lewis, M. Play behavior in the year-old infant: Early sex differences. *Child Development,* 1969, *40,* 21–31.

Goldfried, M., & Davison, G. *Clinical behavior therapy.* New York: Holt, Rinehart, and Winston, 1976.

Goldman, M., & Wallis, D. Restoring freedom when pressured not to select alternatives. *Psychological Reports,* 1979, *44,* 563–566.

Goldstein, A. P., Heller, K., & Sechrest, L. B. *Psychotherapy and the psychology of behavior change.* New York: John Wiley & Sons, 1966.

Goodstadt, M. Helping and refusing to help: A test of balance and reactance theories. *Journal of Experimental Social Psychology,* 1971, *7,* 610–622.

Gordon, R. M. Effects of volunteering and responsibility on perceived value and effectiveness of a clinical treatment. *Journal of Consulting and Clinical Psychology,* 1976, *44,* 799–801.

Gore, P. M. *Individual differences in the prediction of subject compliance to experimenter bias.* Unpublished doctoral dissertation, Ohio State University, 1962.

Götz-Marchand, B., Götz, J., & Irle, M. Preference of dissonance reduction modes as a function of their order, familiarity and reversibility. *European Journal of Social Psychology,* 1974, *4,* 201–228.

Grabitz-Gniech, G. Some restrictive conditions for the occurrence of psychological reactance. *Journal of Personality and Social Psychology,* 1971, *19,* 188–196.

Grabitz-Gniech, G., Auslitz, K., and Grabitz, H. J. Die Stärke des Reaktanz-Effektes als Funktion der absoluten Grösse und der relativen Reduktion des Freiheitsspielraumes. *Zeitschrift für Sozialpsychologie,* 1975, *6,* 122–128.

Grabitz-Gniech, G., & Grabitz, H. J. Der Einfluss von Freiheitseinengung und Freiheitswiederherstellung auf den Reaktanz-Effekt. *Zeitschrift für Sozialpsychologie,* 1973, *4,* 361–365.

Gross, A. E., Wallston, B. S., & Piliavin, I. M. Reactance, attribution, equity and the help recipient. *Journal of Applied Social Psychology,* 1979, *9,* 297–313.

Gruder, C. L., Cook, T. D., Hennigan, K. M., Flay, B. R., Alessis, C., & Halamaj, J. Empirical tests of the absolute sleeper effect predicted from the discounting cue hypothesis. *Journal of Personality and Social Psychology,* 1978, *36,* 1061–1075.

Haley, J. *Strategies of psychotherapy.* New York: Grune & Stratton, 1963.

Haley, J. *Uncommon therapy: The psychiatric techniques of Milton H. Erickson, M.D.* New York: W. W. Norton & Co., 1973.

Hamm, N. H., & Hoving, K. L. Conformity of children in an ambiguous perceptual situation. *Child Development,* 1969, *40,* 773–784.

Hammock, T., & Brehm, J. W. The attractiveness of choice alternatives when freedom to choose is eliminated by a social agent. *Journal of Personality,* 1966, *34,* 546–554.

Hannah, T. E., Hannah, E. R., & Wattie, B. Arousal of psychological reactance as a consequence of predicting an individual's behavior. *Psychological Reports,* 1975, *37,* 411–420.

Hanusa, B. H., & Schulz, R. Attributional mediators of learned helplessness. *Journal of Personality and Social Psychology,* 1977, *35,* 602–611.

Harris, B., & Harvey, J. H. Social psychological concepts applied to clinical processes: On the need for precision. *Journal of Consulting and Clinical Psychology,* 1978, *46,* 326–328.

Harris, M. B., & Meyer, F. W. Dependency, threat, and helping. *Journal of Social Psychology,* 1973, *90,* 239–242.

Harvey, J. H. Attribution of freedom. In J. H. Harvey, W. J. Ickes, and R. F. Kidd (Eds.), *New directions in attribution research* (Vol. 1). Hillsdale, N. J.: Lawrence Erlbaum Associates, 1976.

Harvey, J. H., Barnes, R. D., Sperry, D. L., & Harris, B. Perceived choice as a function of internal-external locus of control. *Journal of Personality,* 1974, *42,* 437–452.

Harvey, J. H., & Harris, B. Determinants of perceived choice and the relationship between perceived choice and expectancy about feelings of internal control. *Journal of Personality and Social Psychology,* 1975, *31,* 101–106.

Harvey, J. H., & Johnson, S. Determinants of the perception of choice. *Journal of Experimental Social Psychology,* 1973, *9,* 164–179.

Hass, R. G., & Grady, K. Temporal delay, type of forewarning, and resistance to influence. *Journal of Experimental Social Psychology*, 1975, *11*, 459–469.

Hass, R. G., & Linder, D. E. Counterargument availability and effects of message structure on persuasion. *Journal of Personality and Social Psychology*, 1972, *23*, 219–233.

Heilman, M. D. Oppositional behavior as a function of influence attempt intensity and retaliation threat. *Journal of Personality and Social Psychology*, 1976, *33*, 574–578.

Heilman, M. D., & Garner, K. A. Counteracting the boomerang: The effects of choice on compliance to threats and promises. *Journal of Personality and Social Psychology*, 1975, *31*, 911–917.

Heilman, M. D., & Toffler, B. L. Reacting to reactance: An interpersonal interpretation of the need for freedom. *Journal of Experimental Social Psychology*, 1976, *12*, 519–529.

Heller, J. F., Pallak, M. S., & Picek, J. M. The interactive effects of intent and threat on boomerang attitude change. *Journal of Personality and Social Psychology*, 1973, *26*, 273–279.

Henion, K. E., & Batsell, R. D. Marketing of blood donorship, helping behavior, and psychological reactance. *Educators' Proceedings*, American Marketing Association, 1976, 652–656.

Herman, G., & Leyens, J. P. Rating films on T.V. *Journal of Communication*, 1977, *27*, 48–53.

Hiroto, D. S. Locus of control and learned helplessness. *Journal of Experimental Psychology*, 1974, *102*, 187–193.

Hiroto, D. S., & Seligman, M. E. P. Generality of learned helplessness. *Journal of Personality and Social Psychology*, 1975, *31*, 311–327.

Hokanson, J., DeGood, D., Forrest, M., & Brittain, T. Availability of avoidance behaviors in moderating vascular stress responses. *Journal of Personality and Social Psychology*, 1971, *19*, 60–68.

Horowitz, I. A. Effect of choice and locus of dependence on helping behavior. *Journal of Personality and Social Psychology*, 1968, *8*, 373–376.

Houston, B. K. Control over stress, locus of control, and response to stress. *Journal of Personality and Social Psychology*, 1972, *21*, 249–255.

Hunt, R. G., & Hunt, G. W. Some structural features of relations between the department of defense, the national aeronautic and space administration, and their principal contractors. *Social Forces*, 1971, *49*, 414–431.

Jacklin, C. N., Maccoby, E. E., and Dick, A. E. Barrier behavior and toy preference: Sex differences (and their absence) in the year-old child. *Child Development*, 1973, *44*, 196–200.

Jackson, D. D. A suggestion for the technical handling of paranoid patients. *Psychiatry*, 1963, *26*, 306–307.

Jellison, J. M., & Harvey, J. H. Determinants of perceived choice and the relationship between perceived choice and perceived competence. *Journal of Personality and Social Psychology*, 1973, *28*, 376–382.

Jenkins, C. D. Recent evidence supporting psychologic and social risk factors for coronary disease. *The New England Journal of Medicine*, 1976, *294*, 987–994, 1033–1038.

Jenkins, C. D., Zyzanski, S. J., & Rosenman, R. H. Progress toward validation of a computer-scored test for the Type A coronary-prone behavior pattern. *Psychosomatic Medicine*, 1971, *33*, 193–202.

Jesness, C. F. Comparative effectiveness of behavior modification and transactional analysis programs for delinquents. *Journal of Consulting and Clinical Psychology,* 1975, *43,* 758–779.

Johns, J. H., & Quay, A. C. The effect of social reward on verbal conditioning in psychopathic and neurotic military offenders. *Journal of Consulting Psychology,* 1962, *26,* 217–220.

Jones, E. E., & Davis, K. E. From acts to dispositions: The attribution process in person perception. In L. Berkowitz (Ed.), *Advances in experimental social psychology* (Vol. 2). New York: Academic Press, 1965.

Jones, E. E., & Gerard, H. B. *Foundations of social psychology.* New York: John Wiley & Sons, 1967.

Jones, E. E., & Nisbett, R. E. The actor and the observer: Divergent perceptions of the causes of behavior. In E. E. Jones, D. Kanouse, H. H. Kelley, R. E. Nisbett, S. Valins, & B. Weiner (Eds.), *Attribution: Perceiving the causes of behavior.* Morristown, N.J.: General Learning Press, 1972.

Jones, R. A. *Choice, degree of dependence, and the possibility of future dependence on determinants of helping behavior.* Unpublished doctoral dissertation, Duke University, 1969.

Jones, R. A. Volunteering to help: The effects of choice, dependence, and anticipated dependence. *Journal of Personality and Social Psychology,* 1970, *14,* 121–129.

Jones, R. A., & Brehm, J. W. Persuasiveness of one- and two-sided communications as a function of awareness there are two sides. *Journal of Experimental Social Psychology,* 1970, *6,* 47–56.

Jones, R. G. *The Irrational Beliefs Test.* Wichita, Kansas: Test Systems, Inc., 1969.

Jorgenson, D. O. *A field test of reactance theory.* Unpublished manuscript. California State University, Long Beach, 1978.

Kanfer, F. H., & Grimm, L. G. Freedom of choice and behavioral change. *Journal of Consulting and Clinical Psychology,* 1978, *46,* 873–878.

Kazdin, A. E. Evaluating the generality of findings in analogue therapy research. *Journal of Consulting and Clinical Psychology,* 1978, *46,* 673–686.

Kazdin, A. E., & Wilcoxon, L. A. Systematic desensitization and nonspecific treatment effects: A methodological evaluation. *Psychological Bulletin,* 1976, *83,* 729–758.

Kelley, H. H. *Attribution in social interaction.* Morristown, N.J.: General Learning Press, 1971.

Kelly, G. *The psychology of personal constructs.* New York: W. W. Norton & Co., 1955.

Kent, R. A methodological critique of interventions for boys with conduct problems. *Journal of Consulting and Clinical Psychology,* 1976, *44,* 297–299.

Kidder, L. H. On becoming hypnotized: How skeptics become convinced: A case of attitude change. *Journal of Abnormal Psychology,* 1972, *80,* 317–322.

Kiesler, C. A. *The psychology of commitment.* New York: Academic Press, 1971.

Kiesler, C. A., & Pallak, M. S. Arousal properties of dissonance manipulations. *Psychological Bulletin,* 1976, *83,* 1014–1025.

Kiesler, C. A., Roth, T. S., & Pallak, M. S. Avoidance and reinterpretation of commitment and its implications. *Journal of Personality and Social Psychology,* 1974, *30,* 705–715.

Kilman, P. R., Albert, B. M., & Sotile, W. M. Relationship between locus of control, structure of therapy, and outcome. *Journal of Consulting and Clinical Psychology,* 1975, *43,* 588.

Kilman, P. R., & Howell, R. J. The effects of structure of marathon group therapy and locus of control on therapeutic outcome. *Journal of Consulting and Clinical Psychology,* 1974, *42,* 912.

Klinger, E. Consequences of commitment to and disengagement from incentives. *Psycho-

logical Review, 1975, *82*, 1–25.

Kohn, P. M., & Barnes, G. E. Subject variables and reactance to persuasive communications about drugs. *European Journal of Social Psychology*, 1977, *7*, 97–109.

Kopelman, R. E. Psychological stages of careers in engineering: An expectancy thesis taxonomy. *Journal of Vocational Behavior*, 1977, *10*, 270–286.

Kruglanski, A., & Cohen, M. Attributed freedom and personal causation. *Journal of Personality and Social Psychology*, 1973, *26*, 245–250.

Kruglanski, A., & Cohen, M. Attributing freedom in the decision context: Effects of the choice alternatives, degree of commitment and predecision uncertainty. *Journal of Personality and Social Psychology*, 1974, *30*, 178–187.

Kukla, A. Foundations of an attributional theory of performance. *Psychological Review*, 1972, *79*, 454–470.

Lacey, H. M. Control, perceived control, and the methodological role of cognitive constructs. In L. C. Perlmuter and R. A. Monty (Eds.), *Choice and perceived control*. Hillsdale, N.J.: Lawrence Erlbaum Associates, 1979.

Lamontagne, Y. Treatment of erythrophobia by paradoxical intention. *Journal of Nervous and Mental Disease*, 1978, *166*, 304–306.

Langer, E. J., & Rodin, J. The effects of choice and enhanced personal responsibility for the aged: A field experiment in an institutional setting. *Journal of Personality and Social Psychology*, 1976, *34*, 191–198.

Lazarus, R. S. *Psychological stress and the coping process*. New York: McGraw-Hill, 1966.

Lefcourt, H. M. Locus of control for specific goals. In L. C. Perlmuter and R. A. Monty (Eds.), *Choice and perceived control*. Hillsdale, N.J.: Lawrence Erlbaum Associates, 1979.

Lerner, M. J., Miller, D. T., & Holmes, J. G. Deserving and the emergence of forms of justice. In L. Berkowitz (Ed.), *Advances in experimental social psychology* (Vol. 9). New York: Academic Press, 1976.

Lerner, M. J., & Simmons, C. H. Observers' reactions to the "innocent victim": Compassion or rejection? *Journal of Personality and Social Psychology*, 1966, *4*, 203–210.

Leventhal, H., & Mace, W. The effect of laughter on the evaluation of a slapstick movie. *Journal of Personality*, 1970, *38*, 16–30.

Lewin, K., Dembo, T., Festinger, L., & Sears, P. Level of aspiration. In J. McV. Hunt (Ed.), *Personality and the behavior disorders* (Vol. 1). New York: Ronald Press, 1944.

Linder, D. E., & Crane, K. A. Reactance theory analysis of predecisional cognitive processes. *Journal of Personality and Social Psychology*, 1970, *15*, 258–264.

Linder, D. E., & Worchel, S. Opinion change as a result of effortfully drawing a counterattitudinal conclusion. *Journal of Experimental Social Psychology*, 1970, *6*, 432–448.

Linder, D. E., Wortman, C. B., & Brehm, J. W. Temporal changes in predecision preferences among choice alternatives. *Journal of Personality and Social Psychology*, 1971, *19*, 282–284.

Lindner, R. *The fifty minute hour*. Toronto: Clarke, Irwin, 1954.

Lohr, J., & Bonge, D. *The relationship of coronary-prone behavior and irrational beliefs in college-age and middle-age males.* Paper presented at the first annual meeting of the Society for Behavioral Medicine, San Francisco, 1979.

Love, L. R., Kaswan, J., & Bugental, D. E. Differential effects of 3 clinical interventions for different socioeconomic groupings. *Journal of Consulting and Clinical Psychology*, 1972, *39*, 347–360.

Lytton, H. Correlates of compliance and the rudiments of conscience in two-year-old boys. *Canadian Journal of Behavioral Science*, 1977, *9*, 242–251.

Lytton, H. Disciplinary encounters between young boys and their mothers and fathers: Is there a contingency system. *Developmental Psychology,* 1979, *15,* 256–268.

Lytton, H., & Zwirner, W. Compliance and its controlling stimuli observed in a natural setting. *Developmental Psychology,* 1975, *11,* 769–779.

Malleson, N. Panic and phobia. *Lancet,* 1959, *1,* 225–227

Manderscheid, R. W. A theory of spatial effects. In R. Trappl & F. R. Pichler (Eds.), Progress in cybernetics and systems research (Vol. 1). Washington, D. C.: Hemisphere Publishing Corp., 1975.

Mandler, G. Helplessness: Theory and research in anxiety. In C. D. Spielberger (Ed.), *Anxiety: Current trends in theory and research* (Vol. 2). New York: Academic Press, 1972.

Mann, M. F., Brasted, W. S., & Geller, E. S. *Limiting conditions on facilitating litter control.* Unpublished manuscript, Virginia Polytechnic Institute and State University, 1979.

Manuck, S. B., Craft, S., & Gold, K. Coronary-prone behavior pattern and cardiovascular response. *Psychophysiology,* 1978, *15,* 403–411.

Mazis, M. B. Antipollution measures and psychological reactance theory: A field experiment. *Journal of Personality and Social Psychology,* 1975, *31,* 654–660.

Mazis, M. B., Settle, R. B., & Leslie, D. C. Elimination of phosphate detergents and psychological reactance. *Journal of Marketing Research,* 1973, *10,* 390–395.

McCord, W., McCord, J., & Zola, I. K. *Origins of crime.* New York: Columbia University Press, 1959.

McGillis, D. B., & Brehm, J. W. *Compliance as a function of inducements that threaten freedom and of modeling behavior that implies restoration of freedom.* Unpublished manuscript, Williams College, 1975.

Miller, A. G. Actor and observer perceptions of the learning of a task. *Journal of Experimental Social Psychology,* 1975, *11,* 95–111.

Miller, D. T., & Norman, S. A. Actor–observer differences in perception of effective control. *Journal of Personality and Social Psychology,* 1975, *31,* 503–515.

Miller, D. T., Norman, S. A., & Wright, E. Distortion in person perception as a consequence of the need for effective control. *Journal of Personality and Social Psychology,* 1978, *36,* 598–607.

Miller, R. L., Brickman, P., & Bolen, D. Attribution versus persuasion as a means for modifying behavior. *Journal of Personality and Social Psychology,* 1975, *31,* 430–441.

Mills, J. Interest in supporting and discrepant information. In R. P. Abelson, E. Aronson, W. J. McQuire, T. M. Newcomb, M. J. Rosenberg, & P. H. Tannenbaum (Eds.), *Theories of cognitive consistency: A sourcebook.* Chicago: Rand McNally, 1968.

Mills, J., & O'Neal, E. Anticipated choice, attention and the halo effect. *Psychonomic Science,* 1971, *22,* 231–233.

Minton, C., Kagan, J., & Levine, J. A. Maternal control and obedience in the two-year old. *Child Development,* 1971, *42,* 1873–1894.

Mirels, H. L. Dimensions of internal vs. external control. *Journal of Consulting and Clinical Psychology,* 1970, *34,* 226–228.

Monson, T. C., & Snyder, M. Actors, observers, and the attribution process: Toward a reconstruction. *Journal of Experimental Social Psychology,* 1977, *13,* 89–111.

Morganstern, K. Implosive therapy and flooding procedures: A critical review. *Psychological Bulletin,* 1973, *79,* 318–334.

Morse, S. J., Gergen, K. J., Peele, S., & van Ryneveld, J. Reactions to receiving expected and unexpected help from a person who violates or does not violate a norm. *Journal of Experimental Social Psychology*, 1977, *13*, 397–402.

Moscovici, S., & Neve, P. Studies in social influence: 1. Those absent are in the right: Convergence and polarization of answers in the course of a social interaction. *European Journal of Social Psychology*, 1971, *1*, 201–214.

Mowday, R. T. The exercise of upward influence in organization. *Administrative Science Quarterly*, 1978, *23*, 137–156.

Moyer, W. W. Effects of loss of freedom on subjects with internal or external locus of control. *Journal of Research in Personality*, 1978, *12*, 253–261.

Mugny, G. La liberté des choix. In W. Doise, J. C. Deschamps, and G. Mugny (Eds.), *Psychologie sociale experimentale*. Paris: Armaud Colin, 1978.

Mugny, G., & Doise, W. Niveaux d'analyse dans l'etude experimentale des processus d'influence sociale. *Social Science Information*, 1979, 6.

Newton, J. R. Considerations for the psychotherapeutic technique of symptom scheduling. *Psychotherapy: Theory, Research and Practice*, 1968, *5*, 95–103. (a)

Newton, J. R. Therapeutic paradoxes. *American Journal of Psychotherapy*, 1968, *22*, 68–81. (b)

Nezlek, J., & Brehm, J. W. Hostility as a function of the opportunity to counteraggress. *Journal of Personality*, 1975, *43*, 421–433.

Nisbett, R. E., Caputo, C., Legant, P., & Marecek, J. Behavior as seen by the actor and as seen by the observer. *Journal of Personality and Social Psychology*, 1973, *27*, 154–164.

Novaco, R. W. Treatment of chronic anger through cognitive and relaxation controls. *Journal of Consulting and Clinical Psychology*, 1976, *44*, 681.

O'Neal, E. Influence of future choice importance and arousal on the halo effect. *Journal of Personality and Social Psychology*, 1971, *19*, 334–340.

O'Neal, E., & Mills, J. The influence of anticipated choice on the halo effect. *Journal of Experimental Social Psychology*, 1969, *5*, 347–351.

Organ, D. Social exchange and psychological reactance in a simulated superior–subordinate relationship. *Organizational Behavior and Human Performance*, 1974, *12*, 132–142.

Pallak, M. S., & Heller, J. F. Interactive effects of commitment to future interaction and threat to attitudinal freedom. *Journal of Personality and Social Psychology*, 1971, *17*, 325–331.

Pallak, M. S., & Sullivan, J. J. The effect of commitment, threat and restoration of freedom on attitude-change and action-taking. *Personality and Social Psychology Bulletin*, 1979, *5*, 307–310.

Pasternack, T. L. Qualitative differences in development of yielding behavior by elementary school children. *Psychological Reports*, 1973, *32*, 883–896.

Patterson, G. R. Interventions for boys with conduct problems: Multiple settings, treatments, criteria. *Journal of Consulting and Clinical Psychology*, 1974, *42*, 471–481.

Patterson, G. R. *Families* (Revised). Champaign, Ill.: Research Press, 1975.

Patterson, G. R. The aggressive child: Victim and architect of a coercive system. In E. Mash, L. A. Hamerlynck, & L. C. Handy (Eds.), *Behavior modification and families*. New York: Brunner/Mazel, 1976. (a)

Patterson, G. R. *Living with children* (Revised). Champaign, Ill.: Research Press, 1976. (b)

Patterson, G. R., Littman, I., & Brown, T. R. Negative set and social learning. *Journal of Personality and Social Psychology*, 1968, *8*, 109–115.

Pennebaker, J. W., Dyer, M. A., Caulkins, R. S., Litowitz, D. L., Ackreman, P. L., Anderson, D. B., & McGraw, K. M. Don't the girls get prettier at closing time: A country and western application to psychology. *Personality and Social Psychology Bulletin*, 1979, 5, 122–125.

Pennebaker, J. W., & Sanders, D. Y. American graffiti: Effects of authority and reactance arousal. *Personality and Social Psychology Bulletin*, 1976, 2, 264–267.

Peterson, R. F., & Whitehurst, G. J. A variable influencing the performance of generalized imitation. *Journal of Applied Behavior Analysis*, 1971, 4, 1–9.

Piliavin, I., & Gross, A. E. The effects of separation of services and income maintenance on AFDC recipients. *Social Service Review*, 1977, 51, 389–406.

Pittman, N. L., & Pittman, T. S. Effects of amount of helplessness training and internal-external locus of control on mood and performance. *Journal of Personality and Social Psychology*, 1979, 37, 39–47.

Pittman, T. S., & Pittman, N. L. Deprivation of control and the attribution process. *Journal of Personality and Social Psychology*, 1980, 39, 377–389.

Proshansky, H. M., Ittelson, W. H., & Rivlin, L. G. (Eds.), *Environmental psychology*. New York: Holt, Rinehart, & Winston, 1970.

Proshansky, H. M., Ittelson, W. H., & Rivlin, L. G. (Eds.). *Environmental psychology* (2nd ed.). New York: Holt, Rinehart, & Winston, 1976.

Quay, H., & Hunt, W. A. Psychopathy, neuroticism, and verbal conditioning. *Journal of Consulting Psychology*, 1965, 29, 283.

Raskin, D. E., & Klein, Z. E. Losing a symptom through keeping it: A review of paradoxical treatment techniques and rationale. *Archives of General Psychiatry*, 1976, 33, 548–555.

Read, R. H. Parents' expressed attitudes and children's behavior. *Journal of Consulting Psychology*, 1945, 9, 95–100.

Redd, W. H. Social control by adult preference in operant conditioning with children. *Journal of Experimental Child Psychology*, 1974, 17, 61–78.

Redd, W. H., & Wheeler, A. J. The relative effectiveness of monetary reinforcers and adult instructions in the control of children's choice behavior. *Journal of Experimental Child Psychology*, 1973, 16, 63–75.

Regan, J. W., & Brehm, J. W. Compliance in buying as a function of inducements that threaten freedom. In L. Bickman and T. Henchy (Eds.), *Beyond the laboratory: Field research in social psychology*. New York: McGraw-Hill, 1972.

Reich, J. W., & Robertson, J. L. Reactance and norm appeal in anti-littering messages. *Journal of Applied Social Psychology*, 1979, 9, 91–101.

Reid, J. B., & Patterson, G. R. Follow-up analyses of a behavioral treatment program for boys with conduct problems. *Journal of Consulting and Clinical Psychology*, 1976, 44, 299–302.

Reizenstein, R. C. A dissonance approach to measuring the effectiveness of two personal selling techniques through decision reversal. *Proceedings*, American Marketing Association, 1971, 176–180.

Rice, D. P., & Schoenfeld, L. S. Aversive conditioning and cognitive mediators with alcoholic respondents. *British Journal of Addiction*. 1975, 70, 165–174.

Ritchie, E., & Phares, E. Attitude change as a function of internal–external control and communicator status. *Journal of Personality*, 1969, 37, 429–443.

Robertson, T. S., and Rossiter, J. R. Children and commercial persuasion: An attribution theory analysis. *Journal of Consumer Research*, 1974, 1, 13–20.

Rodin, J. Density, perceived choice, and response to controllable and uncontrollable outcomes. *Journal of Experimental Social Psychology*, 1976, 12, 564–578.

Rodin, J., Rennert, K., & Solomon, S. K. Intrinsic motivation for control: fact or fiction. In A. Baum & J. E. Singer (Eds.), *Advances in environmental psychology* (Vol. 2). Hillsdale, N. J.: Lawrence Erlbaum Associates, 1980.

Rodrigues, A. Motivational forces of cognitive dissonance and psychological reactance. *International Journal of Psychology*, 1970, *5*, 89–98.

Rosen, B., & Jerdee, T. H. Effects of employee's sex and threatening versus pleading appeals on managerial evaluations of grievances. *Journal of Applied Psychology*, 1975, *60*, 442–445.

Rosen, B., & Mericle, M. F. *The influence of strong versus weak fair employment policies and applicant's sex on selection decisions and salary recommendations in a management simulation.* Unpublished paper, University of North Carolina, 1979.

Rosen, J. *Direct Psychoanalysis.* New York: Grune & Stratton, 1953.

Rosenberg, M. J. Cognitive reorganization in response to the hypnotic reversal of attitudinal affect. *Journal of Personality*, 1960, *28*, 39–63.

Rosenthal, M. J., Finkelstein, M., Ni, E., & Robertson, R. E. A study of mother-child relationships in the emotional disorders of children. *Genetic Psychology Monographs*, 1959, *60*, 65–116.

Rosenthal, M. J., Ni, E., Finkelstein, M., & Berkwits, G. K. Father–child relationships and children's problems. *Archives of General Psychiatry*, 1962, *7*, 360–373.

Rosnow, R. L., & Davis, D. J. Demand characteristics and the psychological experiment. *Et cetera*, 1977, *14*, 301–313.

Roth, S., & Bootzin, R. R. Effects of experimentally induced expectancies of external control: An investigation of learned helplessness. *Journal of Personality and Social Psychology*, 1974, *29*, 253–264.

Roth, S., & Kubal, S. The effects of noncontingent reinforcement on tasks of differing importance: Facilitation and learned helplessness effects. *Journal of Personality and Social Psychology*, 1975, *32*, 680–691.

Rotter, J. B. Generalized expectancies for internal versus external control of reinforcement. *Psychological Monographs*, 1966, *80* (1, Whole No. 609).

Rozen, E. L. *Effects of a reactance manipulation on compliance in an experimental situation.* Unpublished masters thesis, State University of New York at Stony Brook, 1970.

Rubin, Z., & Moore, J. C. Assessment of subjects' suspicions. *Journal of Personality and Social Psychology*, 1971, *17*, 163–170.

Rumm, D. C., & Masters, J. C. *Behavior therapy: Techniques and empirical findings* (2nd ed.). New York: Academic Press, 1979.

Russ, R. C., Gold, J. A., & Stone, W. F. Attraction to a similar stranger as a function of level of effectance arousal. *Journal of Experimental Social Psychology*, 1979, *15*, 481–491.

Ryckman, R., Rodda, W., & Sherman, M. Locus of control and expertise relevance as determinants of changes in opinion about student activities. *Journal of Social Psychology*, 1972, *88*, 107–114.

Samuel, W. Response to bill of rights paraphrases as influenced by the hip or straight attire of the opinion solicitor. *Journal of Applied Social Psychology*, 1972, *2*, 47–62.

Savage, R. E., Perlmuter, L. C., & Monty, R. A. Effect of reduction in the amount of choice and the perception of control on learning. In L. C. Perlmuter and R. A. Monty (Eds.), *Choice and perceived control.* Hillsdale, N.J.: Lawrence Erlbaum Associates, 1979.

Scarboro, M. E., & Forehand, R. Effects of two types of response contingent time-out on compliance and oppositional behavior of children. *Journal of Experimental Child Psychology*, 1975, *19*, 252–264.

Schaps, E. Cost, dependency, and helping. *Journal of Personality and Social Psychology*, 1972, *21*, 74–78.

Schmidt, D. E., Goldman, R. D., & Feimer, N. R. Perceptions of crowding. *Environment and Behavior*, 1979, *11*, 105–130.

Schopler, J., & Matthews, M. W. The influence of the perceived causal locus of partner's dependence on the use of interpersonal power. *Journal of Personality and Social Psychology*, 1965, *2*, 609–612.

Schopler, J., & Thompson, V. D. Role of attribution processes in mediating amount of reciprocity for a favor. *Journal of Personality and Social Psychology*, 1968, *10*, 243–250.

Schulz, R. Effects of control and predictability on the psychological well-being of the aged. *Journal of Personality and Social Psychology*, 1976, *33*, 563–573.

Schwartz, S. H. Elicitation of moral obligation and self-sacrificing behavior: An experimental study of volunteering to be a bone marrow donor. *Journal of Personality and Social Psychology*, 1970, *15*, 283–293.

Schwarz, N. *Experimentelle Untersuchungen zur Reduktion von Reaktanz durch Freiheitswiederherstellung.* Doctoral dissertation, Universität Mannheim, 1980.

Schwarz, N., Frey, D., & Kumpf, M. Interactive effects of writing and reading a persuasive essay on attitude change and selective exposure. *Journal of Experimental Social Psychology*, 1980, *16*, 1–17.

Seipel, C. M. Premiums—Forgotten by theory. *Journal of Marketing*, 1971, *35*, 26–34.

Seligman, M. E. P. Learned helplessness. *Annual Review of Medicine*, 1972, *23*, 407–412.

Seligman, M. E. P. *Helplessness: On depression, development, and death.* San Francisco: W. H. Freeman, 1975.

Seligman, M. E. P., & Maier, S. F. Failure to escape traumatic shock. *Journal of Experimental Psychology*, 1967, *74*, 1–9.

Sensenig, J., & Brehm, J. W. Attitude change from an implied threat to attitudinal freedom. *Journal of Personality and Social Psychology*, 1968, *8*, 324–330.

Seta, J. J., & Seta, C. E. *The relationship between effort or cost and the value of a goal object: An empirical and theoretical analysis.* Unpublished manuscript, University of North Carolina at Greensboro, 1980.

Shaver, K. G. Defensive attribution: Effects of severity and relevance on the responsibility assigned for an accident. *Journal of Personality and Social Psychology*, 1970, *14*, 101–113.

Sheras, P., & Worchel, S. *Clinical psychology: A social psychological approach.* New York: D. Van Nostrand, 1979.

Sherrod, D. R. Crowding, perceived control, and behavioral aftereffects. *Journal of Applied Social Psychology*, 1974, *4*, 171–186.

Sherrod, D. R., Hage, J. N., Halpern, P. L., & Moore, B. S. Effects of personal causation and perceived control on responses to an aversive environment: The more control, the better. *Journal of Experimental Social Psychology*, 1977, *13*, 14–27.

Sistrunk, F., & McDavid, J. W. Sex variable in conforming behavior. *Journal of Personality and Social Psychology*, 1971, *17*, 200–207.

Sloan, L. R., Love, R. E., & Ostrom, T. M. Political heckling: Who really loses? *Journal of Personality and Social Psychology*, 1974, *30*, 518–525.

Sloane, R. B., Staples, F. R., Cristol, A. H., Yorkston, N. J., & Whipple, K. *Psychotherapy versus behavior therapy.* Cambridge, Mass.: Harvard University Press, 1975.

Smith, R. E., & Flenning, F. Need for approval and susceptibility to unintended social influence. *Journal of Consulting and Clinical Psychology*, 1971, *36*, 383–385.

Smith, T. W. *Person perception and the coronary-prone behavior pattern*. Unpublished masters thesis, University of Kansas, 1980.

Smith, T. W., & Brehm, S. S. *Cognitive correlates of the Type A coronary-prone behavior pattern. Motivation and Emotion*, in press.

Snyder, M. L., & Wicklund, R. A. Prior exercise of freedom and reactance. *Journal of Experimental Social Psychology*, 1976, *12*, 120–130.

Snyder, M. L., & Wicklund, R. A. Personal communication, September 1980.

Snyder, M. L., & Wicklund, R. A. Attribute ambiguity. In J. H. Harvey, W. J. Ickes, & R. F. Kidd (Eds.), *New directions in attribution research* (Vol. 3). Hillsdale, N.J.: Lawrence Erlbaum Associates, 1981.

Solomon, S. K. *Control-seeking behavior: Are people motivated to attain control?* Unpublished manuscript, Yale University, 1976.

Solyom, L., Garza-Perez, J., Ledwidge, B. L., & Solyom, C. Paradoxical intention in the treatment of obsessive thoughts: A pilot study. *Comparative Psychiatry*, 1972, *3*, 291–297.

Spitz, C. J., Gold, A. R., & Adams, D. B. Cognitive and hormonal factors affecting coital frequency. *Archives of Sexual Behavior*, 1975, *4*, 249–263.

Stampfl, T. G., & Levis, D. J. Essentials of implosive therapy: A learning theory-based psychodynamic behavioral therapy. *Journal of Abnormal Psychology*, 1967, *72*, 496–503.

Stampfl, T. G., & Levis, D. J. *Implosive therapy: Theory and technique*. Morristown, N.J.: General Learning Press, 1973.

Staub, E. The use of role playing and induction in children's learning of helping and sharing behavior. *Child Development*, 1971, *42*, 805–816.

Staub, E. Effects of persuasion and modeling on delay of gratification. *Developmental Psychology*, 1972, *6*, 166–177.

Stayton, D. J., Hogan, R., & Ainsworth, M. D. S. Infant obedience and maternal behavior: The origins of socialization reconsidered. *Child Development*, 1971, *42*, 1057–1069.

Steiner, I. Perceived freedom. In L. Berkowitz (Ed.), *Advances in experimental social psychology* (Vol. 5). New York: Academic Press, 1970.

Stivers, M., & Brehm, S. S. *The influence of perceived personal control on responses to communications concerning sources of control*. Unpublished manuscript, University of Kansas, 1980.

Stokols, D. A social-psychological model of human crowding phenomena. *Journal of the American Institute of Planners*, 1972, *38*, 72–83.

Storms, M. D., & McCaul, K. D. Attribution processes and emotional exacerbation of dysfunctional behavior. In J. H. Harvey, W. J. Ickes, & R. F. Kidd (Eds.), *New directions in attribution research* (Vol. 1). Hillsdale, N.J.: Lawrence Erlbaum Associates, 1976.

Strassberg, D., & Wiggin, E. Conformity as a function of age in preadolescents. *Journal of Social Psychology*, 1973, *91*, 61–66.

Strickland, B. R. Individual difference in verbal conditioning, extinction and awareness. *Journal of Personality*, 1970, *38*, 364–378.

Sue, S., Smith, R., & Caldwell, C. Effects of inadmissible evidence on the decisions of simulated jurors: A moral dilemma. *Journal of Applied Social Psychology*, 1973, *3*, 345–353.

Suedfeld, P., & Vernon, J. Attitude manipulation in restricted environments: II. Conceptual structure and the internalization of propaganda received as a reward for compliance. *Journal of Personality and Social Psychology*, 1966, *3*, 586–589.

Sullivan, J. J., & Pallak, M. S. The effect of commitment and reactance on action-taking. *Personality and Social Psychology Bulletin*, 1976, *2*, 179–182.

Summers, D. A., Ashworth, C. D., & Feldman-Summers, S. Judgment processes and interpersonal conflict related to societal problem solutions. *Journal of Applied Social Psychology*, 1977, *7*, 163–174.

Swann, W. B., Jr., Stephenson, B., & Pittman, T. S. Curiosity and control: On the determinants of the search for social knowledge. *Journal of Personality and Social Psychology*, 1981, *40*, 635–642.

Taplin, P. *Changes in parental consequation as a function of intervention.* Unpublished doctoral dissertation, University of Wisconsin, 1974.

Taylor, S. E. Hospital patient behavior: Reactance, helplessness, or control. *Journal of Social Issues*, 1979, *35*, 156–184.

Tennen, H., Rohrbaugh, M., Press, S., & White, M. D. Reactance theory and therapeutic paradox: A compliance-defiance model. *Psychotherapy: Theory, Research and Practice*, 1981, *18*, 14–22.

Tetlock, P. E., & Suedfeld, P. Inducing belief instability without a persuasive message: The roles of attitude centrality, individual cognitive differences, and sensory deprivation. *Canadian Journal of Behavioral Science*, 1976, *8*, 324–333.

Thornton, J. W., & Jacobs, P. D. Learned helplessness in human subjects. *Journal of Experimental Psychology*, 1971, *87*, 367–372.

Tjosvold, D. Cooperation and conflict between administrators and teachers. *Journal of Research and Development in Education*, 1978, *12*, 138–148.

Trope, Y. Extrinsic rewards, congruence between dispositions and behaviors, and perceived freedom. *Journal of Personality and Social Psychology*, 1978, *36*, 588–597.

Trope, Y., & Burnstein, E. A disposition–behavior congruity model of perceived freedom. *Journal of Experimental Social Psychology*, 1977, *13*, 357–368.

Turner, C. W., & Simons, L. S. Effects of subject sophistication and evaluation apprehension on aggressive responses to weapons. *Journal of Personality and Social Psychology*, 1974, *30*, 341–348.

Utrech, D. A., & Hoving, K. L. Parents and peers as competing influences in the decisions of children of differing ages. *Journal of Social Psychology*, 1969, *78*, 267–274.

Van Lieshout, C. F. M. Young children's reactions to barriers placed by their mothers. *Child Development*, 1975, *46*, 879–886.

Varela, J. A. *Psychological solutions to social problems.* New York: Academic Press, 1971.

Varela, J. A. Social technology. *American Psychologist*, 1977, *32*, 914–923.

Varela, J. A. Solving human problems with human science. *Human Nature*, 1978, *1*, 84–90.

Ventimiglia, J. C. Career commitment among continuing and exiting seminary students. *Sociological Analysis*, 1977, *38*, 49–58.

Voss, S. C., & Homzie, M. J. Choice as a value. *Psychological Reports*, 1970, *26*, 912–914.

Wahler, R. G. Oppositional children: A quest for parental reinforcement control. *Journal of Applied Behavior Analysis*, 1969, *2*, 159–170.

Wallston, B. S., Wallston, K. A., Kaplan, G. D., & Maides, S. A. Development and validation of the health locus of control (HLC) scale. *Journal of Consulting and Clinical Psychology*, 1976, *44*, 580–585.

Walster, E. Assignment of responsibility for an accident. *Journal of Personality and Social Psychology*, 1966, *3*, 73–79.

Walster, E., Walster, G. W., Piliavin, J., & Schmidt, L. "Playing hard to get": Understanding an elusive phenomenon. *Journal of Personality and Social Psychology*, 1973, 26, 113–121.

Walter, H. F., & Gilmore, S. K. Placebo vs. social learning effects in parent training procedures to alter the behavior of aggressive boys. *Behavior Therapy*, 1973, 4, 361–377.

Wandersman, A. *Participation, choice, and freedom in planning dormitory environments: Exploring concepts concerning freedom.* Paper presented at Southeastern Psychological Association meeting, New Orleans, March, 1976.

Watzlawick, P., Beavin, J. H., & Jackson, D. D. *Pragmatics of human communication.* New York: W. W. Norton, 1967.

Wellins, R., & McGinnies, E. Counterarguing and selective exposure to persuasion. *Journal of Social Psychology*, 1977, 103, 115–127.

West, S. G. Increasing the attractiveness of college cafeteria food: A reactance theory perspective. *Journal of Applied Psychology*, 1975, 60, 656–658.

White, G. D., Nielson, G., & Johnson, S. M. Time-out duration and the suppression of deviant behavior in children. *Journal of Applied Behavior Analysis*, 1972, 5, 111–120.

White, R. W. Motivation reconsidered: The concept of competence. *Psychological Review*, 1959, 66, 297–333.

Wicklund, R. A. Prechoice preference reversal as a result of threat to decision freedom. *Journal of Personality and Social Psychology*, 1970, 14, 8–17.

Wicklund, R. A. *Freedom and reactance.* Potomac, Md.: Lawrence Erlbaum Associates, 1974.

Wicklund, R. A. Objective self-awareness. In L. Berkowitz (Ed.), *Advances in experimental social psychology* (Vol. 8). New York: Academic Press, 1975.

Wicklund, R. A., & Brehm, J. W. Attitude change as a function of felt competence and threat to attitudinal freedom. *Journal of Experimental Social Psychology*, 1968, 4, 64–75.

Wicklund, R. A., & Brehm, J. W. *Perspectives on cognitive dissonance.* Hillsdale, N.J.: Lawrence Erlbaum Associates, 1976.

Wicklund, R. A., Slattum, V., & Solomon, E. Effects of implied pressure toward commitment on ratings of choice alternatives. *Journal of Experimental Social Psychology*, 1970, 6, 449–457.

Willis, J. A., & Goethals, G. R. Social responsibility and threat to behavioral freedom as determinants of altruistic behavior. *Journal of Personality*, 1973, 41, 376–384.

Winett, R. A. Attribution of attitude and behavior change and its relevance to behaviortherapy. *The Psychological Record*, 1970, 20, 17–32.

Winston, A. S., & Redd, W. H. Instructional control as a function of adult presence and competing reinforcement contingencies. *Child Development*, 1976, 47, 264–268.

Wolf, S., & Montgomery, D. A. Effects of inadmissible evidence and level of judicial admonishment to disregard on the judgments of mock jurors. *Journal of Applied Social Psychology*, 1977, 7, 205–219.

Wolosin, R. J., Esser, J., & Fine, G. A. Effects of justification and vocalization on actors' and observers' attributions of freedom. *Journal of Personality*, 1975, 43, 612–633.

Wolpe, J. *Psychotherapy by reciprocal inhibition.* Stanford, Calif.: Stanford University Press, 1959.

Worchel, S. *The effect of simple frustration, violated expectancy, and reactance on the instigation to aggression.* Unpublished doctoral dissertation, Duke University, 1971.

Worchel, S. The effects of films on the importance of behavioral freedom. *Journal of Personality*, 1972, 40, 417–435.

Worchel, S. The effect of three types of arbitrary thwarting on the instigation to aggression. *Journal of Personality*, 1974, *42*, 300–318.

Worchel, S., & Andreoli, V. A. Attribution of causality as a means of restoring behavioral freedom. *Journal of Personality and Social Psychology*, 1974, *29*, 237–245.

Worchel, S., & Andreoli, V. A. Escape to freedom: The relationship between attribution of causality and psychological reactance. In J. H. Harvey, W. J. Ickes, and R. F. Kidd (Eds.), *New directions in attribution research* (Vol. I). Hillsdale, N.J.: Lawrence Erlbaum Associates, 1976.

Worchel, S., Andreoli, V. A., & Archer, R. When is a favor a threat to freedom: The effects of attribution and importance of freedom on reciprocity. *Journal of Personality*, 1976, *44*, 294–310.

Worchel, S., & Arnold, S. E. The effects of censorship and attractiveness of the censor on attitude change. *Journal of Experimental Social Psychology*, 1973, *9*, 365–377.

Worchel, S., Arnold, S. E., & Baker, M. The effect of censorship on attitude change: The influence of censor and communication characteristics. *Journal of Applied Social Psychology*, 1975, *5*, 222–239.

Worchel, S., & Brehm, J. W. Effect of threats to attitudinal freedom as a function of agreement with the communicator. *Journal of Personality and Social Psychology*, 1970, *14*, 18–22.

Worchel, S., & Brehm, J. W. Direct and implied social restoration of freedom. *Journal of Personality and Social Psychology*, 1971, *18*, 294–304.

Worchel, S., Insko, C. A., Andreoli, V. A., & Drachman, D. Attribution of attitude as a function of behavioral direction and freedom: Reactance in the eye of the observer. *Journal of Experimental Social Psychology*, 1974, *10*, 399–414.

Worchel, S., Lee, J., & Adewole, A. Effects of supply and demand on ratings of object value. *Journal of Personality and Social Psychology*, 1975, *32*, 906–914.

Wortman, C. B. Causal attributions and personal control. In J. H. Harvey, W. J. Ickes, and R. F. Kidd (Eds.), *New directions in attribution research* (Vol. 1). Hillsdale, N.J.: Lawrence Erlbaum Associates, 1976.

Wortman, C. B., & Brehm, J. W. Responses to uncontrollable outcomes: An integration of reactance theory and the learned helplessness model. In L. Berkowitz (Ed.), *Advances in experimental social psychology* (Vol. 8). New York: Academic Press, 1975.

Wortman, C. B., & Dintzer, L. Is an attributional analysis of the learned helplessness phenomenon viable?: A critique of the Abramson–Seligman–Teasdale reformulation. *Journal of Abnormal Psychology*, 1978, *87*, 75–90.

Wortman, C. B., & Linder, D. E. *Attribution of responsibility for an outcome as a function of its likelihood*. Paper presented at the 81st Annual Convention of the American Psychological Association, Montreal, 1973.

Wortman, C. B., Panciera, L., Shusterman, L., & Hibscher, J. Attributions of causality and reactions to uncontrollable outcomes. *Journal of Experimental Social Psychology*, 1976, *12*, 301–316.

Wright, H. F. *The influence of barriers upon strength of motivation*. Unpublished doctoral dissertation, Duke University, 1934.

Wright, H. F. The effect of barriers upon strength of motivation. In R. G. Barker, J. S. Kounin, and H. F. Wright (Eds.), *Child behavior and development*. New York: McGraw-Hill, 1943.

Wright, R., & Brehm, J. W. *Difficulty and immediacy of avoidance behavior as determinants of energization and consequent unpleasantness of a potential negative outcome*. Unpublished manuscript, University of Kansas, 1980.

Wrightsman, L. S. The American trial jury on trial: Empirical evidence and procedural modifications. *Journal of Social Issues*, 1978, *34*, 137–164.

Wyatt v. *Stickney*. In B. J. Ennis & P. R. Friedman (Eds.), *Legal rights of the mentally handicapped* (Vol. 1). New York: Practicing Law Institute, 1973.

Yates, J. The application of learning theory to the treatment of tics. *Journal of Abnormal and Social Psychology,* 1958, *56,* 175–182.

Zillman, D. Rhetorical elicitation of agreement in persuasion. *Journal of Personality and Social Psychology,* 1972, *21,* 159–165.

Zillman, D., & Cantor, J. R. Rhetorical elicitation of concession in persuasion. *Journal of Social Psychology,* 1974, *94,* 223–236.

Author Index

Subject Index